Law, Society, Policy series

Series Editor: **Rosie Harding**,
University of Birmingham

Law, Society, Policy seeks to offer an outlet for high quality, socio-legal
research monographs and edited collections with the potential for
policy impact.

Also available in the series:

Death, Family and the Law:
The Contemporary Inquest in Context
By **Edward Kirton-Darling**

Deprivation of Liberty in the Shadows of the Institution
By **Lucy Series**

Women, Precarious Work and Care:
The Failure of Family-friendly Rights
By **Emily Grabham**

Pandemic Legalities:
Legal Responses to COVID-19 – Justice and Social Responsibility
Edited by **Dave Cowan** and **Ann Mumford**

Forthcoming:

D1612599

Intersex Embodiment:
Legal Frameworks Beyond Identity and Patienthood
By **Fae Garland** and **Mitchell Travis**

Polygamy, Policy and Postcolonialism in English Marriage Law:
A Critical Feminist Analysis
By **Zainab Batul Naqvi**

Find out more at
bristoluniversitypress.co.uk/law-society-policy

Forthcoming:

Egalitarian Digital Privacy:
Image Based Abuse and Beyond
By **Tsachi Keren-Paz**

Children's Voices, Family Disputes and Child-Inclusive Mediation:
The Right to Be Heard
By **Anne Barlow** and **Jan Ewing**

Observing Justice:
Digital Transparency, Openness and Accountability in Criminal Courts
By **Judith Townend** and **Lucy Welsh**

Sex Worker Rights Activism and the Politics of Rights:
Within and against the Law
By **Katie Cruz**

Find out more at
bristoluniversitypress.co.uk/law-society-policy

UNSETTLING APOLOGIES

Critical Writings on Apology from South Africa

Edited by
Melanie Judge and Dee Smythe

BRISTOL
UNIVERSITY
PRESS

First published in Great Britain in 2022 by

Bristol University Press
University of Bristol
1–9 Old Park Hill
Bristol
BS2 8BB
UK
t: +44 (0)117 374 6645
e: bup-info@bristol.ac.uk

Details of international sales and distribution partners are available at bristoluniversitypress.co.uk

© Bristol University Press 2022

British Library Cataloguing in Publication Data
A catalogue record for this book is available from the British Library

ISBN 978-1-5292-2795-6 hardcover
ISBN 978-1-5292-2796-3 paperback
ISBN 978-1-5292-2797-0 ePub
ISBN 978-1-5292-2798-7 ePdf

The right of Melanie Judge and Dee Smythe to be identified as editors of this work has been asserted by them in accordance with the Copyright, Designs and Patents Act 1988.

Cover design by Andrew Corbett
Front cover image: William Kentridge, 2005.
Drawing for *Black Box/Chambre Noire*. Courtesy of the artist.

Bristol University Press use environmentally responsible print partners.
Printed and bound in Great Britain by CPI Group (UK) Ltd, Croydon, CR0 4YY

FSC
www.fsc.org
MIX
Paper from
responsible sources
FSC® C013604

About William Kentridge's *Black Box/Chambre Noire*

The development of visual technologies and the history of colonialism intersect in *Black Box/Chambre Noire* through Kentridge's reflection on the history of the German colonial presence in Africa, particularly the German massacre of the Hereros in South-West Africa (now Namibia) in 1904, an event considered by some historians to be the first genocide of the 20th century. In 1885 South-West Africa became a German protectorate. German settlers increasingly encroached upon and expropriated the land of the Hereros. As the tribe's frustration rose, the Hereros, led by their chief Samuel Mahareru, launched a revolt against the ruling Germans. German troops, directed by General Lothar von Trotha, launched a swift counterstrike. Despite objections to General von Trotha's extreme measures by Germans in the colony as well as at home, it wasn't until 1905, after 75 per cent of the Herero population was decimated, that the general was removed from command. In reflecting on this historical incident, Kentridge explores the Freudian concept of 'Trauerarbeit', or grief work, as a labour without end. This ongoing investigation dovetails with the artist's unrelenting and self-reflexive examination of process and meaning. In creating a work that reveals the motors of representation, Kentridge renders these means transparent, removing the veil behind which selective, subjective memories are crafted into grand narratives of history. Resisting closure, the work problematises simplistic constructions of history using binaries of past and present, victim and victimiser, spectacle and spectator.

Credits

Cover image: © William Kentridge, 2005. Drawing for *Black Box/Chambre Noire*. Animated 35 mm film transferred to video, projected front and back onto model theatre with drawings and mechanical puppets. Commissioned by Deutsche Bank AG in consultation with the Solomon R. Guggenheim Foundation for the Deutsche Guggenheim, Berlin.

Text: © 2022 The Solomon R. Guggenheim Foundation.
Maria-Christina Villaseñor, 'William Kentridge: *Black Box/Chambre Noire*', Collection Online, Solomon R. Guggenheim Museum, 2007, https://www.guggenheim.org/artwork/22065

Contents

Series Editor's Preface

The Law, Society, Policy series publishes high-quality, socio-legal research monographs and edited collections with the potential for policy impact. Cutting across the traditional divides of legal scholarship, Law, Society, Policy offers an interdisciplinary, policy engaged approach to socio-legal research which explores law in its social and political contexts with a particular focus on the place of law in everyday life.

The series seeks to take an explicitly society-first view of socio-legal studies, with a focus on the ways that law shapes social life, and the constitutive nature of law and society. International in scope, engaging with domestic, international and global legal and regulatory frameworks, texts in the Law, Society, Policy series engage with the full range of socio-legal topics and themes.

Notes on Contributors

Nurina Ally is Lecturer in the Faculty of Law at the University of Cape Town. Prior to joining the University of Cape Town, Ally served as the Executive Director of the Equal Education Law Centre, a public interest law organisation based in Cape Town. She has practised as an attorney in the public law department of Webber Wentzel Attorneys and served as a research clerk to Justice Cameron and Acting Justice Mhlantla of the Constitutional Court of South Africa. Ally holds BA and LLB degrees from the University of the Witwatersrand, a Master's degree in African Studies from the University of Edinburgh, and a Master's degree in International Human Rights Law from the University of Oxford.

Jaco Barnard-Naudé is Professor of Jurisprudence in the Department of Private Law at the University of Cape Town. Between 2017 and 2020, he was the British Academy's Newton Advanced Fellow in the Westminster Law & Theory Lab, School of Law, University of Westminster. Barnard-Naudé is also a former Honorary Research Fellow of the Birkbeck Institute for the Humanities, Birkbeck College, University of London. His research interests include critical postapartheid jurisprudence, psychoanalytic transitional jurisprudence, law and literature, spatial justice, and queer legal theory. He received the University of Cape Town Fellows' Award in 2008 and the Cliffe Dekker Hofmeyr/UCT Faculty of Law Research Prize in 2010. Barnard-Naudé holds a B2 rating from the South African National Research Foundation (NRF), denoting that he enjoys considerable international recognition for the quality and impact of his research. With Drucilla Cornell and Francois de Bois, he edited the book *Dignity, Freedom and the Post-Apartheid Legal Order*. Barnard-Naudé holds BComm, LLB, and LLD degrees from the University of Pretoria, and an MA in Creative Writing from the University of Cape Town.

Tracey Davies is Executive Director of Just Share, a South African non-profit shareholder activist organisation using engagement, advocacy, and activism to drive urgent action to combat climate change and reduce inequality. She is admitted as an attorney in South Africa and as a solicitor in England and Wales. Davies practised criminal defence and commercial litigation in London prior to joining the South African non-profit Centre for Environmental Rights in 2013. She ran the Centre's Corporate Accountability and Transparency Programme, focusing on research and analysis of the environmental impacts of listed South African companies, including how those impacts are reported, and engaging with investors. Davies sits on the Steering Committee of the Academy of Sciences, South Africa's Just Transition Forum, and is a member of the Advisory Board for the National Business Initiative's Just Transition Pathways Initiative, and the Global Reporting Initiative's Human Rights Technical Committee. She is recognised as an expert on responsible investment, shareholder activism, and corporate governance. Davies holds BA and LLB degrees from the University of Cape Town and an LLM from New York University.

Shireen Hassim is Canada 150 Research Chair in Gender and African Studies at Carleton University, Ottawa. She is also a visiting professor at WiSER, University of the Witwatersrand, Johannesburg. Hassim has written and edited several books, including *No Shortcuts to Power: African Women in Politics and Policy Making*; *Go Home or Die Here: Violence, Xenophobia and the Reinvention of Difference in South Africa*; and *Women's Organizations and Democracy in South Africa: Contesting Authority*, which won the Victoria Shuck Award for Best Book in Women and Politics from the American Political Science Association. Her most recent book, *Fatima Meer: Voices of Liberation*, is an archival recuperation of the work of the South African sociologist, Fatima Meer. She is a member of the Academy of Science of South Africa. Shireen obtained her PhD from York University, Canada.

Diane Jefthas is the Deputy Director of the Centre for Law and Society at the University of Cape Town. At UCT, she has previously worked at the Centre for Criminology, the Gender, Health and Justice Research Unit in the Faculty of Health Sciences, and the Law, Race and Gender Unit in the Faculty of Law. She has also consulted for the Western Cape Department of Justice and Constitutional Development. Jefthas' work has focused on myriad aspects of youth and gender-based violence, with a strong emphasis on empirical research. Her recent work includes a book project centred around the themes of insecurity, navigating violence, marginalisation, and alienation in higher education spaces. Jefthas has a particular interest in monitoring and learning, transformative pedagogies, and the use of non-traditional methodologies to generate new knowledge. She holds Honours and Master's degrees in Social Sciences (Criminology) from the University of Cape Town.

Siphokazi Jonas is a writer and performer who has produced multiple one-woman poetry shows in Cape Town and Johannesburg and has been a featured act at numerous poetry sessions and festivals around South Africa. Her experience with spoken word and performance has led to multiple invitations to judge poetry slam competitions. She is co-producer of the award-winning short film *#WeAreDyingHere*, which is an adaptation of the stage production of the same name, which she co-wrote and directed. In 2016, she was the runner-up for the Sol Plaatje European Union Award. Jonas has lectured part-time on South African literature and isiXhosa oral poetry and is the English Poetry editor for the *New Contrast* journal. She holds an undergraduate degree in Drama and English and a Master's degree in English Literature from the University of Cape Town.

Melanie Judge is a queer and feminist activist and scholar, and Adjunct Associate Professor in the Department of Public Law at the University of Cape Town. She is author of *Blackwashing Homophobia: Violence and the Politics of Sexuality, Gender and Race* and lead editor of *To Have and to Hold: The Making of Same-Sex Marriage in South Africa*. Judge was the 2016 recipient of the Social Change Award, granted by Rhodes University in recognition of her activism and scholarship in the field of sexuality, and serves as trustee of the GALA Queer Archive. She holds a PhD in Women's and Gender Studies and a Master's in Development Studies from the University of the Western Cape, and an Honours in Psychology from the University of Cape Town. Melanie is Senior Policy Advisor on LGBTI Inclusion in Africa for the United Nations Development Programme.

Leila Khan is a researcher, artist, and organiser from Cape Town, South Africa. She currently works at the International Labour Research and Information Group (ILRIG) in Johannesburg, supporting worker and community-based formations through research and popular education. Khan studied politics and economic history at the University of Cape Town, followed by an LLB degree. During her time at UCT, she was involved in student activism through the Palestine Solidarity Forum, the Muslim Youth Movement, and Rhodes Must Fall. She also holds an LLM in Comparative Law, Economics and Finance from the International University College of Turin, Italy.

Peace Kiguwa is Associate Professor in Psychology at the School of Human and Community Development at the University of the Witwatersrand. Her research interests include gender and sexuality, critical race theory, critical social psychology, and teaching and learning. Her current research projects focus on young women's leadership in higher education, in partnership with the African Gender Institute and the Destabilizing Heteronormativity Project in partnership with Aids International. Kiguwa has co-edited three books: *Gender and Migration: Feminist Interventions* (edited with Palmary, Erica, and Katidja); *The Gender of Psychology* (edited with Shefer and Boonzaier); and *Critical Psychology* (edited with Hook, Mkhize, and Collins). She is currently editor of three accredited journals: *Psychology in Society* (PINS), *African Studies*, and the *International Journal of Critical Diversity Studies* (IJCDS). Kiguwa is the current Chair of the Sexuality and Gender Division of the Psychology Society of South Africa (PsySSA), and was the 2015 recipient of the Vice-Chancellor Excellence in Teaching and Learning Award at the University of the Witwatersrand. She obtained her PhD from the University of the Witwatersrand.

Heinz Klug is Evjue Bascom Professor of Law at the University of Wisconsin Law School and a visiting professor in the School of Law at the University of the Witwatersrand. Growing up in Durban, South Africa, he participated in the anti-apartheid struggle, spent 11 years in exile, and returned to South Africa in 1990 as a member of the ANC Land Commission and a researcher for Zola Skweyiya, Chairperson of the ANC Constitutional Committee. Klug served in the ANC political underground and Umkhonto we Sizwe, and was a member of the Medu Art Ensemble in Botswana. He taught Law at the University of the Witwatersrand from 1991 to 1996 and served as a legal advisor after 1994 with the South African Ministry of Water Affairs and Forestry and the Ministry of Land Affairs on water law and land tenure issues. Klug's research interests include constitutional transitions, constitution building, human rights, international legal regimes, and natural resources. His books include *Constituting Democracy: Law, Globalism, and South Africa's Political Reconstruction* and *The Constitution of South Africa: A Contextual Analysis*. More recently, he has co-edited two books on legal realism. The first, co-edited with Sally Engle Merry, is titled *The New Legal Realism: Studying Law Globally*. The latest, the *Research Handbook on Modern Legal Realism*, is co-edited with Shauhin Talesh and Elizabeth Mertz. Klug received a BA(Hons) degree in Comparative African Government and Administration from the then University of Natal in 1978, a JD from the University of California, Hastings, College of the Law in 1989, and an SJD from the University of Wisconsin in 1997. In 2013 he was awarded a Doctor *Honoris Causa* from Hasselt University in Belgium.

Omowamiwa Kolawole is Postdoctoral Research Fellow with the NRF/ DST Research Chair in Intellectual Property, Innovation and Development at the University of Cape Town. Previously, he has been a Junior Research Fellow at the UCT Centre for Law and Society, worked closely with the Democratic Governance Research Unit, and clerked for Malawi's Supreme Court of Appeal. He has co-convened the Master's course on Law and Society in Africa in the UCT Department of Public Law and taught Public Health Law and Human Rights courses in the Master's in Public Health

Programme in the Faculty of Health Sciences. Kolawole's research is at the intersection of law and public health and engages with the right to health and how its realisation influences global health intervention and policies, as well as interpersonal biomedical interactions. He holds an LLB degree from the University of Lagos, and LLM and Master's in Public Health degrees from UCT, where he also obtained his PhD in Public Law, under the auspices of the National Research Foundation Chair in Security and Justice.

Sindiso Mnisi Weeks is Associate Professor of Law and Society at the University of Massachusetts, Boston, and Adjunct Associate Professor in Public Law at the University of Cape Town. Her scholarship has combined research, advocacy, and policy work on women, property, governance, dispute management, and participation under customary law and the South African Constitution. Mnisi Weeks previously clerked for then Deputy Chief Justice of the Constitutional Court of South Africa, Dikgang Moseneke. She is the author of *Access to Justice and Human Security: Cultural Contradictions in Rural South Africa* and co-author of *African Customary Law in South Africa: Post-Apartheid and Living Law Perspectives*. Mnisi Weeks has taught courses in African Customary Law in the Department of Private Law at UCT, and Law and Society in the Department of Political Science at the University of Massachusetts Amherst, as well as teaching for the Consortium for Graduate Studies in Gender, Culture, Women, and Sexuality at the Massachusetts Institute of Technology. She is co-editor of one of the American Anthropological Association's official journals, *Political and Legal Anthropology Review* (PoLAR), on whose editorial board she also previously served. Mnisi Weeks received her DPhil from the University of Oxford's Centre for Socio-Legal Studies, as a Rhodes Scholar.

Nkululeko Nkomo is Senior Lecturer in Psychology at the University of the Witwatersrand. Before joining the university, Nkululeko was a researcher in the social aspects of HIV/AIDS and the Health Division of the Human Sciences Research Council (HSRC). In his research, he aims to bridge normative concerns and reasoning about social justice and transformation with psychosocial research into issues of racialisation, identity, and human health. His most recent publications include 'Bearing the right to healthcare, autonomy and hope' in *Social Science & Medicine* and 'Retrieving grandfathers and histories through objects and affective registers' in *Emotion, Space and Society* (with Canham, Kotze, and S. Nkomo). Nkomo holds BA (Honours) and Master's degrees and a PhD from the University of the Witwatersrand.

Dee Smythe is Professor of Public Law and Director of the Centre for Law and Society at the University of Cape Town. Between 2017 and 2021, she held the National Research Foundation SARChI Chair in Security and Justice. She is an affiliated researcher at the Centro de Investigação e Desenvolvimento sobre Direito e Sociedade (CEDIS) in the Nova School of Law at the University of Nova Lisboa, and a visiting professor at the University of Turin. Her books include *Rape Unresolved: Policing Sexual Offences in South Africa*; *Should We Consent? The Politics of Rape Law Reform in South Africa* (edited with Artz); *Sexual Offences Commentary* (edited with Pithey); *Marriage, Land & Custom: Essays on Law and Society Change* (edited with Claassens); and *In Search of Equality: Women, Law and Society in Africa* (edited with Röhrs). Smythe is an expert on institutional responses to gender-based violence, with a specific focus on sexual offences and sexual harassment. She researches and teaches in the areas of criminal law and procedure, gender, and law and society. Smythe is a trustee of the Women's Legal Centre and the Law and Society Association, and sits on the Advisory Board of the Dullah Omar Institute at the University of the Western Cape. She holds degrees in Political Science and Law from the University of Cape Town, and Master's and Doctoral degrees from Stanford Law School, where she was a Fulbright Fellow.

Yasmin Sooka is a leading human rights lawyer. She currently chairs the Commission on Human Rights for South Sudan, to which she was appointed by the UN Human Rights Council in Geneva in March 2016. Sooka is the former Executive Director of the Foundation for Human Rights in South Africa and serves as an advisor to the Foundation on the Programme on Unfinished Business of the South African Truth and Reconciliation Commission. She served on the South African Truth and Reconciliation Commission from 1996 to 2001 and chaired the committee responsible for the final Truth and Reconciliation Commission (TRC) report from 2001 to 2003. Sooka was appointed by the United Nations to serve on the Truth and Reconciliation Commission of Sierra Leone from 2002 to 2004. Since 2000, she has also been a member of the UN Advisory Body on the Review of Resolution 1325. In July 2010, Sooka was appointed to the three-member panel of experts advising the Secretary-General on accountability for war crimes committed during the final stages of the war in Sri Lanka. In 2015, she was a member of the panel appointed by the UN Secretary-General to investigate allegations of Sexual Exploitation and Abuse (SEA) involving children in the Central African Republic. Sooka obtained her Law degree from the University of the Witwatersrand.

Thuto Thipe is on the faculty of the Department of History at the University of Chicago. Her primary fields of study include land tenure, African cities, local governance systems, race and racial formation, and feminist studies. She previously worked as a researcher in the UCT Law Faculty's Centre for Law and Society. Thipe earned her doctorate from Yale University in History and African American Studies and also holds degrees in History, Gender Studies, and Political Science from the University of Cape Town and Macalester College. Her PhD dissertation, 'Black Freehold: Landownership in Alexandra Township, 1912–1979' won the Yale Afro-American Cultural Center's award for Outstanding Graduate Research in the African Diaspora.

Christi van der Westhuizen is an author, media columnist, and Associate Professor at the Centre for the Advancement of Non-Racialism and Democracy (CANRAD) at Nelson Mandela University. Her professional life started as a journalist at the anti-apartheid newspaper *Vrye Weekblad*. After working as a senior political correspondent in South Africa's democratic parliament, she moved into research. She has held fellowships with various universities, including the University of Cape Town, and previously worked as Associate Professor of Sociology at the University of Pretoria. Her research areas include whiteness, racism, and nationalism in colonial, apartheid, and postapartheid South Africa. Van der Westhuizen's publications include the monographs *White Power & the Rise and Fall of the National Party* (2007) and *Sitting Pretty: White Afrikaans Women in Postapartheid South Africa* (2017), and she is co-editor (with Shona Hunter) of the *Routledge International Handbook of Critical Studies in Whiteness* (2022). Van der Westhuizen obtained her PhD from the University of Cape Town.

Kerry Williams is an Advocate of the High Court and member of the Pan African Bar Association and the Johannesburg Society of Advocates. She is currently a member of the Victoria Mxenge Group of Advocates and was previously an attorney and partner at Webber Wentzel. Williams has litigated a number of hate speech, harassment, and unfair discrimination cases, particularly on behalf of complainants. In addition to being a legal practitioner, Williams writes academically and has contributed to journals and books on issues including LGBTIQ equality, pharmaceutical price regulation, and hate crimes. She holds an LLB from the University of Cape Town, an LLM from the University of London, and an MPA from the John F. Kennedy School of Government at Harvard University.

Acknowledgements

The editors and authors would like to acknowledge the following people and places for their contributions to the making of this book: Viccy Baker, Jill Bradbury, Tsoseletso Bogopa, Leo Boonzaier, Upile Chisala, Kim Gunning, Kate Hofmeyr, Dermod Judge, Mwenya Kabwe, William Kentridge, Antjie Krog, Patrick Lowe, Ahmed Mayet, Anne McIlleron, Racheal Obong, Jill Olivier, Nishal Robb, Ricky Röntsch, Fletcher Smythe-Lowe, Garth Stevens, Jemima Thomas, Christi van der Westhuizen, Katarzyna Zdunczyk, the anonymous reviewers, the Centre for Law and Society, the Mdukatshani Rural Development Project, and the Msinga community.

The research for and writing of this book were assisted by the National Research Foundation of South Africa (Grant no. 47303), through the National Research Foundation SARChI Chair in Security and Justice; the Health Systems Research Initiative, a collaboration between the United Kingdom Medical Research Council, the Economic and Social Research Council, the Foreign Commonwealth and Development Office, and the Wellcome Trust (Grant no. MR/P004725/1); and a grant to the Centre for Law and Society at the University of Cape Town from the Joint Fund to Promote and Advance Constitutionalism in South Africa.

The Power of Apology

Melanie Judge and Dee Smythe

Apologies everywhere ... and nowhere

An apology animates pain – of injury, its story, and effect – and promise – of acceptance, forgiveness, and reparation. As a repository of affective content, when, how, and whether an apology is given invokes fierce interpersonal, public, political, and scholarly debate, the undercurrent of which is often: does it actually matter to those who have been harmed? Defying simple definition and assessment, and multidimensional in how it is both expressed and received, those who are most closely affected by the actions to which the apology is a response are perhaps the ultimate arbiters of its authenticity and value. This is even more so in the age of social media, when apologies are publicly vetted, vilified or verified. The value of apology is mediated by, among others, historical and political dynamics, personal proclivities, legal imperatives, and judicial interpretations. It must be weighed against the gravity of the harm caused and the interpersonal and socio-historical contingencies that shape its impact. As a social act, an apology and the meaning it communicates is tied into how it may, or may not, change the conditions that led to the harm experienced. This makes it necessary to attend to what precisely a given apology seeks to reconcile. And for this reason, context is key.

We live, it has been suggested, in an age of apology (Brooks 1999), with recent years seeing insistent demands for apologies as part of a global reckoning with the enduring legacies of slavery and colonialism (Davis 2014: 271; Faulconbridge 2020; Schaart 2021). But, reduced to mere performance, devoid of reparative content, the significance of the apology for those injured may be overestimated. Moreover, as Wakeham points out, in the context of historical wrongs, apologetic 'practices of atonement' can limit the responsibility of perpetrators by putting the focus on 'historically delimited, specific injuries rather than acknowledging ... systemic ongoing practices', so pre-empting 'sustained investigation of grievances with statements of contrition' (Wakeham 2012: 3). The 'miracle' of South Africa's 'peaceful' transition from apartheid is closely linked in many minds to the Truth and Reconciliation Commission (TRC), led by Archbishop Desmond Tutu, as a definitive moment of truth-telling, contrition, and forgiveness. For others, increasingly, that same process of truth-telling and reconciliation is marked as 'unfinished business' and as having failed to deliver justice for the harms of apartheid. Notwithstanding the postapartheid state's grand plan to enlist law and rights to undo the racial, sexual, and gender inequalities and discriminations of the past (Judge and Smythe 2020), the political narrative has now largely turned away from 'soft option' remedies such as apologies towards the hard retributive edge of law – and particularly criminal law – as a way to address dignity harms.[1] In this regard, legal remedies have closely followed the turn away from apology and forgiveness as being core to national reconciliation. The interpolation of South Africa's opportunity to reconcile with the past and thinking about apology's role in reckoning and remedy for present harms are apparent throughout this book. All of the chapters are situated in a context of the generational harms visited by colonialism and apartheid, even where this is not the focus of the chapter, and the intractability of entrenched power relations as represented in absences of truth and justice. As such, the chapters resist being neatly categorised into timeframes or themes, for each is a meditation on the moment and on the conditions that inform it.

Situated in the precarity of South Africa's present, this book leads us to ask what the cynicism of South Africans towards the reintegrative possibilities of apology (Braithwaite 1989), the increased politicisation of hate, and greater reliance on retributive legal remedies mean for apologies. The question links to concerns that apology alone cannot materially transform the interpersonal, social, political, or economic relationships – past and present, distant and proximate – in which injurious harms are located. Here, history casts a long shadow, in which the ideas of 'forgive and forget' that are frequently associated with politically negotiated apologies can obscure apology's potential in the present. So, the apology comes to take on particular meanings within South Africa's unfinished project of reparation and redistribution within enduring cultures of dehumanisation through which centuries of colonial and apartheid governance were built and sustained. In this sense, the generative possibilities of apology are

---

[1] For more on the personal and political potential for empathic healing though public apologies, see Gobodo-Madikizela (2008).

bound up with an array of socio-political and economic conditions that are historical in nature, bringing under scrutiny what apology does with the past, and what it might in turn do for the future.

As a signifier of remorse and contrition, can the act of apologising lead an individual, a state, or a non-state entity (such as a corporation) to meaningful reform or reparation and spur action towards accountability and the undoing of harm in material ways? In light of South Africa's history of institutionalised discrimination, whether and how apology facilitates the reconstituting of social relations, through reparation and compensation and in tropes of forgiveness and reconciliation, should be central considerations. Can it, as Tarusarira (2019) suggests it must, shift the bedrock – the foundation – underpinning the harm? A critical reading of the South African experience and its legacy of settler-colonialism foregrounds the urgency of doing so, and also its near impossibility, precisely because such a shift is necessarily structural, ideological, and relational, playing out in a context of extreme power disparities. Tarusarira calls this a *transformative* apology (Tarusarira 2019: 213), which is apt for the scale of structural change it urges. In doing so, it echoes South Africa's commitment to a form of transformative rights-based constitutionalism that imagined the possibility of such a bedrock shift. The South African Constitution, suggested Justice Albie Sachs in 2005, 'represents a radical rupture with a past based on intolerance and exclusion, and the movement forward to the acceptance of the need to develop a society based on equality and respect by all for all',[2] an aspiration that remains substantively incomplete. Against this backdrop, our critical engagement with South Africa in this book provides glimpses of the transformative potential of apologies, the political imagination required for their realisation, and the dangerous implications and consequences of their absence.

Enacting apologies

Apologies can be enacted through verbal or public statements, official declarations, court judgments, and apology rituals, monuments, and memorials. They may be expressed by individuals, groups, or institutions, and can be given for something that happened recently or for events in the past. Although apologies take diverse forms, there is some agreement about what makes for a good apology. To start with, apologies are not excuses, justifications, or explanations (Petrucci 2017: 446). Robbennolt (2003: 468) defines an apology 'in its fullest form' as including:

---

[2] *Minister of Home Affairs and Others v Fourie and Others* (CCT 60/04) [2005] ZACC 19 (1 December 2005) para. 59.

expression of embarrassment and chagrin; clarification that one knows what conduct had been expected and sympathizes with the application of negative sanction; verbal rejection, repudiation, and disavowal of the wrong way of behaving along with vilification of the self that so behaved; espousal of the right way and an avowal henceforth to pursue that course; performance of penance and the volunteering of restitution.

In relation to political apologies – such as in response to state-sponsored harms or personal wrongdoing by political actors – scholars identify a more pared-down set of components, including an actual expression of apology, explicit acknowledgement of wrongdoing, acceptance of responsibility, acknowledgement of injury to victims, commitment to not repeating those actions, and offers of reparation (Tavuchis 1991: 19–20; Lazare 2004).

Nick Smith (2008; 2014) offers a detailed and useful account of the elements that he considers to constitute a 'categorical apology'. These are: that the apology should corroborate an agreed upon factual record; that the person apologising should accept 'causal moral responsibility' for the harm caused; that they have the standing to accept blame; that each harm is identified in the apology (as opposed to a sweeping apology or one that deflects to a lesser wrong); that the apology identifies the violated values and principles underpinning the harm and (re)commits the offender to those shared principles; that it recognises and treats the victim as a 'moral interlocutor' worthy of an apology by virtue of their dignity and humanity; that it shows categorical regret for the actions that caused the harm (as opposed to a justification of those actions and associated outcomes); that the apology is expressed to the victim and includes a commitment to not reoffend; and that it involves practical responsibility in the form of redress, with the offender's intention being to benefit the victim's well-being, rather than their own, along with the 'appropriate degree and duration of sorrow and guilt as well as empathy and sympathy for the victim' (Smith 2014: 17–19). Most apologies never meet this categorical standard, with its 'thick conceptions of repentance' (Smith 2014: 19), but Smith suggests that it is a good benchmark against which all apologies might be measured and a number of chapters in this volume do so.

In law, the apology can operate as a remedy and to reduce culpability (and so mitigate liability and punishment) in criminal courts, as well as in other areas that include vernacular law, delict/torts, environmental law, and health law. Because what is said counts materially, there is an industry of experts to advise on how best to tick the mechanistic requirements that allow for a show of remorse (an infamously 'overused, opaque, and imprecise term in law' [Smith 2014: 3]) through apology, without admitting liability. As an ethical and moral concern, the utility of the apology is also connected with the desire to communicate a particular disposition of oneself in respect of a breach or harm, and to repair relationships. If non-defensive, it can turn attention to the value of the relationship and give the victim the opportunity to be heard and to consider their response to the offered apology. Time and space to consider an apology is an important mediator of how it is received (Zechmeister et al 2004; Petucci 2017: 444). Critical too is who offers and who authorises the apology, particularly in the case of wrongdoing by a state, corporation, or institutional entity. The figure offering the apology should be, to use Goffman's term, a 'ratified person' (Goffman 1967; also Thompson 2008: 31) who speaks as a 'representative' and carries sufficient authority to communicate on behalf of the wrongdoer. But, drawing on a content analysis of political apologies, Blatz, Schumann, and Ross (2009) caution that political apologisers typically dissociate the regime they serve from the one that perpetrated the harm, praising victims for their fortitude and forbearance, while ignoring the continuities that inhere in state power. For political apologies, publicity is central to both the performance of the apology and, more critically, in creating a record of contrition and concomitant responsibility. Research shows, however, that while apologies may be effective in restoring trust in interpersonal relations (Fehr et al 2010), they are often less effective in intergroup conflicts (Reinders Folmer et al 2021: 2), with the performance of remorse being treated with suspicion. According to Reinders Folmer et al (2021: 11), victim groups in intergroup situations '… are less inclined to take conciliatory initiatives from outgroups at face value [which] undermines the effectiveness of apologies relative to interpersonal contexts' and may lead to more violence. This is unsurprising, since formal state or corporate apologies are often means to resolve conflict without violence that at the same time expose the fissure between their enactments and a meaningful change in the power relations from which their necessity arises. And yet, as Brooks argues, '[h]eartfelt contrition just might signify a nation's capacity to suppress its next impulse to harm others' (Brooks 1999: 4).

With truth

Giving a full account of the harm for which it is summoned or sought lies at the heart of apology. South Africa's TRC sought to provide official recognition of the truth about the apartheid past and to render an authoritative account of the gross violations of human rights that took place under the apartheid regime. In the end, its capacity to give that full account ended up falling short, as did its ability to provide for meaningful reparations to victims, whether directly or indirectly, of apartheid. The TRC's approach to reconciliation and truth seeking was largely ecumenical, valorising forgiveness and founded on the premise that disclosure, catharsis, and absolution, including bringing together the victim and perpetrator within a confessional frame, would bring resolution. Its granting of amnesty for truth has been linked to 'unrequited expectations for justice' – a 'justice deficit' that precludes reconciliation with the past (Gibson 2002).

Exposing the truth is necessary to reconciliation and has the potential to unmask the denials that lend personal and institutional legitimacy to wrongdoings, in turn connecting abstracted notions of brutal power to the leaders and functionaries through which that power is enacted. The disclosure of the facts of gross violations, and the knowledge of how those atrocities came about, are truth's painful offering. Consequently, the acknowledgement of truth is seen to provide justice to victims and survivors and to restore the wider society (Millar 2011). However, the expression of contrition for the suffering inflicted on another is not a matter of truth alone, for reparation is irreducible to solely the presence or absence of truth. For this reason, a purely positivist approach to evaluating truth revelations is inadequate in that the ultimate objective of those revelations must be to reconcile those members of a society who previously held opposing views of the past regime (Kaminski and Malepa 2006: 386).

The value of the TRC has been critically, and often negatively, assessed in relation to the partiality of the truth it accessed as well as the lack of criminal and social justice, and reparative redress, that followed (Stanley 2001). This criticism, and the deep disappointment it signals, is threaded through many of the chapters in this volume. It is also in this context that the recent apology of the former apartheid leader F.W. de Klerk should be understood. As apartheid's last president, de Klerk led the National Party into a handover of political power that ushered in the democratic rule of the African National Congress (ANC), the former liberation movement. Upon his death in 2021, a pre-recorded "last message, addressed to the people of South Africa" was released, in which de Klerk made a final attempt to apologise for apartheid.[3] De Klerk is considered by some white nationalists to be a sell-out who went too far by ceding state power without defeat, and by some black nationalists as having manipulated the ANC into a constitutional compromise that kept white privilege in place (van der Westhuizen 2021). Until fairly recently, he had refused to concede that apartheid was a crime against humanity. This contested legacy is the scene for how his apology is variously interpreted – as

---

[3] "[L]et me today in this last message repeat, I, without qualification, apologise for the pain and the hurt and the indignity and the damage that apartheid has done to black, brown and Indians in South Africa. I do so not only in my capacity as the former leader of the National Party, but also as an individual. Allow me in this last message to share with you the fact that since the early 80s, my views changed completely. It was as if I had a conversion, and in my heart of hearts realised that apartheid was wrong. I realised that we had arrived at a place which was morally unjustifiable" (de Klerk 2021).

reiterating the obfuscation of apartheid truths, as a defensive strategy without adequate reparative action, or as marking a heartfelt shift in acknowledgement and contrition. In considering the various modalities of truth-telling posited by the TRC,[4] Twidle charges that the Commission was not able to deal with how these multiplicities of truth 'might modify, contradict, unsettle or work against each other', pointing towards all that is 'the unknowable, the unreconciled, the unforgiven' (Twidle 2019: 4), which de Klerk has, in a sense, come to signify. The contending meanings attributed to de Klerk's apology circuit back to the apology's necessary imbrication with both truth and justice. As Norval argues, '[j]ustification of the pursuit of truth and justice derives its strength from an appeal to more fundamental intuitions about the just treatment of citizens in a democratic society' (1998: 252). Such intuitions animate the reception of the apartheid leader's final words at a time when imaginaries of more settled forms of truth and justice, past and present, abound.

Alongside justice

Thinking of apology alongside justice, particularly in the case of harms that are integrally connected to systems and structures of historical injustice, is of particular importance to this volume. The relationship of apology with justice seeking is complex. Central are social commitments to justice and peace in the wake of violence, as 'prerequisite for forgiveness' (Regehr and Gutheil 2002) and a way of making moral amends (Golding 1984–5: 133) that 'signifies a human gesture beyond the structural relationships created by law' (Alberstein and Davidovitch 2011: 154). The apology, then, provides evidence of contrition – proof that 'something was done', responsibility was taken, and redemption was deserved. In this sense, apologies are (or should be) consequential, and can therefore be inhibited by fears of having to pay the price for a particular action by effectively admitting guilt: '(s)ome apologies are not made because of where they could lead; apologies as a path towards reparation, for instance' (Ahmed 2021). Shying away from accountability, bureaucratic apologies, in particular, suggests Ahmed (2021), are 'a way of appearing to recognise harm without really doing so' and of seeing harm without truly seeing it.

The reconciliatory function of apologies focuses on them being reciprocated with forgiveness, referred to as the 'apology forgiveness cycle' (Tavuchis 1991; Shnabel and Nadler 2008), and stresses the delivery of apologies that match the psychological needs of the victim, thus enabling

---

[4]   These include factual and forensic truth, personal and narrative truth, social or 'dialogue' truth, and healing and restorative truth (Twidle 2019).

interpersonal reconciliation. Where there are limited apparatuses to negotiate fraught social relations, such as in South Africa, the dynamic (albeit messy) use of law, including to compel an apology, is inevitably central, with two dominant tracks emerging. The first views apologies within a restorative justice framework that draws on vernacular systems and processes, with both the harm and its remedy seen as embedded within a communal context. Mostly, this approach treats apology and compensation as a 'soft option', suited only for family matters and less serious offences, which are diverted out of the system. The reality, however, as scholars like Mnisi Weeks (2018; and in this volume) have shown, is that vernacular courts in South Africa exercise authority over offences that include murder and rape – often responding to the failure of the state system, but sometimes also as the forum of choice, although Mnisi Weeks urges that these processes should neither be uncritically assumed to be restorative nor taken to be the easier route to remedy. The generative possibilities for justice at the intersection of state and vernacular systems in South Africa remain largely unexplored. The second track builds on the conciliatory/reconciliatory approach of the TRC and is most apparent in South Africa's Equality Courts, the legislative basis for which was laid down in the late 90s, with the explicit object to 'facilitate the transition to a democratic society, united in its diversity, marked by human relations that are caring and compassionate, and guided by the principles of equality, fairness, equity, social progress, justice, human dignity and freedom' (Preamble to the Promotion of Equality and Prevention of Unfair Discrimination Act 2000[5]). These specialised courts are empowered to impose an 'unconditional apology' as a possible remedy, with the most common outcome for successful complainants being payment of monetary compensation to the complainant or to a charity, along with an ordered apology (Emdon and Judge 2018).

Many more of the interpersonal affronts to dignity that could be taken to the Equality Courts in fact come before criminal courts as charges of *crimen iniuria* (an unlawful and intentional affront to the dignity of another). Particularly in respect of racist speech and conduct, there has been a marked shift away from conciliatory remedies, including apology (most apparent in the case of the 'Reitz Four'[6]), and towards harsh retributive measures like imprisonment, as in the case of Vicki Momberg, where the repeated use of the 'k word' led to a two-year prison term.[7] For ordinary South Africans and for the courts it seems, in this regard at least, sorry is no longer enough. This occurs alongside continued demands for the prosecution of perpetrators of

---

[5]   Act 4 of 2000.
[6]   *Van der Merwe and Others v S* (A366/10) [2011] ZAFSHC 88 (23 June 2011).
[7]   *Momberg v S* (A206/2018) [2019] ZAGPJHC 183 (28 June 2019).

apartheid crimes as identified in the TRC report (Truth and Reconciliation Commission 1998), with the opening of inquests into unlawful deaths during apartheid, and the establishment of a dedicated office within the National Prosecuting Authority to prosecute these apartheid-era offences.[8]

We have suggested that meanings and legitimacy are variously assigned to acts of apology and relate to how such acts are received by those who have been injured or aggrieved, as well as to the extent of their transformative potential. As a concentrated point of social connection, apologising can embody explanation or excuse, culpability or contrition, reparation or repentance. The demand it attracts is also deeply connected to the politics of recognition, whereby the humanity of a person, a community, or a people who have experienced a harm linked to the denial of their full humanity might be recognised and acknowledged through apology (see van der Westhuizen in this volume). At the same time, saying sorry does not take the place of reparation and justice; in fact, it might sometimes be deployed to thwart precisely those ends.

Engaging power

The contributions to this volume open up, rather than settle, questions about if and how apologies contest historical and contemporary configurations of power. Approaching the discourse of apology as constitutive of structures and articulations of power draws attention not only to what apology says, but also what it does.[9] Given the injuries that characterise the South Africa condition, apologies are a place where power is contested in historically contingent ways. Here, the act of apologising may reinforce and sustain existing relations of power, or offer counter conduct that opens up new political and relational possibilities. In part, this volume seeks to remedy the lack of attention given to the relationship between apology and the exercise and articulation of power, suggesting ways in which this connection might be theorised to consider how power figures in the discourse and materiality of apology. Questioning the transformative force of the apology in relation to power is also to explore its limits and potential within a force field of contemporary reckoning and recovery.

In the same way that injury and violence may be products of power, so too is the apology. In the social field in which relationships are governed, acts of injury, and of remorse and accompanying reparation, are mediated

---

[8] See, for example, www.ahmedtimol.co.za and www.fhr.org.za/the-unfinished-business-of-the-trc-programme/

[9] This includes its effects on identity and knowledge–power relations as 'it is in discourse that power and knowledge are joined together' (Foucault 1998: 100).

by conditions of power. As this volume shows, particular social, political, legal, and institutional arrangements produce formulations of (non)apology that are embedded in systems and structures of power, reflecting too how the relationship between self/ves and other/s are conceived of therein. By extension, its (im)potency is imbricated with overlapping regimes of inequality that give succour to the injuries to which it is a response. At the same time, as a social practice, the apology draws people into circuits of exchange, reproducing or transforming these (see Nkomo and Kiguwa in this volume). Through the agency of the wronged, and as a counterweight to their denial and silencing, the productive value of apology can serve to put shame and blame where they rightfully belong: at the source of the injury. As both representation and expression, apologies bring into sharp focus the realities of harm and accompanying claims for reparation. These are a means through which rights and recognition can be authorised, and yet apology's deployment may also function as a normalisation strategy to deny such claims. These dynamics may be accentuated in contexts where harms are systemically embedded. Such is the case in settler-colonial states, where apologies may serve to co-opt the recipient into a politics of civility, 'a strategy of containment … substituting rhetorical gestures of atonement for more radical processes of redistributive justice or political power sharing' (Wakeham 2012: 2). In this way, they may 'perform the semblance of rapprochement', says Wakeham, 'without *unsettling* settler privilege … bypassing more radical forms of structural transformation that would destabilize the power asymmetries underpinning white authority' (Wakeham 2012: 3, emphasis in original). Instead, the apology in this context is demanding 'performative responses from those marginalized subjects it addresses', reducing forgiveness to 'acquiescence to the colonial status quo' (Wakeham 2012: 6).

In a similar vein, Tarusarira (2019: 207) argues that, 'while apology and forgiveness are vital for dealing with a violent past, when uncritically undertaken these actions do not transform discourses, narratives, ideas and ideologies that justified the wrongdoing in the first place'. These perspectives serve to situate apology and invite its reconceptualisation as essential to, as Tarusarira puts it, 'actively transforming the conditions that justified the wrongdoing in the first place' (2019: 212). Whether at a personal, political, or structural level, the invocation here is to refuse the conditions and relations of power on which a given apology was contingent, and to not be sorry for that. Such a *transformative* apology (Tarusarira 2019) is one that facilitates fundamental (bedrock) change and requires a rupturing of sorts:

> I killed your goat; I will replace the goat, but also ensure that negative discourses, narratives, ideas and ideologies that made me see it as acceptable to kill your goat are ruptured within me and those who

share the same mentality so that the same wrongdoing does not happen again to you or others. (Tarusarira 2019: 213)

At the same time, Wakeham cautions to the limits placed by apology on discourses of remediation, particularly in respect of land, sovereignty, and the duration of atonement (Wakeham 2012: 5). In this sense, apologies provide (or impose) closures on past wrongs, but they also inscribe an end point for the resolution of those wrongs. In settler states, apologies may therefore '*fore*close upon any need for ongoing anticolonial resistance in the present and future' and, instead, impose on subject groups the responsibility to accept the apology and so to effect conciliation (Wakeham 2012: 6, emphasis in original). Impatient refrains directed at black South Africans to 'move on' from apartheid demonstrate how easily blame for unfinished reconciliation is displaced, further exacerbated by the democratic state's failure to significantly transform persisting inequalities.

Compelled by these realities, this book aims to locate its enquiry of apology in the South African 'epistemic bedrock' (Tarusarira 2019) of enduring conflicts, out of which apologies emerge, while resisting the possibility of foreclosure that is ever-present where apologies land on uneven ground. Locating apology in this way, and through the lens of power, tempers the tendency to view it as an instance – a decontextualised and individualised act – and, instead, to see it as thickly situated in the time and place that produces its appearance (or lack thereof) in particularised ways. This requires a departure from a zero-sum reading of apology as either all or nothing, seeking instead to interrogate its value in exposing how structure, system, agency, and context all mediate its transformative (im)possibilities.

Apology unsettled

As alluded to in the book's title, the ways in which apologies are, if indeed they are, made and received, denied and accepted, and how too they come to matter or not, is unsettled terrain. As already discussed, complex and interrelated social, cultural, legal, and political meanings are given to, and constituted through, them. These meanings also emerge within prevailing cultures of apology and their relationship to histories, politics, and laws that regulate, punish, and also remediate harm.

The chapters in this volume explore various forms of apology – from the most intimate of settings to the level of state and structure – and problematise their consequences for reparation, reconciliation, and justice in South Africa and beyond, opening up wider conversations about impact and import in both practical and theoretical terms. Drawing on contemporary debates on racist hate speech, gender-based violence, and the legacy of the TRC within continued struggles for reparation and decolonisation, the chapters interrogate the value and force of apology in urging and imagining more equitable social relations. Violence is a *leitmotif* in the volume, with the authors capturing the interlacing of structural and intimate violence visited on South Africans through colonialism and apartheid, and their implications for thinking and doing apology. Written in multiple registers, including poetry, personal reflections, fictional accounts, and scholarly treatments, the chapters to follow explore and critique the apology through both historical and contemporary frames.

Siphokazi Jonas situates this volume in the 'burning tongues' and 'tenderised bellies' of Empire, in the death and blood and words that have harvested the old-new South Africa, and throws down the gauntlet: 'we do not "get over" / the fettered trunks of our lost histories, / naked roots and fallen family trees'. It is an intimate meditation on the problematics of apology and the twinned assumption of reconciliation.

Yasmin Sooka explicates how apologies are approached within the field of transitional justice in both international and regional spheres, and as requiring acknowledgement of apartheid as a crime against humanity. She illustrates how the discourse on apologies in South Africa has tended to advance the notion of forgiveness as opposed to accountability for the crimes of the past, exposing the inadequacies of apartheid leaders' apologies and particularly in the absence of reparative measures, and of perpetrators being held criminally to account.

Sindiso Mnisi Weeks sounds a caution on the use of imposed apologies as remedies in judicial processes, contrasting this with mediation processes wherein an apology might arise from one or other party in response to an understanding of the harm and pain caused. Focused on vernacular dispute management forums that are frequently used in rural communities, the chapter interrogates the risks and constraints of creating laws to regulate these forums that rest on normative and colonial ideas about traditional dispute management practices and remedies. Specifically interrogating the value and purpose of apologies in relation to the recognition of traditional communities and their governance, Mnisi Weeks warns against the continuation of repressive harmony mythologies that reiterate colonial discourses.

Nurina Ally and Kerry Williams interrogate why and how a court-ordered apology is an effective remedy through two Equality Court cases concerning hate speech against minority groups. They suggest that compelled apologies – when properly framed and crafted – serve as a potent mechanism to restore and vindicate dignity and equality rights, arguing that it is necessary for the courts to further articulate their remedial value. Recognising that a compelled apology is a dynamic and malleable legal remedy, the authors illustrate how it might be successfully enlisted to further the corrective, restorative, educational, and deterrent goals of equality legislation.

The ethical and moral repair work required in the aftermath of apartheid's destruction are taken up by Shireen Hassim in the figure of Winnie Madikizela-Mandela and her appearance before the TRC. Where reparative burden is placed and how apology may be obstinately refused mark out how the performative resolutions and truth logic of commissions might be disrupted, exposing fractures in the acceptance of the terms of transition itself. In this nuanced reading of Madikizela-Mandela's resistant (non)apology, Hassim exposes the limits of the TRC's apology script, and how it elided other forms of harm and injustice associated with apartheid-era crimes and with violence as a political strategy.

Entering the topic by way of the racist event and its backlash, Nkululeko Nkomo and Peace Kiguwa read a number of contemporary incidents of racism through affect and racialised embodiments, encounters, and social bonds. This affective prism enables an examination of public apologies in relation to historical antipathies towards black bodies, as represented in racist events, and disavowals of past racial injustices. The mobilisation of pain and outrage, as an affective force that underlies the call for apology, is explored as a demand for recognition. In assessing the (im)potency of the apology, the authors underscore how, for a black majority, it is a superficial public gesture to pacify an outrage. They contend that in the absence of radically reimagining the basis of humanity itself, the prospect for public apology as an instrument for conferring meaningful human recognition remains elusive.

Christi van der Westhuizen deals with apology as a knowledge/power construct that is wielded to ensure certain political outcomes. Making the case for how whiteness, as an epistemology of ignorance, is constituted through the denial of racial injustice, the chapter explores how apology can work to disrupt whiteness and enable accountability, remorse, and recognition. Through the (non)apologies of three prominent Afrikaners, van der Westhuizen foregrounds the interaction between apology and humanisation wherein white denialism is dislodged and mutual humanisation is facilitated though the apology's invocation of a recognition of injustice.

Diane Jefthas shifts genres to foreground the violence of intimate apologies. 'I understand that daddy is very sorry' and 'daddy needs me to forgive him' is how Jefthas' fictional account draws us into the cycle of everyday violence in the most ordinary of places, the home. Through the eyes of a child, we see the play of visibility and invisibility, voice and silence, violence and calm, and are thereby provoked to imagine what sorry means inside the spiral of remorse and rage that is characteristic of domestic violence.

Leila Khan and Dee Smythe interrogate reparation in the context of sexual offences and the limits of criminal law. Focusing on a legal system that has both prioritised punitive over restorative approaches to justice and shown itself to be incapable of providing justice to the vast majority of victims of sexual violence in South Africa, the chapter explores the apologetic meaning of compensation for victims. Applying the framework of categorical apologies (Smith 2014), the authors enumerate how compensation is a feature of apology, its meanings for victims, and how it might be a potential remedial pathway that requires more concerted consideration in addressing the harm they experience.

Omowamiwa Kolawole considers the quest for restitution in medical negligence cases that violate patients' dignity. He argues that in this context, proper acknowledgement of suffering is critical to giving effective apologies for medical wrongdoing. Considering the range of motivations that spur litigation and the material harms that are a feature thereof, Kolawole draws on an empirical study of health litigation to argue that apology can be seen as a form of restitution when centred on restoring a patient's sense of dignity and agency, while simultaneously acknowledging the failure of the medical institution or practitioner. In the face of a systemic pattern of refusal by health authorities to acknowledge the facts of any wrongdoing for fear of liability, he argues for more willingness within health systems to accept responsibility, show categorical regret, and commit to reform and reparation.

Turning the line of sight towards corporations, Tracey Davies looks at contemporary failures of business leadership and governance, including through fraud and illegality, linking the associated impunity to a lack of remorse shown by the business sector for their role in gross violations of human rights during apartheid. Interrogating what constitutes an effective corporate apology, Davies also applies Smith's (2014) categorical apology to expose big businesses' handling of apology and reparations in respect of their role in both past and more recent harms and atrocities. Davies asserts a structural connection between the South African corporate sector's unwillingness to accept moral responsibility for its role in apartheid, and the refusal of major corporations to morally apologise for harms caused in the postapartheid era, thus cementing a corporate culture of untouchability.

Central to the question of reconciliation in the settler-colonial state is landownership and property rights, reflected in past laws of dispossession and present laws that provide for compensation and restitution. In her chapter, Thuto Thipe illustrates that black and white freehold landowners are subjected to inequitable financial compensations on the basis of race. Laws intended to provide restitution of land and redress racial discrimination have instead become a vehicle through which black freehold landowners are yet again differentiated from white freehold landowners and receive a fraction of the compensation that the state paid to the latter. Arguing that the democratic state's logic of land compensation has not substantively dismantled the valuing of land rights on the basis of race, the chapter reveals the inherent tension between the promise of postcolonial apologies (as represented in the remedy of land restitution) and the reality of continued land dispossession.

Circuiting back to the TRC, and challenging the normative coupling of apology with forgiveness, Jaco Barnard-Naudé theorises how the discursive context was ideologically loaded with pardon and mercy, which undermined the apology's reparative potential. Viewing the TRC as an institution in which forgiveness was law, including through the mechanism of amnesty and aimed at securing the sovereignty of the new democratic state, it is analysed as representing a 'ridiculous proliferation of mercy' at the cost of shame, as an essential dimension of apology. The importance of shame in the facilitation of reparation is therefore obstructed by the TRC's governing logic of 'forgiveness' and the failure to procure shame, which diminished its capacity to represent the actual victims of apartheid. The chapter argues that this failing is further manifested in a lack of reparation that is a function of the big Other of forgiveness whose presence remains in the postapartheid dispensation.

The final chapter offers a personal reflection on a 23-year-old justification by Heinz Klug, a constitutional law scholar who previously served in the ANC political underground and Umkhonto we Sizwe.[10] In seeking to make sense of the elisions and insufficiencies of apologies, Klug foregrounds the tension between the lived experiences of victims and the denials, avoidances, and justifications of perpetrators. In his reflective evaluation of the process of truth and reconciliation and its ability to give a proper account of the crime of apartheid, Klug asserts that it is only through direct public accountability, remorse, and memory that an acknowledgement of those who suffered can emerge as a necessary barrier against future repetition of past injustice. Outraged at the failure to adequately recognise the lives of those who paid the ultimate sacrifice for freedom, Klug laments the forgetting and denial that risks a more just and sustainable future. While the liberation movement's embrace of constitutionalism is described as a key achievement of the democratic transition and a safeguard against the capture of unaccountable and undemocratic power, Klug emphasises that a common responsibility on the part of all apartheid beneficiaries remains necessary for realising constitutional aspirations.

As editors, we recognise that bringing one's mind (and the rest) to the topic of this book can invoke difficulties, ambivalences, or conflicts for us as writers. So, in the spirit of writing from where one is situated, and as an antidote to approaching apology as solely an abstracted, cerebral, or academic matter, we invited contributors to reflect on the writing process itself. These reflective narratives are presented at the end of some chapters and uncover yet another layer in the diverse terrain of meaning on apology.

---

[10] Umkhonto we Sizwe, 'Spear of the Nation', was the armed wing of the ANC in the apartheid period.

(No) place for sorry

Sorry is never enough, especially if it does little to interrupt similar harm in future or leaves intact the social hierarchies and inequalities that may have produced the need for it in the first instance. Asking more from the apology – at the risk of imbuing it with excessive meaning – turns us back to the persistent conditions that make the call for apology necessary. Perhaps, then, the apology should be scrutinised according to the extent to which it acknowledges, accounts for, and assumes responsibility for past wrongdoing in ways that facilitate a transformative reconstitution of the social, and one that is substantively different from that on which the original injury was premised. This is a tall order for what is effectively a speech act. Yet, again and again, humanity turns to the apology – whether to demand it, distance from it, deploy it, or deny it. As we have argued, its potential, real or imagined, lies beyond its instance and is bound up with aspirations for rights, recognition, repair, and even reconnection, much of which still evades many spheres of interpersonal, community, national, and global life.

As the logics of injustice and harm are never quite out of reach – for anyone, anywhere, and more so in a place wrought from a violent past – one must consider what happens when the apology's potential to repair (or to salvage), however dim, is abandoned altogether. And, if it were to be so, may it be because the injurious inequalities that bring the apology forth have been dismantled, rather than that shame, remorse, contrition, accountability, and reparative obligation are sacrificed for a more harmful future. For apology always returns to show its presence or absence in the places where suffering is made – and, now and then, where life persists and healing begins.

Reflections

It was not clear to me at the start of this project whether to approach the subject of sorry with hope or with despair. This remains so, perhaps because it is in some way, at least for me, bound up with both feelings. There are apologies I ache to give that may never be received. And apologies I yearn for that will never be offered. That our capacities to injure one another are so enduring, that the conditions we create for others so perilous, renders the giving, withholding, accepting, and refusing of apology fraught with ambivalences. Perhaps the inclination to imbue the apology with too little – or too much – meaning reflects something of how historical patterns of harm, and everyday acts of wrongdoing, are at times irreparable, even unforgivable. Yet, as humans, we have in common an embodied experience of the apology's force and failure, of its reckoning with our place in the world and that of others. For me, to write on apology is an attempt to write against the multiple injustices that keep an imagined common ground of liveability beyond reach. A ground that remains an imaginary – endlessly turning on both despair and hope.

Melanie

My earliest memories of apology evoke dusty playgrounds, torn shirts, and bloody noses. The loser held down on the ground; demands to "say you're sorry", to "say it like you mean it"; and the baffling claims on honour that seemed to go along with both the demand for and acquiescence in apology. Sometimes these tussles were trifling – violence was how pretty much everything was settled in the youth of my memory – but regularly there were more serious, generational, battles. The school I went to had five Afrikaans children for every English child. Sporadically, our Afrikaans school mates revisited, with the earnest intent of righting an historical injustice, the *Boere Oorlog* – the South African War of 1899–1902 in which the Boer republics were defeated by the British. On at least one occasion, we squared off after school with pellet guns, but rocks were usually the weapons of choice. We were the *donnerse Engelse* – the damned English – and the end game was to force out of us an acknowledgement of and accountability for the wrongs visited upon their ancestors by ours. From very early in my life, I knew what those wrongs were: the burning of Boer farms, poisoning of wells, and imprisonment of Boer women and children in British concentration camps 80 years before. It was not that the British won the war, but how they did so that mattered to our antagonists. What these early experiences imprinted on me was a deep cynicism about apologies. It was obvious that these apologies were not about righting a wrong – indeed, it was proof to my young self that some wounds were so deep that an apology could perhaps never be enough – but then wherein did their meaning lie?

Questions about the meaning of apology have continued to trouble me through adulthood, as I've navigated a professional space concerned with remediating patriarchal violence and as I've engaged in the personal reckoning that must be made as a white South African with the harms inflicted by my settler-colonial forefathers. In a twist of irony, my great-grandmother had spent the first years of her life in British concentration camps and her father – my great-great-grandfather, a Boer Kommandant – had died as a British prisoner of war on St Helena Island. My great-aunt was married to a nephew of General de la Rey, whose effective guerrilla campaign in the last years of the Boer War had provided the impetus for Britain's inhuman scorched-earth policy and who would, in the 2000s, become a symbol of right-wing Afrikaner resistance to reconciliation in South Africa. Our schoolyard protagonists knew some of this, but they also sensed, I suspect, that my own identity was not attached to *this* history and *these* wrongs in the way that theirs was. My historical attachment lay elsewhere: with my other great-great-grandfather, whose oligarchic Natal government passed the poll tax that sparked the 1906 Zulu Rebellion, oversaw the heavy-handed response to it, and resigned when the Colonial Office tried to override the imposition of the death penalty on the leaders of that Rebellion. The British government backed down, marking a critical moment of imperial acquiescence to the reality – and excesses – of white minority rule in South Africa. The leader of that Rebellion, Chief Bhambatha kaMancinza Zondi, whose head was decapitated and paraded as a trophy by colonial troops, remains to this day a powerful symbol of African resistance to white rule. We are inevitably ensnared in overlapping generational harms, but apologies were beaten out of me for the Boer War, not the Zulu Rebellion. I learnt on those dusty playgrounds that to demand an apology – and all that an apology encompasses – requires the power to do so; that victims can become perpetrators; that current injustices – however slight – attach powerfully to past wrongs; that apology and forgiveness are not inevitably linked; and that bygones are seldom bygones.

Dee

References

Ahmed, S., 2021, 'Apologies for harm, apologies as harm', *FeministKillJoys* 27 January, viewed 20 August 2021 from https://feministkilljoys.com/2021/01/27/apologies-for-harm-apologies-as-harm/

Alberstein, M. and Davidovitch, N., 2011, 'Apologies in the health care system: from clinical medicine to public health', *Law and Contemporary Problems* 74(3), 151–75.

Blatz, C. W., Schumann, K. and Ross, M., 2009, 'Government apologies for historical injustices', *Political Psychology* 30, 219–41.

Braithwaite, J., 1989, *Crime, Shame, and Reintegration*, Melbourne: Cambridge University Press.

Brooks, R. L., 1999, 'The age of apology', in R. L. Brooks (ed.), *When Sorry Isn't Enough: The Controversy Over Apologies and Reparations for Human Injustice*, pp 3–11, New York: New York University.

Davis, A. M., 2014, 'Apologies, reparations, and the continuing legacy of the European slave trade in the United States', *Journal of Black Studies* 45(4), 271–86.

De Klerk, F. W., 2021, 'An ailing FW de Klerk apologises in final video released after his death', *TimesLive*, 11 November, viewed 20 December 2021 from www.timeslive.co.za/news/south-africa/2021-11-11-watch-an-ailing-fw-de-klerk-apologises-in-final-video-released-after-his-death/

Emdon, E. and Judge, M., 2018, *A Snapshot of the Use of South Africa's Equality Courts*, unpublished report. Cape Town: University of Cape Town.

Faulconbridge, G., 2020, 'Exclusive: "Sorry is not enough", Caribbean states say of British slavery apologies', *Reuters*, 19 June, viewed 20 August 2021 from www.reuters.com/article/uk-minneapolis-police-protests-britain-c-idUKKBN23Q10V

Fehr, R., Gelfand, M. J. and Nag, M., 2010, 'The road to forgiveness: a meta-analytic synthesis of its situational and dispositional correlates', *Psychological Bulletin* 136, 894–914.

Foucault, M., 1998, *The History of Sexuality: The Will to Know*, Vol. 1, London: Penguin.

Gibson, J. L., 2002, 'Truth, justice, and reconciliation: judging the fairness of amnesty in South Africa', *American Journal of Political Science* 46(3), 540–56.

Gobodo-Madikizela, P., 2008, 'Empathetic repair after mass trauma when vengeance is arrested', *European Journal of Social Theory* 11(3), 331–50.

Goffman, E., 1967, *Interaction Ritual: Essays on Face-to-Face Behavior*, Garden City: Doubleday.

Golding, M., 1984–5, 'Forgiveness and regret', *Philosophical Forum* 16, 121–37.

Judge, M. and Smythe, D., 2020, 'Striking women: the politics of gender, sexuality and the law in South Africa' in C. Ashford and A. Maine (eds.), *Research Handbook on Gender, Sexuality and Law*, pp 60–75, London: Edward Elgar.

Kaminski, M. M. and Nalepa, M., 2006, 'Judging transitional justice: a new criterion for evaluating truth revelation procedures', *Journal Of Conflict Resolution* 50(3), 383–408.

Lazare, A., 2004, *On Apology*, Oxford: Oxford University Press.

Millar. G., 2011, 'Local evaluations of justice through truth-telling in Sierra Leone: postwar needs and transitional justice', *Human Rights Review* 12, 515–35.

Mnisi Weeks, S., 2018, *Access to Justice and Human Security: Cultural Contradictions in Rural South Africa*, New York: Routledge.

Norval, A. J., 1998, 'Memory, identity and the (im)possibility of reconciliation: the work of the Truth And Reconciliation Commission in South Africa', *Constellations* 5(2), 250–65.

Petrucci, C., 2017, 'Apology in the criminal justice setting', *Oñati Socio-Legal Series* 7(3), 437–54.

Regehr, C. and Gutheil, T., 2002, 'Apology, justice, and trauma recovery', *Journal of the American Academy of Psychiatry and the Law* 30, 425–30.

Reinders Folmer, C. P., Wildschut, T., Haesevoets, T., De Keersmaecker, J., van Assche, J., and Van Lange, P. A. M., 2021, 'Repairing trust between individuals and groups: the effectiveness of apologies in interpersonal and intergroup contexts', *International Review of Social Psychology* 34(1), 1–15.

Robbennolt, J. K., 2003, 'Apologies and legal settlement: an empirical examination', *Michigan Law Review*, 102, 460.

Schaart, E., 2021, 'The Netherlands told to apologize for slave trade past', *Politico* 1 July, viewed 20 August 2021 from www.politico.eu/article/neth erlands-slave-trade-apology-demand/

Shnabel, N. and Nadler, A., 2008, 'A needs-based model of reconciliation: satisfying the differential emotional needs of victims and perpetrators as a key to promoting reconciliation', *Journal of Personality and Social Psychology* 94, 116–32.

Smith, N., 2008, *I Was Wrong: The Meanings of Apologies*, New York: Cambridge University Press.

Smith, N., 2014, *Justice through Apologies: Remorse, Reform, and Punishment*, New York: Cambridge University Press.

Stanley, E., 2001, 'Evaluating the Truth and Reconciliation Commission', *Journal Of Modern African Studies* 39(3), 525–46.

Tarusarira, J., 2019, 'The anatomy of apology and forgiveness: towards transformative apology and forgiveness', *International Journal of Transitional Justice* 13, 206–24.

Tavuchis, N., 1991, *Mea Culpa: A Sociology of Apology and Reconciliation*, Stanford: Stanford University Press.

Thompson, J., 2008, 'Apology, justice, and respect: a critical defense of political apology' in M. Gibney, R. E. Howard-Hassmann, J. Coicaud, and N. Steiner (eds.), *The Age of Apology: Facing Up to the Past,* pp 61–76, Philadelphia: University of Pennsylvania Press.

Truth and Reconciliation Commission, 1998, *Report*, Vol. 5, viewed 20 May 2021 from www.justice.gov.za/trc/report/finalreport/Volume5.pdf

Twidle, H., 2019, Experiments with Truth: Narrative Non-Fiction and the Coming of Democracy in South Africa, Rochester: James Currey.

Van der Westhuizen, C., 2021, 'FW de Klerk: a defender of his roots until the end', *News24*, 11 November, viewed 20 December 2021 from www. news24.com/news24/obituaries/christi-van-der-westhuizen-fw-de-klerk-a-defender-of-his-roots-until-the-end-20211111

Wakeham, P., 2012, 'Reconciling "terror": managing indigenous resistance in the age of apology', *American Indian Quarterly* 36(1), 1–33.

Zechmeister, J. S., Garcia, S., Romero, C., and Vas, S. N., 2004, 'Don't apologize unless you mean it: a laboratory investigation of forgiveness and retaliation', *Journal of Social and Clinical Psychology* 23(4), 532–64.

2

We Speak in the Shadow of the Tongues They Took

Siphokazi Jonas

Death

Chimera

Neither river nor custodian can
recall the first bite of the flame. Only the
blaze of teeth gnawing at the riverbank.

At Lovedale Mission Station, cinder sons
of chiefs were consumed (daughters and common
folk are always last to catch strange fires)

languishing on an altar of flint-hard
school desks. Civilisation was: Bantu
bellies tenderised by the alien

cuisine of living embers and Trojan
Horse syllabi – recitations of Lear
and Lamentations. And conversion was:

learn to be impervious to the smoke
eclipsing the old trails to the river.

***

On some renaissance day, they find their way
to the blistering lip of the bank, their
mouths full of burning tongues (the Empire

denies setting them alight), unable
to translate themselves to the other side:
they drank, and drank to quench the flame. They sank.

Can you Caliban?

Oh Chthonia, who then shall rescue you?
Erectheus, an oracle, and wars
made muti of your bones. Your death secured
your sire eternal lips. Alas, here too
they've slain their young since 1994's
demand to forge a tender peace. On doors
they nailed then threshed the tongue until taboo.
Split the 'coconut' and 'Oreo' child
in half, unearth a colony of gall
and lies of English–mild and kaffir–wild.
From corridors to belly of school hall
in Prospero's image will they be carved, with
the blood of Chthonia upon the wall.

Mambhele's harvest

My grandmother was a guardian
tending a kingdom of cabbages;
leafy, layered planets in constant orbit emasimini.
uMamBhele was a general, rearing
a battalion for survival at 50c a head.
In imitation of Genesis,
she could craft a field into her image long before the sun had
    sobered to rise.

Her husband, uNcotshe, was himself a spade
toiling in the tunnels of Jozi – the colon of Gauteng –
which is constipated with gold, and the bodies of black men.
Spewing them out on opposite ends:
one to the baas, the other to the grave.
My grandfather was an intercessory prayer, praying in picks;
his penance paid inside a rock.
His sweat would flow like rivers of provision and sacrifice, but
sometimes like signals of smoke; all the way to Keiskammahoek
where they were funnelled into grandmother's veins
    of steel,
and a back as broad as the mountains of uQoboqobo.

Here she would midwife a harvest, all Canaan-like,
all giant-headed paradise-like.
This cabbage connoisseur
could craft seven variations of cabbage dishes –
there were revelations between those leaves
chopped fine like sermons.

Umakhulu noTamkhulu babengabantu bomhlaba.
And my inheritance lay underneath their fingernails.
Even now, when it rains, I find that I crave the soil three times a day.
Some call it anaemia, but I know it to be communion.

My mother is a pillar of soil
with tendrils for fingers.
The plants at home gravitate towards her as if
she is the sun setting into the room.
Perhaps they are descendants of cabbages
packed solar system tight on the back of ibakkie yakwa Mampinga
on Saturday mornings, while grandmother's soldiers
rattled along to the backtrack of an exhaust pipe harmonising,
"50 cents! 50 cents amakhaphetshu! Two for R1!"

But now she must study Agriculture in Afrikaans.
This mother of mine who can swing a hoe in cursive
with more finesse than a pencil,
who learned of the cradle of land
from the canyons in her parents' hands,
must learn the only thing she understands
in a language her tongue does not.

1988
Grandfather's body turns to gold.
Six-feet deep.
But he will not be mined.

1992
John Vorster Primêre Skool.
One of the first blacks in an Afrikaans school
all dolled up in white and blue,
a sign of a South Africa new.
Juffrou reads out the register and non-existent clicks intimidate her –
"Sifokazi Jonas?"
Sifo – disease. Kazi – big.

'Big Disease Jonas.'
"Here ma'am."
My father will explain.

1995
Still in white and blue, now with added red;
English schools are the new means to an end.
On introduction night, our names sit on our tongues like trays.
Flashback.
"Sifokazi Jonas."
Maybe a twang is the antidote?
"Hi, my name is Siphowkarzy Jonas."
Laughter rolls off the other trays: *She's trying to be white.*

1999
My sister is a new recruit to a post-TRC world
where searching for a better life still left us sitting on the back
of Oom Koos' red botsotso bakkie as red as our school ties.
Nathi singamakhaphetshu. We too are cabbages.
Two for R1!

2001
Grandmother is planted.
Six-feet deep.
She will not be harvested.

Now,
My mother is proud of how finely I chop cabbages.
She says, it's the time and care I take to disassemble planets.

Mourning

Of dreams and mielie meal
You might have wished to be a poet,
before you were wife, and mother of so-and-so.
Pressed as you were between the dark mountain
of Verwoerd's embargo on native ambition, and
the flooded valley of a world fashioned for the whims of men.

Contemplated your resemblance, perhaps,
to bruised bodies of grain ushered into the gluttonous belly of
   a grinding stone –

a single kernel pitched back and forth under the press of history.
Wished yourself to be a grinding stone.
Wished your daughters to be grinding stones.

Still,
in the discretion of night strangling fire,
you imagine the grass mat beneath to be
woven page. And you, a praise poem,
improvising endless ways to thutha yourself away from this place,
unsheathing dreams like dry grass from the rondavel's thatched sky
above you.

The moon and the wind declare us gathered around
bowls of umqa, nepapa, nomphokoqo;
all the contingencies we forge
when our grandmothers are food for grinding stones.
In these poems I am sifting through mielie meal with my fingers,
with my back to the mountain.

We do not 'get over'

The fettered trunks of our lost histories,
naked roots and fallen family trees.
In this unapologetic winter,
we recast what remains of black bodies as fuel,
weigh which of our ancestors' bones are still good for wood,
and inherit their propensity to survive the fire:
I, my grandfather's lungs, and encounters with gold,
bequeathed in silicosis.
she, her mother's heels, kneading the ground, subduing
the protesting mud with the 4/4 of a toyi-toyi.
Them, their grandmother's eyes, haunted by spectres of the
    old houses
unavenged on District Six streets.
In Alex, Bizana, eDutywa, Mafikeng, Nyanga East, eQoboqobo,
    Umlazi, and Mitchells Plein
we do not 'get over' the past without betraying ourselves
for bowls of soup.

Making bread

When all is mixed to dough,
I hold a pinch of every isiXhosa poem I write

up to my mother's mouth
to knead between her teeth.
We deliberate on dry ingredients:
that idiom there
this translation here
these puns here, and those ones there.
But she is mum on substitution of self-raising flour for yeast –
knows it is the best I can do in the circumstance
of a tongue baked in surrogacy.
Every December,
in exchange for a Tupperware dish full of roosterkoek
tried over coals,
I present uMama with English poems
to match the decadence of the season.
(English with its heavy hand of sugar
corrodes my vernacular.
English poems do not let me forget
that this bowl I work in is borrowed.)

When we break bread
at the kitchen table,
we slather slices of my mother's tongue with margarine,
steer it along a steaming tide of *Rooibos* tea
or glass sweating with ice and *Oros*:
I do not know how to make this meal last all year long.
I want to pray in isiXhosa,
"give us this day, our daily bread. And
when we commune with you, never let us need grace again".

Big shoes

Do you remember playing dress-up
in Mama's too big shoes and bag,
and how her satin blouse wore you to the knees?
Eventually you grow into her,
then outgrow things neither of you are willing to undress.
You are still an imposter
in your mother's tongue.
There are things you want to unpack
out of this bag,
but you don't have the language to do so.
When you write in isiXhosa
you feel as if everyone is looking at how tight and narrow

English is on your feet.
Rubbing you so raw you are now
a bone out of place, and
a bunion of cultures at war.
All you want is to wear your mother tongue around town
    without limping.

The unveiling

Mending
    Things you have never seen your mother do:
    sitting at a sewing machine,
    making kingdom of table and chair.
    Brown paper patterns and chalk
    spread before her like maps or battle plans,
    dividing fabric along its natural borders
    to style clothes into the countries
    of her imagination.

    Things in which you have never heard your mother speak:
    the language of pencil sketches and scissors
    with the resonance of a polyglot
    soothing the stuttering tongues of
    cashmere and cotton, satin or silk,
    along some unseen dreamscapes.

    Things you cannot count about your mother:
    the number of buttons restored,
    the splits she has sealed, seams under strain, and
    the lengths she has hemmed,
    needle in one hand and thread in the other.
    How many times she has licked one end of that thread
    into a point sharp enough to fit through an eye.

    Things you do know about your mother:
    she never mends without first unravelling.
    She listens to both sides of the wound, and
    lets it breathe until it can speak,
    until it tells her the kind of stich needed for healing.
    You also know that after all the unravelling and speaking,
    and speaking and unravelling,
    she ties a knot so tight; it is a living will.

That knot holds together what is lost between two pieces of fabric
between your woven worlds.

It is how you know your mother is a storyteller,
by how she seeks the best point from which
to pierce a narrative without wounding it again.
The pathways she finds between characters as stubborn as denim
the new ones she must make.
The healing that comes with new thread
making its way through ancient hurt;
how she follows the path of piercing.

There are other things she has stitched in you with the
    same precision
along the seam of tearing skin.
She turns you inside out and stiches from within.
She grapples with the fraying, reconciling
threads imperfectly, but always
on the end of this story is a knot as tight as a prayer.
I would have to tear myself up again to undo it.

My grandmother, my mother, and I are turned inside out
    and pierced.
Tracing the torn places and finding
how they might speak to each other again.
Reminded that a stitch only follows an unravelling.
We are unravelling,
forced to gather at needlepoint, and
to remember all the days
we sat at our mothers' feet,
not quite paying attention as she taught us
how to thread an eye,
how to tie a knot tight enough to hold our tongues,
to mend a village through its children.
We are remembering healing ways disguised as hemming stiches.

3

Can an Apology Ever Be Enough for Crimes of the Past?

Yasmin Sooka

Introduction

The South African Truth and Reconciliation Commission (TRC) has become almost synonymous with the notion that an apology for the past is sufficient to obtain forgiveness, even for the gravest of crimes, given the equating of the amnesty process with forgiveness. This is in complete contradiction to the notion that an apology should be victim-centred and not compromise the rights of victims to justice, truth, and reparations, and should instead facilitate the delivery of those rights. Victims should also not be coerced into accepting apologies in the name of societal goals, such as social cohesion, reconciliation, and national unity (United Nations Special Rapporteur 2019). This chapter sets out how apologies have been dealt with in the field of transitional justice, including individual apologies before regional bodies and international tribunals, and those by heads of state to populations at large for the crimes orchestrated or committed by them directly (in the case of individual perpetrators), or by their predecessors or their state. The chapter then turns to how apologies were tendered in the context of the South African TRC, and advances the argument that an apology in this context is inappropriate without the acknowledgement that apartheid was a crime against humanity and that the apartheid state was a criminal state, with death squads operating outside the rule of law. The chapter makes the point that to apologise without coupling it to measures acknowledging responsibility for reparations is despicable and unjust.

Apologies and transitional justice

Apologies have long been considered an important aspect of transitional justice. But, as Carranza et al (2015: 3) note, 'their impact on victims and society has varied according to whether the apologies were accompanied by other forms of reparation or were part of a broader transitional justice agenda' designed to transform a society. Historically, transitional justice is associated with accountability for the crimes of the past. The normative understanding of transitional justice was formalised in 2004 by the United Nations (UN) Secretary-General, who defined it as 'the full range of processes and mechanisms associated with a society's attempts to come to terms with a legacy of large-scale past abuses, in order to ensure accountability, serve justice and achieve reconciliation' (UN Security Council Secretary-General 2004: 4). The updated principles to combat impunity expanded this framework, setting out the obligations of states and rights of victims in response to gross violations of human rights and serious violations of international humanitarian law, through the four complementary pillars of the right to truth, the right to justice, the right to reparation, and the guarantee of non-recurrence.[1] In 2006 the rights of victims were further strengthened, when the UN General Assembly adopted a set of Basic Principles and Guidelines on the Right to a Remedy and Reparations for Victims of Gross Violations of International Human Rights Law and Serious Violations of International Humanitarian Law.[2] This document provides that victims should receive 'full and effective reparation', which includes: 'restitution, compensation, rehabilitation, satisfaction and guarantees of non-repetition' (art. 18). One form of 'satisfaction' set out in the principles and guidelines is an apology that is public, acknowledges the facts, and accepts responsibility (art. 21(e)).

Public apologies in the field of transitional justice have tended to be 'solemn and, in most cases, public acknowledgement that human rights violations were committed in the past, that they caused serious and often irreparable harm to victims, and that the state, group, or individual apologizing is accepting some or all of the responsibility' for the violation (Carranza et al 2015: 4). Carranza et al explain further that acknowledgement in this context is both a factual and moral recognition that victims' rights were violated, that these victims suffered harm, and that the state, as well as individuals

---

[1]   UN Commission on Human Rights, *Updated Set of Principles for the Protection and Promotion of Human Rights through Action to Combat Impunity*, UN Doc. E/CN.4/2005/102/Add.1, 8 February 2005.

[2]   A/RES/60/147, 21 March 2006.

who are legally accountable for committing or enabling the violations, are obligated to repair the harm done.[3]

As Carranza et al (2015: 4) argue, 'at their best, apologies can help to mark a before and after period, acting as a symbolic turning point', characterised by debate and reflection among 'political elites, different identity groups, or social classes, or across an array of social, economic, and political divides'. In the context of transitional justice, apologies raise critical questions such as who the audience is, the motivation for the apology, the timing and language, and whether the apology is accompanied by an acknowledgement of the truth and responsibility for reparations (Carranza et al 2015).

Apologies by heads of state

In post-conflict societies, political leaders, frequently on behalf of the state, commonly proffer public apologies to victims of human rights abuses (Carranza et al 2015).

There have been many heads of sovereign states who have apologised for their nation's prior conduct, domestically and internationally (Stoltz and van Schaak 2021). As in Chile (Roniger and Sznajder 1999: 101), Indonesia (Rondonuwu 2008) and South Africa (Sly 1993), most apologies have been offered many years after the violations occurred, and often only after the conclusion of criminal and civil trials, or truth-seeking processes. Prime Minister Tomiichi Murayama offered Japan's first full apology for its wartime conduct a full 50 years after Japan's surrender in the Second World War (Murayama 1995), admitting that Japan had 'through its colonial rule and aggression, caused tremendous damage and suffering to the people of many countries, particularly to those of Asian nations', and expressing his 'feelings of deep remorse', 'heartfelt apology', and 'profound mourning for all victims' (Murayama 1995), but failing to provide for concrete reparation.

The impact of these apologies on survivor communities and the international standing of states is varied, as will be seen from examples in this chapter. Apologies have, in certain instances, served important foreign and domestic policy interests. However, the moral imperative to apologise and express remorse for human rights abuses must be accompanied by

---

[3] For example, the UN *Basic Principles and Guidelines on the Right to a Remedy and Reparation for Victims of Gross Violations of International Human Rights Law and Serious Violations of International Humanitarian Law* provides in article 16 that states should endeavour to establish national programmes for reparation.

measures on reparations that acknowledge the violations and harm done to the victims and communities, in order to reinforce credibility.

Apologies by states are frequently associated with demands for monetary reparations, including compensation. There is no doubt that the field of reparations has been greatly influenced by the example of how successive German governments concretely linked their remorse for the Holocaust to reparations to Israel and to Jewish Holocaust victims around the world (Jewish Virtual Library n.d.). Despite these examples, the international debate around apologies and compensation has continued to be a controversial one, particularly in relation to colonialism, as most governments are deeply fearful that apologies to their former colonies might result in the demand that they pay reparations. In 2013, after a lengthy legal campaign waged by the survivors of the Mau Mau Rebellion in Kenya, which included litigation and lasted for more than four years, the UK government eventually tendered a settlement (Wessley 2017). The settlement included an expression of 'sincere regret' and payment of £2,600 each to around 5,000 people imprisoned and tortured during this Rebellion in the 1950s (Wessley 2017). In 2016 in Canada, Grand Chief Stewart Phillip of the Union of British Columbia Indian Chiefs declined to attend a reconciliation ceremony with the Duke and Duchess of Cambridge when they paid their first state visit to Canada, stating: 'Reconciliation has to be more than empty symbolic gestures ... the chiefs-in-assembly just didn't feel that it was appropriate to feed into that public illusion that everything is okay' (Kassam 2016).

Following bilateral negotiations between the German Foreign Ministry and the Namibian government, the German government admitted that Germany had waged a war against the local communities of the Ovaherero and Nama (and the Damara and San) between 1904 and 1908 in German South West Africa (now Namibia), recognising that it was a genocide. In May 2021 the special envoys of Germany and Namibia signed a joint declaration, which stated that: 'Germany apologises and bows before the descendants of the victims ... The Namibian Government and people accept Germany's apology and believe that it paves the way to a lasting mutual understanding and the consolidation of a special relationship between the two nations' (Joint Declaration 2021). Both governments have been criticised for using the joint declaration to 'seek ... forgiveness without listening to descendants' and for making no reference to the return of land to the dispossessed as part of restitutive justice (Hitchcock and Kelly 2021). The declaration avoids the term 'reparations', committing an amount of €1.05 billion (US$1.18 billion) over a period of 30 years to development projects in Namibian regions with the descendants of the genocide victims, without dealing with individual reparations (Joint Declaration 2021).

Apologies before international criminal courts, tribunals, and regional bodies

As comprehensively detailed in the 2019 Report of the UN Special Rapporteur on the Promotion of Truth, Justice, Reparation and Guarantees of Non-Recurrence, apologies are a key feature in the jurisprudence of a number of international courts (United Nations Special Rapporteur 2019). The International Criminal Tribunal for the former Yugoslavia (ICTY) is a case in point, where one third of the 90 sentenced defendants made statements of apology, 19 of which were part of their guilty pleas (United Nations Special Rapporteur 2019: 7). One particular case before the ICTY draws attention to the authenticity and credibility of apologies. It involved the former president of Republika Srpska, Biljana Plavšić, pleading guilty to crimes against humanity and making a statement of apology that led the prosecution to drop some of the charges against her, in particular the charge of genocide (United Nations Special Rapporteur 2019). A number of those present disputed whether Plavšić's statement amounted to an apology, and ICTY Prosecutor Carla Del Ponte recounted: '[Plavšić] got up during her sentencing hearing and read out a statement full of generalized mea culpas but lacking compelling detail. I listened to her admissions in horror, knowing she was saying nothing' (Del Ponte and Sudetić in United Nations Special Rapporteur 2019: 7). Following the granting of her early release from prison, Plavšić confessed that her apology had been a strategic move to avoid a harsher sentence, reiterating that she had done nothing wrong. The Report of the UN Special Rapporteur also notes that senior transitional justice figures, including former US Secretary of State Madeleine Albright and Alex Boraine, the former Deputy Chair of the South African TRC, gave evidence in support of Plavšić, as they regarded her apology as critical to reconciliation in the region.

In the case of the International Criminal Tribunal for Rwanda (ICTR), one sixth of the 62 defendants expressed some remorse for their past crimes; however, none of the highest-ranking defendants apologised (United Nations Special Rapporteur 2019). The former Prime Minister of Rwanda at the time of the genocide, Jean Kambanda, offered no apology, contrition, or regret for his active involvement in the genocide, despite the court having given him the opportunity to do so.[4]

An apology also featured in the International Criminal Court (ICC) when Ahmad Al Faqi Al Mahdi was convicted for the war crime of intentionally directing attacks against historic religious monuments and buildings in

---

[4] *Prosecutor v Jean Kambanda*, ICTR 97-23-S, Judgment and Sentence, 4 September 1998, para. 51.

Tombouctou, Mali, in July 2012.[5] At his sentencing hearing, Al Mahdi expressed remorse and regret at the damage his actions had caused, and the ICC ordered that his statement of apology be published on its website as a symbolic measure of reparation (United Nations Special Rapporteur 2019).[6] While the court considered the apology to be 'genuine, categorical and empathetic', some victims publicly rejected it, questioning the sincerity, timing, and place of delivery.[7]

In another case before the ICC involving Germain Katanga, who was sentenced to 12 years' imprisonment for crimes against humanity and war crimes in the Democratic Republic of the Congo,[8] the accused did not apologise during the trial or at sentencing.[9] However, later, while in detention, Katanga did issue a public apology for the sentence review hearing (United Nations Special Rapporteur 2019). His apology was not accepted by his victims, who indicated that it was not specific to the crimes Katanga had committed and was only a strategic move to avoid a harsher sentence.

There is no doubt that apologies and remorse play a significant role in the acknowledgement of wrongdoing and in the healing process. It is, however, extremely problematic if they are taken into account as a factor impacting on sentencing, given that it is exceptionally difficult for judges to assess the credibility of an apology.

The most developed jurisprudence on apologies before regional human rights courts has emerged from the Inter-American Court of Human Rights. In a number of its decisions on reparations, the Inter-American Court has ordered public apologies to compel states to acknowledge their responsibility for past human rights violations and to apologise to victims.[10] A case in point is *Plan de Sánchez Massacre v Guatemala*,[11] which concerned the killing of Mayan villagers by the Guatemalan armed forces in 1982. The court held that 'to be fully effective as reparation to the victims and serve as a guarantee of non-recurrence, … the State must organize a public act

---

[5]   *Prosecutor v Ahmad Al Faqi Al Mahdi*, ICC-01/12-01/15-171, Judgment and Sentence, 27 September 2016.

[6]   *Prosecutor v Ahmad Al Faqi Al Mahdi*, ICC-01/12-01/15-236, Reparations Order, 17 August 2017, para. 71. For further discussion of reparations in the *Al Mahdi* case, see Capone (2018).

[7]   *Prosecutor v Ahmad Al Faqi Al Mahdi*, Reparations Order, 17 August 2017, para. 70.

[8]   *Prosecutor v Germain Katanga*, ICC-01/04-01/073436, Judgment pursuant to art. 74 of the Statute, Trial Chamber II, 7 March 2014.

[9]   *Prosecutor v Germain Katanga*, ICC-01/04-01/073728, Order for Reparations pursuant to art. 75 of the Statute, Trial Chamber II, 24 March 2017, para. 315.

[10] *Bámaca Velásquez v Guatemala*, (Reparations and Costs), IACHR Series C No 70, 22 February 2002, para. 84.

[11] *Plan de Sánchez Massacre v Guatemala*, Judgment (Reparations), IACHR Series C No 116, 19 November 2004.

acknowledging its responsibility for the events that occurred' (para. 100). While the African Commission on Human and Peoples' Rights has issued reparation orders, it has not sought nor required an official apology in any case (Redress 2013: 71).[12]

In examining these examples of apologies, there is a notable difference between apologies made by individuals (such as Al Mahdi and Katanga) and those made by heads of state on behalf of the state or state structures. In the case of individuals, the impact of their apology is measured by the satisfaction of victims who often consider the apology as irrelevant or opportunistic with regard to its impact on sentencing. The apologies of heads of state, usually for historical crimes and injustices, have the impact of recognition and acknowledgement for past state crimes, which decisively ends cultures of denial, even where individual victims may reject such apologies.

Apologies in the South African context

South Africa's negotiated settlement in 1993 brought an end to an internal armed conflict that had lasted more than 350 years, and conclusively drew a line under more than three decades of rule by the apartheid government (South African History Online 2019). There were no winners of the conflict, posing critical questions to the negotiators on how to deal with the crimes of the past and heal a highly unequal nation with deep racial and political divides (Boraine et al 1994; Sooka 2007). As can be seen from the Explanatory Memorandum to Parliament accompanying the TRC Bill,[13] the amnesty deal was framed as a bridge between the past and the future, and a necessary prerequisite to achieving reconciliation. This link was explicitly reflected in the postscript of South Africa's transitional Interim Constitution.[14] And it was taken up in the preamble to the new

---

[12] For example, African Commission on Human and Peoples' Rights, Communication No. 295/04, Zimbabwe Human Rights NGO Forum/ Zimbabwe, paras. 131 and 136; African Commission on Human and Peoples' Rights, Communication No. 295/04, Abdel Hadi and others/Sudan.

[13] Memorandum on the Objects of the Promotion of National Unity and Reconciliation Bill, 1995. Available at www.justice.gov.za/trc/legal/bill.htm.

[14] 'The acceptance of this Constitution creates a solid foundation for the people of South Africa to bridge the divisions and discord of the past that had led to severe violations of human rights, the breaking of the principles of humaneness during violent conflict and a legacy of hate, fear, guilt and revenge. The opportunity now presents itself to put it right on the basis that there is a need for understanding and not for a thirst for revenge, a need for recovery and not for retribution, a need for ubuntu and not for victimisation. In order to promote this reconciliation and restructuring, amnesty has to be granted with regard to acts, omissions and misdemeanors connected to political aims and that was perpetrated in the course of the conflict of the past.' Postscript, Constitution of the Republic of South Africa Act 200 of 1993.

Constitution.[15] Ingeniously, the provisions of the amnesty would only be determined when the new democratic government was established following elections, an acknowledgement that neither the liberation movements nor the illegitimate apartheid government enjoyed the legitimacy to finalise the process of reconciling South African society.

The year-long consultations on the scope of the amnesty deal eventually introduced a conditional approach, requiring that individuals make individual voluntary applications for amnesty, based on two requirements: full disclosure about the crimes they were involved in, and proof that those were carried out in pursuit of the political objectives of either the former state and its agencies, or the liberation movements.[16] To ensure that their rights were protected, victims and their families could oppose an amnesty application and cross-examine amnesty applicants before the Amnesty Committee, composing of judges of the High Court and operating as a quasi-judicial body.[17] The amnesty deal was incorporated in legislation establishing the South African TRC. This legislation was linked to the goals of truth recovery and investigations into past violations, reparations, victim recognition, and recommendations for non-recurrence through institutional reform to ensure national healing and reconciliation.[18] The South African TRC was established in 1995 in the aftermath of the earlier Latin American Truth Commissions, in Chile, Argentina, and El Salvador, all of which had been set up in the context of military dictatorships making way for civilian governments, and focused mainly on civil and political rights violations (Neier et al 1994: 1, 8; Arthur 2009).

The amnesty law did not require an apology or even an expression of regret to secure an amnesty. In return for a full disclosure of their crimes, individual perpetrators were granted amnesty and escaped prosecution and any claim for damages; and if they had been convicted and were in prison, they would be released and their conviction and sentence expunged. The Human Rights Violations Committee provided for the documentation of gross human rights violations perpetrated during the apartheid years and also supplied a forum for victims to testify to their suffering. Together with the Reparations and Rehabilitation Committee, these Committees facilitated the restoration of human dignity and recognition for South African citizens. However, there is no doubt that the emphasis on *ubuntu* and reconciliation, particularly by Archbishop Tutu, the Chair of the Commission, perversely saw South

---

[15] Constitution of the Republic of South Africa Act 108 of 1996.

[16] The Promotion of National Unity and Reconciliation Act 34 of 1995.

[17] Explanatory Memorandum to Parliament accompanying TRC Bill, www.justice.gov.za/trc/legal/bill.htm.

[18] The Promotion of National Unity and Reconciliation Act 34 of 1995.

Africa's unique experience of transitional justice become defined by the notion that an apology tendered by a perpetrator entitled that perpetrator to forgiveness by victims. This unfair exchange constituted a substitute for justice. The Human Rights Violations Committee often found itself at odds with the Amnesty Committee's emphasis on the rights of perpetrators, to the detriment of the rights of victims.

As the amnesty process unfolded, a notable distinction emerged between truth recovery and satisfying the criteria for full disclosure, which the amnesty law required, as many perpetrators who came before the Amnesty Committee obtained amnesty without necessarily disclosing the full truth. This is evidenced in the Nokuthula Simelane case, where the applicants were granted amnesty for her abduction, and where the Amnesty Committee failed to make the link with the international crime of an enforced disappearance (South African Broadcasting Corporation 1999). Furthermore, the perpetrators were not put on terms by the Amnesty Committee to disclose her final whereabouts and confirm their responsibility for her murder, as would be required under the legal obligations relating to an enforced disappearance (Patino and Huhle 2020). The case exemplifies the complexity of the search for the truth when it is separated from justice. Truth is not always easy to establish and, as Argentinean lawyer Juan Mendez has noted, it 'does not necessarily emerge from a commission or an exercise in truth telling' (Mendez in Boraine et al 1994: 89). Mendez argued that it was 'misguided to separate truth and justice, because prosecutions provide a measure of truth that is more complete and more undeniable than that which is achievable through a truth commission' (Mendez in Boraine et al 1994: 89). This was certainly true for the numerous cases involving enforced disappearances in the apartheid period. In Colombia, the Colombian Special Jurisdiction for Peace (JEP) also noted the distinction between victims wanting a recognition of the truth and receiving a factual account by a perpetrator of an event or incident, which angered victims as it did not constitute acknowledgement of the crime perpetrated.[19] The JEP, responding to the challenge that this created, worked incredibly hard to ensure that perpetrators would not just provide a factual account, but would own and acknowledge that they had perpetrated serious international crimes amounting to both war crimes and crimes against humanity (Liévano 2021).

The mandate of the TRC in South Africa focused primarily on civil and political violations (a legacy of the Latin American experience). This mandate was too narrowly construed, as it obscured the structural and pervasive legacy of violations, failing to recognise that the South African

---

[19]   Special Jurisdiction for Peace and Foundation for Human Rights Dialogue, 2021, 'Building a Community of Practice', Confidential Virtual Consultation, 7 May 2021.

conflict was intrinsically about the systemic crimes of apartheid as set out under the Apartheid Convention. The United Nations had in 1966 declared 'apartheid' a crime against humanity (Dugard 2008). There is no doubt that the laws and structural policies underpinning apartheid in South Africa went far beyond civil and political rights violations to encompass structural violations, which remain the most bitter legacy that the country lives with today (Dugard 2008).

Unfortunately, the transition in South Africa and the work of the TRC has been characterised by the lack of any meaningful apology to those who suffered under the apartheid system, particularly black South Africans. There has also been a complete and utter failure of the leadership of white apartheid South Africa, including former presidents P. W. Botha and F. W. de Klerk and politicians of the old order, to acknowledge that apartheid was a crime against humanity (Sooka 2007). Antjie Krog, a South African journalist who covered the work of the TRC, made the point that '[t]he [families of the] victims ask the hardest of … questions: How is it possible that the person I loved so much lit no spark of humanity in you?' (Krog 1998: 36).

The South African TRC heard the apologies of numerous amnesty applicants, including those from politicians. These apologies have been extremely difficult to deal with. They include F. W. de Klerk's apology with reservations and qualifications (South African Press Association, 1997a); the apology wrung from Winnie Madikizela-Mandela by the Chair of the Commission, Archbishop Desmond Tutu (TRC 1997); and the apology tendered by the killers of Amy Biehl before the TRC (Biehl and Nofomela n.d.). Then, when the Commission handed over its final report to him, President Mandela made a gracious apology to our nation in an extremely difficult and volatile context, and amid having been taken to court by the ruling party to stop the report from being published (Mandela 1998). Another example arose in the aftermath of the work of the Commission, when the former apartheid Minister of Law and Order, Adriaan Vlok, apologised to his victims by washing their feet (Fairbanks 2014). In addition, Gideon Niewoudt, a security branch member in the Eastern Cape, went to the home of slain student leader Simphiwe Mtimkulu to ask for forgiveness (Matyu and Bamford 2004).

At the time of the transition, Rev. Beyers Naude, a Dutch Reformed minister and one of the first Afrikaners to speak out against apartheid and who served seven years' house arrest under a banning order, said an apology by the National Party was essential from the Christian perspective: 'Just three words – "we are sorry" – will do more to restore meaningful relations between blacks and whites in South Africa than all the sermons I or anyone else could preach' (Wren 1991). Sadly, President F. W. de Klerk himself was intransigent. Speaking on state-run television in 1991, he said that the decision to undertake fundamental change was prompted by soul-searching in the National Party and the realisation within those ranks that separate development of racial groups could not succeed (O'Malley 1991). It was unhelpful to apportion blame for the past, he said, because the nation's problems could only be confronted by looking ahead.[20] In response, Sampie Terreblanche, an economist at Stellenbosch University, a leading Afrikaans-speaking academic institution, remarked that 'it's a bizarre state of affairs … the unwillingness, the unpreparedness of De Klerk and his people to make a confession for the National Party and its guilt for this suffering … they are convinced about the unworkability of apartheid, not about the immorality or exploitive character of apartheid' (Wren 1991).

Former president de Klerk died on 11 November 2021 at the age of 85 years at his home in Cape Town after a battle with cancer. Following his death, his foundation released a pre-recorded farewell message, in which de Klerk says he "defended separate development in his early years" but "had a conversion" in the 1980s and realised apartheid was wrong (de Klerk 2021). And he apologised: "I, without qualification, apologise for the pain and the hurt and the indignity and the damage that apartheid has done to black, brown and Indians in South Africa," a frail-looking de Klerk says in the undated video (de Klerk 2021).

It is tragic that even in death, former president de Klerk's video from the grave fails to address critical questions around his own role during apartheid, leaving the families of victims and South Africa with many untold secrets about how his government functioned, and without properly and honestly accounting to the families whose loved ones were murdered by his party and the government he served for decades. His deathbed apology still does not acknowledge that apartheid had been declared a crime against humanity and that the apartheid state had been a criminal one. De Klerk also makes no mention of the need for acknowledgement and restitution for the wrongdoing and harm done to countless victims and their families. His attempt to clean up his legacy through a video from the grave fails utterly, and continues to mislead South Africans about his role during apartheid, spinelessly abrogating his responsibility to subordinates. His greatest crime is that he failed to deal with the truth of the past in the spirit of real truth and reconciliation.

In examining his apologies, it is noteworthy that throughout his life, the former president consistently denied having any knowledge of the setting up of death squads. Rather, he claimed that as Commander in Chief he must have been lied to, stating that 'the activities of units like the Civil Cooperation Bureau (CCB), the Directorate of Covert Collection Operations (DCC) and Vlakplaas were deplorable and inexcusable' (de Klerk 1999). He consistently

---

[20] Interview with F.W. de Klerk, 21 May 1996.

refused to acknowledge that these units were established and funded death squads, and that their activities – including killings, massacres, torture, and enforced disappearances – were condoned by the apartheid state (de Klerk 1999). It was extremely difficult for de Klerk to credibly maintain his denial, as he served in the National Assembly of the apartheid government from 1972 and held numerous cabinet posts from 1979 onwards. He was also alleged to have participated, from its inception, in more than 98 per cent of meetings of the State Security Council, which constituted a parallel structure running apartheid South Africa under former president P.W. Botha (de Klerk 1999). De Klerk was allegedly present at a meeting of the State Security Council in May 1986, which discussed the setting up of a 'third force', effectively death squads (South African Broadcasting Corporation n.d.). The State Security Council was responsible for establishing death squads under the apartheid government and de Klerk arguably exercised both command and superior responsibility for the crimes perpetrated by these squads (Pauw 1991; TRC 1998, vol. 6). Under international law, command and superior responsibility are modes of liability, which entail the responsibility of a military or civilian commander for serious crimes committed by their subordinates (Bantekas 1999; Case Matrix Network 2016). The responsibility of the commander arises from an omission: their failure to prevent or punish serious international crimes.

De Klerk's denial of apartheid as a crime against humanity was particularly noteworthy when he appeared before the TRC a second time on 14 May 1998, and repeated, in more impassioned terms than before, his apology for apartheid (South African Press Association 1997a). De Klerk (1999) reiterated his belief that apartheid was wrong and said:

> I apologize ... to the millions of South Africans who suffered the wrenching disruption of forced removals in respect of their homes, businesses and land. Who over the years suffered the shame of being arrested for pass law offences. Who over the decades and indeed centuries suffered the indignities and humiliation of racial discrimination. Who for a long time were prevented from exercising their full democratic rights in the land of their birth. Who were unable to achieve their full potential because of job reservation. And who in any other way suffered as a result of discriminatory legislation and policies. (p 378)

De Klerk's apology was rejected by both the TRC and the victims of apartheid crimes, given his denial and refusal to acknowledge that the apartheid state had become a criminal state and that the crimes perpetrated by the apartheid government constituted crimes against humanity (TRC 1997a). De Klerk continued to maintain that he did not know who authorised the activities of the death squads, despite the testimony to the contrary of senior officials within the apartheid state (de Klerk 1999: 378).

Incensed at the findings regarding his conduct, which the TRC was proposing to publish in its final report, and which was to be handed over to President Mandela on 29 October 1998, de Klerk threw the Commission a curveball. While its report was being transported from Cape Town to Johannesburg for the handover, former president de Klerk approached the courts to compel the Commission to remove the findings dealing with the denial of his role as an accessory to human rights violations, specifically in the bombing of Khotso House and COSATU House in the 1980s (South African Press Association 1998a; Daley 1998; BBC 1998; van Zyl 1999). The Commission, on the advice of its lawyers, decided to remove its findings on de Klerk from the Commission's final report and replace it with a black page reminiscent of the days of apartheid government censorship when the media would publish a symbolic black page where the censored/banned article would have appeared (South African Press Association 1998a). The Commission's lawyers advised that withdrawing the finding temporarily would allow the Commission an opportunity to publish and disseminate its report and engage with de Klerk in the future over the proposed findings.[21] The Commission finally published its findings against de Klerk in its final volume 6, handed over to President Mbeki on 21 March 2003, and revealed that he had failed to make full disclosure when testifying about human rights violations (TRC 1998, vol. 6). It also found that de Klerk was an accessory to these violations, given his admission that he knew of former Police Commissioner Johan van der Merwe and former Law and Order Minister Adriaan Vlok having been involved in the bombings and didn't report them because they had applied for amnesty (TRC 1998, vol. 6). De Klerk was also among those implicated by Eugene de Kock in crimes perpetrated by the apartheid state and was alleged to have been present at a meeting of the State Security Council when the authorisation was given to kill the Cradock Four (Amnesty International/Human Rights Watch 2003).[22]

On reviewing the evidence that came before the TRC 27 years later, it is clear that the Commission's findings should have detailed de Klerk's role as the head of state with command and superior responsibility for the crime of apartheid, bearing in mind that he had been a cabinet minister in

---

[21] Legal advice provided to the Commission by Advocate David Soggot, October 1998. On file with the author.

[22] Eugene de Kock is a former police colonel of the apartheid regime. He commanded the infamous Vlakplaas unit which specialised in executing and torturing anti-apartheid activists. The Cradock Four are a group of four anti-apartheid activists who were abducted and murdered by South African security police in 1985 in the town of Cradock, Eastern Cape province.

the apartheid government for more than 16 years and had participated in numerous meetings of the State Security Council. While apologies play a critical role in acknowledging the painful truth of a country's history, in the case of de Klerk, critics have suggested that the former president regarded an unequivocal apology as signifying weakness and making him potentially vulnerable to criminal proceedings.

The Commission's removal of the finding against de Klerk emboldened the ruling party, the African National Congress (ANC), to also contest the TRC's proposed finding against itself. On the eve of the handing over of the five-volume report to President Mandela on 27 October 1998, the ANC filed an application to stop the publication of the findings against it. This would inevitably prevent the handover of the TRC report (South African Press Association 1998a; South African Press Association 1998b). The ANC filed a 25-page affidavit accusing the TRC of trying to criminalise the struggle for the liberation of South Africans (O'Malley 1998). This action was premised on the Commission's proposed finding that a distinction could be drawn between a just war and the means used to conduct that just war. The finding was based on the ANC's own submissions, that it had in certain instances violated international humanitarian law (O'Malley 1998). In its application the ANC argued that this was to protect itself and the national liberation struggle (South African Press Association 1998b; Guelke 1999). The ANC also argued that the TRC had not given adequate time to rebut the proposed findings of gross human rights violations against it, this despite having received notice of the proposed finding three months in advance, within which time the ANC could have made further submissions to the TRC, but decided not to respond (Deegan 2015). The Commission, and in particular the Archbishop and his deputy, were devastated by the ANC's legal action and opposed the application. The Cape High Court, on 28 October 1998, upheld the Commission's right to publish the finding and hand over the final report, which took place in an incredibly tense environment with a large number of cabinet ministers boycotting the ceremony. President Mandela, gracious as always, accepted the report and indicated his willingness to assume responsibility for the crimes perpetrated against the South African population, even though most of these crimes were committed by the former apartheid government (Mandela 1998).

One of the greatest challenges for the TRC was its interactions with Winnie Madikizela-Mandela who appeared before the Commission in an eight-day hearing (South African Press Association 1997b). The hearing also saw the ANC divided in its support for Madikizela-Mandela, despite the fact that she was regarded as the 'mother of the nation'. Ironically, the Commission itself did not want a public hearing and ventilation of the allegations that had been raised and offered her a closed, in-camera hearing (TRC 1997b). Madikizela-Mandela perversely dared the Commission to take her on and demanded a public hearing (South African Press Association 1997c). The public hearing, which began on 24 November 1997 and ended on 4 December 1997, witnessed devastating testimony from prominent United Democratic Front (UDF) leaders, including Murphy Morobe, Azhar Cachalia, and Frank Chikane, to name but a few (TRC 1997b).[23] The UDF leadership spoke of the complete lack of accountability that Madikizela-Mandela displayed in dealing with the Mandela United Football Club. Countless victims and their families testified to the reign of terror sowed by the Mandela United Football Club in Soweto during the 1980s, leading the community to even burn down the Mandela house (TRC 1997b). At the hearing, evidence emerged of the numerous informers, including Jerry Richardson, the coach of the Football Club, who had surrounded Madikizela-Mandela and infiltrated her circle in order to compromise her – an obvious Stratcom operation by the apartheid state.[24] The hearing, however, came to a dramatic end when the Chair of the Commission, Archbishop Desmond Tutu, pleaded with her to take responsibility for the wrongs committed, to acknowledge that things had gone wrong, and to say that she was sorry. Under the Archbishop's tearful entreaty to her, Madikizela-Mandela conceded that 'things went horribly wrong' and said she was 'deeply sorry' (TRC 1997b).[25] Looking back, it is extremely difficult to analyse what motivated her expression of regret and whether it was genuine or, as author Njabulo Ndebele described, 'a minor concession to the moral authority of the man of God who stood before you' (Ndebele 2003: 63).

Many years later, in a conversation with Winnie Madikizela-Mandela at a social event, she admitted that she had apologised under duress and that she really hated the Archbishop in that moment.[26] She stated explicitly that she did not consider herself to be a victim and therefore decided not to testify before the Commission. She was also enraged that the Commission itself never took the trouble to explore the brutal repression unleashed against her and her daughters by the apartheid state in total violation of their rights, including torture and harassment, when her husband went to prison. She reiterated this statement in a documentary on her life, where she said that she hated Tutu and that her subpoena to appear before the Commission was part of a Stratcom operation against her. The apology wrung from her by

---

[23] The United Democratic Front was an anti-apartheid body that included many anti-apartheid organisations and leaders, and formed part of the broader internal liberation movement in support of the banned and exiled ANC.

[24] Stratcom, also known as Strategic Communications, was a police unit that was set up to produce and disseminate false information against political enemies of the National Party government.

[25] For more on the Madikizela-Mandela apology, see Hassim in this volume.

[26] Private communication, July 2012.

an emotional Archbishop, deeply pained by the testimony at the hearings, raises the question of whether it was genuine and whether she took political responsibility for her actions and that of the Club, as Karl Jaspers suggests politicians have a responsibility to do (Jaspers 1966). Whatever the answer, one cannot help but contrast her conduct with that of de Klerk, who self-righteously threatened to walk out of the TRC hearings. Did Madikizela-Mandela become responsible in the minds of white South Africans for the activities of the ANC, waged in its war against the apartheid state, and why was her apology necessary when no other ANC leader was asked to apologise? One cannot but ask whether gender played a role in how she was treated.

In another controversial incident in 2007, Adriaan Vlok, the last serving Minister of Law and Order in the apartheid government between 1986 and 1991, negotiated a plea bargain with the National Prosecuting Authority (NPA) for the attempted murder of Rev. Frank Chikane.[27] His plea bargain was made in exchange for a ten-year suspended sentence, but shockingly did not provide any new disclosures, including the name of the person who supplied the paraxon (a deadly poisonous substance) to the operatives who laced Frank Chikane's clothes with it, or who had authorised the operation (Groenewald 2007: 10; Govender 2007: 10). Chikane became so ill that he had to be flown to Paris for treatment, narrowly escaping death (Groenewald 2007: 10; Govender 2007: 10). Vlok, however, was the only apartheid politician to be convicted of apartheid crimes (Fairbanks 2014). Years later, Vlok underwent a life-altering conversion (his words) to 'Born Again Christianity' and consequently decided that God required him to apologise to his victims. On 1 August 2006, Vlok made his way to the Union Buildings to tender an apology to Rev. Frank Chikane, by washing his feet and recreating the biblical story of Jesus washing the feet of his disciples (Fairbanks 2014). Rev. Chikane, the former Secretary-General of the South African Council of Churches, had been the target of the apartheid government given the pivotal role he played in the 1980s in opposing apartheid and campaigning for sanctions against South Africa (Balcomb 2004). Chikane fortunately survived the assassination attempt and surprisingly allowed Vlok to wash his feet. Vlok's act of washing the feet of victims,[28] while applauded by many, was heavily criticised by many families of victims, who questioned the value of an apology unaccompanied by a full disclosure about who developed and supplied the poison and gave the orders for its use (Fairbanks 2014). These questions have remained unanswered even today.

---

[27] On the plea bargain and the outcome, see Groenewald (2007: 10) and Govender (2007: 10).
[28] Vlok also washed the feet of the Mamelodi mothers who lost their sons at the hands of the death squads.

The discourse on apologies in South Africa

The discourse on apologies in South Africa is morally and legally repugnant as it has tended to advance the notion of forgiveness rather than accountability for the crimes of the past. However, as these examples illustrate, an apology without an acknowledgement that the apartheid state was criminal in nature, establishing and funding death squads to operate outside of the law, is untenable. To compare the criminal nature of the apartheid state with that of Nazi Germany, it is useful to turn to Karl Jaspers. In his dialogue on the nature of Nazi Germany, he suggests that '[t]he decisive point is whether one acknowledges that the Nazi state was a criminal state, and not merely a state that committed crimes' (Jaspers 1966). Jaspers argues that 'a criminal state is one which, in principle, neither establishes nor acknowledges the rule of law' and that 'what it calls justice, and what it produces in a flood of laws, is for it a means to the pacification and subjugation of masses of men, and not something that the state itself honors and observes' (Jaspers 1966). The apartheid state behaved exactly as the Nazi German state did, passing unjust, discriminatory, criminal, and immoral laws under the pretext that the mere legislating of laws would establish its legality to operate under rule by law rather than rule of law. Indeed, the attribution of responsibility to individual perpetrators is understood to be the fundamental task of justice after mass atrocity crimes, as was articulated by the Nuremberg tribunal: 'crimes ... are committed by men, not by abstract entities, and only by punishing individuals who commit such crimes can the ... law be enforced' (International Military Tribunal Nuremberg 1947: 223; Bonafè 2009: 37).

The debate around apologies, however, also raises the issue of the responsibility of the beneficiaries. This question, and whether all Germans are collectively responsible for Nazi crimes, was asked at the end of the Second World War by the Allied Forces. Schaap reads Arendt and Jaspers as agreeing that, 'by virtue of their membership in a political community, all citizens are ... collectively responsible for reparations to those wronged by their state', while holding to the critical distinction between 'collective guilt' and 'collective responsibility' (Schaap 2001: 750). Collective responsibility attaches to individuals *as citizens* of a state and is therefore not unjustly imposed, while collective guilt is unjust, because it imposes individual blame, regardless of intention, for the conduct of others (Schaap 2001). As Jaspers writes, 'a people must answer for its polity' (Jaspers 1961: 55).

If one draws an analogy with South Africa, the majority of white South Africans voted successive National Party governments into power with overwhelming majorities and therefore have a responsibility for the crimes perpetrated by the state they voted into power. Collectively, they too have a responsibility to apologise to those who were oppressed by the apartheid state and to make reparations.

Furthermore, the evidence available before the TRC suggests that de Klerk and his cabinet colleagues bear both political responsibility for the crimes perpetrated by the apartheid state and also criminal responsibility, given their roles as cabinet ministers and members of the State Security Council, the body which authorised death squads and crimes against humanity (TRC n.d.). Nevertheless, most apartheid politicians, like de Klerk and his colleagues, have consistently refused to acknowledge that apartheid was a crime against humanity, despite the declaration by organs of the United Nations and the international community[29] that they presided over a criminal state. Indeed, de Klerk himself only changed his stance in 2020, when challenged by the human rights community and the media and when the American Bar Association disinvited him from giving their annual lecture (DW.com 2020).

In the case of the leadership of the apartheid state, an apology can never be sufficient to deal with the crimes of apartheid.[30] Apartheid-era cabinet ministers and officials holding high political appointments during apartheid must be held criminally accountable, none of whom, barring Adriaan Vlok, have been convicted. Moreover, none of them to date has offered reparations for the crimes of the past. The failure by the democratic state to hold the late President de Klerk and his colleagues accountable, for both command and superior responsibility for apartheid crimes, as well as those officials and foot soldiers who did not apply for amnesty or who were refused amnesty, remains a stain on the South African state. In truth, the language of reconciliation may have allowed the perpetrators of apartheid to believe that they would never have to accept any kind of responsibility, including criminal accountability, for the crimes of the past. Any apology in these circumstances would be totally obscene.

Reflections

Writing the piece on apologies brought home the impunity that existed in South Africa under the apartheid state and equally that of the democratic state. This has led to the political suppression of cases emanating from the TRC, the Marikana massacre, the

---

[29] In 1966, the General Assembly labelled apartheid as a crime against humanity (UN General Assembly, *The Policies of Apartheid of the Government of the Republic of South Africa*, A/RES/2202 (XXI), 16 December 1966), and in 1984 the Security Council endorsed this determination (UN Security Council, *Security Council resolution 556 (1984) [South Africa]*, S/RES/556 (1984), 23 October 1984).

[30] See *France and ors v Göring (Hermann) and ors,* Judgment and Sentence [1946] 22 IMT 203.

Esidimeni tragedy, as well as sexual and domestic violence impacting on women and LGBTI+ people.[31] Impunity is also manifest in endemic corruption including the looting and pillage of COVID-19 funds by state officials and private corporations. Impunity for apartheid-era crimes in South Africa is indelibly linked to the failure to implement the recommendations of the TRC – particularly the failure to prosecute apartheid criminals, which compromises the rule of law. The discourse on forgiveness and reconciliation is offensive as it is not accompanied by remorse or a commitment to reparations. The impunity emanating from the political suppression of the TRC cases by the democratic state has entrenched my view, in line with that of international law, that amnesties should never be allowed for serious international crimes. Numerous victims testifying in the reopened Ahmed Timol, Neil Aggett, Ernest Dipale, and Hoosen Haffejee inquests described the brutal torture they experienced at the hands of the security branch during the apartheid years, including the pain, humiliation, disempowerment, and loss of self. Torture is dehumanising and its victims never fully recover from their experiences. It is also exacerbated by the denial by security branch torturers of the torture. The failure to acknowledge their crimes is deeply repugnant, and must be punished. Furthermore, those responsible for systemic crimes must also be held accountable. Louis Joinet, a UN authority on the question of the impunity of perpetrators of violations of civil and political rights, points out in his influential work on impunity that '[a]ction to combat impunity has its origins in the necessity that justice be done, … and must respond to three imperatives: sanction those responsible, satisfy the right of the victims to know and to obtain reparation and, allow the authorities to discharge their mandate as the power which guarantees public order'. Impunity in South Africa was a political choice by the apartheid state to hide their criminality, but in the case of the democratic state we have an enigma – why is the democratic government intent on protecting apartheid-era perpetrators?

Yasmin

---

[31] Esidimeni concerns the cruel and inhumane treatment at psychiatric facilities in the Gauteng province of South Africa in 2015–16 that resulted in the deaths of 144 mental health patients and over 1,400 being exposed to torture, trauma, and severe human rights violations. The Marikana massacre refers to the killing of 34 miners by the South African Police Service in 2012 during a wildcat strike at the Lonmin platinum mine in Marikana, North West Province.

References

Amnesty International/Human Rights Watch, 2003, 'Truth and justice: unfinished business in South Africa', briefing paper February 2003, viewed 12 May 2021 from www.hrw.org/legacy/backgrounder/africa/truthandjustice.pdf

Balcomb, A., 2004, 'From apartheid to the new dispensation: evangelicals and the democratization of South Africa', *Journal of Religion in Africa* 34, 1–2.

Bantekas, I., 1999, 'The contemporary law of superior responsibility', *The American Journal of International Law* 93(3), 573–95.

BBC, 1998, 'De Klerk accusations cut from report', *BBC News*, 28 October, viewed 12 May 2021 from http://news.bbc.co.uk/2/hi/africa/202367.stm

Biehl, L. and Nofomela, E., n.d., 'Stories', viewed 12 May 2021 from www.theforgivenessproject.com/stories/linda-biehl-easy-nofemela/

Bonafè, B. I., 2009, *The Relationship between State and Individual Responsibility for International Crimes*, Leiden: Martinus Nijhoff.

Boraine, A., Levy, J., and Scheffer, R. (eds.), 1994, *Dealing with the Past: Truth and Reconciliation in South Africa*, Cape Town: IDASA.

Capone, F., 2018, 'An appraisal of the Al Mahdi order on reparations and its innovative elements: redress for crimes against cultural heritage', *Journal of International Criminal Justice* 16(3), 645–61.

Carranza, R., Correa, C., and Naughton, E., 2015, *More than Words: Apologies as a Form of Reparation*, New York: International Centre for Transitional Justice.

Case Matrix Network, 2016, *International Criminal Law Guidelines: Command Responsibility*, Brussels: Centre for International Law Research and Policy. Also available at www.legal-tools.org/doc/7441a2/pdf/

Daley, S., 1998, 'South Africa truth commission may withhold its report', *New York Times*, 29 October 1998, viewed 12 May 2021 from www.nytimes.com/1998/10/29/world/south-africa-truth-commission-may-withhold-its-report.html

Deegan, H., 2015, *Politics South Africa*, Abingdon: Routledge.

De Klerk, F. W., 1999, *The Last Trek: A New Beginning*, New York: St. Martin's Press.

De Klerk, F. W., 2021, 'An ailing FW de Klerk apologises in final video released after his death', *TimesLive*, 11 November, viewed 20 December 2021 from www.timeslive.co.za/news/south-africa/2021-11-11-watch-an-ailing-fw-de-klerk-apologises-in-final-video-released-after-his-death/

Dugard, J., 2008, 'Introductory note – convention on the suppression and punishment of the crime of apartheid', Geneva: United Nations Audiovisual Library of International Law, viewed 12 May 2021 from https://legal.un.org/avl/pdf/ha/cspca/cspca_e.pdf

DW.com, 2020, 'Ex-South African president de Klerk withdraws apartheid comments after backlash', *DW.com News*, 17 February 2020, viewed 12 May 2021 from www.dw.com/en/ex-south-african-president-de-klerk-withdr aws-apartheid-comments-after-backlash/a-52410923

Fairbanks, E. 2014, ' "I have sinned against the Lord and against you! Will you forgive me?" ' *The New Republic*, 19 June 2014, viewed 12 May 2021 from https://newrepublic.com/article/118135/adriaan-vlok-ex-aparth eid-leader-washes-feet-and-seeks-redemption

Govender, P., 2007, 'Vlok not completely off the hook', *Sunday Times*, 19 August 2007, 10.

Groenewald, Y., 2007, 'Vlok's walk to freedom', *Mail and Guardian*, 17–23 August 2007, 10.

Guelke, A., 1999, 'Truth for amnesty? The Truth and Reconciliation Commission and human rights abuses in South Africa', *Irish Studies in International Affairs* 10, 25.

Hitchcock, R. and Kelly, M., 2021, 'Reconciliation between Germany and Namibia: towards reparation of the first genocide of the 20th century', *IWGIA*, 12 October 2021, viewed 26 February 2022 from www.iwgia. org/en/news/4538-reconciliation-between-germany-and-namibia-towa rds-reparation-of-the-first-genocide-of-the-20th-century.html

International Military Tribunal Nuremberg, 1947, *Trial of the Major War Criminals before the International Military Tribunal Nuremberg, 14 November 1945–1 October 1946*, Vol. 1, Nuremberg: Secretariate of the International Military Tribunal Nuremberg. Also available at www.loc.gov/rr/frd/Milit ary_Law/pdf/NT_Vol-I.pdf

Jaspers, K., 1961, *The Question of German Guilt*, New York: Capricorn Books.

Jaspers, K., 1966, 'The criminal state and German responsibility', abridged version, trans. Dannhauser, W. J., *Commentary*, February 1966, viewed 12 May 2021 from www.commentarymagazine.com/articles/karl-jaspers/ the-criminal-state-and-german-responsibility-a-dialogue/

Jewish Virtual Library, n.d., 'Holocaust restitution: German reparations' viewed 11 May 2021 from www.jewishvirtuallibrary.org/german-holoca ust-reparations

Joint Declaration, 2021, 'Joint declaration by the Federal Republic of Germany and the Republic of Namibia: united in remembrance of our colonial past, united in our will to reconcile, united in our vision of the future', May, viewed 23 February 2022 from www.parliament.na/wp-cont ent/uploads/2021/09/Joint-Declaration-Document-Genocide-rt.pdf

Kassam, A., 2016, 'Canada First Nations chief won't join UK royals for "empty gesture" ceremony', *The Guardian*, 26 September, viewed 25 February 2022 from www.theguardian.com/world/2016/sep/26/canada-first-nations-prince-william-kate-middleton-british-columbia

Krog, A., 1998, *Country of my Skull*, Johannesburg: Random House.

Liévano, A. B., 2021, 'Kidnappings in Colombia: FARC leaders acknowledge full responsibility', *JusticeInfo.Net*, 7 May, viewed 12 May 2021 from www.justiceinfo.net/en/76928-kidnappings-colombia-farc-leaders-acknowledge-full-responsibility.html

Mandela, N., 1998, 'Statement by Nelson Mandela on receiving Truth and Reconciliation Commission report', 29 October, viewed 12 May 2021 from www.mandela.gov.za/mandela_speeches/1998/981029_trcreport.htm

Matyu, J. and Bamford, H., 2004, 'Family relives pain after Niewoudt video', *IOL*, 7 March, viewed 12 May 2021 from www.iol.co.za/news/politics/family-relives-pain-after-niewoudt-video-207281

Murayama, T., 1995, 'Statement by Prime Minister Tomiichi Murayama "on the occasion of the 50th anniversary of the war's end"', Ministry of Foreign Affairs of Japan, 15 August, viewed 26 February 2022 from www.mofa.go.jp/announce/press/pm/murayama/9508.html

Ndebele, N., 2003, *The Cry of Winnie Mandela*, Cape Town: David Philip.

Neier, A., Zalaquett, J., and Michnik, A., 1994, 'Why deal with the past', in A. Boraine, J. Levy and R. Scheffer (eds.), *Dealing with the Past: Truth and Reconciliation in South Africa*, 2nd ed., pp 3–21, Johannesburg: IDASA.

O'Malley, P., 1991, 'De Klerk, FW – press conference', *O'Malley Archive*, 30 July, viewed 12 May 2021 from https://omalley.nelsonmandela.org/omalley/index.php/site/q/03lv00017/04lv00344/05lv00511/06lv00525.htm

O' Malley, P., 1998, 'TRC report released', *O'Malley Archive*, November, viewed 12 May 2021 from https://omalley.nelsonmandela.org/omalley/index.php/site/q/03lv02424/04lv02730/05lv02918/06lv02951.htm

Paige, A., 2009, 'How "transitions" reshaped human rights: a conceptual history of human rights', *Human Rights Quarterly*, 31(2), 321–67.

Patino, M. C. J. and Huhle, R., 2020, 'The rights of the victims of enforced disappearance do not have an expiration date', *OpinioJuris*, 7 July, viewed 12 May 2021 from http://opiniojuris.org/2020/07/07/the-rights-of-the-victims-of-enforced-disappearance-do-not-have-an-expiration-date/

Pauw, J., 1991, *In the Heart of the Whore: The Story of Apartheid's Death Squads*, Johannesburg: Jonathan Ball.

Redress, 2013, *Reaching for Justice: The Right to Reparation in the African Human Rights System*, London: Redress.

Rondonuwu, O., 2008, 'Indonesia, "East Timor leaders regret vote bloodshed"', *Reuters*, 15 July, viewed 30 June 2022 from www.reuters.com/article/uk-indonesia-timor-idUKJAK5503420080715

Roniger, L. and Sznajder, M., 1999, *The Legacy of Human Rights Violations in the Southern Cone: Argentina, Chile, and Uruguay*, Oxford: Oxford University Press.

Schaap, A., 2001, 'Guilty subjects and political responsibility: Arendt, Jaspers and the resonance of the "German question' in politics of reconciliation', *Political Studies* 49(4), 749–66.

Sly, L., 1993, 'De Klerk apologizes for apartheid's abuses', *Chicago Tribune*, 30 April, viewed 25 February 2022 from www.chicagotribune.com/news/ct-xpm-1993-04-30-9304300330-story.html

Sooka, Y., 2007, 'E pluribus unum? Race and reconciliation', in A. Adebajo, A Adedeji, and C. Landsberg (eds.), *South Africa in Africa: The Post-Apartheid Era*, pp 78–91, Durban: University of KwaZulu-Natal Press.

South African Broadcasting Corporation, n.d., 'Special report, transcript episode 66, Section 1', viewed 12 May 2021 from https://sabctrc.saha.org.za/tvseries/episode66/section1/transcript40.htm&t=de+klerk&tab=tv?tab=hearings

South African Press Association, 1997a, 'De Klerk apologises again for apartheid', *SAPA*, 14 May, viewed 12 May 2021 from www.justice.gov.za/Trc/media/1997/9705/s970514a.htm

South African Press Association, 1997b, 'Winnie remains unmoved during testimony at TRC', *SAPA*, 24 November, viewed 12 May 2021 from www.justice.gov.za/trc/media/1997/9711/s971124l.htm

South African Press Association, 1997c, 'Winnie told to appear before Truth Commission', *SAPA*, 23 September, viewed 12 May 2021 from www.justice.gov.za/trc/media/1997/9709/s970923h.htm

South African Press Association, 1998a, 'TRC deletes FW de Klerk criticism from final report', *SAPA*, 28 October, viewed 12 May 2021 from www.justice.gov.za/trc/media/1998/9810/s981028a.htm

South African Press Association, 1998b, 'ANC interdict throws TRC's final report into disarray', *SAPA*, 28 October, viewed 12 May 2021 from www.justice.gov.za/trc/media/1998/9810/s981028n.htm

South African Broadcasting Corporation, 1999, 'Amnesty hearing transcript of day 9 of the amnesty hearing of Wilhelm Coetzee', 17 May, *SABC*, viewed 12 May 2021 from https://sabctrc.saha.org.za/hearing.php?id=53362&t=Nokuthula+simelane+coetzee&tab=hearings

South African History Online, 2019, 'Negotiations and the transition', viewed 12 May 2021 from www.sahistory.org.za/article/negotiations-and-transition

Stoltz, D. and van Schaak, B., 2021, 'It's never too late to say "I'm sorry": sovereign apologies over the years', *Just Security*, 16 March, viewed 11 May 2021 from www.justsecurity.org/75340/its-never-too-late-to-say-im-sorry-sovereign-apologies-over-the-years/

Truth and Reconciliation Commission, n.d., 'Transcript of security hearing on 14 October', viewed 12 May 2021 from www.justice.gov.za/trc/special/security/1securit.htm

Truth and Reconciliation Commission, 1997a, 'Transcript of the National Party, party political recall, 14 May 1997', viewed 12 May 2021 from www.justice.gov.za/Trc/special/party2/np2.htm

Truth and Reconciliation Commission, 1997b, 'Transcript of day 1 of the human rights violation hearing of Nomzamo Winnie Madikizela Mandela' 24 November, viewed 12 May 2021 from www.justice.gov.za/trc/special/mandela/mufc1.htm

Truth and Reconciliation Commission, 1998, *Report*, Vol. 6, Cape Town: Truth and Reconciliation Commission, viewed 30 June 2022 from https://www.justice.gov.za/trc/report/finalreport/vol6_s5.pdf

United Nations Security Council Secretary-General, 2004, *Report of the Secretary-General on the Rule of Law and Transitional Justice in Conflict and Post-Conflict Societies*, UN Doc S/2004/616, 3 August.

United Nations Special Rapporteur, 2019, *Report of the Special Rapporteur on the Promotion of Truth, Justice, Reparation and Guarantees of Non-Recurrence*, UN Doc. A/74/147, 12 July 2019.

Van Zyl, P., 1999, 'Dilemmas of transitional justice: the case of South Africa's Truth and Reconciliation Commission', *Journal of International Affairs* 52(2), 647–67.

Wessley, A., 2017, 'The Mau-Mau case – 27 years on', *Leigh Day*, 6 October, viewed 11 May 2021 from www.leighday.co.uk/latest-updates/blog/2017-blogs/the-mau-mau-case-five-years-on/#:~:text=In%20mid%202013%20the%20government,that%20these%20abuses%20took%20place%E2%80%9D

Wren, C. S., 1991, 'The world; South Africa and apartheid: no apologies, *New York Times,* 24 February, viewed 18 May 2021 from www.nytimes.com/1991/02/24/weekinreview/the-world-south-africa-and-apartheid-no-apologies.html

4

In Pursuit of Harmony:
What Is the Value of a
Court-Ordered Apology?

Sindiso Mnisi Weeks

Introduction

It was the crack of dawn and thus barely light in Msinga, KwaZulu-Natal, when MaMakhe's son, Mfana, saw their neighbour, MaMsolwa, near the gate of his family's homestead. Their dog's bark had woken him and prompted him to go out to see what was the matter. Mfana returned to alert his mother; it was then that he realised that it was MaMsolwa standing by the gate of MaMakhe's home in conversation with another neighbour. Mfana concluded that the situation was harmless and returned to bed. Yet other members of his family were not as easy to placate; already awake, MaMakhe, her daughter Buhlungu, and her other son went to the gate. It was clear – or so it seemed to them – that MaMsolwa was up to no good; in fact, Buhlungu averred that MaMsolwa wanted to kill her mother.

MaMsolwa brought the matter to the headman's council because of the accusation that she had been performing witchcraft at MaMakhe's gate at dawn.[1] In her defence, MaMsolwa said that she had just been standing there in conversation. Finding against MaMakhe, the headman's council ordered MaMakhe's family to cleanse MaMsolwa's name and household in ritual practice. This would be done by giving a goat to be slaughtered on behalf of her daughter for this purpose, which cleansing ceremony the headman said would make it possible for the parties to forgive each other, be reconciled, and 'return to living alongside each other as neighbours as

---

[1]   This case is discussed in Mnisi Weeks (2018: 59–60 and 222).

before'. In the headman's assessment, their dispute had not been a 'case' but rather an instance of neighbours (and, thus, friends) 'correcting each other'.

It is of some interest as to why MaMakhe and most of her children had promptly concluded that MaMsolwa was up to mischief at their gate. As it happened, this very fact was canvassed in discussions before the headman's court. According to Buhlungu, MaMsolwa had said to MaMakhe, 'If I die, I will have died at your home, MaMakhe', to which Buhlungu had responded, 'If my mother dies, she will have died at your hand'. The headman asked why Buhlungu had made such a statement, to which she replied that she knew that her mother disliked MaMsolwa. With some probing, the headman's council learnt that the reason for the mutual animosity between MaMakhe and MaMsolwa was a rumour that had reached the ears of MaMakhe, according to which MaMsolwa had allegedly said, when lightning had struck her home, that MaMakhe had sent it (thus implying that MaMakhe practised witchcraft).

What had caused such deep and enduring offence, however, was not this particular rumour but another that turned out to be worthy of further investigation. It turned out that MaMakhe had initially been accused of issuing a witchcraft accusation against MaMsolwa following a separate set of injurious events. In particular, MaMakhe's family had reported that a mobile phone had gone missing, which MaMakhe alleged to have been taken by MaMsolwa's children. MaMsolwa alleged that, although she had permitted MaMakhe's children to search for the phone at her home and they had failed to locate it there, MaMakhe's children had not conducted themselves appropriately. She reported that MaMakhe's children had threatened destruction of MaMsolwa's phone, at which point she had started calling out for the assistance of neighbours (who also unsuccessfully searched her home for the missing mobile phone). Against this backdrop MaMsolwa had heard a rumour that she had been seen coming to perform witchcraft outside MaMakhe's home.

MaMsolwa had reported this first witchcraft accusation to the headman and ultimately taken the matter to the chief's council for hearing. At that point, MaMakhe was found to be without sufficient proof for her allegation of witchcraft. Thus, Buhlungu's accusation, this second time, was a re-enactment, of sorts, of her mother's prior alleged accusation against MaMsolwa. In turn, MaMsolwa's reporting to the headman was itself a re-enacted event in a repeating cycle of neighbourly conflict marked by unresolved resentments and unhealed wounds concerning difficult words exchanged in the face of unexplained property loss. In essence, MaMakhe was persuaded against the available evidence that, enabled by MaMsolwa, MaMsolwa's child had stolen the phone belonging to a child of MaMakhe.

Considering the history between these neighbours, the headman's reflections on the value of an apology, grounded in a ceremony in which the blood of a goat, paid for by MaMakhe, would be shed to cleanse MaMsolwa's home, seemed somewhat hollow. In particular, the dispute between MaMsolwa and MaMakhe raises all sorts of questions about the value of an apology that is not grounded in a process in which the parties fully air and effectively address the initial source of conflict between them and the enduring (indeed, compounding) pain that gave rise to the original conflict. It is from this place that it is necessary to trouble the use of apologies as remedies in judicial processes, wherein parties are ordered to apologise, as contrasted with mediation processes, wherein an apology might arise from one or other party in response to developed understanding of the harm caused to and pain inflicted on one another.

Vernacular dispute management forums (that is, locally developed spaces for dealing with disputes in deep rural South African communities) often order their parties to apologise to one another. Furthermore, in its 2008/ 2012 and 2017 versions, the Traditional Courts Bill has consistently provided for an apology as an order that can possibly be issued by these forums. However, there has been little reflection on what the value is of an apology when it is ordered in such contexts. It turns out that this is an important consideration in the face of empirical evidence from vernacular forums, which shows that ordered apologies do not bear a necessary relationship with reconciliation, being the articulated goal, as well as alternative dispute resolution literature, which shows that reconciliation is best achieved by other means.

This interrogation has become even more urgent as the South African government quickly moves to pass into law legislation that takes for granted that apologies are suitable remedies in vernacular forums. In December 2020, the Traditional Courts Bill (TCB) (B1-2017) was approved by the National Council of Provinces and sent on to the National Assembly's Portfolio Committee for final processing before it becomes law, which was expected to occur on 16–17 March 2021, but has since been repeatedly delayed.[2] Despite all of the arguments that have been presented, by ordinary rural people and civil society over the last 12 years, as to why vernacular forums should not be regulated as 'courts', in the sense in which that term is used in s. 166(e)

---

[2] After two failed attempts to pass the version of the Traditional Courts Bill embodied in B8-2008 and B1-2012, the latest version of the Traditional Courts Bill (B1-2017) was introduced in the National Assembly (NA) in January 2017. Since then, it has been passed by the NA in March 2019 and the National Council of Provinces (NCOP) in December 2020. The Select Committee on Security and Justice's vote to approve the Bill, with minor edits, was based on mandates from seven provinces in support of the bill (Eastern Cape, Limpopo, Mpumalanga, Free State, Northern Cape, Gauteng, and North West), and two provinces not in support (KwaZulu-Natal and the Western Cape, the latter ultimately abstaining from the vote).

of the Constitution,[3] but rather as alternative dispute management 'forums' under s. 34,[4] the legislature has thus far seemed insistent on recognising them as 'courts of law'.[5] What comes with this is the power to *impose* the *penalty* of an apology, even alongside a description of 'traditional courts' as conciliatory spaces[6] that focus on 'maintaining harmony'[7] and achieving 'restorative justice', which itself is described in terms of reconciliation.[8]

---

[3] Section 166 of the Constitution of the Republic of South Africa Act 108 of 1995 reads: 'Judicial system. The courts are *(a)* the Constitutional Court; *(b)* the Supreme Court of Appeal; *(c)* the High Courts, including any high court of appeal that may be established by an Act of Parliament to hear appeals from High Courts; *(d)* the Magistrates' Courts; and *(e)* any other court established or recognised in terms of an Act of Parliament, including any court of a status similar to either the High Courts or the Magistrates' Courts'.

[4] Section 34 of the Constitution reads: 'Access to courts. Everyone has the right to have any dispute that can be resolved by the application of law decided in a fair public hearing before a court or, where appropriate, another independent and impartial tribunal or forum'.

[5] Section 1 of the TCB defines this term as follows: ' "court" means any court established in terms of section 166 of the Constitution'. It says ' "traditional court" means a customary institution or structure, which is constituted and functions in terms of customary law, for purposes of resolving disputes, in accordance with constitutional imperatives and this Act, and which is referred to in the different official languages as *(a)* "eBandla" in isiNdebele; *(b)* "Huvo" in Xitsonga; *(c)* "Inkundla" in isiZulu; *(d)* "iNkhundla" in siSwati; *(e)* "iNkundla" in isiXhosa; *(f)* "Kgoro" in Sepedi; *(g)* "Kgotla" in Sesotho; *(h)* "Khoro" in Tshivenda; *(i)* "Kgotla" in Setswana; and *(j)* a tribunal for Khoi-San communities'.

[6] Section 2 states that '[t]he objects of this Act are to *(a)* affirm the values of customary law and customs in the resolution of disputes, based on *restorative justice* and *reconciliation* and to align them with the Constitution; *(b)* affirm the role of traditional courts in terms of customary law by (i) promoting co-existence, peace and *harmony* in the community; …' (emphases added).

[7] In describing the 'nature of traditional courts', s. 6 of the TCB states:
'(1) Traditional courts—
(a) are *courts of law* the purpose of which is to promote the equitable and fair resolution of certain disputes, in a manner that is underpinned by the value system applicable in customary law; and *(b)* function in accordance with customary law, subject to the Constitution.
(2) Traditional courts must be constituted and function under customary law so as to—
(a) promote access to justice;
(b) prevent conflict;
(c) maintain harmony; and
(d) resolve disputes where they have occurred, in a manner that promotes *restorative justice*, Ubuntu, peaceful co-existence and *reconciliation*, in accordance with constitutional imperatives and the provisions of this Act' (emphases added).

[8] As s. 1 of the TCB defines it, ' "*restorative justice*" (emphases in original) *(a)* means an approach to the resolution of disputes that aims to involve all parties to a dispute, the families concerned and community members to collectively identify and address harms, needs and obligations by accepting responsibility, making restitution and taking measures to prevent a recurrence of the incident which gave rise to the dispute and promoting *reconciliation* (emphasis added); *(b)* does not extend to measures which, in good faith, purport to give effect to the objectives contemplated in paragraph *(a)* but which, in

The entwined ironies here should not be lost on the reader. First, is an apology truly 'a regretful acknowledgement of an offence or failure' (as the *Oxford English Dictionary* defines 'apology'), and thus sincere, when it is imposed as a penalty by a court of law rather than organically emergent from the wrongdoer? This prompts a subordinate question: does it matter whether or not an apology is sincerely 'regretful' for it to be valuable? Secondly, does a so-called harmonious community truly qualify as being 'free from disagreement or dissent', possessing 'the quality of forming a pleasing and consistent whole', or in 'the state of being in agreement or concord' (as the *Oxford English Dictionary* defines 'harmony' and 'harmonious') when its dispute management forums must be legally assigned the punitive powers of courts and its members must be compelled to apologise by means of a court order? Furthermore, if court-ordered apologies are inconsistent with harmonious community, then what values and purposes do they really serve in the recognition of traditional communities and their governance? It is these questions to which this chapter responds.

Thus, the chapter explores the motives behind the desire of parties, courts, and legislators for the use of an ordered apology as a remedy. It interrogates the conditions that produce the endurance of this desire, and challenges the conventional wisdom surrounding traditional dispute management practices and their relationship with harmony ideology (Nader 1990). In so doing, it engages with the nature of dispute resolution processes as socio-politically performative environments in which social constructs are instantiated (Mnisi Weeks 2011). It simultaneously considers the nature of customary law and the political economy of communities that continue to live under traditional normative arrangements in 21st-century South Africa.

The argument presented is essentially that the ways in which 'harmony' is used in descriptions of traditional communities and the authority of traditional leaders to govern them, including by resolving disputes as described by the Traditional Courts Bill (TCB), are not benign. In fact, these uses of 'harmony' are nefarious as the concept is fundamentally used for oppressive purposes. That is, traditional community harmony cannot be 'maintained' because it cannot exist or persist under the enduring conditions of the historical and contemporary political economy of rural South Africa in the first place. In that respect, the embeddedness of MaMakhe and MaMsolwa's conflict in material loss is important to acknowledge here.

---

fact, do not meaningfully restore the dignity of, or redress any wrong-doing against, any person involved in the dispute; and *(c)* results in redressing the wrong-doing in question and ensuring the restitution of the dignity of the person in question in a just and fair manner'.

Furthermore, vernacular forums cannot achieve the goals of achieving 'harmony' as adjudicative structures (a la 'traditional courts'), but rather as hyphenated mediatory and arbitration spaces (which they have always been). This implies that vernacular forums should be supported in operating as structures that facilitate disputants fully airing and effectively addressing the original sources of their conflicts and the wounds they leave behind, so that returning to good neighbourliness becomes a realistic hope.

In other words, by recognising them as 'courts', and comparing them to Magistrates' Courts, the TCB increases the pressures on vernacular forums to formalise and subjects them to the axiological, ontological, epistemological, and temporal logics of Western dispute resolution and relationships with people and things. It does this all while disguising this imperialist move in the language of tradition, as was done by colonial authorities under the principle of 'indirect rule' (Mamdani 1996). But, in fact, the axiological, ontological, epistemological, and temporal logics of vernacular dispute management lean heavily towards informality, negotiability, relationality, complexity, longevity, and multi-generationality.

This skewing of logics towards the colonial is already prevalent in rural communities, their governance structures and their disputing processes, after generations of pressure to formalise and professionalise in order to be seen as legitimate by colonial and apartheid authorities and thus defend their very existence. This unrelenting pressure to conform to colonial logics over the *longue durée* is, after all, why the mediatory airing of the dispute was not evidenced in the multiple layers of institutional vernacular management of the conflict between MaMakhe and MaMsolwa. This failure led to theirs being an enduring conflict, simmering under the surface as it awaited the next opportunity to find expression in yet another dispute.

In fact, a key insight from these women's case is that the repeated punishments that were imposed on MaMakhe only heightened her sense of being the aggrieved party in the conflict because, after all, she still believed that her child's mobile phone had been stolen by MaMsolwa's family and this purported wrong had never been remedied. On top thereof, she believed that MaMsolwa had accused her of sending lightning to strike her home, thus amplifying her resentment which, as seen, then extended to some of her children. Despite repeated court appearances, the source conflict between these women and their progeny had not been addressed and thus, even with ordered apologies, relations between them had not been restored.

Apology and harmony: in theory

While apologies typically fall into a values assessment that conceptualises them as inherently good, there is much evidence to suggest that they are more complex than first thought. They fall into a complex array of political speech acts that can be violently oppressive. At their best, apologies can certainly be good. As Aaron Lazare observes, 'The result of an apology process, ideally, is the reconciliation and restoration of broken relationships' (Lazare 2005: 1). However, he goes on to question:

> Why do people apologize? Why is it so difficult to apologize? Why do some apologies heal while others fail? Why do some attempts at apologies offend, making matters worse? Do apologies have to be sincere to be effective? What do apologies mean to the offended parties? How is apology related to forgiveness? Is it ever too late to apologize? Is the ability to apologize a sign of strength or weakness? In what ways are public apologies different from private ones? (p 17)

Many of these questions delving into the ambiguities and other complexities relating to apologies will be canvassed below in this section.

Acknowledgement of the potentially repressive uses of apology is appropriate, not only with reference to apology and forgiveness, but with reference to harmony as well. In that vein, Laura Nader (1990: 1) wrote: 'My research suggests that compromise models and, more generally, the harmony model are either counter-hegemonic political strategies used by colonized groups to protect themselves from encroaching superordinate powerholders or hegemonic strategies the colonizers use to defend themselves against organized subordinates'. In this way, harmony can be seen to be strategically used by both colonisers and the colonised in their respective struggle for power over the other (control) or over self (autonomy). This section therefore focuses on the theoretical discussions relevant to understanding the meanings of apology, forgiveness, and harmony in legal and court processes, and their significance in law, politics, and society at large.

Can dignity be found in a coerced apology?

The subject of apology has been extensively canvassed in disciplines ranging from psychology to law over decades (Tavuchis 1991; Levi 1997; O'Hara and Yarn 2002; Govier and Verwoerd 2002; Frantz and Bennigson 2005). In fact, as scholars record, there was a tremendous rise in interest in public apologies across the spectrum, from local to international politics, around the turn of the century (Lazare 2005; Gibney et al 2008). This is all understandable. After all, apologies play a significant role in human interaction and successful – as well as failed – relationships.

In this respect, Deborah Levi argues that 'thinking about apology as exchange, and particularly as ritual, helps to account for apology's role in transforming relationships' (Levi 1997: 1209). As Lazare (2005: 19) aptly summarises, 'the phenomenon of apology can be a window into the human emotions and behaviors that maintain and restore human dignity'. Similarly, in her book on dignity, Donna Hicks narrates a story:

> Once, a participant was describing a horrible experience, and no one from the other side of the table responded. There was no expression of remorse or compassion, not to mention an apology. I realized that if I wanted a more complete understanding of the ways people felt that their dignity was violated, I had to add to Burton's initial list [of basic human needs]. What about the desire to be understood? The desire for suffering to be seen and acknowledged? The desire to feel free from domination so that a sense of hope and possibility could blossom? The desire to be given the benefit of the doubt? The desire to be apologized to when wronged? (Hicks 2011: 28)

There is evident agreement that, in apologies, a basic human need (Burton 1990) can potentially be met: namely, restoration of dignity to the wronged.

Yet, there is also agreement that this need is infrequently met. In fact, recounting a different story in which the need was met, Hicks (2011: 90–1) observes:

> My colleague and I ... were surprised because many years of convening parties in conflict have shown that apologies do not happen very often. The need to save face ... is one of the most primal aspects of our evolutionary legacy, and it has caused much harm for us as human beings, holding us back from doing what a part of us knows, deep inside, is right. It takes great strength to fight the impulse to save face. Very few people want to admit that they have done something wrong. The fear of looking bad in the eyes of others and the fear of losing dignity are nearly insurmountable.

Hicks then reflects on the question of what it is about the receipt and witnessing of an apology that can shift the receiver and perceivers' perception of the issuer. Among the questions posed to neuroscientists, she asks: 'Can our neurons sense when someone's remorse is genuine?' (p 91). And, further still, does this then generate true forgiveness in the receiver? In fact, these questions have long plagued scholars.

For a time, scholars believed that apologies could only be achieved under extremely constrained circumstances. As Levi put it in 1997, the story of a mediation heart-warmingly resolved by a well-executed apology 'is far from typical. Because apology is a delicate interaction, it can only be effective when certain conditions are fulfilled' (p 1166). Likewise, more recently in 2016, Mandeep Dhami (2016) presented a detailed analysis of victim–offender mediation agreements in the United Kingdom to see how often partial or full apologies formed part thereof.[9] She found such references in just over half of these restorative justice agreements.

Summarising a view that is representative of much earlier work on apology, Levi proceeds to write of 'happy ever after' apologies. Under that restrictive theory of apologies, it is believed that what is needed, primarily, is the issuer's sincerity, which is extremely difficult to predict or secure, especially in a formal conflict resolution scenario. Thus, she observes, some scholars holding to such a view were led to conclude that it is 'misguided' for others to prescribe apology as a legal solution to pursue.

> Apologetic ritual is a delicate process that requires the participation of suitable parties, the absence of obstructive lawyering, well timed gestures and sensitive intervention, a climate that permits honest, vulnerable communication, efforts to reconstruct past events rather than letting wounds fester over time, and a belief that apology will not preclude satisfaction of stronger desires for compensation, restitution, or retribution. (Levi 1997: 1209)

All of the criteria raised by Levi come to mind in thinking about MaMakhe and MaMsolwa's dispute and the lack of success had by each of the vernacular dispute management interventions in their efforts to resolve the conflict. Further still, these criteria suggest a low likelihood that the TCB's prescripts would have changed the outcome of their dispute cycle.

Central to the debate on sincerity is what Levi described above as 'honest, vulnerable communication', which Hicks and others also acknowledge. At base, the concern is about coercion of the party who has to make the court-ordered apology (thus undermining their freedom of expression, among other rights) and the impact on the receiver of the apology. As concerns the coercion experienced by the issuer, Dhami notes:

> There have been several concerns expressed about the role of apology in victim–offender mediation, including the idea that offenders may feel pressured to apologise (Blecher, 2011), and that they may apologise for self-serving reasons (Blackman and Stubbs, 2001). In the present study, the low frequency of partial and full apologies in the agreements, suggests that offenders did not feel pressured to apologise either by victims or facilitators. It also demonstrates that offenders were not simply viewing apology as an easy, self-serving approach to deal with the situation. (Dhami 2016: 39–40)

---

[9]   Also see Dhami (2012).

Thus, she concludes that soft coercion did not really occur in the mediations which she reviewed. But, more importantly still, for the purpose of the present chapter, Gijs van Dijck notes that, even where coercion does occur through an explicit court order, the fact that the apology from the issuer lacks sincerity does not necessarily mean that it is of no benefit to the receiver (van Dijk 2017: 586). It is this turn in the recent literature on apology upon which I will focus for the remainder of this discussion.

While continuing to draw on a range of sources *in toto*, the remainder of this review will focus primarily on two recent metasyntheses that summarise the literature on apologies vis-à-vis the law. The first of these, by Robyn Caroll, Alfred Allan, and Margaret Halsmith (2017), centres on what mediators need to know about the psychology of apology and its effects in order to mediate disputes most effectively and how to ensure that parties coming to mediation, needing an apology as one of the main outcomes for them to consider the mediation a success, have the best chance of getting that. Their review of the literature relates particularly to civil disputes. The second metasynthesis is authored by van Dijck (2017) and is focused specifically on whether there is value in court-ordered apologies. Both were published in 2017 and are in agreement that, based on the evidence, it is inappropriate to wholly dismiss apologies as products of formal disputing processes but it is also important to understand what such apologies do and do not achieve.

As briefly introduced, van Dijck responds to critiques centred on the lack of sincerity in a court-ordered apology by saying:

> Is this concern valid? Yes and no. Yes, because court-ordered apologies do cause sincerity concerns. No, because ordered apologies can serve a purpose even if they lack sincerity. The widespread belief that an apology needs to be sincere in order for it to have a positive effect on the receiver of the apology has to be rejected, at least as a general rule. The fact that court-ordered apologies can serve a purpose even if they are not offered voluntarily suggests that the sincerity concern should not prevail when considering court-ordered apologies. (p 586)

In this bold statement, van Dijck rejects the idea that the value in court-ordered apologies is only found in sincerity, because these apologies can give effect to much more than feelings of remorse.

What then is the gamut of goods or values that can emerge from a coerced apology? Carroll et al summarise it as follows:

> There is consensus that a full apology incorporates an expression of heartfelt regret and remorse for what has happened, sympathy for the victim and acknowledges the wrongdoer's transgression. For some, it is important that the apology also offers some form of recompense

and a commitment to change in the future. Psychological research establishes that what constitutes an acceptable apology is a unique and subjective experience for each individual. Exactly which components need to be present for an apology to be beneficial in any particular circumstance will depend on many variables. (p 572)

In their conclusion, Carroll et al (2017: 573), as do van Dijck and Levi, argue for recognition of a place for ' "Tactical/Cynical", "Explanation" and "Formalistic" apologies'.[10] In support of this position, van Dijck (2017: 586) recommends that a coerced apology should be delineated as follows:

The ordered apology is a fulfilment of a legal requirement rather than a statement of genuinely held feelings. Since the law can only recommend or impose apologies on a wrongdoer, and because compensation is already commonly provided by courts and adjudicators, an ordered apology should be defined as an order directed at the wrongdoer to provide an affect-apology (eg an expression of regret), an affirmation-apology (eg an admission of fault) or an affect-admission-apology. Recognising that ordered apologies are a fulfilment of a legal requirement and that they can serve a purpose even if they are not sincere calls for a legal framework that assists in assessing the appropriateness of court-ordered (coerced) apologies.

Key to van Dijck's argument, as to Carroll et al's, is the fact that coerced apologies are not always appropriate. In fact, van Dijck closes his article by saying that '[m]ore work is required to evaluate or further integrate victims' needs in relation to legal procedures, and to consequently bridge the gap between the needs that victims have and what the law has to offer' (p 587). In essence, that is the contribution of this chapter.

Put simply, my argument pertains to the appropriateness of context – social and institutional – for coerced apologies. From a social perspective,

---

[10] Also see Levi (1997: 1175). As Carroll et al (2017: 489) put it:

'We suggest that it is consistent with the role of a facilitative mediator to work with the psychological concept of the "good enough" apology rather than a binary view of apologies as either authentic, meaningful and of value on the one hand or as unauthentic, not meaningful and therefore without value on the other. ... Whether an offer of apology, viewed by a third party, might be considered to be an explanation, an account, or a defence, and whether it might be offered for instrumental or strategic reasons for example, does not determine the value of an apology to its recipient.'

I have previously argued that the nature of social proximity and intimacy of relations in Msinga make effective resolution of disputes, as is best achieved by mediation, essential (Mnisi Weeks 2018). The fact that people's safety and security (both physical and material) are grounded in people's relationships means that relationships must be effectively restored as a means to addressing any conflicts. Put differently, people's mutual dependency for survival under extremely precarious conditions is profoundly contingent upon strong social trust, which is only achievable through interactions that are autonomous and sincere. Healthy, genuine relationships are therefore crucial.

From an institutional perspective, vernacular forums are ill-placed to serve as courts; and courts are ill-placed to produce the genuine apologies that the social context of customary communities such as Msinga demands (Mnisi Weeks 2018). Almost all conflicts in this context occur between people who know each other intimately and those tasked with managing the disputes – those who constitute the vernacular dispute management forums – are also people with whom they share many aspects of communal life. Furthermore, a substantial part of what the dispute management forums are tasked with is the work of restoring healthy relationships in order to achieve a healthy society that predominantly follows a collective way of life.

The research is clear that mediation has the best chance of achieving these outcomes. In that respect, Carroll et al draw out three themes from the literature concerning the connection between mediation and genuine apologies, and law's role therein: (1) 'mediation is an ideal forum for authentic and meaningful apologies'; (2) 'the value of apologies will be lessened if they are legally protected and mediation is used for instrumental or strategic purposes'; and (3) 'mediation can be used oppressively and result in unfair outcomes and re-victimisation of parties' (Carroll et al 2017: 588–90).

With respect to the first theme, Carroll et al note, of mediation, that 'the process can accommodate rights and power-based perspectives to provide an emotionally safe and legally protected environment for an exchange which seems fundamental to equanimity in the human condition' (p 588). Under the second theme, they observe that '[t]he concept of a "good enough" apology means that it may satisfy a party's interests to accept an apology that an objective bystander would not perceive to be sincere, complete or self and other focused' (p 589). On the third theme, they find that '[w]hile a mediator cannot control whether or not apologies will be offered and accepted, the sincerity with which they are offered (and accepted) and how they are composed, a mediator ultimately controls the mediation process and must bring it to an end if necessary' (p 590). It goes without saying that all of these factors would be extremely difficult, if not impossible, for adjudicatory processes to fulfil because of the adversarial and typically positivist approach that courts take to managing disputes.

It is for this reason, among others, that vernacular forums are best placed to act as mediatory-arbitrational spaces if they are to facilitate genuine apologies and real reconciliation. Carroll et al summarise this point well:

> mediation is a process that provides an opportunity for parties to have their interests relating to apologies met in a way that adversarial, rights based legal proceedings does not. The law has a significant, albeit indirect, role to play in supporting the opportunity that mediation presents and protecting parties where the process is unsuitable or misused. It is important, therefore, for mediators to have a sound understanding of significant psychological features of apologies and the law's underpinning role in civil dispute resolution. (p 590)

While the virtues of mediation, as contrasted with adjudicatory process, can be overly romanticised, there is general acceptance that mediation has distinct benefits, especially when the preservation of relationships beyond the intervention is required. When we talk about maintenance of good relations in traditional communities, interlocutors often jump to the conclusion that what is under discussion is harmonious communal relations; yet this is far from what is meant. The next subsection therefore canvasses the ways in which harmony ideology is often (mis)understood and (mis)used.

Deconstructing colonial logics of harmony ideology

When not described as savage and barbaric, 'tribal' communities have been idealised by descriptions using the language of harmony for decades. Nader summarises the point well: 'Ethnographies have taken harmony for granted while seeking to explain disharmony' (Nader 1996: 1). Yet, as three decades of research have now shown, there is nothing to be taken for granted about claims of 'harmony' or conventional explanations of 'disharmony' (see, for example, Nader 1990; Leung et al 2002; Lee 2004; Tam 2006; Tan 2007; Miyasaka Porro and Shiraishi Neto 2014; Beyer and Girke 2015; Porter 2016). Overwhelmingly, the research concludes with Nader (1990: 1–2) 'that the uses of harmony are political', specifically linking 'harmony with autonomy or harmony with control' (p 2). As Nader writes, 'harmony can come in many forms [and] may be part of a local tradition or part of a system of pacification that has diffused across the world along with Western colonialism, Christian missions, and other macro-scale systems of cultural control' (p 2).

This observation of the relationship between harmony and colonialism – as a function of both political and religious missionary activity that was geared toward the pacification of local populations in the would-be colonies – is continued in Nader's later work. In that work, she elaborates and extends this argument, about rural Mexico, globally. She writes that, in her efforts to 'unpack theories of harmony and controversy to see if, how, and when harmony legal models were used to suppress peoples by socializing them toward conformity in colonial contexts' (Nader 1996: 2), she had reviewed classic ethnographic work pertaining to former British colonies, such as South Africa.

She cites, specifically, her encounter with the work of South African legal historian Martin Chanock, who she credits with synthesising:

> the data on the missionary presence in British African colonies from the 1830s onward, revealing the early connections between local law and Christian missions. Chanock uses the term 'missionary justice' to call attention to the fact that from the early 1800s missionaries were heavily involved in the settlement of disputes according to a Victorian interpretation of biblical law which they generally fitted with English procedures as they knew them. According to Chanock, the missionaries were glad to be peacemakers and to hand down Christian judgment. (Nader 1996: 2)

What is most fascinating about this observation is the clarity with which it makes the connection, which Chanock (1985; 2001) has long advocated, between customary law and common law as being extensions of the same colonial imagination.

Complementing this connection, made by Chanock's work, between colonial and customary logics in law as expressed through the actions of courts, Nader adds that she found the same to be true in Talea. In fact, she writes that '[t]he contemporary relationship of harmony ideology, local solidarity, and resistance is embedded in the social organization of the local community and reflected in the workings of its courts' (Nader 1990: 2–3). Yet it is not only seen in the actions of the courts but also in other political machinations in which community representatives participate. As Nader describes it, '[i]n Talea, political elites compete successfully against agents of the state, preserving local solidarity and cultural identity, partly because of their harmony ideology' (p 1).

When the African National Congress (ANC) buys into and cynically exploits the belief that traditional leaders in South Africa bring the rural vote, it is tapping into a well-worn set of colonial logics that are premised on notions of despotic 'chiefs' and docile, unthinking black 'subjects' who do not internally contest authority structures in their locales and whose identities are simple and flat. The harmony ideology – in terms of which local identity, intra-community loyalty, and solidarity, as well as a somewhat coerced unity, were promoted, effected, and preserved in the face of external state oppression – served two functions, at least. On one hand, imposition of the political and cultural hegemony of the state and, on the other, strategic resistance thereto by leaders in the victim communities. In the latter sense, harmony ideology becomes mobilised in claims of autonomy and refusal of state interference in the governance of cultural enclaves that are claimed as not requiring state intervention. These are the very terms in which the traditional leader lobby in South Africa lays claim to state non-interference in their governance of their customary law 'subjects' (Mamdani 1996).

This harmony ideology around conflict processes has the same potency and mythical, if fictive, power that *ubuntu* carries in South African legal philosophy (Mokgoro 1998: Cornell and van Marle 2005; Mnyaka and Motlhabi 2005; Bennett 2011; Metz 2011; Gade 2011; Himonga et al 2014; Cornell 2014; Mwipikeni 2018). As Rushiella Songca (2018: 92) describes it:

> an apology is an important element of restorative justice, and is tantamount to restoring the dignity of the victim. This view received judicial recognition in the case of *Dikoko v Mokhatla* (2006). The case concerned a civil case for damages arising from defamation. In their minority judgments, Justices Mokgoro and Sachs expressed the view that an apology would have sufficed and been more in keeping with African notions of *Ubuntu* and South Africa's commitment to dignity.

This idealised principle of harmony expresses itself repeatedly in the emphasis on reconciliation and unity in a country in which, as numerous studies have ironically shown, the approach to justice is a pluralistic and paradoxical one, in which punitive and vengeful sentiments and approaches coexist with the language of human rights and reconciliation (Wilson 2000; Posel and Simpson (eds.) 2002; Buur and Jensen 2004; Oomen 2004; Ashforth 2005; Smythe 2015; Smith 2019). Moreover, as the literature on the Truth and Reconciliation Commission (TRC) has shown, the transition from process to reconciliation (that is, 'the restoration of friendly relations'[11] and reunion) is made relatively glibly, with forgiveness being assumed with the issuance of an apology rather than considered with real seriousness or in detail (Wilson 2001; Gobodo-Madikizela 2008; Tutu 2009; Smith 2019).

As I write in my 2018 book, *Access to Justice and Human Security: Cultural Contradictions in Rural South Africa*, it is also true in Msinga, South Africa, that '[h]armony ideology can be powerful even when it contradicts the common realities of disputing' (p 2). Msinga is a place where people experience a comprehensive sense of violence due to the overlapping forms of vulnerability and human insecurity with which they are constantly

---

[11] This being the explanatory meaning given to the word 'reconciliation' by the *Oxford English Dictionary* (2019).

confronted. Yet, the normative ideals are strong. Furthermore, as part thereof, the notion of a harmony to be maintained, which is communicated by traditional leaders and held on to by lawmakers whenever there is a discussion of regulating traditional courts, arises in Msinga too. This fiction has shaped the content of every iteration of the TCB since it was first introduced in 2008,[12] reintroduced in 2012,[13] and then redrafted and introduced again[14] in 2017.[15]

Conclusion: Apology and harmony in the Traditional Courts Bill

I have asked, in this chapter, whether court-ordered apologies are consistent with harmonious community. I have also proposed that, if they are not, then we must closely interrogate what values and purposes they really serve in the recognition of traditional communities and their governance. With the literature cited, I have found that it would be inappropriate to wholly dismiss apologies as sometimes legitimate and purposive products of formal disputing processes. Likewise, I have also argued that it is important to understand what such apologies do and do not achieve. In this vein, I have emphasised the particularities of deep rural contexts such as that in which MaMakhe and MaMsolwa's cycle of conflict arose, and argued that coerced apologies are inconsistent therewith. Furthermore, I have argued that some of the purposes to which such apologies and broader discourses of harmony give effect, are repressive.

Much as pertains to the literature on apology and discussions of harmony, there is much idealisation, in law and society, of vernacular dispute management forums. This has been repeatedly represented in the process and debates over the adoption of legislation to regulate so-called traditional courts in South Africa. Harmony[16] and reconciliation[17] are at the core of what is described as the nature and purpose of 'traditional courts'. Indeed, the memorandum of objects at the end of the TCB says of the section dealing with the powers of the court to impose orders: 'Clause 8 sets out the orders that a traditional court may make. The type of orders provided for in this clause is (sic) restorative in nature, for instance compensation and

---

[12] Traditional Courts Bill B8-2008.

[13] Traditional Courts Bill B1-2012.

[14] Traditional Courts Bill B1-2017. For the latest version of the Bill, see B1D-2017.

[15] See various drafts of the Bill as provided by the Parliamentary Monitoring Group at https://pmg.org.za/bill/680/. For analysis, see Mnisi Weeks (2011a); Mnisi Weeks (2011b); Mnisi Weeks (2012).

[16] Sections 2(b)(i) and 6(2)(c) of the Traditional Courts Bill B1-2017.

[17] Sections 1(1)(a), 2(a), 3(d), and 6(2)(d) Traditional Courts Bill B1-2017.

redress, which are aimed at restoring relations between parties and promoting harmony'.[18] Yet these forums were given adjudicative responsibilities and punitive powers that would make it difficult for them to achieve such harmony and reconciliation even if the oppressive political economy and socio-economic circumstances in which traditional communities, such as those in Msinga, allowed for it.

In this chapter, I have been concerned particularly with the nature of coercively ordered apologies in vernacular dispute management forums. In this respect, s. 8(1) of the TCB (B1-2017) states: 'A traditional court may make any of the following orders after having deliberated on a dispute before it: ... (e) an order that an unconditional apology be made'. As I wrote in my submission to the Portfolio Committee on 14 March 2017:

> Research shows that compelled apologies are ineffectual and even counterproductive. This is understandable because it is contrary to the very nature of an apology that it should be ordered. People therefore should not be ordered to apologise or to reconcile; rather the provision can provide for the traditional court to recognise and accept an apology if that is the settlement between the parties themselves and is arrived at voluntarily.

As it turns out, my recommendation on this narrow point was accepted. Hence, s. 8(1) of the TCB (B1D-2017) states: 'A traditional court may make any of the following orders after having deliberated on a dispute before it: ... *(e)* an order *accepting* an unconditional apology *where such an apology is a voluntary settlement between the parties themselves*' (emphasis added).

This is an important modification to the prior assumptions that were operative in the TCB's employment of coerced apologies, as an order that could be handed down by the courts. However, as shown by the detailed overview of the research on apology and harmony canvassed above, while this amendment to the Bill is a win, voluntariness is heavily constrained in contexts such as Msinga by, on the one hand, the comprehensive violence described above and, on the other, a pervasive harmony ideology that is so totalising that it precludes even debate on the terms of engagement.

The TCB demonstrates this very clearly, as the legislature accepted reforms that were consistent with the harmony ideal, which was pushed by traditional leaders (Nader's [1990: 1], 'political elites', and government representatives who are now the inheritors of colonial structures of government). Yet the legislature vehemently rejected reforms or amendments to the Bill that were inconsistent with this ideal. They

---

[18]   Point 2.7 of the Memorandum of Objects on the Traditional Courts Bill B1-2017.

went so far as to disallow oral submissions from dissident voices, such as those of rural activists concerned with not allowing rural people to opt out of having their disputes resolved in traditional courts[19] and/or having traditional courts 'presided over' by traditional leaders with power to ban conduct. These activists were fearful of more cases like that which went to the Constitutional Court in *Pilane and Another v Pilane and Another*.[20] Yet their expressions of resistance were fiercely silenced in the face of harmony ideology's unquestionable dominance.

Thus, the change made to Clause 8(1)(e) of the TCB is but a token and does not reflect a change in the legislature's misconception of vernacular dispute management forums and how to help them in a manner that supports their effectiveness or the well-being of rural communities. Harmony ideology expresses itself in many ways – both direct and indirect, external and internal – to vernacular groupings commonly referred to as traditional communities. These expressions are most evident in the fact that the legislature rejected the call of rural people (such as the Alliance for Rural Democracy members, who marched to the executive offices at the Union Buildings to deliver a petition to the president in June 2019) to choose whether they wanted to bring their cases to 'traditional courts' or state courts. It also rejected rural activists' calls for 'traditional courts' to be untethered from the 'tribal' boundaries that were put in place under apartheid and according to which traditional leaders and courts are recognised under the TCB.[21] When the language of harmony and reconciliation, which saturates the TCB, is read in the context of these and other changes to the Bill, which were advocated by rural activists and vehemently rejected by the legislature, it becomes clear that the colonial logics inherent in harmony ideology continue to prevail.

---

[19] See, for example, Makinana (2018).

[20] *Pilane and Another v Pilane and Another* (CCT 46/12) [2013] ZACC 3) (28 February 2013). In this case, two men were interdicted from holding meetings with a group of community members they led who objected to the traditional leader's corrupt administration of village affairs and sought to secede and establish their own traditional community and governing council. The Constitutional Court lifted the interdicts that were instated by the North West High Court.

[21] Section 1 of the TCB says ' "traditional leader" means any person who, in terms of customary law of the traditional community concerned, holds a traditional leadership position and is recognised in terms of the applicable legislation providing for such recognition'. Section 28 of the Traditional Leadership and Governance Framework Act 2 of 2019 and the Traditional and Khoi San Leadership Act 3 of 2019 make it clear that these are effectively the same authorities recognised under apartheid legislation. Also see ss. 4(1)(b), 5(1)(b), and 6(3) of the TCB.

Reflections

There is something strange (dare I say, out of place) about writing about conflicts happening in impoverished communities in deep rural South Africa while quarantined due to COVID-19 in one of the most privileged and protected corners of the globe, my house in the north-east of the United States of America. It reminds me of how simultaneously global and local contemporary experiences are; we are, as I've recently heard it said, caught 'in the same storm, but not in the same boat'. One of the ways in which my situational position shapes my writing about apologies as a means of conflict management and/or resolution is based on how front-of-mind questions of redress for historical and ongoing injustices against multigenerational victims of imperialist logics, pursuits, and exploits are in public debates on #BlackLivesMatter and indigeneity in America today. Hence, I find myself steeped in exploration and interrogation of redress from a vantage point daring to imagine abolition of carcerally minded criminal 'justice' institutions and payment of reparations as possibilities. As I write from a perspective that takes the insights of critical race theory to be a given (observations of fact as well as analyses of their implications), I am cognisant of the raging political debate on the sacredness of the colonial and white logics that imbue the field of law, which is the subject of my critique, even in South Africa. At the same time, writing as a Christian by faith about the imperialist legacy of missionaries – of which my spiritual beliefs are largely a product – in the ways in which people who look like me and share my mother tongue think about conflict, harmony, and apology, I wrestle with my own multifaceted identity and the inner conflicts with which it riddles me. I am reminded, as though I ever were able to forget, that I am always in both South Africa and Euro-America at once because both places are ever in me.

Sindiso

References

Ashforth, A., 2005, *Witchcraft, Violence, and Democracy in South Africa*, Chicago: University of Chicago Press.

Bennett, T. W., 2011, 'Ubuntu: an African equity', *Potchefstroom Electronic Law Journal/Potchefstroomse Elektroniese Regsblad* 14(4), 30–61.

Beyer, J. and Girke, F., 2015, 'Practicing harmony ideology: ethnographic reflections on community and coercion', *Common Knowledge* 21(2), 196–235.

Blackman, M. C. and Stubbs, E. C., 2001, 'Apologies: genuine admissions of blameworthiness or scripted, sympathetic responses?', *Psychological Reports*, 88, 45–50.

Blecher, N. J., 2011, 'Sorry justice: apology in Australian family group conferencing', *Psychiatry, Psychology, and Law*, 18, 95–116.

Burton, J., 1990, *Conflict: Human Needs Theory*, New York: Springer.

Buur, L. and Jensen, S., 2004, 'Introduction: vigilantism and the policing of everyday life in South Africa', *African Studies* 63(2), 139–52.

Carroll, R., Allan, A., and Halsmith, M., 2017, 'Apologies, mediation and the law: resolution of civil disputes', *Oñati Socio-Legal Series* 7(3), 569–600.

Chanock, M., 1985, *Law, Custom, and Social Order: The Colonial Experience in Malawi and Zambia*, Cambridge: Cambridge University Press.

Chanock, M., 2001, *The Making of South African Legal Culture 1902–1936: Fear, Favour and Prejudice*, Cambridge: Cambridge University Press.

Cornell, D. and van Marle, K., 2005, 'Exploring ubuntu: tentative reflections', *African Human Rights Law Journal* 5(2), 195–220.

Cornell, D., 2014, *Law and Revolution in South Africa: uBuntu, Dignity, and the Struggle for Constitutional Transformation*, New York: Fordham University Press.

Dhami, M., 2012, 'Offer and acceptance of apology in victim–offender mediation', *Critical Criminology* 20(1), 45–60.

Dhami, M. K., 2016, 'Apology in victim–offender mediation', *Contemporary Justice Review*, 19(1), 31–42.

Frantz, C. M. and Bennigson, C., 2005, 'Better late than early: the influence of timing on apology effectiveness', *Journal of Experimental Social Psychology* 41(2), 201–07.

Gade, C. B. N., 2011, 'The historical development of the written discourses on ubuntu', *South African Journal of Philosophy* 30(3), 303–29.

Gibney, M., Howard-Hassmann, R. E. Coicaud, J.-C. and Stiener, N. (eds.) 2008, *The Age of Apology: Facing Up to the Past*, Philadelphia: University of Pennsylvania Press.

Gobodo-Madikizela, P., 2008, 'Transforming trauma in the aftermath of gross human rights abuses: making public spaces intimate through the South African Truth and Reconciliation Commission', in A. Nadler, T. Malloy and J. D. Fisher (eds.), *Social Psychology of Intergroup Reconciliation*, pp 57–75, Oxford: Oxford University Press.

Govier, T. and Verwoerd, W., 2002, 'The promise and pitfalls of apology', *Journal of Social Philosophy* 33(1), 67–82.

Hicks, D., 2011, *Dignity: The Essential Role It Plays in Conflict Resolution*, New Haven: Yale University Press.

Himonga, C., Taylor, M., and Pope, A., 2014, 'Reflections on judicial views of *ubuntu*', *Potchefstroom Electronic Law Journal/Potchefstroomse Elektroniese Regsblad* 16(5), 369–427.

Lazare, A, 2005, *On Apology*, Oxford: Oxford University Press.

Lee, A., 2004, *In the Name of Harmony and Prosperity: Labor and Gender Politics in Taiwan's Economic Restructuring*, Albany: SUNY Press.

Leung, K., Koch, P. T., and Lu, L., 2002, 'A dualistic model of harmony and its implications for conflict management in Asia', *Asia Pacific Journal of Management* 19(2–3), 201–20.

Levi, D. L., 1997, 'Note: the role of apology in mediation', *New York University Law Review* 72, 1165–210.

Makinana, A., 2018, 'Presenters belittled at traditional courts hearing', *City Press*, 28 May, viewed 28 May 2021 from www.news24.com/citypress/news/presenters-belittled-at-traditional-courts-hearing-20180318

Mamdani, M., 1996, *Citizen and Subject*, Princeton: Princeton University Press.

Metz, T., 2011, 'Ubuntu as a moral theory and human rights in South Africa', *African Human Rights Law Journal* 11(2), 532–59.

Miyasaka Porro, N. and Shiraishi Neto, J., 2014, 'Coercive harmony in land acquisition: the gendered impact of corporate "responsibility" in the Brazilian Amazon', *Feminist Economics* 20(1), 227–48.

Mnisi Weeks, S., 2011, 'Securing women's property inheritance in the context of plurality: negotiations of law and authority in Mbuzini customary courts and beyond', *Acta Juridica*, 140–73.

Mnisi Weeks, S., 2011a, 'Beyond the Traditional Courts Bill: regulating customary courts in line with living customary law and the Constitution', *South African Crime Quarterly*, 35, 31–40.

Mnisi Weeks, S., 2011b, 'The Traditional Courts Bill: controversy around process, substance and implications', *South African Crime Quarterly*, 35, 3–10.

Mnisi Weeks, S., 2012, 'Regulating vernacular dispute resolution forums: controversy concerning the process, substance and implications of South Africa's Traditional Courts Bill', *Oxford University Commonwealth Law Journal* 12(1), 133–55.

Mnisi Weeks, S., 2018, *Access to Justice and Human Security: Cultural Contradictions in Rural South Africa*, Abingdon: Routledge.

Mnyaka, M. and Motlhabi, M., 2005, 'The African concept of ubuntu/botho and its socio-moral significance', *Black Theology* 3(2), 215–37.

Mokgoro, J. Y., 1998, 'Ubuntu and the law in South Africa', *Potchefstroom Electronic Law Journal/Potchefstroomse Elektroniese Regsblad*, 1(1), 1–11.

Mwipikeni, P., 2018, 'Ubuntu and the modern society', *South African Journal of Philosophy* 37(3), 322–34.

Nader, L., 1990, *Harmony Ideology: Justice and Control in a Zapotec Mountain Village*, California: Stanford University Press.

Nader, L., 1996, 'Coercive harmony: the political economy of legal models', *Kroeber Anthropological Society Papers* (80), 1–13.

O'Hara, E. A. and Yarn, D., 2002, 'On apology and consilience', *Washington Law Review* 77(4), 1121–92.

Oomen, B., 2004, 'Vigilantism or alternative citizenship? The rise of Mapogo a Mathamaga', *African Studies* 63(2), 153–71.

Porter, H., 2016, *After Rape: Violence, Justice, and Social Harmony in Uganda*, Cambridge: Cambridge University Press.

Posel, D. and Simpson, G. (eds.), 2002, *Commissioning the Past: Understanding South Africa's Truth and Reconciliation Commission*, Johannesburg: Wits University Press.

Smith, N. R., 2019, *Contradictions of Democracy: Vigilantism and Rights in Post-Apartheid South Africa*, Oxford: Oxford University Press.

Smythe, D., 2015, *Rape Unresolved: Policing Sexual Offences in South Africa*, Cape Town: Juta and Company Ltd.

Songca, R., 2018, 'The Africanisation of children's rights in South Africa: Quo Vadis? *International Journal of African Renaissance Studies – Multi-, Inter- and Transdisciplinarity* 13(1), 77–95.

Tam, C.-L., 2006, 'Harmony hurts: participation and silent conflict at an Indonesian fish pond', *Environmental Management* 38(1), 1–15.

Tan, E. K., 2007, 'Harmony as ideology, culture, and control: alternative dispute resolution in Singapore', *Australian Journal of Asian Law* 9(1), 120–51.

Tavuchis, N., 1991, *Mea Culpa: A Sociology of Apology and Reconciliation*, California: Stanford University Press.

Tutu, D., 2009, *No Future without Forgiveness*, New York: Image.

Van Dijck, G., 2017, 'The ordered apology', *Oxford Journal of Legal Studies* 37(3), 562–87.

Wilson, R. A., 2000, 'Reconciliation and revenge in post-apartheid South Africa', *Current Anthropology* 41(1), 75–87.

Wilson, R. A., 2001, *The Politics of Truth and Reconciliation in South Africa: Legitimizing the Post-Apartheid State*, Cambridge: Cambridge University Press.

5

Penance and Punishment: Apology as a Remedy for Hate Speech

Nurina Ally and Kerry Williams

You cannot dive into their
mouths and fish out a 'sorry';
it's never worked that way.
And what good is a 'sorry' you had to drown for?

Upile Chisala 2020: 9

Introduction

Equality Courts in South Africa are specifically empowered to order an unconditional apology where hate speech, unfair discrimination, or harassment has been perpetrated. But is a court-ordered apology (also referred to as a compelled apology) an effective remedy against hate speech?

Opinions on the effectiveness of apology as a remedial measure diverge starkly. On one end of the spectrum, saying sorry is dismissed as a weak form of redress letting violators off scot-free (Delgado and Stefancic 1996). On the other, apology is cast as a potentially potent mechanism to shame and punish transgressors (Baker 1999). For some, apology carries the promise of restorative healing and broader reconciliation but only when voluntarily and sincerely made (Skelton 2013). For others, even a compelled and insincere apology can vindicate rights and transform community norms (White 2006).

Drawing on these debates, we critically reflect on the role of court-ordered apologies as an effective remedy for hate speech. We do so through the lens of two Equality Court cases, each involving the publication of hate-filled bigotry against minority groups and each including a demand for an apology.

In the first case, a prominent public figure, Jon Qwelane, published an opinion piece titled 'Call me names – but gay is not okay' (Qwelane

75

2008: 14). In the article, Qwelane expressly demeans and debases lesbian and gay relationships as being against the 'natural order of things', compares homosexuality with bestiality, calls for the Constitution to be amended so that gay marriage will be outlawed, and praises Robert Mugabe's 'unflinching and unapologetic stance over homosexuals'.[1] The column was printed together with a cartoon depicting a man marrying a goat with a caption reading: 'When Human Rights Meets Animal Rights'. Knowing that he will be called upon to retract his article, Qwelane pre-emptively taunts: 'by the way, please tell the Human Rights Commission that I totally refuse to withdraw or apologise for my views' (p 14). In response, the South African Human Rights Commission (SAHRC) sought just that – an apology. Following 12 years of litigation, Qwelane passed away in December 2020, while his appeal was still pending before the Constitutional Court. The Constitutional Court's eventual judgment in July 2021 declared Qwelane's comments to be hate speech but did not issue the apology that was originally sought.

Following almost a decade later, the theme of apology also features prominently in the case of *The Chinese Association (Gauteng) v Henning and 11 Others*.[2] The Chinese Association (TCA) launched the challenge in response to hate-laden vitriol (including genocidal sentiments) posted on Facebook and directed at the Chinese community. The jarring flurry of anti-Chinese commentary was generated after a documentary was aired about the killing of donkeys in South Africa. TCA launched an Equality Court challenge, demanding an apology as part of a package of remedial interventions. Even though some respondents admitted that the utterances constituted hate speech and consented to all of the remedial measures sought, TCA considered it essential that the court conduct a full inquiry so that the extent of the hurt and pain felt by the community could be ventilated. Judgment is pending in the Equality Court.

We suggest that these cases offer useful reflections on the effectiveness of apology as a legal remedy in relation to three 'types' of hate speech transgressors. The *Qwelane* case highlights the role of an apology order against a recalcitrant

---

[1] An excerpt from Qwelane's opinion piece reads:

> 'Homosexuals and their backers will call me names, printable and not, for stating as I have always done my serious reservations about their "lifestyle and sexual preferences", but quite frankly I don't give a damn: wrong is wrong! I do pray that some day a bunch of politicians with their heads affixed firmly to their necks will muster the balls to rewrite the constitution of this country, to excise those sections which give licence to men "marrying" other men, and ditto women. Otherwise, at this rate, how soon before some idiot demands to "marry" an animal, and argues that this constitution "allows" it?' (Qwelane 2008: 14)

[2] (EQ2/2017) [2019] ZAGPJHC 145 (20 March 2019).

hate speech transgressor who expressly refuses to apologise. The *TCA* case raises the prospect of transgressors who may concede to an apology based on genuine and sincere remorse, or those who – more cynically – may agree to apologise merely as a quick and cheap escape route from genuine reckoning.

We argue that in respect of each of these 'types' of transgressors, compelled apologies – when properly framed and crafted – can serve as a potent mechanism to restore and vindicate the dignity and equality rights of the target group. Where an offender is unrepentant for their constitutionally offensive speech acts, the punitive dimension of a compelled apology – which limits the transgressor's freedom of expression – can vindicate complainants' rights and underscore society's thresholds for constitutionally acceptable speech. Where a sincerely remorseful transgressor concedes to an apology order, the act of public penance (following the *process* of a full Equality Court inquiry where the experience of the complainants is ventilated) can serve to restore the dignity and equality of complainants as well as to transform the offender through a confrontation with their own prejudice.

Before turning to an analysis of the cases, we set out the legal framework within which to assess apology as a remedial measure in response to hate speech in South African law.

Apology as an effective remedy under the Equality Act

As a remedial response to hate speech, apology finds a statutory home under the Promotion of Equality and Prevention of Unfair Discrimination Act (Equality Act).[3] Ambitious in its goals – the preamble describes its aim as being to create a more 'caring and compassionate' society – the Act prohibits unfair discrimination, harassment and hate speech in all spheres. High Courts and designated Magistrates' Courts are entrusted to serve as Equality Courts in their areas of jurisdiction, with proceedings specifically intended to be informal, easily accessible, and participatory.[4]

In light of their mandate to address systemic discrimination and inequalities, Equality Courts have been described as 'a transformative tool for bringing about greater justice for all' and 'not merely special rooms for dealing with equality matters' (De Jager 2011: 109). To this end, the courts are afforded wide remedial discretion to make 'any appropriate order' including, for example, declaratory orders, damages awards, prohibitory or mandatory interdicts, and policy audits.[5] Significantly, the Act expressly contemplates

---

[3]   Act 4 of 2000.

[4]   Equality Act, ss. 4(1)(a)-(b).

[5]   Equality Act, s. 21(2).

an 'unconditional apology' as a potentially appropriate remedy in response to harassment, unfair discrimination, and hate speech.[6]

But how do we assess whether and when an apology order may serve as an 'appropriate' remedy? The Constitutional Court in *Fose v Minister of Safety and Security*[7] has provided guidance on this score, emphasising that an 'appropriate remedy must mean an effective remedy' (para. 69). As Justice Ackermann stated:

'Particularly in a country where so few have the means to enforce their rights through the courts, it is essential that on those occasions when the legal process does establish that an infringement of an entrenched right has occurred, it be effectively vindicated' (para. 69). In other words, effective relief is 'relief that leaves no gap between right and remedy' and that 'makes the constitutional ideal a reality' (Bishop 2014: 67). Moreover, a court's order is constitutionally required to always be just and equitable in the given circumstances. As Justice Madlanga commented in *Electoral Commission v Mhlope and Others*:[8] 'The outer limits of a remedy are bounded only by considerations of justice and equity' (para. 83). Therefore, when an apology is ordered as a remedial response to hate speech by Equality Courts, it is necessary for such a remedy to be just and equitable and to effectively vindicate the rights that the Act seeks to further and protect.

Significantly, the Equality Act itself offers a framework for assessing whether the rights impaired by hate speech, harassment, and unfair discrimination are effectively vindicated. In terms of the Act, Equality Courts should be guided by the principle of applying 'corrective or restorative measures in conjunction with measures of a deterrent nature' in the adjudication of proceedings under the Act.[9] In addition, one of the aims of the Act is to provide for 'measures to educate the public and raise public awareness' around the importance of overcoming unfair discrimination, hate speech, and harassment.[10] The Act sets up signposts, then, indicating that remedial measures should serve corrective, restorative, educational, and/or deterrent functions in order to further the purposes of the Act. In light of this framework, it is apt that the Equality Court's remedial repertoire has been described as 'forward-looking, community-oriented and structural' (Parliament of South Africa 2017: 329). And it is within this constitutional and statutory setting that

---

[6] Equality Act, s. 21(2)(j). Equality Courts are also empowered to refer cases of hate speech to the Director of Public Prosecutions for the possible institution of criminal proceedings, as per s. 10(2).
[7] (CCT14/96) [1997] ZACC 6 (5 June 1997).
[8] (CCT55/16) [2016] ZACC 15 (14 June 2016).
[9] Section 4(1)(d).
[10] Section 2(e).

the effectiveness (or not) of an apology as a legal remedy in response to hate speech should be assessed.

However, while Equality Courts have granted apology orders in a number of hate speech cases, it is striking that the purpose, role, and value of such a remedy has rarely been articulated in judgments. To the extent that it has, and despite court-ordered apologies falling squarely within their remedial wheelhouse, some Equality Court judges and magistrates have expressed open scepticism around whether apology can serve as an effective remedy in hate speech matters.

In the notorious case of Penny Sparrow, who sparked nationwide anger after she made racist references to black people as 'monkeys' on social media (Singh 2019), the presiding magistrate – in dialogue with counsel – pointedly questioned the efficacy of coerced court-ordered apologies:

> Where an apology is contrived, in other words, through an order of Court, what is the purpose of that? You know, where a person does not come of their own accord and they have enough time to apologise for conduct, and we understand all human beings are fallible, but what is the purpose of the Court making an order that the respondent issues a written apology?[11]

Doubtful of the value of a coerced or 'contrived' apology, the court ultimately declined to make such an order. However, in parallel *criminal* proceedings (in which Sparrow was convicted of the offence of *crimen injuria*) she was ordered to make a public apology in addition to the imposition of a fine and sentence of imprisonment (Marias 2017: 31), thus signalling that apology orders may be considered as an effective punitive measure by some courts.

The scepticism expressed by the Equality Court in *Sparrow* was echoed in the 2019 case of *South African Human Rights Commission v Khumalo*.[12] In *Khumalo*, a public official apologised for a racist rant on social media, but when the matter came before the Equality Court, he recanted his apology and withdrew any acknowledgement that his comments constituted hate speech. In the context of the official's about-turn, Justice Sutherland opined that it 'is difficult to pin down' the 'true value' of a compelled apology (para. 108) and that '[t]he husk of an empty apology carries no weight' (para. 43). Yet, despite having cast the effectiveness of apology as remedy in serious doubt, the Equality Court nevertheless proceeded to order exactly that.

The *Khumalo* court's approach is constitutionally unpalatable. Fundamental rights that are infringed by hate speech, including the rights to equality

---

[11] *ANC v Sparrow* (01/16) [2016] ZAEQC 1 (10 June 2016) p 29.

[12] (EQ6-2016; EQ1-2018) [2018] ZAGPJHC 528 (5 October 2018).

and dignity, can scarcely be vindicated by a public apology where the court *itself* suggests the remedy is ineffective. This runs the risk of leaving the gap between right and remedy wide open. In so doing, the court not only dilutes the potency of the relief granted but also the seriousness of the rights violations inflicted by hate speech. As the Constitutional Court in *Fose* warned, 'without effective remedies for breach, the values underlying and the rights entrenched in the Constitution cannot properly be upheld or enhanced' (para. 69). Moreover, casting remedies that have been ordered in response to hate speech as ineffectual has the potential to erode the very legitimacy of Equality Courts as a mechanism to advance the elimination of discrimination and inequality. However, because the court in *Khumalo* ultimately ordered an apology, this suggests apology does perform a function and may be effective particularly when combined with other relief – even if the value of apology is difficult to identify.

It is critical, then, for courts (when granting apology orders) and litigants (when praying for such relief) to attempt to 'pin down' the 'true value' of such a remedy as a response to hate speech. As we discuss below, the jurisprudence of the Constitutional Court has expressly cast the remedial role of apology in restorative justice terms.[13] However, the question of whether a compelled apology (which may well be insincere) can serve those goals has been brought into question. We suggest that in relation to hate speech, compelled apology is a multivalent remedy which (in respect of both sincere and unrepentant transgressors) gives effect to the Equality Act's focus on, not only restorative, but also corrective, educational, and/ or deterrent remedial goals.

The effectiveness of compelled insincere apologies

In the field of defamation law (where injury to an individual's dignity and reputation draws focus), several judges of the Constitutional Court have linked apology orders to restorative justice goals.[14] While a detailed

---

[13] Mia Swart explains restorative justice in the following terms: 'Restorative justice has been defined as "a process whereby all the parties with a stake in a particular offence come together to resolve collectively how to deal with the aftermath of the offence and its implications for the future". Apology can clearly be one such action. Restorative justice accords primary attention to healing the victim and secondary attention to punishment' (Swart 2008: 53, citing Braithwaite 1999).

[14] In minority opinions in *Dikoko v Mokhatla* (CCT62/05) [2006] ZACC 10 (3 August 2006), Justices Bess Nkabinde and Albie Sachs suggested that apology could serve as a restorative justice remedy in defamation cases. Their views were subsequently cited with approval by the majority of the Constitutional Court in *Le Roux and Others v Dey* (CCT45/10) [2011] ZACC 4 (8 March 2011).

consideration of these cases is beyond the scope of this chapter, we discern at least three remedial roles for apology from the court's evolving jurisprudence.

The first is the restoration of harmonious social relationships and 'mutual understanding' between the parties, which is for the 'good of both the plaintiff and defendant', as articulated in *Dikoko v Mokhatla*.[15] This has been explicitly linked to the project of reconciliation, and the 'recantation of past wrongs and apology for them', as held in *Le Roux and Others v Dey*.[16] As we discuss below, the capacity of a compelled apology to keep complainants and respondents in some form of relationship with each other – forcing a reckoning or engagement where it may be difficult – can lend to the effectiveness of apology as a restorative remedy in hate speech cases. The second remedial role of apology articulated by judges of the Constitutional Court is 'securing redress' (*The Citizen 1978 (Pty) Ltd and Others v McBride*)[17] for the complainant through the restoration of their dignity so that they can 'walk away with head high, knowing that even the traducer has acknowledged the injustice of the slur' (*Dikoko* para. 109). We also highlight the role that compelled apology plays in restoring equality or equalising social relations in hate speech cases. And the third role envisaged by members of the court has been the possible sensitisation of the defendant to the hurtful impact of their actions (*Dikoko* para. 68). While keeping in mind the uncertain meaning of 'sensitisation', we suggest that an apology may also hold the possibility of a 'freedom from denial' (Tippett 2017) for perpetrators of hate speech, whereby a person's confrontation with their own prejudice also educates and frees them from such prejudice.

While these restorative outcomes appear particularly viable in relation to a willing, sincere, and genuinely remorseful respondent, can a court-ordered apology, which may well be *insincere*, achieve these restorative purposes? In her thoughtful analysis of the Constitutional Court's restorative justice jurisprudence, Ann Skelton (2013) welcomes the court's embrace of a restorative approach in civil matters but is sceptical of the ability of *coerced* apologies to serve that aim. She suggests that apologies must be allowed to emerge from a restorative justice *process* rather than simply being imposed through court sanction. In her words: '[An apology's] sincerity and, flowing from that, its power to heal and achieve reconciliation depends on it being allowed to "well up". Without an engagement that provides such an opportunity, the apology may not be sincere, and may achieve little in terms of restorative justice aims' (Skelton 2013:142, citing Braithwaite 2003). Indeed, in a gloss to his minority judgment in *Dikoko*, Justice Sachs

---

[15] (CCT62/05) [2006] ZACC 10 (3 August 2006) para. 69.

[16] (CCT45/10) [2011] ZACC 4 (8 March 2011) para. 202.

[17] (CCT 23/10) [2011] ZACC 11 (8 April 2011) para. 134.

recognised that where a defaming party apologises because 'it is just words' and 'costs them nothing' (para. 120), then the goals of the remedy may not be met. However, in *McBride* (where a series of newspaper articles were challenged as defamatory),[18] the Constitutional Court suggested (without deciding) that there may still be an important restorative role for a compelled apology even against an unremorseful defendant. Justice Cameron, writing for the majority of the court, indicated that '[i]t is by no means clear that ordering an unrepentant media defendant to apologise to a defamed plaintiff serves no purpose' (para. 130), and that even in such cases the role of an apology order 'in securing redress and in salving feelings cannot be under-estimated' (para. 134). However, the plaintiffs, Robert McBride's, own rejection of an apology ultimately weighed against ordering one in that case.[19]

The court's consideration of the complainant's view on the effectiveness of an apology is significant. Where an injured party rejects an offer of apology as an insufficient remedy to the harm caused, then the apology is unlikely to be effective in those circumstances. One such example emerged during proceedings of the Truth and Reconciliation Commission (TRC). While the legislation establishing the TRC did not require perpetrators to show remorse (Swart 2008: 50), apology and forgiveness were recurrent themes during public hearings (Weisman 2006). One of the more interesting interactions around a proffered apology occurred between Dirk Coetzee and Charity Khondile (the mother of the child Coetzee murdered). Coetzee offered an apology during his amnesty application. The apology was resolutely rejected by Khondile and she reasoned that the apology was *evidence* of a lack of real remorse. From her perspective, Coetzee would have chosen to stand trial and potentially receive criminal punishment had he been truly remorseful and sincere in his apology (Weisman 2006: 237–8).[20] Khondile's refusal of

---

18 In September and October 2013, *The Citizen* newspaper published various articles and editorials opposing McBride's candidacy for a senior police post. The articles referred to McBride as a criminal and a murderer (in respect of acts for which he had been granted amnesty by the TRC) and alleged that he had been detained in Mozambique on suspicion of gunrunning.

19 While McBride had originally sought an apology in the High Court, he disavowed his desire for one in the Constitutional Court, in part because of his view that in the absence of remorse the apology would 'be hollow' (*McBride* para. 133).

20 The exchange between Coetzee and Khondile is quoted by Weisman (2006: 237) as follows:

'Dirk Coetzee: I hope to in future meet up with her one day and look her in the eye, and the pathetic sorry all I can say, but generally one just wants to meet someone of the calibre of Mrs. Khondile.

Lawyer for Mrs. Khondile: Mrs. Khondile asks me to convey to you that this is an honour that she feels you do not deserve and that if you were really remorseful you would not have applied for amnesty, but in fact stood trial for what you did with her son.'

the apology suggests that it could not appropriately punish or function as an appropriate form of penance. This is unsurprising considering Coetzee's murderous actions. However, in contrast and as we suggest below, apology for hate speech may be well suited as a form of penance or punishment.

In her comprehensive work on court-ordered apologies, Robyn Carroll (2013) has offered useful insights around the multivalent nature of apology as legal remedy:

> When seeking ways to give meaning to apologies within a legal context, we need to acknowledge that the law is simultaneously pragmatic, instrumental and aspirational. We know that law can guide, influence and direct behaviour, but it cannot compel emotions and heartfelt speech. It is in this context that the meaning of an apology as a legal remedy needs to be understood and it is why, from a legal viewpoint, it is helpful to understand apology as having multiple meanings. (Carroll 2013: 322)

In other words, the value of apology as a legal remedy and the purposes it may serve are neither monolithic nor static. The remedial efficacy of a compelled apology may in some cases be dependent on the wrongdoer's sincere expression of remorse (as Robert McBride and Charity Khondile made clear was necessary). In other cases, it may be the very fact that an unrepentant wrongdoer has been *compelled* (with the punitive dimension that this entails) to apologise and publicly acknowledge their wrong that may vindicate and restore the dignity and equality of the complainant, as well as serving the corrective, educational, and/or deterrent goals of the Equality Act.[21]

In this regard, Swart (2008: 51), drawing on the work of John Austin (1962), argues that because of the 'essentially performative nature of apologies', even an insincere apology can have potent symbolic and restorative

---

[21] Marais (2017: 25, 48) suggests that the Equality Act is 'primarily aimed at transformation instead of punishment' and 'aims to give effect to the constitutional values of human dignity and equality outside the judicial realm of the punishment of crime or delictual liability for the violation of personality rights'. We agree that the Equality Act does not concern itself with the imposition of criminal sanctions (other than through the possibility that hate speech cases may be referred to the Director of Public Prosecutions (s. 10(2))). However, this should not be read to suggest that the punitive dimension of remedial measures contemplated by the Act should be ignored or excluded. Indeed, given the seriousness of unfair discrimination, hate speech, and harassment, the Act clearly contemplates the need for a package of restorative, corrective, and deterrent measures to achieve its transformative goals (thus eschewing a strict distinction between punishment and transformation).

value, particularly where the wrongdoer 'exhibits shame or if the apology involves public humiliation'. As she suggests, 'A properly constructed apology can satisfy the victim's need for a public acceptance and admission of responsibility even if it is not sincere. Such apology can also help to restore the victim's sense of pride' (Swart 2008: 60). Similarly, Brent White (2006: 1274–5) argues that the dignity of victims may be restored when a perpetrator apologises through 'a symbolic transfer of humiliation and power between the offender and victim', and that this restorative effect may be particularly relevant for *public* (as opposed to private) apologies where the transgressor 'is forced to admit his faults publicly'. Indeed, it is important to recognise that a compelled apology forces the perpetrator to speak words which may not be voluntary, thus encroaching on their freedom of speech. In our view, such an infringement is justified and properly balanced by the effect such compelled apology has on respecting, protecting, and promoting equality and dignity of those affected by the hate speech.

Moreover, the performance of public apologies – even if insincere – has an important 'expressive utility', serving to confirm and affirm society's normative commitments (White 2006: 1278–9). While a declaratory order by a court may also serve this goal to some extent, White (2006: 1283–4) offers an important reminder that the legalese of court judgments may not always be widely accessible or easily comprehensible. By contrast, apologies are 'culturally embedded moral signifiers that convey clear messages of right and wrong' (White 2006: 1284) with which all members of society are familiar.

Thus, while a genuine acknowledgement and realisation of wrongdoing may be a desirable outcome of court-ordered apologies, the effectiveness of a compelled apology as legal remedy does not entirely depend on the transgressor's sincerity. The nature of the compulsion, the nature of the apology, and the role that the victim plays in seeking the compelled apology also determines if dignity and equality are ultimately upheld.

Where a transgressor is genuinely repentant, a compelled apology may serve as a form of performative penance, understood as 'a kind of self-imposed suffering that serves to express the offender's contrition for the offence and to restore his bonds with the society from which he has been separated by his offence' (Baker 1992: 312). Where the transgressor is unrepentant then the punitive element of a compelled public apology may lend to its role as a powerful – albeit not always complete – mechanism to (i) express and reinforce the constitutional threshold where the right to freedom of expression gives way to the protection of the rights to dignity and equality of those against whom the speech is directed; and (ii) to protect and promote these rights.

To draw out these various dimensions of apology as court-ordered relief in hate speech cases more fully, we turn to a consideration of the two cases we introduced at the beginning of this chapter. In *Qwelane*, the value of apology against an unrepentant transgressor is squarely raised. In *TCA*, we see the careful framing of apology as the outcome of a *process*, which: (i) in the case of an insincere respondent, ensures that the tender of an apology is not used as an escape route to avoid accountability; and (ii) in the case of a genuinely remorseful respondent, creates the possibilities of a restorative encounter whereby the transgressor comes to recognise the full impact of their prejudice and harm.

The role of apology in two hate speech cases

Refusing to apologise: compelling Jon Qwelane's apology as an effective remedy

When John Qwelane published his homophobic tirade in the pages of the *Sunday Sun* in 2008, a flood of complaints was received by the South African Human Rights Commission (SAHRC) as well as the Press Ombudsman (Ombud).[22] The Ombud held that the newspaper and Qwelane had breached the Press Code by publishing denigrating and discriminatory references to people based on sexual orientation. In terms of redress, the Ombud took the view that the *Sunday Sun* had 'already gone a long way to making amends' (by drawing attention to the backlash Qwelane had received in a subsequent edition of the paper), but that an apology was required in order to 'complete the amends' (Thloloe 2008).

The publisher proceeded to print a full-page summary of the ruling together with an 'apology' (the wording of which was approved by the Ombud). Published under the heading '[W]e didn't break the law but for our sins I apologise', the publisher's 'apology' suggested that Qwelane's column had generated valuable debate and that the paper had actually been vindicated by the Ombud's ruling (which held that the publication fell short of hate speech). To the extent that any regret was expressed, it was for 'sinning against the [Press] Code' and for the 'uproar that clearly hurt some people's feelings', but not for the affront to the equality and dignity of gay and lesbian people (du Plessis 2008). The sub-editor of the *Sunday Sun* would later describe the publisher's apology as 'one of those apologies that he [the publisher] likes to write – that he says he did nothing wrong but I do apologise'.[23]

---

[22] The Ombud received almost 1,000 complaints in response to Qwelane's article (Thloloe 2008) and the SAHRC received 350 complaints, which was reported to be the greatest number of complaints received by the SAHRC in relation to any one matter (South African Human Rights Commission 2017).

[23] See the Record of Appeal (p 938) in *South African Human Rights Commission v Jonathan Dubula Qwelane & Another* (EQ44/2009; EQ13/2012) [2017] ZAGPJHC 218 (18 August 2017).

With the publisher's cynical apology adding insult to injury, the SAHRC instituted proceedings in the Equality Court against Qwelane and Media24 (the owner of the *Sunday Sun*) for violating the Equality Act's prohibition against hate speech and harassment. An order was sought requiring Qwelane to 'make an unconditional apology to the gay and lesbian community, [the] terms of which will be agreed upon by the parties' and with the apology being 'made an order of the court and published in the Sunday Sun as well as one other national newspaper'.[24]

Protracted legal skirmishes and offshoot litigation ensued, including a challenge to the constitutionality of the Equality Act. It would take eight years – with an intervening approach to the Constitutional Court to resist postponement efforts – before the Equality Court finally heard the matter (Williams and Judge 2018). When the seven-day hearing began in March 2017, the role of apology took centre stage on several occasions with various (and differing) views on what remedial role, if any, an apology by Qwelane would serve.

In response to a question from the SAHRC's counsel on the role of an apology, the SAHRC's head of legal services, Pandelis Gregoriou, cast an apology order as a measure to signal acknowledgement of wrongdoing by Qwelane and a transformation of his views, thus achieving some form of reconciliation: 'We would want to pursue [an outcome] where we actually see how parties have reconciled. That they have attempted to reflect on their conduct, they understood the error of their ways and they want to make an apology internally'.[25] In a similar vein, Professor Juan Nel of the Psychological Society of South Africa (PsySSA), which had intervened as *amicus curiae* in the matter, linked apology to healing and restoration. As he stated, 'I don't think we must underestimate the importance of a platform where somebody can ask for an apology and where forgiveness can be given'.[26]

The framing of apology and restorative justice in these terms appears to centre primarily on possibilities for reconciliation and, as the Constitutional Court has framed it, 'mutual understanding' (*Dikoko* para. 69). But this particular restorative role of apology is closely tied to the sincerity of, and

---

[24] See the Founding Affidavit in *South African Human Rights Commission v Jonathan Dubula Qwelane & Another* (EQ44/2009; EQ13/2012) [2017] ZAGPJHC 218 (18 August 2017). The SAHRC also sought damages in the amount of R100,000 from Qwelane and Media24 to be paid to the 777 campaign (focused on raising awareness around gay and lesbian rights), as well as an order requiring the respondents to be enrolled in a journalism sensitivity training programme and having to report to the SAHRC on such attendance.

[25] See the Record of Appeal (p 771) in *Qwelane & Another* (CCT 13/20) [2021] ZACC 22 (31 July 2021).

[26] Record of Appeal (p 1098) in *Qwelane & Another* (CCT 13/20) [2021] ZACC 22 (31 July 2021).

genuine acknowledgement of wrongdoing by, the transgressor. Where this is obviously lacking, then the reconciliation role of apology would appear to be extinguished.

This scepticism around the value of an insincere apology was expressed by MN, a lesbian woman, whose *in camera* testimony described the physical and psychological violence and abuse that she had experienced as a result of her sexual orientation. For MN, an apology would offer cold comfort against Qwelane's incendiary utterances:

> I wouldn't accept the apology that is extended by him after making such utterances. And in the media, he reflected that he doesn't care, and he wouldn't apologise. This was said on many occasions and this is a waste of time especially for people who find this very offensive. Especially those who were hurt very badly by this.[27]

In light of the reticence expressed around the value of an apology, Judge Moshidi questioned the SAHRC's counsel on the efficacy of apology as a remedial order. In response, Advocate Tembeka Ngcukaitobi indicated that the value of a compelled apology need not lie in Qwelane's sincerity, but rather in the significance of having an unrepentant Qwelane submit to the very act he resists: 'This is precisely the point that we make, my lord, because the value behind this apology is exactly that … even those people that are skeptical about the efficacy of the act would learn that in fact the law has teeth, the law has to protect them'.[28] He went on to add:

> In order for this Court to provide some kind of remedy for people like MN, it is vital that its own remedial jurisdiction is effective. Notwithstanding their skepticism, and notwithstanding the disdainful attitude that has been illustrated by Mr. Qwelane in telling the Commission, in his own article, that they can do whatever they want, he is not going to apologise and not showing up for his trial to this Court. Not only showing contempt to the Commission but also showing contempt to the Court as well.[29]

Cast in these terms, Qwelane's compelled apology is not a stillborn attempt at influencing his views on homosexuality and motivating him to request

---

[27] Record of Appeal (p 900) in *Qwelane & Another* (CCT 13/20) [2021] ZACC 22 (31 July 2021).

[28] Record of Appeal (p 1214) in *Qwelane & Another* (CCT 13/20) [2021] ZACC 22 (31 July 2021).

[29] Record of Appeal (pp 1214–15) in *Qwelane & Another* (CCT 13/20) [2021] ZACC 22 (31 July 2021).

forgiveness. Rather, because it can be compelled, its force is focused on affirming and vindicating the equality and dignity of gay and lesbian people regardless of Qwelane's sincerity. And a compelled public apology is a particularly potent remedy, exactly because Qwelane was so resistant to it. For Qwelane himself, an apology would not have been just words that 'cost nothing'.[30]

In addition, a compelled apology by Qwelane would play a significant value-expressive role as envisioned by the Act's call for measures that educate and raise awareness around unfair discrimination and inequality. As Advocate Kate Hofmeyr (counsel for the PsySSA) emphasised, apology also serves another important purpose, in that it 'marks speech' which is detrimental to constitutional values.[31]

On 18 August 2017, the Equality Court held that Qwelane's utterances constituted hate speech.[32] A declaratory order was made and Qwelane was ordered to publish an unconditional apology (the terms of which were to be agreed on by the parties).[33] Disappointingly, however, Justice Moshidi did not deal in any depth with the effectiveness of the final relief granted. Without substantive explanation, he declined to order sensitivity training, nor did he award damages. Most of the remedial work of the relief therefore centred on an unconditional apology, and yet the judgment did not articulate why the remedy would be an effective one in the circumstances.

This is particularly surprising since, in his judgment in *South African Human Rights Commission obo South African Jewish Board of Deputies v Masuku and Another* 2017,[34] which was handed down just two months before *Qwelane*, Justice Moshidi expressly set out why a compelled public apology, even against an unrepentant defendant, may be considered as an effective remedy in response to hate speech. In that case, the judge emphasised his view that 'an order for an unconditional apology is by no means lenient, and should not be viewed in the light of the proverbial slap on the wrist' (para. 62). Instead, he indicated, apology plays a restorative role for victims and that requiring a transgressor to recognise their statements as hate speech constitutes 'a notable move towards compensating the target groups' (para. 62). Significantly, he also linked the purpose and value of apology as a remedial measure to

---

[30] See *Dikoko* para. 120.

[31] Record of Appeal (p 1468) in *Qwelane & Another* (CCT 13/20) [2021] ZACC 22 (31 July 2021).

[32] *South African Human Rights Commission v Qwelane; Qwelane v Minister for Justice and Correctional Services* (EQ44/2009; EQ13/2012) [2017] ZAGPJHC 218 (18 August 2017).

[33] The SAHRC and PsySSA handed up a draft apology to the court before the conclusion of the hearing (Record of Appeal (p 1371) in *Qwelane and Another* (CCT 13/20) [2021] ZACC 22 (31 July 2021).

[34] (EQ01/2012) [2017] ZAEQC 1 (29 June 2017).

the broad systemic goals of the Equality Act and emphasised that its order should 'create awareness' and 'change the mindset of our society, and certain unrepenting people or groups of people' (para. 62).[35]

It is possible that Justice Moshidi's reflections in *Masuku* may have similarly motivated his order of an apology in *Qwelane*. However, his failure to articulate this in the *Qwelane* judgment is not only regrettable but constitutionally unsustainable. As we have sought to argue, in order for compelled apologies to have legitimacy as a response to hate speech, Equality Courts need to clearly explain the effectiveness of that remedy in any particular hate speech case. Qwelane passed away in December 2020, never having publicly apologised. He successfully appealed the Equality Court judgment to the Supreme Court of Appeal, but this was eventually overturned by the Constitutional Court in July 2021.[36] The Constitutional Court declared Qwelane's comments to constitute hate speech, although it declined to issue an apology order in light of Qwelane's passing.[37]

Notably, during the very period that appeals in the *Masuku* and *Qwelane* matters were being considered by the Constitutional Court,[38] the country's Chief Justice at the time (Chief Justice Mogoeng Mogoeng) became embroiled in a controversy for which he was called upon to publicly apologise.[39] In response, the Chief Justice dug in his heels. He declared at a prayer meeting that he would not apologise:

'Even if 50 million people can march every day for the next 10 years for me to retract or apologise for what I said, I will not do it … There will be no apology. Not even this political apology that "in case I have offended anybody without meaning to offend them for that reason …". I will not apologise for anything. There is nothing to apologise for, there is nothing to retract; and I can't apologise for loving, I can't

---

[35] The Equality Court's judgment in *Masuku* was appealed, with the Constitutional Court handing down final judgment in the matter on 16 February 2021 (*South African Human Rights Commission obo South African Jewish Board of Deputies v Masuku and Another* CCT 14/19) [2022] ZACC 5 [16 February 2022]. The Constitutional Court held that the impugned comments in that matter amounted to hate speech and ordered the respondents to tender an unconditional apology to the Jewish community within 30 days of the order.

[36] *Qwelane v South African Human Rights Commission and Another* (CCT 13/20) [2021] ZACC 22 (31 July 2021).

[37] The Constitutional Court held that the apology order was a personal remedy against Qwelane and could not be enforced against third parties (*Qwelane* para. 192).

[38] The Chief Justice was one of the Constitutional Court justices who heard the *Masuku* appeal, but the Chief Justice did not hear the *Qwelane* appeal.

[39] A furore erupted over comments (see Judicial Conduct Committee 2021: 4) made by the Chief Justice regarding South Africa's foreign policy stance towards Israel.

apologise for not harbouring hatred, I will not. If I perish, I perish.' (Judicial Conduct Committee 2021: 45)

He repeated his refusal to apologise in his official response to complaints lodged with the Judicial Conduct Committee (JCC). In March 2021, the JCC ruled that the Chief Justice's initial comments had breached various provisions of the Code of Judicial Conduct and that he should publicly apologise (Judicial Conduct Committee 2021). Moreover, the JCC ruled that the Chief Justice's declarations that he was unrepentant and would never apologise were aggravating and should be unreservedly retracted and withdrawn (p 66). The Chief Justice was ordered to circulate a scripted apology and retraction (as per wording specified in the JCC ruling) by way of media statement and to read the apology aloud at a meeting of the justices of the Constitutional Court (p 66).

While we do not take a view on the merits of the JCC's order, in our view the Chief Justice's resistance to the ruling reveals not only the power and potency of being ordered to publicly apologise, both to the general public via a media statement and before his colleagues via reading aloud, but also highlights its punitive potential, particularly against unrepentant respondents. In public comments explaining his appeal, the Chief Justice is reported to have referred to the scripted apology as 'a most unusual remedial action', which appeared to be designed as if 'to trash you, to reduce you to nothing, to put you in your place' (Erasmus 2021). In other words, as with Qwelane, the Chief Justice did not view an apology order as a mere 'slap on the wrist' but recognised the 'symbolic transfer of humiliation and power' (White 2006: 1274–5) that such an order invokes – particularly where it required the Chief Justice to read aloud a scripted apology in front of fellow justices.[40]

---

[40] On appeal, the JCC upheld certain aspects of the initial decision but found that the Chief Justice's statements regarding a refusal to apologise had not been assessed in its full context and should not have been considered as aggravating (Judicial Conduct Committee 2022: 32). In a minority opinion, Justice Victor explicitly agreed with the Chief Justice that the original apology order 'was calculated to humiliate and crush' (Judicial Conduct Committee 2022: 66). The JCC appeal committee revised the initial order and did not require the Chief Justice to read his apology aloud before fellow justices, but only required him to circulate a scripted apology by media statement. While the Chief Justice (who was, by that stage, retired) subsequently issued a media statement, the apology was preceded by written comments that arguably served to signal his ongoing view that he had not been in the wrong in relation to the views he expressed, but was only wrong in relation to his involvement in a political controversy/participating in extra-judicial activity, which was incompatible with *inter alia*, the independence of judges (Office of the Chief Justice 2022).

Agreeing to apologise: The Chinese Association (TCA) case and apology as a restorative justice process

As one of the first hate speech cases instituted in the Equality Courts, the pursuit of apology in the *Qwelane* matter charted new territory. Following a decade later, the *TCA* case demonstrates a maturing practice around apology as a remedial measure in hate speech litigation, particularly in cases where transgressors agree to apologise, either as a result of having sincerely acknowledged wrongdoing or in an effort to escape a full reckoning.

In early 2017, *Carte Blanche* (a weekly investigative journalism show) aired a segment on the illicit trade of donkey skins in South Africa. During the segment, it was reported that some of the skins were allegedly being sent to China. This unleashed a torrent of anti-Chinese commentary on social media, with hate-filled comments being posted on the Facebook pages of *Carte Blanche* and the Karoo Donkey Sanctuary (which had featured in the segment). Some of the comments were egregiously bigoted, propagating various negative stereotypes about people of Chinese origin, advocating for Chinese people to leave South Africa, calling for Chinese people to be 'wiped' off the earth and for their children to be killed.[41]

An Equality Court challenge was launched by TCA, an organisation established in 1903 with the aim of promoting and protecting Chinese culture within South Africa. TCA complained that the social media posts of 12 individuals, in particular, constituted hate speech, unfair discrimination, and harassment. An unconditional apology (the terms of which were to be approved by TCA) was sought as part of a package of remedial interventions, which included a declaratory order, interdict, requirement that the respondents pay damages and/or render service to a charitable organisation nominated by TCA, and a requirement that the respondents attend an anger management course. TCA also sought to have the matter referred to the Director of Public Prosecutions for the possible institution of criminal proceedings.

In response to the litigation, five of the respondents confessed that their comments constituted hate speech, which infringed the dignity and equality of Chinese people. As part of their confession statements, four of the respondents agreed to the relief sought by TCA, including an apology (the terms of which had been drafted by TCA). One respondent's apology read as follows:

---

[41] Particulars of Complaint, *The Chinese Association (Gauteng) v Henning and 11 Others* (EQ2/2017) [2019] ZAGPJHC 145 (20 March 2019).

Following communications with the Chinese Association and proceedings in the Equality Court, I acknowledge that my comment was extremely hurtful and harmful to the members of the Chinese Community of South Africa and that it had the potential to incite racial hatred and harm against the Chinese Community.

I unconditionally apologise to the Chinese Community, its members and all other persons that might have read my comment for the harm that I have or might have caused, including violating the Chinese Community's right to human dignity and equality.

I acknowledge that animal cruelty is not part of the character or culture of Chinese people or the Chinese community in South Africa.

I am sincerely sorry for making any member of the Chinese Community feel threatened, unwelcome and unsafe in South Africa, their home, especially in view of the long history of unfair discrimination against Chinese people in South Africa under colonialism and apartheid.

I undertake not to make or endorse such insulting, ignorant and intolerant comments on Facebook or anywhere else. I hope that this apology will help others to understand how hurtful and harmful such comments can be, and to refrain from making such statement in the future.[42]

Even though the acknowledgement of wrongdoing was accepted by TCA, this was not the end of the matter. Notwithstanding the confessions, TCA proceeded on the basis that the Equality Court still needed to conduct an inquiry in respect of *all* of the respondents before handing down a final order and judgment. In practical terms, this meant that each of the respondents, even those who confessed, would be required to attend court, and to hear the evidence and arguments presented.

The 12th respondent opposed this vigorously. Picking up on the issue as a point *in limine*, she argued that, in light of her confession, the court should swiftly make a final order and dispense with any further proceedings against her. TCA, in turn, argued that confessions by respondents were not a 'proverbial get out of jail free card'.[43] Instead, the Equality Act requires courts to conduct a full inquiry and ventilate all relevant evidence (of which the confessions may form part) before any order is handed down. Critically, TCA emphasised that the Equality Court is a *sui generis* forum, the proceedings of which should be geared towards victim-centred, restorative processes. As such, the *process* of the Equality Court inquiry – where respondents

---

[42] Ninth Respondent's Confession Statement in the *TCA* case.
[43] Transcript of Proceedings of 25 March 2019.

listen to testimonies from those who have been pained and injured by the impugned speech – is itself necessary to fully serve the restorative purposes of the Equality Act. Advocate Faizel Ismail, acting on behalf of TCA, put it to the court as follows:

> I can think of nothing more restorative than to have the proponents of the hate speech listen to the harm that is caused. Listen to the members of the community who have been here for generations. Listen to their pain. Listen to why it is wrong. Be educated about it.[44]

In other words, the tender of an apology by a hate speech transgressor does not simply let them off the hook. Instead, a truly repentant transgressor will understand the need for complainants to express their hurt. And a transgressor who is simply looking to 'helter-skelter get out of court'[45] by tendering an apology will be required to listen to and perhaps come to properly acknowledge the harm of their hate speech. As Advocate Ismail emphasised, 'An apology means precious little particularly coming from some of these Respondents, especially the 12th respondent, if she is not prepared to listen to the person whom she has injured egregiously. To hear their pain, to experience what they experience'.[46]

There were some respondents who did exhibit such willingness. The 10th respondent had submitted a confession and apology and attended court for the full duration of the inquiry. Drawing this to the court's attention, counsel for TCA noted that the 10th respondent 'had the courage to be present and remain present through these proceedings'.[47] In this way, the TCA case demonstrates the potential for Equality Courts to, as Melanie Judge and Juan Nel have argued, facilitate 'an encounter with prejudice and its impacts, and for victims/survivors to speak back to hateful speech' (Judge and Nel 2018: 16).

The *TCA* case also demonstrates the importance of the process by which the *terms* of an apology order are crafted. The potency and effectiveness of such orders depends on litigants and courts carefully framing and constructing their relief so that it fully vindicates the rights that have been infringed. Where a hate speech offender is simply ordered to make an unconditional public apology, there is no guarantee that a clear and unequivocal statement of wrongdoing will be made. Even worse, the offender may use the opportunity to negate responsibility or reinforce their position by a variety

---

[44] Transcript of Proceedings of 25 March 2019.
[45] Transcript of Proceedings of 25 March 2019.
[46] Transcript of Proceedings of 25 March 2019.
[47] Transcript of Proceedings of 2 December 2019.

of non-apology tactics. One example is politician Julius Malema's public apology following a judgment that declared certain of his utterances as hate speech and harassment against women.[48] In addition to damages, Malema was ordered to apologise within two weeks. Over a year later, Malema's eventual 'apology' included the disclaimer 'it doesn't matter whether you are right or not, you must have the capacity to say sorry' (Roehrs 2011: 16). As Roehrs (2011) argues, Malema's 'apology' failed to effectively vindicate rights as it eschewed any real acknowledgement of wrongdoing.

Anticipating these types of non-apology tactics, the framing of relief in the *TCA* case sought to ensure that complainants approve the terms of an apology before a final order was handed down, with the prayer cast in the following terms: 'ordering the Respondent, within 10 days, to make an unconditional apology in an appropriate form and forum, to be approved in advance by TCA.'[49]

Notably, the 12th respondent insisted that negotiation over the specific terms of the apology should take place *after* an order requiring such apology is granted. The 12th respondent went further and argued that *she* would proffer a draft of the apology, with TCA providing input thereafter. Unwilling to accept this approach, TCA argued that negotiation regarding the terms of the apology had to be undertaken *upfront* (before final judgment) so that the wording of the apology, as agreed upon by TCA, would be clear when the court's order was handed down. To adopt the 12th respondent's approach, submitted TCA, would 'denude' the apology order of its remedial effectiveness, with the complainants shouldering the burden of having to return to court in order to determine the appropriate wording of an apology.[50] Moreover, TCA considered it remarkable that a self-confessed perpetrator of hate speech would seek to dictate the terms of an apology to the complainants whose very rights had been infringed. As TCA's legal representatives explained in correspondence with attorneys for the 12th respondent:

> It is entirely untenable for the wording of the apology or the nature of the community service to be left to a negotiation between the parties after the court order is granted … this will precipitate the real risk that the hurt and harm that has been caused by the conduct will not be remedied and will only be exacerbated. This is because the aggressor (your client) will be allowed to dictate the remedy to the victim, once again reinforcing the power of the aggressor whose unfortunate and

---

[48] See *Sonke Gender Justice Network v Malema* [2010] ZAEQC 2 (15 March 2010).
[49] See Particulars of Complaint of the *TCA* case.
[50] See the Transcript of Proceedings of 25 March 2019 of the *TCA* case.

despicable comments were made with every expectation that she had the power to wield such hateful and hurtful words against others with impunity. Frankly it is through the Court sanctioned order that our client will feel redres.[51]

While the *TCA* case is still to be decided, the approach adopted by the litigants offers useful reflections on how carefully crafted apology orders, viewed as part of a restorative *process* and not merely outcome, can ensure that (i) consenting to an apology order is not simply an easy escape route for insincere transgressors, and (ii) genuinely repentant transgressors confront their prejudice and deepen their understanding of the damaging impact of their hate speech.

Conclusion: The effectiveness of apology

The role of apology as legal remedy is dynamic and malleable. Reflecting on the *Qwelane* and *TCA* cases, we have suggested some of the ways in which compelled apologies can serve as an effective remedial measure in response to hate speech. In cases where transgressors are genuinely repentant, a court-ordered apology – as a form of performative public penance – holds the restorative potential to vindicate the rights of complainants as well as to transform the transgressor. Where a transgressor is entirely unrepentant, a court-ordered apology's limitation on the offender's freedom of expression and the resulting 'symbolic transfer of humiliation and power between the offender and victim', to return once again to White's powerful phrasing (2006: 1274–5), serves to affirm society's thresholds for constitutionally acceptable speech. Carefully framing apology orders as part of a restorative *process* rather than mere outcome can ensure that transgressors who adopt a cynical approach to apology (as a means to escape accountability) are in fact required to reckon with the impact of their hate speech. In addition, crafting apology as part of a broader package of remedial interventions, including, for example, damages, community service, and sensitivity training, can add to and reinforce the effectiveness of compelled apologies in hate speech cases. In these ways, apology as a remedial measure can, to varying degrees and depending on the circumstances of each case, further the corrective, restorative, educational, and/or deterrent goals of the Equality Act.

While we have sought to respond to scepticism around the 'true value' of a compelled apology in hate speech cases, we recognise that law and legal processes can perpetuate injustice. Marginalised communities may 'use law to

---

[51] See letter from attorneys for the complainant to attorneys for the 12th respondent in the *TCA* case.

resist social injustices', but may be 'confronted, and at times defeated, by the injustices of law in practice' (Williams and Judge 2018: 257). Indeed, in both the *Qwelane* and *TCA* cases, the desire for final remedial closure remained unfulfilled years after the offending speech was first published – in part due to the trappings of formal, adversarial legal procedures. It is important, then, for Equality Court judges and magistrates to embrace the Equality Act's promise of enhanced access to justice through accessible and participatory processes, which places the restoration of the dignity and equality of complainants at its centre. Where the process of pursuing an apology exhausts and depletes complainants themselves, then we are reminded of Upile Chisala's (2020) caution: 'what good is a "sorry" you had to drown for?'

Reflections

We both are often conflicted about the role (and importance) of the law generally, and apology orders specifically. We were involved in the *Qwelane* matter when it first began almost a decade ago, and Kerry is currently involved in the *TCA* case. We have each (separately and together) fluctuated between enthusiasm and cynicism around the potential of courts to meaningfully vindicate rights in hate speech cases as well as many other cases in which constitutional rights are claimed. Following the writing process, and particularly with the judgment in the *Qwelane* matter being handed down, we remain conflicted. The judgment is great for South Africa as the bar for harmful speech is not set too high and is victim-centred (for want of a better term). But Mr Qwelane died without apologising and it is not clear that the judgment can replace a compelled personal apology from the man himself. But this ongoing internal tension is vital – for now it seems that there must be value in the apology-seeking *process* and it is probably blinkered to just focus on outcome – as it is in the process that individuals confront, engage, learn, and reckon with our personal and collective vision of justice. The difference between apology and other legal remedies is that apology keeps us engaged with each other in a way that is true to both our ongoing humanity and the ongoing difficulties South Africans are likely to have with each other. For this reason, it seems a dynamic remedy – unpredictable in its content and unpredictable in the way it may be delivered, received, and what all of this may collectively produce for a better society.

Nurina and Kerry

References

Austin, J. L., 1962, *How to Do Things with Words*, London: Oxford University Press.

Baker, K. K., 1999, 'Sex, rape, and shame', *Boston University Law Review* 79(3), 663–716.

Baker M. B., 1992, 'Penance as a model for punishment', *Social Theory and Practice* 18(3), 311–31.

Bishop, M., 2014, 'Remedies' in S. Woolman and M. Bishop (eds.), *Constitutional Law of South Africa*, 2nd ed., pp 1–199, Cape Town: Jutastat e-publications.

Braithwaite, J., 2003, 'Principles of restorative justice' in A. von Hirsch, J. Roberts, A. Bottoms, J. Roach, and M. Schiff (eds.), *Restorative Justice and Criminal Justice: Competing or Reconcilable Paradigms* (pp. 1-20). Oxford: Hart Publishing.

Carroll, R., 2013, 'Apologies as legal remedy', *Sydney Law Review* 35(2), 317–47.

De Jager, J., 2011, 'Addressing xenophobia in the Equality Courts of South Africa', *Refuge* 28(2), 107–16.

Delgado, R. and Stefancic, J., 1996, 'Apologize and move on? Finding a remedy for pornography, insult, and hate speech', *University of Colorado Law Review* 67, 93–111.

Du Plessis, D., 2008, 'We didn't break the law, but for our sins I apologise', *Sunday Sun*, 3 August 2008, p 16.

Erasmus, D., 2021, ' "The Lord gave me grounds to appeal": Chief Justice Mogoeng rejects Judicial Conduct Committee finding', *Daily Maverick*, 15 March, viewed 23 March 2021 from www.dailymaverick.co.za/arti cle/2020-07-02-the-mogoeng-mogoeng-blowup-what-judges-say-does-matter/

Judge, M. and Nel, J., 2018, 'Psychology and hate speech: a critical and restorative encounter – editorial', *South African Journal of Psychology* 48(1), 15–20.

Judicial Conduct Committee, 2021, *African 4 Palestine, SA BDS Coalition, Women's Cultural Group v Chief Justice Mogoeng Mogoeng*, JSC 819/20 and 825/20 and 827/20, 4 March, viewed 3 May 2021 from www.judiciary. org.za/images/news/2021/Judicial_Conduct_Committee_decision_on_complaints_against_the_Chief_Justice.pdf

Judicial Conduct Committee, 2022, *Appeal Decision in Terms of s. 17 of the Judicial Service Commission Act 9 of 1994 in African 4 Palestine, SA BDS Coalition, Women's Cultural Group v Chief Justice Mogoeng Mogoeng*, JSC 819/20 and 825/20 and 827/20, 20 January.

Marais, M. E., 2017, 'A constitutional perspective on the Sparrow judgments', *Journal for Juridical Science* 42(2), 25–64.

Office of the Chief Justice, 2022, 'Media statement by former Chief Justice Mogoeng Mogoeng', 3 February, viewed 16 February 2022 from www.judici ary.org.za/index.php/news/press-statements/2022

Parliament of South Africa, 2017, Report of the high level panel on the assessment of key legislation and the acceleration of fundamental change', viewed 13 January from www.parliament.gov.za/storage/app/media/Pages/2017/october/ High_Level_Panel/HLP_Report/HLP_report.pdf

Qwelane, J., 2008, 'Call me names, but gay is NOT okay …', Sunday Sun, 20 July, p 14.

Roehrs, S., 2011, 'Waiting and watching: Malema's delayed apology and compensation payment and their broader implications', Agenda 25(4), 112–17.

Singh, K., 2019, 'Penny Sparrow, whose racist post sparked fury, has died' News24, 25 July, viewed 13 January 2021 from www.news24.com/new s24/SouthAfrica/News/breaking-penny-sparrow-has-died-20190725

Skelton, A., 2013, 'The South African Constitutional Court's restorative justice jurisprudence', Restorative Justice: An International Journal 1(1), 122–45.

South African Human Rights Commission, 2017, 'Complaints on gay article the biggest complaint before SAHRC', viewed 13 January from www.sahrc. org.za/index.php/sahrc-media/news/item/591-complaints-on-gay-arti cle-the-biggest-complaint-before-sahrc

Swart, M., 2008, 'Sorry seems to be the hardest word: apology as a form of symbolic reparation', South African Journal on Human Rights 24(1), 50–70.

Thloloe, J., 2008, 'Lesbian, gay, bisexual and transgender community vs Sunday Sun', Ruling by Press Ombudsman, 29 July, viewed 13 January 2021 from www.politicsweb.co.za/party/lesbian-gay-bisexual-and-tran sgender-community-vs-

Tippett, K., 2017, 'Layli Long Soldier – the freedom of real apologies', audio recording, viewed 4 May 2021 from https://onbeing.org/programs/ layli-long-soldier-the-freedom-of-real-apologies/

Upile, C., 2020, 'Swim class' in A Fire Like You, Kansas City: Andrews McMeel Publishing.

Weisman, R., 2006, 'Showing remorse at the TRC: towards a constitutive approach to reparative discourse', Windsor Yearbook of Access to Justice 24(2), 221–40.

White, B. T., 2006, 'Say you're sorry: court-ordered apologies as civil rights remedy', Cornell Law Review 91(6), 1261–312.

Williams, K. and Judge, M., 2018, 'Happy (n)ever after? Public interest litigation for LGBTI equality', in J. Brickhill (ed.), Public Interest Law in South Africa, pp 239–57, Cape Town: Juta.

6

On Not Apologising: Winnie Madikizela-Mandela and the TRC Hearing into the Mandela United Football Club

Shireen Hassim

Introduction

What kind of ethical gestures are required for a nation on the cusp of a new set of institutional forms and norms, and yet haunted by a violent past?[1] The Truth and Reconciliation Commission (TRC), established in South Africa in 1995, sought to stage the transition from apartheid to democracy by framing truth, accountability, apology, and forgiveness as the necessary ethical dimensions for national rebirth. The TRC suggested that something more than democratic institutions was necessary for the postapartheid state. Moving into the future would require moral repair, an attention to the ways in which apartheid had transgressed the very notion of humanity by rendering people into disposable objects of state policies. Moral repair rested on the twinned gestures of acknowledgement of harm (recognising that it existed, and taking responsibility for it) and forgiveness (amnesty, or through mechanisms of restorative justice). In this sense, testimonies before the TRC provided a metaphorical bridge between the past, in which a range of unacceptable actions manifested, and the future, in which a just,

---

[1]   This chapter is a reworking of my 2018 paper 'Not Just Nelson's Wife: Winnie Madikizela-Mandela, the TRC and radicalism in South Africa', *Journal of Southern African Studies*, 44(5), 895–912.

inclusive, and caring society would be based on shared understanding of the past and would be underpinned by new, democratic values. Moral repair is not unidirectional: the assumption is that both perpetrators and victims would be rehumanised by the process, and would be more likely to recognise shared humanity in the future. Perpetrators of gross human rights violations – defined as 'the killing, attempted killing, abduction, severe ill treatment, or torture' (TRC 1998a: 60) arising from political conflict – testified to the TRC and in some cases requested amnesty, dependent on full disclosure.

Although an apology was not necessary for amnesty, one TRC hearing dramatically demanded an apology: not from an agent of the apartheid state, but from one of its most high-profile victims, Winnie Madikizela-Mandela. In a process that was globally significant for debates about post-conflict reconciliation, Madikizela-Mandela's obstinate refusal to apologise for her actions during the 1980s stands out with clarity. It was a rare moment in which a reparative burden was placed on a black woman, and in her refusal to apologise, Madikizela-Mandela appeared to refuse the very terms on which postapartheid South Africa was being constituted.

Political apologies are most frequently extended by people in positions of state authority towards collectives of people that have been harmed by state actions. It is rare for a political apology to be demanded of a person who had no formal political authority. In a context where there appeared to be a clear and binary distinction between perpetrators and victims, Winnie Madikizela-Mandela presented a complex figure: someone to whom an apology was owed by the agents of the apartheid state was put into the position of having to apologise, being both a victim and a perpetrator. This hearing was one of a very small number that explored tensions between black protagonists. It was also the only one in which a woman was required to account for acts of violence. Most TRC testimonies made by women dealt with instances where it was women to whom violence was done, either personally or to their male relatives (Ross 2003; Lazare 2005).[2] Winnie Madikizela-Mandela is a rare, indeed only, example of a woman having to account for her own culpability in acts of violence (Lazare 2005: 17). The TRC intended an apology to be made not only to the families of the people affected by the activities of the Mandela United Football Club (most notably, but not only, the families of Lolo Sono and Abubaker Asvat) but generally to the nation. Madikizela-Mandela's dogged refusal, followed

---

[2] Gendered harms, including the burdens imposed on women as a result of forced removals, and trauma caused by sexual harassment in the workplace, among others, were not considered gross human rights violations. Aaron Lazare (2005) argues that women in general apologise more than men.

by a mild apology,[3] did not in any way achieve the performative national resolution that had been staged in several other instances in the TRC, and decades later remains unresolved for the victims at the heart of the story.[4] Elsewhere, I focused on the significance of the hearing for debates on national unity, arguing that her refusal to offer a political apology was both emblematic of and anticipated a rupture with the celebratory narrative of the postapartheid state (Hassim 2018). In resisting the demand to provide a narrative of culpability, Madikizela-Mandela disallowed the TRC's own narrative of truth-telling and personal accountability as an accompaniment to the new governance mechanisms that established democracy. This stance illuminated the emerging fault lines in democratic South Africa between those who accepted the terms of the transition and those for whom the TRC sidelined justice in favour of reconciliation.

This chapter addresses the complicated and multifaceted nature of the apology demanded of Winnie Madikizela-Mandela, and the reasons given for her (non)apology both by herself and her supporters. I argue that there was an implicit gendered script in the Mandela United Football Club hearing, and in the ways in which the appeal for an apology was made, and tease out the main elements of this script. The chapter untangles some elements of the affective structure of the hearing, focusing on the ways in which Archbishop Tutu engaged Winnie Madikizela-Mandela as an intimate member of a family rather than as a criminal. I propose that there are two affective moves at work in the testimony of Winnie Madikizela-Mandela, both of which are processes of reattribution, that is, ways of shifting the causal relationship for violence away from the individual to the structural features of an unjust society. First, responsibility is reattributed to the apartheid state, in a move that resonates with a large part of the intended audience for the apology. A second narrative reattribution, more evident after the hearing than at it, invokes the patriarchal double standard by which Madikizela-Mandela was judged. This recalibration resonates with young

---

[3]   After Archbishop Tutu made his heartfelt appeal to Madikizela-Mandela to take responsibility for the harms caused by the Football Club, she said to the Asvat family that she 'was deeply sorry'. Her apology to Caroline Sono, mother of Lolo Sono, was equally brief and without elaboration. Immediately after the hearing, Nicodemus Sono (Lolo's father) and Caroline Sono questioned the sincerity of the apology. See SAPA (1997) 'Winnie complies with Tutu's appeal for her to say sorry', at www.justice.gov.za/trc/media/1997/9712/s971204v.htm, viewed 13 February 2022.

[4]   These include Katiza Cebekhulu, who claimed to have seen Winnie Mandela stab Stompie Seipei. He was due to testify at her trial in 1991 but absconded and fled from South Africa. He was famously 'rescued' from Zambia by British MP Emma Nicholson and is currently living in a state of destitution in England. He continues to hold the African National Congress (ANC) and Winnie Mandela responsible for his plight (Bridgland 1997).

feminists critical of the failures of the postapartheid state to address gender harms.[5] Thus, although the intention of the TRC hearing may have been to acknowledge the harms caused by the Mandela United Football Club, and to hold the leader of the Club morally accountable in order to effect a common narrative, Madikizela-Mandela became the figure around whom a narrative rupture of the reconciliation project coalesced.

The affective and reconciliatory work of political apologies

The political apology is a particular category in the genre of writing about apologies. A political apology is part of a distinct process in which harms are recognised to have been committed, and in which some degree of public responsibility is taken. Such an apology may be formally offered by an official on behalf of a group of people, for a historical wrong (such as the apology offered by Canadian Prime Minister, Stephen Harper, in 2008 to indigenous Canadians for previous government policies of confining indigenous children in residential schools), or may be a non-verbal gesture (such as Willy Brandt's genuflection at the Holocaust memorial in Warsaw in 1970). Alice MacLachlan, drawing on the work of Hannah Arendt, treats political apologies as acts that are part of creating the conditions necessary for people to live together. In a meticulous examination of the ways in which political apologies constitute political communities, MacLachlan shows the ways in which apologies are part of creating a new public record, and in the process, enable deeply fractured societies to reconvene around common values (MacLachlan 2014).

Nicholas Tavuchis outlines what has become a standard set of criteria about what is entailed in an effective apology: the unqualified (and for the purposes of this chapter, public) acknowledgement of harms, the expression of regret and the acceptance of responsibility, and the naming of the moral norm that has been violated (Tavuchis 1991). Public apologies are forms of political speech, in that they assert the standing of victims as equals in the moral community. They are ways of validating and naming harms, but go beyond this by recognising the worth and integrity of people who were in positions of unequal power. Read as

---

[5]   One of the first breaks with the celebratory nationalist narrative of progress was with feminists, who queried the state's failure to deal with gender-based violence, the disproportionate responsibility for health care during the AIDS pandemic, and the persistence of gender inequalities in the economy (Moffett 2006; Gqola 2007; Hassim 2008).

political in this way, apologies are not simply a means of complying with a legal requirement. Nor does a political apology necessarily rest on an admission of guilt; it is sufficient to express remorse for actions taken in the name of an ideology or a movement of which one has been a leader. Apologies operate performatively; they invoke an affective structure in which tone, demeanour, and narrative devices signal the extent of sincerity of the leader who is apologising. Gender is a key feature of the affective structure, Lachlan argues, noting that:

> people of different genders are likely to be socialized differently when it comes to the rhetorical spaces of apology: that is, situations of conflict, anger, and resentment. Women – that is, persons socialized to see themselves as feminine and who are treated as feminine by others – face pressures to be 'compassionate and giving' rather than 'angry and vindictive' victims that men in positions of privilege do not. (MacLachlan 2013: 136)

These gendered expectations were heightened in the case of Winnie Madikizela-Mandela, who is firmly located within the nationalist script as mother of the nation (Meintjes 1998; Hassim 2018; Msimang 2018). She appeared before the hearing as someone about whom public opinion was firmly decided. Although she was deeply loved by many, she was seen to have violated the code of motherhood, having already been convicted as an accomplice in the abuse and death of children. In the next section, I trace the period before the TRC in order to sketch the deeply complex context in which Madikizela-Mandela was formed as both victim and perpetrator.

Background to the TRC hearing

In 1985, after years of banishment by the state to Brandfort, Winnie Madikizela-Mandela returned to her home in Orlando, Soweto. By this stage, she was not simply the wife of Nelson Mandela, but a political leader in her own right, with a following among the youth in the townships and a global status as an outspoken critic of the apartheid regime. She returned to Soweto at a time of heightened conflict between the apartheid state and its opponents, which had spillover effects on relationships between residents in black townships. Many of the conflicts between black people were fuelled by the state, via nefarious practices of the stoking of differences between, and at times arming, particular political factions (Swilling and Phillips 1989; Hamber and Lewis 1997; Duncan 2008). For reasons that are unclear – perhaps she felt that the threats against her had increased, or perhaps someone in Orlando wanted to honour her – a football club known as the Mandela United Football Club (MUFC) was formed a year later, with many of its members living on Winnie Madikizela-Mandela's property (Gilbey 1993). It was styled as a social club, a means of providing structured activities for the many young people who clustered around 'Mam'Winnie', as she was known. However, members of the MUFC also took on the role of being Winnie's bodyguards, and when she went out of the household, they accompanied her, carrying weapons. Lodge (2006: 183) comments that the MUFC 'began behaving in the fashion of a territorial gang, conducting turf wars with other groups of youths. It abducted adherents of rival groups and acquired a reputation for torturing its opponents'. Within a short space of time, township residents began to complain that the members of the Football Club were lawless and operated as a gang. Among the activities of the MUFC, for example, was the abduction of young activists that the Club deemed to be state informers. So-called informers would be taken to Winnie Madikizela-Mandela's house, beaten and, it was alleged, tortured. In one gruesome incident in May 1987, Peter Makanda and his brother were tortured; Peter Makanda's chest was carved with an 'M' and 'Viva ANC', and battery acid was poured into the wounds (Meredith 2010: 377). Madikizela-Mandela's house was burnt down by unknown persons – possibly opponents of the MUFC, possibly by security police agents – and she moved from the Orlando section to the neighbourhood of Diepkloof, taking the members of the Club with her.

The burning of the Mandela home, and the complaints of Soweto residents about the activities of the MUFC, alarmed the leadership of the internal resistance movement, loosely gathered under the name of the Mass Democratic Movement, including the United Democratic Front (UDF) and the trade unions (TRC 1998b). By 1987, anti-apartheid organisations such as the UDF were concerned about the extent to which violence was spreading in the townships, and especially with the targeting of so-called collaborators and informers for violent reprisals. Although the ANC had issued a call to make the country 'ungovernable' (ANC n.d.) – that is, by the apartheid state – it was fast retreating from this position, as kangaroo courts began to spring up in the townships and, increasingly, the targets of violence were not the manifestations of white power but fellow black people (ANC 1986). The ethical line between violence that enables the end of repression and violence that exists in and for itself (Roy 2009) was constantly breached. The actions of the MUFC certainly fitted the pattern of self-appointed arbiters of political justice, people who Nancy Scheper-Hughes has termed instruments of 'social or community hygiene' (Scheper-Hughes 1995: 418). A group called the Mandela Crisis Committee was set up, including some of the most respected political leaders in the community.[6] They sought to control Winnie Mandela's actions and to shut down the MUFC. They approached the imprisoned Nelson Mandela, who protested Madikizela-Mandela's innocence in the activities of the Club, although privately he did urge her to dissociate from the Club, counselling that 'it is poor judgement to have them near you' (Lodge 2006: 184). They also approached Winnie Madikizela-Mandela directly, and asked her to release the abducted youths; it took several days before she acceded to the request (Mass Democratic Movement 1989).

The attempts to curb the activities of the Club were unsuccessful. Lolo Sono, a teenage boy, was beaten so badly that his father, glimpsing him in the back of a van, could barely recognise him. Madikizela-Mandela had taken Lolo to his father's home to inform him that she was taking him away. Lolo was never seen again. Other deaths followed: Siboniso Shabalala, Sizwe Sithole, Kuki Zwane, Sicelo Dhlamini, Sibusiso Chili. Matters spiralled to a head in December 1988, when four boys – Stompie Seipei, Thabiso Mono, Kenny Kgase, and Pelo Megwe – were abducted from the Methodist Mission Manse in Orlando. By her own account, the abduction was ordered by Madikizela-Mandela on the grounds that they were being sexually abused by the priest, Paul Verryn (AP Archive 2015). She said she had been told that one of the four, 13-year-old Stompie Seipei, was an informer. Stompie Seipei had been beaten so badly by members of the Mandela United Football Club that his head was described by one observer as being 'swollen like a football' (Wren 1990; TRC 1998c). He was later found dead in a field. Dr Abubaker Asvat, dubbed 'the people's doctor', was killed in his surgery in Soweto in January 1989. Asvat was a supporter of the Black Consciousness Movement and a member of the Azanian People's Organisation, a rival to the ANC. Although the police arrested two men on charges of theft and murder in relation to the attack on Dr Asvat, many believed that the deaths of Seipei and Asvat were connected, and that this connection was the figure of Winnie Mandela. It was alleged by several people who appeared before the TRC that Winnie Mandela wanted Dr Asvat to testify to Seipei's and three other boys' sexual abuse at the hands of a priest, and that he was killed because there was no such evidence. None of these allegations were proven.

In 1991, a short year after the release of political prisoners from Robben Island and with her husband Nelson by her side, Winnie Madikizela-Mandela was charged with complicity in the murder of Stompie Seipei and the abductions of Kenny Kgase, Pelo Megwe, and Thabiso Mono. Also charged were her driver, John Morgan, coach of the Mandela United Football Club,

---

6   They included Azhar Cachalia, Murphy Morobe, Frank Chikane, Rev. Beyers Naude, Aubrey Mokoena, Sister Bernard Ncube, and Sidney Mufamadi.

Jerry Richardson, and Winnie Madikizela-Mandela's erstwhile friend, Xoliswa Falati. Madikizela-Mandela was found guilty of four charges of kidnapping and being an accessory after the fact to assault and sentenced to six years in prison. Richardson was found guilty of the murder of Seipei. On appeal,[7] the jail sentence was set aside, and instead a fine and suspended sentence was imposed.[8] For some, the trial was an illegitimate sham by an apartheid court to smear the Mandela name, while for others, Madikizela-Mandela was let off lightly because she carried the Mandela name. Whatever the position, neither side felt that the entire truth had been told about the Football Club's activities or about the role of Madikizela-Mandela herself, from whose name the Club derived its authority.

Interrogating violence: the Mandela United Football Club hearing

The Winnie Mandela TRC hearing, a drama within a drama, sought to uncover the extent of the Mandela United Football Club's complicity in various forms of violence in Soweto during the 1980s. The allegations included 13 counts of murder, among them the killing of Stompie Seipei, and a range of other abuses of rights, such as physical abuse of people in the home of Winnie Mandela. Unusually, as previously discussed, the death of Stompie Seipei and the abductions of Kgase, Megwe, and Mono had already been prosecuted in 1991 and this reinterrogation was not fully explained by the TRC. Madikizela-Mandela was offered the option of a closed hearing; after an initial testimony without the media or public present, she decided that she would prefer to have the hearing in public. Her approach to the TRC from the outset was one of defensive refusal. Msimang captures very well the affective posture with which Winnie Madikizela-Mandela presented herself in the early 1990s, and which may well describe her appearance in the hearing:

> You seem unmoved by the events related to Stompie. You seem not to know that you have gone too far, and so you have no impulse to make amends. You carry your attitude of unrepentant superiority with

---

[7] In her appeal, Madikizela-Mandela justified the abduction of the four youths from the Methodist manse by claiming that she had removed the four youths from the manse because she had been informed by Xoliswa Falati, who lived there, that they were being sexually abused by the white priest, and that the youths were engaging in homosexual activities of their own accord, in addition to being coerced. There was no evidence of such activities. Nor is there any evidence that Madikizela-Mandela was directly involved in the murder of Seipei.

[8] *S v Morgan and Others* (644/91) [1993] ZASCA 94 (2 June 1993).

you wherever you go. It protects you like a shawl. This is strength in action. You stay warm, protected by your wilfulness. (Msimang 2018: 122)

This set the scene for a hostile nine days, in which Madikizela-Mandela stonewalled all attempts to get her to acknowledge that there had been abuses in her name and in her home, and that several people accused her of being directly involved in physical assaults and in creating a climate of fear. She wore dark glasses throughout the testimonies by a parade of complainants, and showed almost no emotion on her face. For days, her answers to allegations made by various witnesses, and to questions posed by lawyers, were made in the briefest of terms. She continually used the words 'ludicrous' and 'ridiculous' in response to the allegations, deflecting critiques by questioning the sanity of her accusers. For example, when asked whether she had ordered the death of Stompie Seipei, as claimed by Jerry Richardson, she replied 'That is ridiculous and the worst lunacy' (Sono 2018). Asked of the allegation that she had assaulted a woman of whom she was jealous (Phumlile Dlamini was pregnant by a man who was also Madikizela-Mandela's lover), her answer was simple: 'I regard that statement as totally ludicrous'. In relation to Dr Asvat, her own lawyer, Ishmael Semenya asked: 'there was an allegation of an altercation, is this correct?' Madikizela-Mandela's response was dismissive: 'It is one of those hallucinations I have heard here for the first time' (Sono 2018). In sum, Madikizela-Mandela's testimony provided absolutely no clue as to the nature of her motivations, and she constantly reiterated her position that all the allegations were simply untrue and part of a co-ordinated attempt to cast her in a bad light, and therefore required no explanation. Although she repeated her understanding that the boys had taken refuge in her house because they had been sexually assaulted, she denied any involvement in the assault.

What was described were extreme manifestations of violence in the sphere of the intimate-political. They were not acts of resistant violence against the state, but inwardly turned violence that bred generalised fear in Soweto. Nicodemus Sono, Stompie's father, articulated the views of many who thought that there was a particular harm in a woman attacking a child: 'She used to be a mother, she used to be a loving person. You will go to Winnie with your grievances she will help you if she can. But what has turned now, now lately, I don't know what happened to her' (Sono 2018). This was a moment that encapsulated the dilemma that Srila Roy points to in her study of revolutionary violence in postcolonial South Asia: violent political action is deeply imbued with unresolved ambiguities about 'good' and 'bad' violence (Roy 2009: 318). When victims become perpetrators, they may suspend those ambiguities in ways that disavow their own agency and that suspend normative questions for political efficacy. It is, as a consequence, a form of action that is not easily contained within democratic norms, or within the patriarchal norms of how women should behave in leadership positions. In effect, what was in operation here was a seizure of sovereign power by a small group. Winnie Madikizela-Mandela and the MUFC decided what was political, what was criminal, what was within the boundaries of 'black culture', what was to be punished, and what was to be forgiven. There was no recourse here to any form of community beyond the household, and indeed where the broader community did seek to articulate a view, it was often in opposition to the activities of the MUFC. As Palesa Morudu puts it:

These were the tears of black parents who were deeply hurt by our heroine. Their story and others should not be erased because Madikizela-Mandela has become a feminist icon. Nor is it acceptable to argue that 'bad things happen in war'. To do so is nothing short of rationalising violence. (Morudu 2018)

Madikizela-Mandela offered no alternative explanation at the TRC hearing for what might have occurred in her home, other than her lack of knowledge. 'My evidence is well known, my evidence is that I was not there when they (the boys) were brought there forcibly and that I found youths there' (Morudu 2018). (This assertion was disputed by contradictory evidence.) As Sisonke Msimang describes her affect at the hearing, she appeared to be 'a woman who considers herself not simply innocent but morally superior to those who have called [her] here' (Msimang 2018: 136). As she observed the testimony, Msimang wrote, 'disdain is written all over [her] face' (p 136).

Five harrowing days of testimony followed, detailing the violent behaviour of the Mandela United Football Club, Winnie Madikizela-Mandela's supporters, and, some said, her personal bodyguard detail. At the end of it, Archbishop Desmond Tutu pleaded with Madikizela-Mandela:

'I speak as someone who loves you deeply. ... Many would have rushed out in their eagerness to forgive you and to embrace you. I beg you, I beg you please … You are a great person and you don't know how your greatness would be enhanced if you were to say sorry, things went wrong, forgive me. I beg you.' (SABC 1997)

After days of refusing any culpability for any of the actions of her supporters, and certainly not of herself, Madikizela-Mandela responded:

I will take this opportunity to say to the family of Dr Asvat, how deeply sorry I am. To Stompie's mother, how deeply sorry I am. I have said so to her a few years back, when the heat was very hot. I am saying it is true, things went horribly wrong. I fully agree with that and for that part of those painful years when things went horribly wrong and we were aware of the fact that there were factors that led to that, for that I am deeply sorry. (SABC 1997)

This was an apology that met none of the conditions for a good political apology. She rendered the accounts of the witnesses dubious, and gave no succour to the families of the victims. For Nicodemus Sono, the father of Stompie, her testimony merely confirmed what he already knew: there would be no justice.

Partial and self-exculpatory, Madikizela-Mandela's apology was given as an act of closure to end what Madikizela-Mandela had experienced as a violation of her integrity, rather than offering any form of closure to the victims' families. She said as much in an interview in 2015 with the Swedish journalist Malou von Sivers, in which she called the witnesses state agents:

They were all plants by the system. My own life to this day is still of people who were working for the previous regime who still continue to try and undermine those of us who were seen as the backbone of the ANC. It's absolute rubbish. Nothing of the sort happened. I explained to the TRC and to everyone else who was interested in that statement that it was made in the context of that time. Anyone who disbelieves that can go jump. I am not prepared to apologise for anything we did whilst we were fighting. I will continue being the white man's enemy for as long as I am alive. (von Sivers 2015)

Winnie Madikizela-Mandela is presenting, here, an argument that the fundamental antagonism in South Africa remains that of race, and that the transition to democracy did not change the terms of the race power relationship in any way. In this framing of 'we' as black and 'them' as white, all other struggles are either erased, subsumed, or cast as oppositional to an imputed notion of hegemonic blackness. Any temporal differences between the apartheid state and the democratic state are also dissolved, as the enemy remains the same, 'the previous regime' and 'the white man'. All her critics, from those who certainly were racist and intent on harming her, to those who articulated a different path to overthrowing apartheid and worked alongside her in the trenches of political struggle, were cast together in the same group: they were 'plant[ed] by the system'. All her accusers are linked, she suggests, by a conspiracy against her, and this conspiracy is no different to the attacks on her by the apartheid state. Even her ex-husband was made part of the conspiracy. Nelson Mandela, she claimed, had instructed George Fivaz, the National Police Commissioner, to 'dig up all the dirt against her'. In a closed hearing before the TRC commissioners, she claimed: 'When the commission treats me like a leper and its chairperson hugs our former oppressors, then I worry about what type of reconciliation we are fostering' (Mbhele 1997). She is wronged, and they are all-powerful. In this framing of blackness, and of friends and enemies defined on the basis of apartheid, in the hearing and in the preceding trial, it is clear that Madikizela-Mandela's refusal is based on a notion of community posed, not just against the impositions of the apartheid state, but also against the scripts of citizenship and community that were offered by the TRC, or the ANC itself. Here, the framing of the 'people' articulated in the ANC's Freedom Charter ('we, the people of South Africa, black and white') is replaced with a far narrower, and yet much bolder, conception. It rejects the inclusive, non-racial nationalism of the ANC and makes a claim for a nation founded on autochthony.

Madikizela-Mandela's testimony used the distinction between violence employed by an oppressive state and violence used by revolutionary organisations *against* an oppressive state. Her defence turned on the harms done to her by an illegitimate state, and the harms done to a 'pure' black culture by white supremacy. However, this framing falls apart when it is used in connection with actions against members of her own community. The target of physical violence was not the illegitimate state (or even white people), but young black men. To be sure, these men were seen as agents of or collaborators with the state, but in conditions where such a judgment in fact was not made through any collective community mechanism. This slippage in the uses of violence from ethically justifiable revolutionary arguments to indiscriminate targeting of people considered dangerous without proper evidence went to the heart of the problems that the UDF was attempting to address.

At the TRC hearing, leaders of the anti-apartheid movement gathered again to make the argument that such indiscriminate violence went against the norms of their organisations.[9] It was a moment in which to make the necessary and nuanced arguments that might explain how and why such acts were perpetrated. Madikizela-Mandela had provided some explanations in the past, offering a Fanonian justification for revolutionary violence as a necessary response to the violence of apartheid. For example, in 1985 she asserted:

I will speak to you of violence … I will tell you why we are violent. It is because those who oppress us are violent. The Afrikaner knows only one language: the language of violence. The white man will not

---

9   This was articulated most eloquently by Azhar Cachalia, who had been part of the Crisis Committee: 'The UDF had very little direct control over the development of this phenomenon, its capacity and ability to intervene was limited due to the negative impact to the state of emergency on our organisations. We made public statements distancing ourselves from the conduct' (TRC 1998b).

hand over power in talks around a table . ... Therefore, all that is left
to us is the painful process of violence. (Bezdrob 2011: 220)

In the context of a state of emergency, and an apartheid state that was bent on
militarised use of state power against the people, Madikizela-Mandela offered
a compelling argument. The Manichean reading of the moment – black
resistance against white supremacy – helped to create a shared subjectivity
among black people, and many were attracted to the notion that the
moment had arrived for a renewed violent struggle conducted from within
the townships rather than by an exiled ANC. At the TRC, however, she
would have needed to extend this argument to a justification for shifting the
ethical line, for acting against fellow black people; not the abstractions of 'the
Afrikaner' or 'the white man', but Stompie Seipei, Lolo Sono, and Abubaker
Asvat. Rather than reciprocating the invitation to justify and explain, in
her own terms, she took a position of non-cooperation. She placed herself
outside of the symbolic order of a society grappling with new ways to live
together in community, and thereby effaced the hurt inflicted on the victims.
After all, the demand being made at the TRC was not that Madikizela-
Mandela should submit to the law, or that the law was indisputably correct.
Issues of legal culpability had, after all, been resolved in the 1991 trial. The
TRC hearing was an invitation to another kind of logic, one that valorised
knowing rather than discipline, and redemption rather than incarceration.
It involved answering the questions of the mother of Lolo Sono – 'What
happened to my child? Where is his body?' – rather than answering the legal
question of guilt. To refuse to accord knowledge to the survivors and the
families of the deceased was an act more akin to the arrogant sovereignty
of the authoritarian state than to the popular leader of the radical left. It is
difficult, in this context, to romanticise Winnie Madikizela-Mandela's refusal
as an act of radical courage. Rather, the position of Madikizela-Mandela in
the hearing can only be read as a subversion of the radical logics of refusal,
a logic bent to evade justice rather than to invoke justice against the law.

Several versions of what happened to Stompie Seipei, Lolo Sono, and
Abu Asvat were presented at the TRC hearing. In all versions, although
there was a lack of definitive proof, Madikizela-Mandela was implicated in
beatings, in kidnapping, and in the cover-up of violent actions. The TRC
was not a court of law, and no formal findings were made. But neither
did any definitive truth emerge to explain the murder of Dr Asvat; it
remains a mystery despite the conviction of two young men. At the very
least, there were questions of fact that could have been cleared up by the
testimony of Madikizela-Mandela. Instead, she chose silence and refusal,
and justified these in the language of radical refusal, of questioning of the
very terms of the TRC and of the postapartheid state, and by claiming
that all the witnesses were, to some or other extent, fabricating their

stories. She turned attention to her own experience of being hounded and tortured by the police. Was Madikizela-Mandela saying 'choose my loss, my grief, my suffering as the point of reference, not that of Lolo Sono or Stompie Seipei or Aþu Asvat'? The grieving families found no answers to their questions. The harms done to other people in her community were compounded – excised from community first by allegations that they were informers, and then by the denial of the violence done to them. The failure to accept her role – to attempt an explanation, *in any terms*, of what may have been at stake in those awful years between 1987 and 1989 – had the effect that she colluded in denial of the value of the lives of those affected by the events.

Madikizela-Mandela's choice to shift the narrative from the harms supposedly done *by* her to a narrative of the harms done *to* her was effective in a number of respects. First, it is a classic example of reattribution – a process of displacing responsibility to other sources, such as apartheid and colonialism. In her study of the International Criminal Court, Kamari Clarke (2019) argues that reattribution is an affective gesture to deal with internal contradictions in the positions and actions of perpetrators. It resonates because it invokes sentimentalised narrative strategies that imply that formal justice processes are a form of perversion of the justice principle.

> Various justice imaginaries – such as the 'perpetrator' and the 'freedom fighter' – operate through emotionally infused icons that draw on deep-seated histories and psychosocial feelings that compel social action. The freedom fighter becomes an icon of justice, a redemptive body who preserves the traces of past actions and brings them into the present as potentials … Through the vehicle of the iconic body, constructed through sentimentalised affect, we experience the embeddedness of history in future socio-political affects. (p 34)

This is a moment of narrative rupture that depends on the act of refusal. Madikizela-Mandela's reattribution strategy could be read as self-serving because it allowed her to evade the key elements of an apology – acknowledgement of harm, taking responsibility, regret, reinscribing shared moral norms – but that kind of reading does not fully encapsulate the impact of her refusal. Nor does a narrow reading of accountability fully grasp the political dimensions of her disruptive refusal. At least as significant was the way in which she redirected attention to the fact that the terms of the TRC did not include addressing the everyday harms and violence of apartheid: the forced removals, Bantustan policies, and the humiliations of racial capitalism. These structural features shaped how ordinary people experienced apartheid. While the audience imagined by Archbishop Tutu was the amorphous 'nation' apparently longing to move past apartheid, Madikizela-Mandela addressed another audience for whom the act of putting the archetypal victim on the stand was unfair and painful.

This is not to suggest that there was only one way of telling truths; the TRC itself was a particular kind of political device. It produced its own mode of rendering life narratives into a public sphere. It aimed at uncovering particular kinds of truths, those that restored dignity, that empowered victims to come to terms with the past and to continue to live a life subsequent to healing (Posel and Simpson 2002; Ross 2003; Cole 2009). Fiona Ross argues that the TRC encoded good and evil, and entailed performances of loss, grief, culpability, heroism, and victimhood (Ross 2003). These were necessary performances, modes for scripting a nation: by articulating what was done and how and by whom, the nation would 'confront its divided past' – to use a common tagline of the TRC – and imagine a future both healed by the acts of public storytelling and liberated from its worst selves. The ritualised storytelling of the TRC was central, then, to staging a future nation. One of the knottiest problems for the TRC was how to deal with forms of violence within national liberation movements and within black communities. On the one hand, such actions complicated the narrative of perpetrators and victims. On the other hand, to equate such forms of violence as emerged in conditions of despair, fear, and mistrust with the systematic and deliberate violence of the state would be to do an injustice. The ANC resisted revealing, for example, abuses in exile camps on the grounds that it implied moral equivalence and the TRC steered away from the issue. It also chose to make a blanket submission on its activities to the TRC, notably leaving the Mandela United Football Club and Winnie Madikizela-Mandela out of the submission. In this way, acts of violence, and choices by activists on the ground that defied the official prescripts of the movement's leadership, were externalised to, and contained within, the figure of the irrational woman.

The Winnie Madikizela-Mandela hearing was a rare moment, perhaps, in which to make the case for understanding the unintended consequences of advocating violence in the mid-1980s in terms of the conditions of life in the townships, and the impatience with the pace of change. It could have been a moment in which to reflect on the traumatic consequences of torture of activists by the state, including Winnie Madikizela-Mandela's own experiences during her 18 months of solitary confinement.[10] It is not far-fetched to argue that at the TRC, Madikizela-Mandela was narrating not only her own choices and actions, but also the choices of collectivities who thought violence was an acceptable tactic.

Christian Tileaga argues that in societies coming out of periods of trauma, interpreting the lives of individuals is inextricably tied with the evaluation

---

[10] For a more detailed discussion of this period, see Hassim (2018).

of the political choices of the community that she represents (Tileaga 2011). Writing about narratives of Eastern Europe under communism, Tileaga notes that biographies can play an important role in understanding polities as a whole. Narratives of guilt have a particular import for political history, he argues: 'what is at stake is not so much reducing and relativizing feelings of guilt but managing moral self-assessment and moral accountability' (p 201). Read in this way, the Stompie Seipei incident stands in for a larger story of violence in the townships, of the viability of strategies of the targeting of collaborators with the apartheid state, and of tactics such as the 'necklace'. These unresolved questions of violence are all encapsulated in the Stompie incident. In this respect, the testimony of Winnie to the TRC and indeed her entire life stands as a symbol – a kind of moral test, this time not of the state but of the liberation movements. When Archbishop Tutu says 'her hands are dripping with blood', does he also mean to indict township activists? Thinking of the hearing in this way helps to illuminate some of Winnie Madikizela-Mandela's resistance to answer the questions posed, and the trust many activists place in her may have been reinforced by her refusal to account for her choices, and therefore for theirs, in an arrangement of power that they deemed to be unjust. Her refusal to apologise had, in other words, affective resonances with many people, independent of the facticity of the accusations against her.

To be sure, Madikizela-Mandela may not have been easily able to separate the hearing from the innumerable humiliating appearances she had made before apartheid's courts. The hearing was not technically a court of law, but its idioms mimicked the courtroom. There was an accused, who was also a defendant, there were witnesses, and there were prosecutors. There were demands for certain kinds of evidence, and especially for certain kinds of confession, for an admission of guilt. All these actors within the drama played their part except for Madikizela-Mandela. The hearing demanded of Madikizela-Mandela that she provide motivations and explanations. By refusing this, she broke the discursive power of the TRC. Indeed, this accounts for the register in which Tutu addressed Madikizela-Mandela at the end of the frustrating week of testimonies. Tutu, although cast in the somewhat abstracted role of judge, stepped out of the mode of the law to make his appeal. He appealed not to the authority of the state, or the justice of the newly adopted Constitution. He spoke, rather, in the voice of kinship, in the terms of familial intimacy, and of love. It was a paternalistic approach, as a father might appeal to a wayward daughter, steeped in reassurances of reacceptance into the fold. In this way, he seemed to be placing himself outside of the terms of the law that Madikizela-Mandela had been resisting, traversing over to her own logic outside of politics into the logic of community that stood outside and prior to the law. This, finally, cracked her implacable façade and led to her qualified apology.

Conclusion

The chapter offers a multifaceted reading of Winnie Madikizela-Mandela's non-apology at the TRC. While the TRC might have considered the audience for the Mandela United Football Club to be 'the nation', Madikizela-Mandela addressed a different audience, no less significant: her supporters, disaffected by the meagre goods that seemed to be offered by democracy and angered by the failure of the TRC to put the most senior leaders of the apartheid state on the stage. Although she turned away from the pain of the direct victims of the activities of the Mandela United Football Club, she turned towards her supporters, achieving an affective resonance with their pain. For that audience, Madikizela-Mandela's refusal to apologise validated their sense of a historical injustice being perpetrated. Read within the large political context of the transition from apartheid to democracy, she achieved something that was noteworthy, rejecting the script that was offered because it was compromised in her terms, and rewriting it in a register that foregrounded another set of harms. Her actions may be read as confirming Aaron Lazare's (2005) argument that when making (or not) an apology, leaders speak not only *for* but also *to* their supporters. Whether or not the lack of a meaningful apology to the families of the victims is judged to be a moral lapse by Madikizela-Mandela, for her supporters her stance righted a larger wrong. Read this way, we might conclude that while Madikizela-Mandela failed to achieve one part of the TRC's aims, she may well have achieved its most fundamental demand for truth-telling about apartheid-era crimes. The tragedy is that no reconciliation was achieved either for the families, who do not believe that the whole truth was told, or for the supporters of Madikizela-Mandela, for whom the failures of the transition mean that violence remains a viable political strategy.

Reflections

I have been intrigued by Winnie Madikizela-Mandela for as long as I can remember. She was a ubiquitous figure, loud and proud no matter what life and the apartheid security apparatus threw at her. When she made her 'matchboxes and necklaces' speech, her moral authority broke for some people and strengthened for others. That piqued my curiosity about this unusual female political activist, who seemed to be carving her own fearless path in response to apartheid. She was *sui generis*, defying easy comparisons (though many have been made, from Penelope to Antigone to Evita Peron). Perhaps it was only through the figure of a woman that the tensions of living in violence could be so completely embodied: the contradictory forces of nurturing and harming, the power of giving life and its shadow of taking it away. Violence seems unresolvable, when viewed as grand human drama. Watching Madikizela-Mandela's testimony to the TRC distilled that drama to the scale of the intimate. What is required of us when the harm is not so much to a system but to individuals? For a nation seemingly used to casual apologies – South Africans say 'sorry' at the sight of spilt water, 'sorry' to strangers if they drop a napkin, 'sorry' if they see someone stumble in the distance – Madikizela-Mandela's refusal to apologise seemed breathtaking. In seeking to understand this, it seemed obvious that a refusal to apologise was not merely a lapse in accountability. It was primarily a political act. What appeared as a moral lapse (and maybe it actually is one – I do not discount that) became transformed into the basis for moral authority, this time to a new generation of activists. I learnt a huge amount from her, retrospectively, about the politics of symbolism and performance, a repertoire of actions that could hold a nation in a breathless pause. For this research, I read and watched days of traumatic testimony at the TRC, surfacing the pain of so many, and evoking in me again the shock when I had first stood at the back of the JISWA Centre in Mayfair, watching the hearing. I remain alternately shocked and impressed at the ability of this strong woman to refuse the terms on which the social contract is negotiated, working into rupture and pain rather than plastering over the wound. The past is not done with us, the future not yet ready for her (or us) to step into.

Shireen

References

ANC, n.d., 'Render South Africa ungovernable! Message of the National Executive Committee of the ANC on the 73rd anniversary of ANC by O. R. Tambo, 8 January 1985', *South African History Online*, viewed 6 May 2018 from www.sahistory.org.za/archive/render-south-africa-ungoverna ble-message-national-executive-committee-anc-73rd-anniversary

ANC, 1986, 'A.N.C. calls to the nation: from ungovernability to people's power', *South African History Online*, viewed 7 May 2018 from www.anc. org.za/content/ungovernability-peoples-power-anc-call-people

AP Archive, 2015, 'South Africa: Winnie Mandela Truth Commission hearing update', viewed 11 April 2018 from www.youtube.com/watch?v= XM7smNNuJR4

Bezdrob, A., 2011, *Winnie Mandela: A Life*, Alexandria: Zebra Press.

Bridgland, F., 1997, *Katiza's Journey: Beneath the Surface of South Africa's Shame*, London: Macmillan.

Clarke, K., 2019, *Affective Justice: The International Criminal Court and the Pan-Africanist Pushback*, Durham: Duke University Press.

Cole, C., 2009, *Performing South Africa's Truth Commission*, Bloomington: Indiana University Press.

Duncan, N., 2008, 'Understanding collective violence in apartheid and post-apartheid South Africa', *African Safety Promotion* 3(1), 5–22.

Gilbey, E. G., 1993, *The Lady: The Life and Times of Winnie Mandela*, London: Jonathan Cape.

Gqola, P. D., 2007, 'How the "cult of femininity" and violent masculinities supports endemic gender-based violence in contemporary South Africa,' *African Identities* 4(1), 111–24.

Hamber, B. and Lewis, S., 1997, *An Overview of the Consequences of Violence and Trauma in South Africa*, Braamfontein: Centre for the Study of Violence and Reconciliation.

Hassim, S., 2008, 'Social justice, care and developmental social welfare in South Africa: a capabilities perspective', *Social Dynamics* 34(2), 104–18.

Hassim, S., 2018, 'Not just Nelson's wife: Winnie Madikizela-Mandela, violence and radicalism in South Africa', *Journal of Southern African Studies* 44(5), 895–912.

Lazare, A., 2005, *On Apology*, Oxford and New York: Oxford University Press.

Lodge, T., 2006, *Mandela: A Critical Life*, Oxford and New York: Oxford University Press.

MacLachlan, A., 2013, 'Gender and public apology', *Transitional Justice Review* 1(2), 126–47.

MacLachlan, A., 2014, 'Beyond the ideal political apology', in M. Mihai and M. Thaler (eds.), *On the Uses and Abuses of Political Apology*, pp 13–31, Basingstoke Hampshire: Palgrave Macmillan.

Mass Democratic Movement, 1989, 'Statement by Mass Democratic Movement on Winnie Mandela', *South African History Online*, viewed 18 January 2021 from www.sahistory.org.za/archive/statement-mass-democra tic-movement-winnie-mandela

Mbhele, W., 1997, 'Winnie accuses Mandela at TRC', *Mail and Guardian*, viewed 15 November 2020 from https://mg.co.za/article/1997-10-23-win nie-accuses-mandela-at-trc/

Meintjes, S., 1998, 'Winnie Madikizela Mandela: tragic figure? Populist tribune? Township tough?', *South African Report* 13(4), 14, viewed 20 January 2021 from https://web.archive.org/web/20131213002850/http://www.africafiles.org/article.asp?ID=3791

Meredith, M., 2010, *Mandela: A Biography*, Boston: Hachette Book Group.

Moffett, H., 2006, '"These women, they force us to rape them": rape as a aarrative of social control in postapartheid South Africa', *Journal of Southern African Studies* 32(1), 129–44.

Morudu, P., 2018, 'Has truth become a casualty of Winnie's rejection of accountability?', *BusinessDay*, viewed 12 November 2020 from www.busin esslive.co.za/bd/opinion/2018-04-13-has-truth-become-a-casualty-of-winnies-rejection-of-accountability/

Msimang, S., 2018, *The Resurrection of Winnie Mandela*, Johannesburg: Jonathan Ball.

Posel, D. and Simpson, G., 2002, *Commissioning the Past: Understanding South Africa's Truth and Reconciliation Commission*, Johannesburg: Wits University Press.

Ross, F., 2003, *Bearing Witness: Women and the Truth and Reconciliation Commission in South Africa*, London: Pluto Press.

Roy, S., 2009, 'The ethical ambivalence of resistant violence: notes from postcolonial South Asia', *Feminist Review* 91(1), 135–53.

Scheper-Hughes, N., 1995, 'The primacy of the ethical: propositions for a militant anthropology', *Current Anthropology* 36(3), 409–40.

Sono, N., 2018, 'South Africa: Winnie Mandela Truth Commission hearing update', *Politicsweb*, viewed 14 November 2020 from www.politicsweb.co.za/documents/i-pleaded-with-winnie-not-to-take-my-son-away--nic

South African Broadcasting Corporation, 1997, 'Special hearings: Mandela United Football Club hearings day 5' (transcript), in *SABC Truth Commission Special Report*, viewed 11 April 2018 from http://sabctrc.saha.org.za/hearing.php?id=56342&t=winnie+mandela&tab=hearings

Swilling, M. and Phillips, M., 1989, 'State power in the 1980s: from total strategy to the counter-revolutionary warfare', in J. Cock and L. Nathan (eds.), *War and Society: The Militarization of South Africa*, pp 134–48, New York: St. Martin's Press.

Tavuchis, N., 1991, *Mea Culpa: A Sociology of Apology and Reconciliation*, Stanford: Stanford University Press.

Tileaga, C., 2011, '(Re)writing biography: memory, identity, and textually mediated reality in coming to terms with the past', *Culture and Psychology* 17(2), 197–215.

Truth and Reconciliation Commission, 1998a, *Truth and Reconciliation Commission of South Africa Report, Volume 1*, viewed 11 April 2018 from www.justice.gov.za/trc/report/finalreport/Volume%201.pdf

Truth and Reconciliation Commission, 1998b, *United Democratic Front Submission* (transcript), viewed 7 May 2018 from www.justice.gov.za/trc/special/udf/udf.htm

Truth and Reconciliation Commission, 1998c, 'Special investigation into the Mandela United Football Club', in *Truth and Reconciliation Commission of South Africa Report, Volume 2, Chapter 6*, viewed 11 April 2018 from www.justice.gov.za/trc/report/finalreport/Volume%202.pdf

Von Sivers, M., 2015, 'Interview with Winnie Mandela', *Dialogues Select*, viewed 11 April 2018 from www.dialogues.org/interview/10/24/2015/interview-with-winnie-mandela-by-malou-von-sivers1/1465769619

Wren, C., 1990, 'Winnie Mandela named in beatings', *New York Times*, viewed 11 April 2018 from www.nytimes.com/1990/05/10/world/winnie-mandela-named-in-beatings.html

7

(Mis)Recognitions in the Racial Apology: Reading the Racist Event and its Fallouts

Nkululeko Nkomo and Peace Kiguwa

Introduction

In February of 2016 in Northriding, Johannesburg, a distraught white woman named Vicki Momberg, the latest victim of a smash-and-grab crime incident in the city, is on the phone with a 10111 emergency call centre agent that she has dialled to assist her. She is also surrounded by a group of black policemen who have arrived to assist her. Captured on video, her encounter with the police, including her interaction with the call agent, would quickly go viral. Vicki Momberg is recorded to have hurled racist abuse at the policemen, calling them the *K-word*[1] word 48 times. In response to the policemen's repeated offers to help, she responds: 'I am happy for a white person to assist me or a coloured person or an Indian person – I do not want a black person to assist me' (Cowan 2018). Before the police officers arrived to her aid, she was similarly abusive with the emergency call centre agent, asking the agent 'Is this a white person speaking?', and proceeded to insist 'please don't send a bunch of k****s … so send me white people or Indian people, but don't send me a k****r' (Cowan 2018). It is also during her interaction with the emergency call centre agent that she bemoaned 'k****s are everywhere'

---

[1] South African racially derogatory term to refer to black people. In 2000, the South African parliament passed the Promotion of Equality and Prevention of Unfair Discrimination Act 4 of 2000, which has among its primary objectives the prevention of hate speech, such as the label of kaffir. To safeguard or protect from its injurious quality, the label is recoded as the *K-word* or k****r.

and expressed her deep mistrust in them. Hence, when she was advised by the call centre agent to drive to the nearest petrol station for her safety until the police could arrive to assist her, she was unwilling to do so because she anticipated that the employees would be black people.

A month before a video of Momberg's racist outburst goes viral, igniting increased racial tension in the country, a social media rant by KwaZulu-Natal South Coast estate agent Penny Sparrow has already sparked nationwide fury and division. In her social media post, she writes:

> These monkeys that are allowed to be released on New Year's eve and New Year's day on to public beaches, towns etc obviously have no education what so ever, so to allow them loose is inviting huge dirt and troubles and discomfort to others. I'm sorry to say I was amongst the revellers and all I saw were black on black skins what a shame. I do know some wonderful and thoughtful black people. This lot of monkeys just don't want to even try. But think they can voice opinions about statute and get their way dear oh dear. From now on, I shall address the blacks of South Africa as monkeys as I see the cute little wild monkeys do the same pick, drop and litter. (Nemakonde 2016)

Two years later, businessman Adam Catzavelos, holidaying in Greece, posts a video of himself on the beach. The camera pans across the beach, meant as an illustration of the words that Catzavelos utters for his audience: 'Let me give you the weather forecast here. Blue skies, beautiful day, amazing sea, and not one *k****r* in sight' (Jordaan 2018). All three would later be charged and found guilty of *crimen injuria*[2] and ordered to pay fines, with Momberg sentenced to two years in jail,[3] although she did not serve the full sentence. After much pressure and public outcry, all three also apologised.

What makes a racial apology meaningful? If one of its aims is to signify some type of remorse, how does this feeling work to materialise the communities associated with the demand for it and its issuing? In this chapter, we consider the affective composition of the racial apology in a postapartheid context by engaging with how race is constituted in the events of the racial encounter. In the first section of the chapter, we ask: what are the dynamics of racial assemblage within which the racist event may be read through an affective lens? How may the interactions and encounters surrounding the online rants of Sparrow and Catzavelos or between Momberg, the emergency call centre

---

[2]   *Crimen injuria* is a unique South African common law offence that consists of 'unlawfully and intentionally impairing the dignity or privacy of another person' and which may include use of racial offensive language (Milton 1996: 492).

[3]   *Momberg v S* (A206/2018) [2019] ZAGPJHC 183 (28 June 2019).

agent, and on the streets of Johannesburg with the black police officers who came to her aid, be read as not only racist but also affective events? We also examine the public backlash to these racist encounters. Against the backdrop of the divergent affective logics grounding their non-recognition of black people and the ensuing public outcry, we conclude with a critical appraisal of the public apologies made by Momberg, Sparrow, and Catzavelos. The racist outburst and the public backlash to it therefore offer a way of examining the possibilities and limits of public apologies in an evolving postapartheid South African context.

Reconfiguring the racially affective event

Ahmed's theory of affective economies provides a provocative perspective for considering how emotions work to reveal collective identifications, including how the vexing outbreaks of emotive racist events that characterise contemporary South Africa might be thought about in relation to particularly marked and visceral attachments to the country's history of racial privilege and oppression. The theory amalgamates elements of the logic of Marx's critique of the accumulation of value in the commodity cycles of market economies, as well as the psychoanalytic notion of unconscious ideas and the conscious feelings associated with them. For Ahmed (2004a, 2004b and 2004c), emotions do things. They reveal our visceral attachments, psychologically and socially, although they are not reducible to them, as if what we feel originates from inside our bodies and moves outwards or from the outside moving inwards to take up residence in our bodies.

In contact with other subjects, emotions configure our bodily 'responsiveness' to them. Contact can be face to face or physically unavailable, taking place virtually and involving sensorial rather than physical proximity between bodies; or, as Massumi (2002) points out, contact is recaptured from an earlier experience through the transference of a previously registered context of perception to the moment of the interface of bodies in proximity to one another. Whether contact is in proximity, remote, or virtual, it is always contingent, suggesting that it involves negotiation between impressions generated forthwith and brought into the relational context. Our orientations to others are mediated by us, transforming them into objects of feeling. Implied through the translation is that the objects of our emotions move us, and their moving involves attachment, or conversely, dissociation. What moves us makes us feel, and what makes us feel 'holds us in place', affords us residence (Ahmed 2004b: 11), and concurrently draws us away from *other* others.

Racist encounters are 'peculiar' because moving towards another is usually followed by distancing (see Ahmed 2004b), and so they are by their formation confrontational or tense. Bhabha (1984) contends that they could also be described as at once recognition and misrecognition – seeing and not seeing the racialised other. Indeed, the very thought of a racist encounter elicits in the imagination a scene of interchange between visibility and invisibility. Our analysis of the three incidents engages this interchange to understand the public outcry and some of the cynical reaction to the public apologies by Momberg, Sparrow, and Catzavelos, considering, too, that emotions have a crucial function in racial objectification and the response to it.

Consider Momberg. Her calling of the black police officers by the very racially derogatory and historically loaded word k****r, and refusing their assistance, is very telling of her racial social bonds. She wanted the black police officers to hear her racial tirade against them. Her recognition that they are present to receive her abusive comments is a deliberate act of (mis)recognition of their humanity as well as their authority as police officers. She consciously distances herself to render them invisible to her. By refusing their help, she also figuratively 'puts them in their place'.

If we think of the way Momberg's hatred of black people influenced how her encounter with the black police officers and interaction with the emergency call centre agent unfolded, situating where the bodies involved belong, then we might read how this functioned to both distance her from black people, while also affiliating her with white people, like Sparrow and Catzavelos, who are similarly nauseated and enraged by the presence of black people. The revelation of this common body (racialised as white) through its reading of another collective body (racialised as black) is magnified with intensity in the racist event. The example of Momberg helps to illustrate that emotions work to align individual bodies with a collective body at once, while differentiating them from other collective bodies (Ahmed 2004a, 2004b and 2004c). Through the alignment, bodies are configured this way or that way, depending on schemas of recognition and association (see Ahmed 2004c). The racist event and its fallouts revolve around the circulation of objects or signs of emotions, and because of this, the surfacing of collective identifications.

The origin of the word 'emotion' in Latin is *movere*, denoting either agitation or movement. Emotions are mobile; they do not remain fixed, even though they hold bodies in place. Instead of being *in* bodies, as objects or signs of feeling, emotions move or circulate *between* bodies. They are associated with the movement of objects or signs, but they are not vested in them. Produced in this movement, through communicability or contagion, such that there is an appearance of possession of feelings, is emotion. The word contagion or communicability is important: it alludes to what moves between rather than seeps through bodies. The contagiousness or communicability of objects or signs attached with social or cultural significance generates feelings. As Ahmed (2004b: 45) points out, emotions are 'an effect of the circulation between objects and signs'. Their circulation accumulates worth or value.

Objects or signs of emotions move sideways, forwards, and backwards in constituting the multiple worlds and bodies we inhabit. The movement sideways and forwards is enabled through the discursive or narrative-based frames of reference and thought that shape how we do or could react to others in the moment of contact. Ahmed (2004a: 119) calls this movement 'the rippling effect of emotions', which entails 'sticky associations between signs, figures, and objects'. For illustration, we could think of how Momberg is repulsed through a 'sticky association' between different figures of black bodies she encountered that evening of the smash-and-grab incident. This association produced her reaction. The association is also retrogressive, pivoting backwards by rekindling a historical representation of the black body as the object of abjection.

Before we explain further what we mean by the circulation backwards, we would like to expand on what is involved in the constitution of reactions when we encounter other subjects. Our reactions to others assemble the impressions they make or leave on us, which are also markers of the ways we are touched or moved by them. Impressions incorporate our perceptual evaluations and judgments. They mediate our experiences and sensory perceptions of others (see Deleuze and Guattari 1994; see also Massumi 2002). In the racist events with Momberg, Sparrow, and Catzavelos, we can see, for instance, that their impressions are also filtered through the sight of black bodies. Impressions also include our intentions, revealed by the readings we bring to encounters with others. In this interstice – our readings of others, culminating in the impressions formed on us by others – the negotiation between moving towards or away from others is staged.

Impressions might also be productively thought about in similar terms to the way Spinoza (1985) uses the word 'affect', which is subsequently taken up by Deleuze and Guattari (1987, 1994). Being 'impressed upon' or to be 'under an impression' indicates change effected to bodies when they make contact, 'increasing' or 'diminishing' our ability for action. That action can involve moving towards or negating the other because of how we are impressed upon, or the impression created through the contact. Echoing Spinoza (1985), Deleuze and Guattari (1987: 284) state:

> We know nothing about a body until we know what it can do, in other words what its affects are, how they can or cannot enter into composition with other affects, with the affects of another body, either to destroy that body or be destroyed by it, either to exchange actions and passions or to join with it in composing a more powerful body.

Impressions in this way denote mutual definition between subjects or bodies, even in rejection, during contact. By underscoring the bodily location and activity of impressions, we are suggesting that affects and emotions are interchangeable; they both work with and between bodies, and in the Spinozan sense, open different possibilities for action, depending on the way the bodies involved read one another and are moved in the moment of contact.

We can also describe the circulation backwards by how impressions assemble. Our impressions of others are often filtered through their priming by prior or repeated associations we carry in our bodies and into contact with other bodies. When we are with others, as Ahmed (2004a: 19) writes, they are 'encountered as having certain characteristics'. We read others through prior associations that structure how we will approach them. Prior associations constitute what Massumi (2002, 2015a, and 2015b) calls our 'readiness potential' or pre-existing affective tendencies, set in motion or activated by previous encounters or experiences, including inherited sociocultural and political narratives and histories, and prior influences. These surface as marks on our bodies. Our impressions of others, moreover, can persist even in their absence. Contact does not only involve the subjects in contact at that moment, but is also shaped by prior social, cultural, and personal histories that may work their way into the present, giving contact a 'haunted effect' (see Cheng 2001).

We suggest that racist encounters and events, both in their physicality or virtuality of movement through space, bring into sharp relief the affective dynamics set out above. To illustrate, let us turn to Catzavelos and Sparrow. When he celebrated the absence of black bodies on the beachfront during his vacation in Greece, Catzavelos could preserve them as objects of disavowal. This illustrates the attachment of revulsion to the collective bodies that are the subject of negation by Sparrow and Catzavelos and those who subsequently jumped to their defence: the white Afrikaner lobby group and trade union Solidarity eagerly defended Sparrow. It is this attachment that surfaces the black body as an object of anxiety for them. In addition, Sparrow and Catzavelos are joined together by hostility and suspicion against a common foe. The affinity between them and their sympathisers is materialised by the black body as the object of renunciation.

The formation of the apartheid regime in 1948, and colonialism before it, entailed a history of institutionalised discrimination (see Bonner et al 1994), including the segregation of social spaces, such as beaches where black bodies were restricted from 'whites only' beachfronts. This is the history that is reproduced by Sparrow, Catzavelos, and their sympathisers. This history, moreover, constitutes a foundation that materialises a contemporary collective identification of black bodies with spoliation of spaces that were previously restricted for them. Catzavelos further demonstrates that this stigmatisation can apply even when black bodies are physically absent from spaces. The absence that he celebrates, which we can also read as repudiation, might as well have been a presence, because what carried over from Sparrow to him – or moved intensely between them – gathers variously iterated historical impressions about the imagined threat of presence. If we recall that, for Fanon (1986), in a colonial context the black body evokes horror or terror through the white gaze, what he aptly terms 'negrophobia', then what we have with Catzavelos, Sparrow, and the collective they surface is an embodied contemporary rendition of this projection of black bodies. The black body effectively becomes what Fanon describes as a 'phobogenic' body (inducing fear and disgust). For Sparrow and Catzavelos the black body is already a phobogenic body, invested with fear and disgust.

Catzavelos illustrates another inheritance of historical racism: the dialectic of aversion and obsession with the other. With rejection, there is equally a need or dependence on the other in the racist imaginary. Cheng (2001: 12) explains: 'racism is hardly ever a clear rejection of the other' – it needs the other that it fears or hates. For Ahmed (2004b: 51), with racially motivated hatred, 'for the destructive relation to the object to be maintained the object itself must be conserved in some form … an expulsion or incorporation that requires the conservation of the object itself in order to be sustained'. Probably another reason why, even in their absence, Catzavelos could recall black bodies as threatening or defiling objects is because what the recollection does is to say that white people are under threat or endangered in the postapartheid political order. The recollection enacts the fantasy that, unlike in the past, when white people were afforded securities and privileges denied to black people, in postapartheid South Africa they live precariously. For him, this is like hell, in that 'not one k****r in sight' is comparable to 'heaven on earth …'. Implied also in his remarks is that the futurity of the 'solution to the problem' of belonging for white South Africans lies in immigration to countries where, in contrast with South Africa, white people constitute most of the population. Catzavelos' fantasy reveals a besieged mentality.

Sparrow's racialising and dehumanising diatribe at the sight of black bodies on South African beaches is arguably animated by the same fantasmatic persecutory disposition of an imminent threat to white people in South Africa. As someone who claims to 'know wonderful and thoughtful black people', unlike this 'lot of monkeys' whom she was among at the beach and who 'just don't want to even try', in a discursive move that Ahmed (2004a: 119) describes as manifesting a 'relationship of displacement and difference', Sparrow's fictional threat is only posed by some black bodies and not others. The fantasy or fiction for both Catzavelos and Sparrow summons an embodied aversive impulse towards black bodies and simultaneously brings forth an affective investment in constructing them as the cause of the displeasure and unhappiness aggregating around an imagined risk to the enjoyment of South Africa by white people.

Hook (2017) offers a useful point of orientation in our account of the constitutive role of enjoyment in the fantasy of persecution by Sparrow and

Catzavelos: a libidinal economy that takes shape in the form of property, through which their enjoyment of the country means exclusion of those who either do not look like them or share their values. Black bodies' enjoyment of some spatial sites engenders a feeling of space invasion. In describing this perceived theft of enjoyment, Hook notes:

> This alerts us to something crucial in the intersubjective economy of enjoyment. In such a situation, not only have I been deprived of what I take to be my rightful enjoyment (enjoyment experienced here as a kind of property); someone else has enjoyed in my place. There is, in short, invariably an intersubjective dialectic at play in relations of enjoyment. Other people seem to enjoy at my expense. (p 607)

Harris (1993) makes a similar point when she argues that whiteness has evolved from an exclusively racial signifier of identity to one of property. Whiteness comes to be solidified as an identity worthy of protection in the law and, relative to the discrimination and oppression of enslaved populations, through recourse to the notion of property. This sense of racial privilege and hierarchy persists in post-slavery periods and may be entrenched in white opposition to shared rights and policies of retributive justice. The consequence of this feeling of displacement for Sparrow and Catzavelos is that it draws out and fuels a passionate dislike of black revellers for supposedly (mis)appropriating and subverting the exclusive racial coordinates of their possessive enjoyment of South African beachfronts. This libidinal fantasy of enjoyment fulfils itself through aversion by enjoying the repudiation of black bodies. The loathing is a source of pleasure for Sparrow and Catzavelos.

Momberg's rant is also theoretically instructive. During her trial, she had supporters, mainly white South Africans and organisations like Solidarity and Afriforum.[4] When interviewed for a television news channel, one of her supporters dismissed the verdict of the court that found Momberg guilty of racism and sentenced her to two years in prison. As her supporter put it, 'she wasn't thinking clearly, things were just coming out of her mouth. She can't even recall what she said. I know, I've said to them … I have said the word …' (eNCA 2019). For the supporter, and others who rallied behind Momberg, her racist rant was just a reaction, justified by the trauma she had endured during the smash–and–grab incident. The supporter sees Momberg's outburst that evening as a *faux pas*, justified because of the high levels of

---

[4] Afriforum mainly provides litigation services, specifically private prosecutions. Although recently it has taken on a range of prosecutorial cases for a diversity of clients, it is also common cause or knowledge that it exists to serve the interests of the white Afrikaner community.

crime in the country and the inefficiency of the police services in managing it. That Momberg's verbal rant is tainted by racism is of less concern for the supporter. 'Everyone is racist', she declares, looking straight at the news reporter, confidently, as if expecting him to agree with her. Startled by her generalisation and the presumption that he will meekly agree with her, as if it is a self-evident truth, the news reporter quickly retorts that this does not apply to him. For the rest of the brief interview, she stumbles over her words, not letting up in her defence of Momberg. The transgressions for her were the crime perpetrated on Momberg and the government's failure to reign in the beggars on the streets, not Momberg's racist outburst. Her refusal to acknowledge the gravity of the racial offence committed by Momberg preserves the black body as the object of abjection, because, for all her unhappiness about lawlessness in South Africa, it is also accompanied by a racially coded unease. The support for Momberg unveils a negative racial sentiment towards black people, impelling the alliance that is ostensibly about safety and security.

Our perspective is that Momberg's rant, seemingly 'couched in bodily feeling ... bound up with unfolding sensation' (Massumi 2015b: 9), suggests an already existing inclination to objectify black bodies as threatening or fearsome. Given South Africa's political history of racial oppression, it is perhaps not surprising that her outburst is filtered through racially insulting language. As Ahmed (2004c: 63) would argue, the loathing and hostility with which she behaved towards the police officers during the interaction 'opens up past histories of association'. Notwithstanding the obvious trauma of her ordeal that evening, her dismissive interaction with the emergency call centre agent, who likely was a black person, and her rejection as well as verbal abuse of the black police officers who wanted to assist her, reveals an already racially biased evaluation and perception of black bodies more generally. Her aggrievance recapitulates an inability to see humanity in the black bodies that, reluctantly, she now depends on to assist her through the trauma she endured. The probability that the perpetrators were also black only prompted her predilection by metonymic translation for conflating different black bodies as equally threatening and hateful. Ahmed (2006) reminds us that histories are reproduced at the level of embodiment, and as Momberg and her coterie of defenders embody it, South African history carries a tremendous reservoir of denigration and hostility towards black bodies.

How then can we understand the reading of black bodies through the excessive anxiety of Momberg, Sparrow, and Catzavelos, and their defenders or sympathisers? What enables it? The model of affective economies helps us comprehend the circulating revulsion as a dynamic interaction between history and presence. Here we see the denouncing of black bodies opening on to the affective terrain of nostalgia for a segregated South Africa. The nostalgia entails a begrudging identification with the postapartheid present. In this affective economy of identification with the past and dis-identification with the present, we see re-emerging an affective politics of fear, echoing the erstwhile National Party's '*Swart Gevaar*' ('*Black Peril*') 1948 campaign slogan, which eventually morphed into its governing doctrine (see Brown 1987). As Biko (2004: 98) commented on its rationale and teleology, what the 'imaginary bogey' of the apartheid biopolitical strategy of the *swart gevaar* constructed in the imagination of white South Africans is that 'there is something to fear in the idea' of black people taking their 'rightful place at the helm of the South African ship'. What is striking in the three incidents of Sparrow, Momberg, and Catzavelos is the way their bodies substitute for the doctrine, as its contemporary living embodiment, revealed by their collective bodily response of being repulsed, agitated, and threatened by black bodies. We have already noted, through Catzavelos, that this response is not only set off by the proximity of black bodies; it can also be active even in their absence.

Through the affective dynamic of presence and absence, bringing together Sparrow, Momberg, and Catzavelos, the black body is projected as repulsive, agitating, and threatening, and thus retrieving, and reinstating, a contemporary version of its abjection from the era of the *swart gevaar*. We agree with Menninghaus (2003: 1) that what is at issue in disgust and revulsion is '... [a] fundamental schema [concerning] the experience of a nearness that is not wanted'. Racial disgust as affective register functions as a social distinction signifier that clearly demarcates the place and function of racialised bodies. Moreover, racial disgust adheres to the logic of the sensory or visceral push and pull elicited by its object. To borrow Kolnai's (2004) theorisation of disgust as a contradictory affective response, this logic vacillates between aversion and obsession with the object of disgust. We see this demonstrated by Sparrow, Momberg, and Catzavelos. Their disgust exposes an anxiety with the dissolution of boundaries – racial, moral, or behavioural – they imagine or believe separate them from black people. The fixation with observing or elevating these boundaries betrays their instability. Racial disgust comes not from its authenticity or credibility in representing the object of disgust, but from the risk of cessation of the boundary that it constructs.

In reconfiguring the affective racist event in the way that we have done in the discussion above, we are compelled to think through what underwrites the intense antipathy to black bodies that is so frequently evinced by some white South Africans in contemporary society. What we are proposing is that the outbreaks of anti-black racist events at this stage of our democracy perhaps also denotes the complex admixture of an embodied and conscious attachment to a past ideality that is preserved into a destructive sign or object of identification with the present – at least by some groups in the white community. If we think of nostalgia as both a restorative and performative idealisation of the past (see Boym 2007), for racist white South Africans the reflexive and conscious identification with the country's colonial and apartheid pasts allows them to disregard profound racial injustices against black people. This translates into imaginary threats, attacks, and discrimination against white people in the present, and against the civilisation they believe only emerged with colonialism and apartheid.

By recalling and idealising this constitutive negative South African past, in a sense, white South Africans such as Sparrow, Momberg, and Catzavelos are also enacting their desire to relive that past. Rather than only idealised or revered, much less grieved, the past is also their way of embodying and inhabiting the present postapartheid South African context. Racist *jouissance* or enjoyment is never only individual or intra-psychic, but also social (Hook 2017). That is, it always stands in relation to transgression of the law and social values, which makes the public transgressions of Sparrow, Momberg, and Catzavelos, and similar public racist tirades, invite an even more interesting reading. This is more so considering that, while apartheid's social logic endorsed the racist rant, postapartheid social logic does not. The public transgressions unmask a sentimental longing for apartheid. Hence, we must consider that beyond the anger of the backlash over these transgressions, and some very vocal dismissals of the apologies they eventually offered, there is a deeper grievance about this unremitting identification with apartheid in present South Africa.

Pain and injury in/as outrage

We now turn to the backlash generated by the three incidents. We start off with the extract by South African commentator and writer Sisonke Msimang. The open editorial by Msimang reflects on Sparrow's Facebook post. She problematises the text's underlying affective longing for a segregated South Africa that motivates Sparrow's racial diatribe:

> Sparrow ... reminds us all that there was a time, not too long ago, when 'public' beaches were segregated ... She is asserting that black people do not know how to behave when they are given permission to occupy public spaces ... In the early days of the transition, there might have been more voices calling for South Africans to understand that Penny Sparrow's hysteria is based on fear, and that all fear is underpinned by vulnerability. They might have argued that Sparrow needs pity rather than vitriol. Those days are over. Twenty years after the end of apartheid, this generation isn't interested in understanding the roots of white vulnerability. Their eyes are on accountability and building a new political culture based on justice rather than nostalgia and sentimentality. (Msimang 2016)

The second extract is by a commentator on Twitter and also focuses on Sparrow's Facebook post. Like the other comments on Twitter that are included in the discussion that follows, we get an even stronger sense of the level of discontent generated by Sparrow's post: 'I have No and I repeat No respect for Penny Sparrow. I am disgusted by her statement ... If she is unhappy, she must leave this country ... She will destroy and discourage our future generation. She is what we call poison' (News24 2016). Msimang draws a line in the sand: the 'nostalgia' and 'sentimentality' of those who are stuck in the apartheid past, like Sparrow, Momberg, and Catzavelos, differentiates them from those working towards racial healing, transformation, and justice in the postapartheid context. For the commentator on Twitter in the second extract, hope for South Africa's future generation lies in exorcising 'disgusting' figures like Sparrow. There is an attempt to rearticulate disgust here, no longer as an embodied abject body (Sparrow) but within a discursive moral and affective economy that can dismiss the racist figure for its lack of moral character and insensitivity. At the same time, the designation of an abjected body is being resisted or reattributed. The black body as the object of a historical racial denigration is already registering the necessity to overhaul the terms of its future construction. Beyond resisting the attribution of racial abjection, both the extracts remind us that black and white racial embodiments are an inheritance of an ignominious history and its contemporary re-enactment.

We mostly act out of emotions, and they provide us with our sense of belonging or place in the world by 'sticking' us together with others. Emotions structure the alignment of individual bodies to collective bodies. The alignment surfaces the collective as a body (see Ahmed 2004b). Emotions become crucial in establishing social bonds with others, creating a collective body. What is more, as Ahmed (2004b: 29) points out, collective bodies take shape or form through 'the way in which they read the bodies of others'. When emotions align us with others through 'actions and passions' that effectively 'compose one body', they can also align us against other bodies, to borrow Deleuze and Guattari's (1987: 284) words. Very little that issues from our emotional life can be separated from the emotional lives of others. Even when we are disconnected from others, it is because we are connected to *other* others. The thinking that guides our actions reflects intentions that are shaped by our relationships with other people.

Therefore, much as emotions worked to surface and stick together Momberg, Sparrow, Catzavelos, and their sympathisers as a collective body, they also mobilised another affective community, materialised through the outrage their actions and words generated. Two emotive and temporally bound orientations are at play that are opposed. There is nostalgia, superimposed into the present and future by Sparrow, Catzavelos, and Momberg. For Msimang and the commentator on Twitter in the extract above, as well as other responses that we examine, of those who also took to Twitter to express their aggrievance, the feeling of loss associated with the past is mapped on to the transformation of the postapartheid present and future. The racist event and its fallouts put in sharp relief the racially coded affective and temporal sensibilities that structure identifications with and attachments to colonial, apartheid, and postapartheid South Africa.

The question that we examine in this second section therefore asks: what affective force underlies the demand for apology? What are we to make of the outrage that characterised the response to the three incidents on social media platforms? The function of digital and mediatised affective activism that can galvanise and transmit affective force also bears noting here. While it is tempting to read these as fleeting and almost populist reactions – generally taken to be the way of engagement on online platforms – we argue that something more is at stake. For beneath the outrage and hankering for an apology lies a demand for recognition of humanity for black bodies. The demand, or expectation, for a public apology is further inextricably bound to a sense of past and continuing loss. Rendered semantically, it is a loss described in terms of subjective pain and injury. Fanon (1986: 89) offers insight into the profundity of the loss and its affective implications: 'Sealed into that crushing objecthood, I turned beseechingly to others … the glances of the other fixed me there, in the sense in which a chemical solution is fixed by a dye. I was indignant; I demanded an explanation. Nothing happened. I burst apart … .'

In the actions and words of Sparrow, Momberg, and Catzavelos, it is precisely this non-recognition of the black body that is enacted, and their racist events expose the unravelling of the hope and promise for restoration and the reason that paved the way to the postapartheid state. Essentially these events trigger what Berlant (2011) might term states of 'affective impasse' for race relations in postapartheid South Africa. It is not only that this promise goes awry or is continually deferred; what the incidents also make visible is the difficulty of realising the promise without recognition of, and a full reckoning with, the triple knot of racial pain, injury, and grief. This triple knot configures a desire for recognition of a humanity that is denied and, for Wynter (2003), Braidotti (2013), and Walcott (2014), may also be beyond reach to those who were never, from its inception, figured within its boundaries.

We can examine the work that the deployment of pain and injury do in the response to the racist event. If pain is an invalidating impression created through contact with other bodies, involving an exchange of sensations and feelings that are interpreted as injurious, then we would argue that the response to the events with Sparrow, Momberg, and Catzavelos indexes the way race is historically and viscerally sedimented. The response is an act of recollection of past pain. With reference to the visceral emotions that

Sparrow's words ignited for black people, the extract above by Msimang illustrates this point in its allusion to Sparrow's social media post as a reminder of the past. In an experience or encounter that evokes pain 'one might search one's memories for whether one has had it before' (Ahmed 2004b: 25). It is a painful memory that Msimang highlights and contrasts with a nostalgic and sentimental attachment to the past that is depicted in Sparrow's social media post. For the subjects addressed in the words and actions of Sparrow, Momberg, and Catzavelos, their response is already linked to 'past bodily experience'. In contrast to the nostalgia and sentimentality that joins Sparrow, Momberg, and Catzavelos, it is a sense of woundedness that mobilises a collective response to the racial disgust of their words and actions. Brown (1995) calls these intensely affective relationships to histories of oppression and exclusion 'wounded attachments', including the forms of collective identity associated with and mobilised for political action from them. The outrage can only therefore make sense if it is understood as a reaction to words and actions that reopen a wound that can hardly be described as healed, the attachment to which is also a means for measuring the potential for recognition of black people within the bounds of humanity.

Like in the two extracts, particularly in terms of their orientation towards some sort of redirection of anger towards productive action, even by the shaming through exclusion of perpetrators of racism, one of the people on Twitter who responded to Catzavelos' post starts off by noting that '[w]e have the power'. Let us develop this further. Recall Momberg's reinstating of the apartheid-era racial hierarchy during her racist tirade in the previous discussion. Although not commenting on Momberg, the commentary recapitulates the power relationship in terms that seek to reverse or pull down what previously would have been acceptable to being unacceptable behaviour in postapartheid South Africa. If we draw out one of the implications of the commentary, it is that the repulsive body, one deserving of being disinvested with power in the current postapartheid moment, becomes the racist body.

The commentator proceeds to catalogue options for politicised action to enforce consequences for people like Catzavelos, which included to 'boycott the companies that support his business, write to his kids' school for suspension, his gym for cancellation, his bank where his house is financed' (Twitter 2018). In this instance, we can ask: how is the racist body and the black body reconstituted in relation to one another in this commentary? What transpires in this reconstructive movement, to reinterpret Ahmed (2004b: 57), is a 'sealing' of people like Catzavelos 'as objects of hate' for their racism. Catzavelos, as well as others like him, come to be perceived as effectively *standing in* and *standing for* the egregious legacies of colonial and apartheid rule. Based on the reaction to his video, people like Catzavelos become placeholders for systems which, to be continually reminded of, reinstall and aggravate the immense pain, injury, and loss linked to them.

They put a face on our past and its logic of denigrating the black body. Not wholly implying or limited to the personification of perpetrators of racism, the commentator's 'move' is nevertheless clouded by individualising accountability for racist action. The commentator concludes by pointing out that 'we have to move the action from our thumbs on Twitter to the real world' (Twitter 2018). It is time for a recalibration. 'This is perhaps because the country has been here before – it seems it is yet another lesson not learned,' another commentator reminds us (Twitter 2018). There is an affective release and circulation of pent-up anger in this response. A disenchantment with the tenuous state of race relations in postapartheid South Africa. Twitter is a medium that enables the release of the anger that can then go viral. A crisis of racial embodiment, argues Khanna (2020: 149), can trigger 'a moment of historical catharsis'. This clamour, beyond denoting only a condition of agitation, also expresses the desire for self-determination. As Cheng (2001: 75) states, 'the denigrated body comes to voice, and the pleasure of that voice, only by assuming the voice of authority'. Here, we can paraphrase Msimang's closing remark in her opinion article: in the current moment of the postapartheid dispensation, there is probably less sympathy for white fear or the sense of precariousness that underlies it than there might have been in the early years of the transition to a democratic South Africa. There is now much more of a willingness to confront the historic denigration embodied by Sparrow, Catzavelos, and Momberg. One cannot, however, overlook the racial grievance and sense of loss linked to this collective outrage, even while it portrays itself with a sense of agency. The outrage is a symptom of racial wounding. That is, we see the public backlash or outrage substituting for what Eng and Han (2019) describe as melancholia, accruing from an ontologically based non-/mis-recognisability. The demand for an apology and retributive action recuperates that loss through identification with it. At the heart of the public backlash lies the more profound problem of racial melancholia or mourning.

The transition in 1994 represented a new political and social chapter for South Africa. There was hope that the country would turn the page after years of systemic racism and its injustices. Through the call for reconciliation, framed by the Truth and Reconciliation Commission (TRC) and embodied by the former president, Nelson Mandela, we were asked to move on and focus on building a new South Africa. The incidents with Sparrow, Momberg, and Catzavelos and the public reaction to them reflect a profound and still unresolved historical racial tension evolving into the pulse of the present. As the following tweet commenting on the apology issued by Catzavelos illustrates, this ongoing tension complicates, rather than enables, the value of racial apologies in constituting mutual recognition: 'A fine of 150,000 is an insult. That guy is an unapologetic racist jackass who is not gonna abandon his racial bull just because it cost him 5,000 a month. He's only gonna be careful not to get caught'

(Sibanda 2019). The challenge is to create conditions that make the offering of public apologies truly conciliatory and enable genuine recognition of the humanity of all. Postapartheid South Africa is still confronted with this task.

The (im)potency of racial apologies

This last section of the chapter returns to the function of racial apologies within the public domain. In addressing apology's (im)potency, we consider its normalisation as a standard mode of engagement, post the racist event. From Sparrow, Momberg, and Catzavelos, to more recent events surrounding Clicks and H&M racialising adverts[5] (The Guardian 2018), the public apology has come to enjoy an almost normative status in the social and political imaginary. Mihai and Thaler (2014), for example, observe that the political apology has come to be part of liberal democratic practice and may often take the form of state recognition and apology for historical abuse of human rights. Justin Trudeau's apology to former students of residential schools in Canada in 2017 (Prime Minister of Canada 2017) is an example of such a political apology that recognises historical injustice against a population. In some instances, states may also offer reparations as a means of redress. In other contexts, public figures may also publicly express contrition to a social group to which they have caused offence and following public backlash. South African TV personality Zodwa Wabantu's recent apology to the LGBTI+ community, following an outcry against comments made on her reality show, is a good case in point (Entertainment Reporter 2019). What these examples demonstrate is how the public apology seems to have assumed an evidential role that is par for the course in how public offence and injury is treated. And yet within this normalisation lie troubling meanings and effects that attest to its intrinsic failures.

MacLachlan's (2014) useful distinction between apology and apology as political practice alerts us that the practice of apology is far from neutral, but rather is framed within a history and politics of social engineering. In this latter sense, the public apology is framed in reference to a historical and political logic and practice that is aimed at the deliberate and strategic deployment of subjects for specific social engineering projects, such as separate development, ethnic cleansing, and genocide, among others. Apology that does political work via redress and state recognition is different in political meaning and import than the public apology to which MacLachlan draws our attention. While historical injury may be claimed and/or disavowed, what are we to make of the racial apology that is not

---

[5] In 2018, H&M franchise stores in South Africa were forcibly shut following protest over an advert featuring a black child with a 'coolest monkey in the jungle' inscription on wear.

configured in the features of the state's political apology? More importantly, how do we assess its successes and failures within the public sphere? Drawing on Arendt's (1958) understanding of the political as encompassing more than state power, but also involving business, public institutions, and social relations between subjects in the public sphere, MacLachlan invites us to consider public apology's failures or successes as always *in situ* and contingent on diverse and shifting contexts. This is useful to consider. Nonetheless, in drawing out some key dimensions of what we may consider to be meaningful apologies, we specifically hone in on one critical dimension: recognition.

In our reading, at least the following five key dimensions must be evident in the racial apology: 1) recognition and acceptance of harm/injury inflicted; 2) recognition of oneself as having caused harm/injury; 3) recognition of an Other as being injured; 4) gestures towards some form of reparation, whether by saying sorry publicly, or through financial reparation, volunteering of service, expression of regret, and so on; and lastly 5) an assurance that the offence will not be repeated. Arguably, most if not all of these dimensions were present in the public apologies of the three case studies that frame this chapter. In her court appearance, Sparrow's read apology noted that 'it is difficult to put into words the regret I feel ... I accept that in comparing black people to monkeys in my Facebook post earlier this year I have impaired the dignity of African people. Please accept my heartfelt apology' (Singh 2016).

Similarly, in a read statement, Catzavelos acknowledges that he has 'caused unspeakable pain to every single person in South Africa', describing his actions as 'thoughtless and insensitive'. He further states: 'I have watched my video and feel total shame. It's hard to put into words what I want to say and genuinely apologise. I don't expect people to forgive me, but I will spend the rest of my life repenting and trying to make up for my total lack of respect and judgement' (Alfreds 2018).

Momberg offered some form of apology during her first court appearances, stating: 'There are no words to explain how I feel about the situation. I realised that it had affected the people and it is not something that I want to put myself and anyone else through again' (Pijoos 2017). Since her release, she has embarked on a lawsuit against the state, claiming her arrest and detention were unlawful (Ngqakamba 2020). Appearing on Newzroom Africa, she has defended her actions on the day as those of a traumatised person who is not racist and did not intend to cause (racial) injury: 'Racism is not a crime ... I'm not guilty of a crime, I'm guilty of lashing out because of the trauma that I was under' (Friedman 2019).

On the surface, the following dimensions of apology are present in Sparrow's and Catzavelos' statements: acknowledging harm and injury, recognising oneself as having caused this harm and injury, recognition of an Other that is hurt, acceptance of the need for a reparation, and a promise to never repeat the offence. This suggests that these apologies should be read as successful.

Indeed, the presiding magistrate, Vincent Hlatshwayo, endorsed Sparrow's apology as authentic because 'these things are coming from the bottom of your heart. We all make mistakes. It is important to identify the mistake and rectify it', adding that he was able to 'see the truth' in her apology (Singh 2016).

And yet there remains the nagging feeling, echoed within much social media dialogue, that these apologies were/are futile and inauthentic. Despite the shame expressed and the regret at causing injury (incidentally, but perhaps not surprisingly, expressed as a revelation to the offender given race's psychosocial, ideological, and psychic constitution), there is still a sense, at least for the public who have been the targets of such racist vitriol, that these apologies are superficial and meaningless. And so, we must ask: what makes an apology meaningful? Reading these five dimensions alongside Arendt's (1958) notion of meaningful political speech and Smith's (2014) idea of recognition of victims as worthy moral interlocutors, we return to (absence of) recognition of the human as being at the heart of both woundedness and meaningful apology. Even in the event of the public apology, the felt absence of recognition as human remains a vexing impediment to meaningful apology.

While it does benefit to read events in their particularities, the argument can still be made that the continuous 'obstinacy' of racism and racialisation in South Africa attests to a raced repetition (Stevens 2018: 42) that confirms for a black majority that racial apologies are nothing more than superficial public gestures made to pacify an outraged public. Indeed, it is only following threats of legal action that these apologies were offered by the three individuals. Meaningful apology must then offer to the injured not only a sense of authenticity but also a recognition that sees the injured as human and so will 'treat them as humans deserving dignity rather than as mere means to some end [and] understand and interact with the injured not as abstractions …' (Smith 2014: 39). The public apology becomes meaningful when not performed as a public goodwill gesture but as a willingness to reimagine the very ontology of the human from its historical exclusion of the other: 'When I harmed you, I saw you as somehow unworthy of sufficient consideration, but now I turn to you in humility to discuss the very values and principles that give meaning to my life' (p 40). Without a radical reimagination of the basis of our humanity, and with it a reconceptualisation of 'existence anew' (Warren 2018: 172), a public apology will remain an ineffective instrument for conferring meaningful human recognition.

Reflections

Writing on race is not an easy task. It is emotionally extremely taxing. Throw in the topic of apology and the task becomes even more complicated. What struck me is the impossibility of that which it is intended to do or achieve in the light of our history or histories and their legacy or legacies. An apology, whether offered in public or privately, is supposed to bring closure. What is closure? Can we ever agree on it? Can an apology help? Our feelings tell us a lot about ourselves and our time in postapartheid South Africa. Through our feelings, our pasts persist in the present. The racist events and the backlash we analysed show me there is still a lot of mutual distrust between the different groups of people in South Africa. I doubt that apologies will help diffuse it and bring us closure anytime soon. The time it will take for apologies to bring closure, or to move on, is beyond our own lifetime. The past, present, and future are intertwined in the actions and the outrage that result in the giving of an apology. There can be no redemptive possibility in the apology without recognition of this temporal dimension to our feelings. We are subjects of our histories and their unfolding in the present. We embody our histories. Our feelings bear this out. Our future depends on our ability to reckon with this conjoining of the past and present. Does an apology help us face this temporal aspect of our feelings? I think it is maybe a start, but not enough. We soon quickly 'move on' until there is another offending event or incident, and an apology is demanded or issued, yet there is no meaningful closure. Our feelings might once again bear this out.

Nkululeko

Writing this reflection in the context of recent unrest in the country is sobering for me. Perhaps because it signals at something that I can only describe as the failure of apology or public gesturing. We clash against each other, in both public and private domains. We also apologise to each other, sometimes because we independently choose to and sometimes because we are made to. Nonetheless, we apologise. For hurts caused. For misunderstandings. With a promise to do and be better with/for each other. Revisiting the three events that we write about in our chapter, I face, once again, the failure of apology and the failure of the public gesture. It is a grim task to tamp down my tenacious belief and hope that spaces between conflicting groups can be bridged and to confront head-on the failure of apology to bring this about. Apology takes on a shadowy life of its own – teasing in its promise to bridge a gap, precious in its conditional life, mysterious in its furtive elucidation of what these conditions could be. I ended the chapter with a feeling of urgency about what gets excavated when we hurt and thinking of a gap that inevitably remains empty, filled with empty gestures and words that can never be enough. And so, even now, as we continue to clash against each other, maybe an apology or two will be thrown in, post-conflict. But the gaps also seem to have a shadowy life of their own.

Peace

References

Ahmed, S., 2004a, 'Affective economies', *Social Text*, 22(2), 117–39.

Ahmed, S., 2004b, *The Cultural Politics of Emotion*, Abingdon-on-Thames: Routledge.

Ahmed, S., 2004c, 'Collective feelings: or, the impressions left by others', *Theory, Culture & Society*, 21(2), 25–42.

Ahmed, S., 2006, *Queer Phenomenology: Orientations, Objects, Others*, Durham: Duke University Press.

Alfreds, D., 2018, 'Adam Catzavelos issues apology over k-word video, vows to repent for the rest of his life', *News24*, viewed 9 December 2020 from www.news24.com/news24/SouthAfrica/News/adam-catzavelos-issues-apology-over-k-word-video-vows-to-repent-for-the-rest-of-his-life-20180824

Arendt, H., 1958, *The Human Condition*, 2nd ed., Chicago: University of Chicago Press.

Berlant, L., 2011, *Cruel Optimism*, Durham and London: Duke University Press.

Bhabha, H., 1984, 'Of mimicry and man: the ambivalence of colonial discourse', *Discipleship: A Special Issue on Psychoanalysis*, 28, 125–33.

Biko, S., 2004, *I Write what I Like*, Johannesburg: Picador Africa.

Bonner, P., Delius, P., and Posel, D., 1994, *Apartheid's Genesis, 1935–1962*, New York: Raven Press.

Boym, S., 2007, 'Nostalgia and its discontents', *The Hedgehog Review* 9(2), 7–19.

Braidotti, R., 2013, *The Posthuman*, Cambridge: Polity Press.

Brown, B. B., 1987, 'Facing the "black peril": the politics of population control in South Africa', *Journal of Southern African Studies* 13(2), 256–73.

Brown, W., 1995, *States of Injury: Power and Freedom in Late Modernity*, Princeton: Princeton University Press.

Cheng, A. A., 2001, *Melancholy of Race: Psychoanalysis, Assimilation, and Hidden Grief*, New York: Oxford University Press.

Cowan, K., 2018, 'The call that sealed Momberg's fate: "please don't send a bunch of k*****s"', *Times Live*, viewed 13 December 2020 from www.timeslive.co.za/news/south-africa/2018-03-31-the-call-that-sealed-mombergs-fate-/

Deleuze, G. and Guattari, F., 1987, *A Thousand Plateaus*, trans. B. Massumi, Minneapolis: University of Minnesota Press.

Deleuze, G. and Guattari, F., 1994, *What is Philosophy?* New York: Columbia University Press.

eNCA, 2019, 'Malungelo Booi hears from a Vicki Momberg sympathizer', viewed 2 September 2020 from www.youtube.com/watch?v=_ZCL igw3DYU

Eng, D. and Han, S., 2019, *Racial Melancholia, Racial Dissociation*, Durham: Duke University Press.

Entertainment Reporter, 2019, 'WATCH: Zodwa Wabantu issues apology for homophobic comments', *IOL*, viewed 9 December 2020 from www. iol.co.za/entertainment/celebrity-news/local/watch-zodwa-wabantu-iss ues-apology-for-homophobic-comments-29229936

Fanon, F., 1986, *Black Skin, White Masks*, trans. C. L. Markmann, London: Pluto Press.

Friedman, B., 2019, '[WATCH] "racism is not a crime," says Vicki Momberg during TV interview', viewed 9 December 2020 from www.capetalk. co.za/articles/351663/watch-racism-is-not-a-crime-says-vicki-momb erg-during-tv-interview

Harris, C., 1993, 'Whiteness as property', *Harvard Law Review*, 1707–91.

Hook, D., 2017, 'What is "enjoyment as a political factor"?' *Political Psychology* 38(4), 605–20.

Jordaan, N., 2018, '[WATCH] 5 funny responses to racist Adam Catzavelos' video', *Times Live*, viewed 13 December 2020 from www.timeslive.co.za/ news/south-africa/2018-08-23-watch--5-funny-responses-to-racist-adam-catzavelos-video/

Khanna, N., 2020, *The Visceral Logics of Decolonization*, Durham: Duke University Press.

Kolnai, A., 2004, *On Disgust*, trans. Barry Smith and Carolyn Korsmeyer, Chicago: Open Court.

MacLachlan, A., 2014, 'Beyond the ideal political apology', in N. Smith, Mihaela Mihai, and Mathias Thaler (eds.), *On the Uses and Abuses of Political Apologies*, pp 13–31, London: Springer.

Massumi, B., 2002, *Parables for the Virtual: Movement, Affect, Sensation*, Durham: Duke University Press.

Massumi, B., 2015a, *The Power at the End of the Economy*, Durham: Duke University Press.

Massumi, B., 2015b, *Politics of Affect*, Cambridge: Polity Press.

Menninghaus, W., 2003, *Disgust: Theory and History of a Strong Sensation*, trans. E. Howard and J. Golb, New York: State University of New York Press.

Mihai, M. and Thaler, M., 2014, *On the Uses and Abuses of Political Apologies*, London: Springer.

Milton, J. R. L., 1996, *South African Criminal Law and Procedure, Vol. II, Common Law Crimes* 3rd ed., Johannesburg: Juta.

Msimang, S., 2016, 'South Africa has no patience for Penny Sparrow's apartheid nostalgia', *The Guardian*, 7 January, viewed 6 September 2020 from www.theguardian.com/commentisfree/2016/jan/07/south-africa-penny-sparrow-apartheid-nostalgia-racist

Nemakonde, V., 2016, 'Penny Sparrow calls black people "monkeys"', *Citizen*, viewed 13 December 2020 from https://citizen.co.za/news/south-africa/927765/kzn-estate-agent-calls-black-people-monkeys/

News24, 2016, 'Twitter revolts over #PennySparrow "monkey" comments', *News24*, viewed 7 September 2020 from www.news24.com/news24/video/southafrica/news/pennysparrow-trends-as-twitter-comes-down-on-racism-20160104

Ngqakamba, S., 2020, 'Vicki Momberg sues SAPS, justice ministers, NDPP for R8.5m for 'unlawful arrest', *News24*, viewed 9 January 2020 from www.news24.com/news24/SouthAfrica/News/vicki-momberg-sues-saps-justice-ministers-ndpp-for-r85m-for-unlawful-arrest-20200109

Pijoos, I., 2017, 'My apologies fell on deaf ears – Vicki Momberg', *News24*, viewed 9 December 2020 from www.news24.com/news24/SouthAfrica/News/my-apologies-fell-on-deaf-ears-vicki-momberg-20171130

Prime Minister of Canada, 2017, 'Prime Minister delivers apology to former students of Newfoundland and Labrador residential schools', website of the Prime Minister of Canada, News, viewed 9 December 2020 from https://pm.gc.ca/en/news/news-releases/2017/11/24/prime-minister-delivers-apology-former-students-newfoundland-and#:~:text=On%20June%2011%2C%202008%2C%20on,%2C%20their%20families%2C%20and%20communities

Sibanda, O., 2019, 'Sorry, Adam Catzavelos, but your apology and fine are not enough', viewed 30 December 2020 from www.dailymaverick.co.za/opinionista/2019-09-02-sorry-adam-catzavelos-but-your-apology-and-fine-are-not-enough/

Singh, K., 2016, ' "I will strive to be a better citizen" – Penny Sparrow', viewed 9 December 2020 from www.news24.com/news24/southafrica/news/i-will-strive-to-be-a-better-citizen-penny-sparrow-20160912

Smith, N., 2014, 'Political apologies and categorical apologies' in N. Smith, Mihaela Mihai, and Mathias Thaler (eds.), *On the Uses and Abuses of Political Apologies*, pp 32–51, London: Springer.

Spinoza, B., 1985, *The Collected Works of Spinoza*, ed. and trans. E. Curley, Princeton: Princeton University Press.

Stevens, G., 2018, 'Raced repetition: perpetual paralysis or paradoxical promise?', *International Journal of Critical Diversity Studies*, 1(2), 42–57.

The Guardian, 2018, 'H&M stores in South Africa trashed by protesters after "racist" ad', *The Guardian*, viewed 9 December 2020 from www.theguardian.com/world/2018/jan/14/hm-stores-in-south-afrtica-trashed-by-protesters-after-racist-ad

Twitter, 2018, 'On the #Adam Catzavelos issue', viewed 6 September 2020 from https://twitter.com/vusithembekwayo/status/1032135976968175 616?lang=en

Walcott, R., 2014, 'The problem of the human: black ontologies and the coloniality of our being', in S. Broeck and C. Junker (eds.), *Postcoloniality-Decoloniality-Black Critique: Joints and Fissures*, pp 93–105, Frankfurt and New York: Campus.

Warren, C. L., 2018, *Ontological Terror: Blackness, Nihilism, and Emancipation*, Durham: Duke University Press.

Wynter, S., 2003, 'Unsettling the coloniality of being/power/truth/ freedom: towards the human, after man, it's overrepresentation – an argument', *The New Centennial Review* 3(3), 257–337.

8

Apology as a Pathway
Out of White Unknowing

Christi van der Westhuizen

my past crawls forth on its deadly knees without once looking up
Litany by Krog 1998: 264, line 8

Africa, past and present, suffers under a humanism that has dehumanised. This limited the definition of 'the human' to select Westerners, with humanism in law historically turning people, racialised as black, into 'a race doomed to wretchedness, degradation, abjection and servitude' (Mbembe 2011: 188). It is demonstrated in South Africa by the ongoing resistance of white people against the notion that apartheid was a 'crime against humanity', a recognition that would enable apology. This stance transpired in a response from the last apartheid president, F. W. de Klerk, when he rejected the notion as an 'agitprop project' of the now defunct Soviet Union, in tandem with his old foes, the African National Congress (ANC) and the South African Communist Party (SACP), aimed at 'stigmatis[ing] white South Africans by associating them with genuine crimes against humanity' (Gerber 2020). His long-held position had been against casting guilt over 'whole classes of decent [white] people and communities', as they did not know about apartheid state violence (van der Westhuizen 2007: 318). After public outrage and pressure from the Desmond and Leah Tutu Foundation, de Klerk apologised with the ambivalent concession that 'this is not the time to quibble about the degrees of unacceptability of apartheid' (Etheridge 2020). He confirmed the Rome Statute of the International Criminal Court's definition of apartheid as a crime against humanity, even though it is a codification of the United Nations resolutions against which he had railed. He revisited this question one last time, in a video that was released upon his death on 11 November 2021. In the video, de Klerk denied that he had continued to justify apartheid and instead insisted that 'on many occasions, I apologised for the pain of the indignity that apartheid has brought to persons, to persons of colour in South Africa' (de Klerk 2021). In the video, he offered an apology 'without qualification … for the pain and the hurt and the indignity and the damage that apartheid has done to black, brown and Indians in South Africa' (de Klerk 2021). The wording of this apology would indicate a shift in relation to the recognition of black people's humanity. However, the apology was tainted by his insistence that his personal realisation that apartheid was 'morally unjustifiable' happened in the early 80s, a claim not borne out by his actions as cabinet minister during that time (van der Westhuizen 2021).

Opposition to the notion of apartheid as a violation of humanity is widely held among white people. An overview of the Institute for Justice and Reconciliation's (IJR) annual surveys (van der Westhuizen 2016) shows that white South Africans consistently diverge from other racial groups on this point, with 30 per cent to 50 per cent of white people, as opposed to 5 to 30 per cent of black people, refuting that it was a crime against humanity (p 175). This opposition can be read, as I have argued, as either that apartheid was not a crime, or that black people should not be understood as part of humanity. Either way, black people's humanity is placed in question, which continues colonial humanism's exclusion of black people from the definition of 'human'. This racism also speaks to questions of knowledge, that is, the knowledge of the crimes committed to sustain apartheid. It is echoed in other IJR survey questions, such as in 2003 when fewer than a third of white respondents agreed that white people should apologise for 'what happened' under apartheid, as opposed to 60 per cent to 75 per cent of black respondents in agreement (p 176). This amounts to a 'white opportunism of denial', to 'acquit whiteness from culpability, reinstate its inherent innocence and relieve white people of all responsibility, including reparation' (p 180).

The confluence of this persistent racism with the lack of substantive transformation of economic inequality has provoked a clamour of denunciations of the project of reconciliation. Reconciliation held sway as a socio-political aim during the transition to democracy in the 1990s, hand in hand with the notion of apology. While the focus in the field of law is placed on retributive justice through the prosecution of apartheid-era ministers, soldiers, and civil servants, the other burning question remains the vast challenge of socioeconomic justice. In exploring the latter challenge (van der Westhuizen 2007), I have argued that this possibility was mostly postponed when the ruling ANC opted for neoliberal capitalist policies in the early 1990s. Such policies have globally deepened socioeconomic inequality. Ironically, the ANC entrenched the neoliberal trajectory that the National Party (NP) establishment had embarked upon already in the 1970s. Hence, South Africa's Gini coefficient has globally been the worst since the 1990s, with coloniality perpetrated in patterns of dispossession and impoverishment of racialised people, continued from the past almost four centuries. Only the upper echelons of postapartheid[1] society have been deracialised.

The relative lack of redistribution to overturn apartheid's racial division of material resources is linked with white people's overall lack of remorse. Apology is not toothless, as the case of German colonial violations in Namibia shows: Germany has tiptoed around apology, as apology sets off reparation (*Deutsche Welle* 12 October 2020). Apology is about accountability over the past. I argue here that it works as a knowledge/power construct, in that knowledges are wielded in a bid to ensure certain outcomes over others, including to prevent certain material repercussions. Knowledge of apartheid state violence has been presented in white discourse as a precondition for apology. It is true that different knowledges exist depending on the location of the knower (van der Westhuizen 2007: 293–319). But the emphasis on knowledge of state violence obscures the question of knowledge of the everyday injustices of apartheid, hinging as it did on what Posel (2001) calls a 'common sense' form of racism. The political and social impact of South Africa's Truth and Reconciliation Commission (TRC) was limited in part due to its emphasis on perpetrators and victims as opposed to beneficiaries and victims (Mamdani 1996). The focus was limited to the NP leadership's violently oppressive use of the state apparatus and its lack of transparency about that use. The TRC turned contrition into an opportunity to gain amnesty, but 'lack' (suppression) of knowledge was used to sidestep this offer of forgiveness. Moreover, with the attention paid to perpetrators of egregious apartheid violence, what was lost from sight was the wider white citizenry's active complicity in reproducing and keeping apartheid intact through everyday acts of omission and commission. Lack of knowledge was operationalised as a device to distance and exonerate Afrikaners and white people generally from the crimes of the regime. Obfuscated were the ordinary and normalised dehumanisations of apartheid, and the denial that apartheid disadvantaged black people while privileging white people – a denial which still serves to rationalise the negation of socioeconomic redress. Thus, two plains of knowledge are created: of apartheid state crimes and of the everyday violences to sustain apartheid. The conflation of the two enables white ignorance and obviates the need for apology and, hence, for redress.

Whiteness is constituted through the denial of racial injustice. The unlocking of knowledge through apology fractures whiteness, as apology works as an admission of knowledge of racial injustice as underpinning the constructed 'superiority' of 'whites'. Therefore, in this chapter I look at how apology opens the possibility for knowing what it takes to sustain white

---

[1] Postapartheid is used without a hyphen, to emphasise that no radical division can be made between apartheid and what follows.

supremacy, and how admitting to this knowing opens the way for apology, and hence the recognition of the black Other as fully human. In exploring how knowing informs apology, I draw on critical whiteness theories of 'epistemologies of ignorance', which approach ignorance as generative of whiteness (Mills 2007; Steyn 2012). By homing in on how remorse unlocks what is known and not known, one can expose the workings of power that underpin (un)knowing. Integral to whiteness as an epistemology of ignorance is misrecognition, in the sense of refusing to regard racialised others as human and therefore not needing to know what was done to black and brown people under apartheid. White ignorance becomes white innocence, obviating the need for apology and hence the need for redress, while perpetuating the colonial division of racialised recognition and white people's refusal of shared humanity, which underpins the material division of resources. White people's avoidance of apology, and therefore collective and individual responsibility for apartheid, serves as the bedrock for the resurgence of an intransigent whiteness reproclaiming supremacy 27 years into democracy.

Ways of knowing and humanisation, and how these reflect in and through apology, are here explored through the exemplars of three Afrikaners, prominent for divergent reasons during the transition to democracy: apartheid assassin Eugene de Kock, as analysed by Pumla Gobodo-Madikizela; former NP Deputy Minister of Law and Order and, later, Human Rights Commissioner Leon Wessels; and poet, author, and journalist Antjie Krog. All three figures cut through the TRC's too-narrow divisions of knowledge, and show the complex interaction between apology and humanisation. The next section briefly discusses whiteness as produced through ignorance.

Whiteness: an epistemology of ignorance

Premesh Lalu (2009: 138) observes that narratives of empire are at their core beset by a 'contradictory impulse', due to 'attempts to justify acts of violence'. The avoidance of apology is one among various strategies deployed by white people in general, and Afrikaners in particular, to avoid culpability and redress for apartheid and colonial violences. Apprehensiveness about apology can be explained using theorisations of whiteness as constituted, in part, by epistemologies of ignorance, given the imbrication of knowledge with power.

Drawing on Mills (2007), Steyn's (2012) discussion of an 'ignorance contract' as being at the heart of whiteness is useful. First, she explains whiteness as 'a structurally privileged positionality (un)informed by ignorance/blindnesses – taking for granted unearned entitlements that come at the expense of racialized others, and generally lacking insight into the normalized racial order that shapes life opportunities and conditions imperceptibly around the comfort, convenience and advancement of whites' (p 11). Ignorance is here understood as similar to knowledge, as ignorance is *not* an absence of knowledge but rather a 'product of deliberate practices' (p 10). Ignorance is also similarly produced: created and circulated intersubjectively through communication in different settings and through social networks, in the interest of white people (p 10). The ignorance contract underpins white collusion that sustains racial hierarchies, and therefore is not accidental, but a choice (p 12). The white epistemology of ignorance extends to what Mills (2007: 22) calls 'moral non-knowings': 'incorrect judgments about the rights and wrongs of moral situations themselves'. It also works conceptually: the 'nonwhite Other is so located in the guiding conceptual array that different rules apply', to the extent of European colonialism's conjecture of ' "empty" lands that are actually teeming with millions of people, of "discovering" countries whose inhabitants already exist' (p 27). '[T]he concept is driving the perception, with whites aprioristically intent on denying what is before them' (p 27). Memory work is pivotal to whiteness as an epistemology of ignorance, with the suppression of past racial injustices to normalise present white privilege and preclude any corrective action – what Mills calls 'the mystification of the past [that] underwrites a mystification of the present' (p 31).

The active construction of white superiority and black inferiority has been 'unremembered', to use Gqola's (2010: 8) phrase, for 'a calculated act of exclusion and erasure'. White unknowing derives from unremembering, which emphasises the active engagement in knowing and not knowing, the turning away so as not to know the injustice on which white privilege is founded. Memory is about forming identities in the present: in the case of postapartheid whiteness, the aim is an identity that is not blameworthy (van der Westhuizen 2017). Wessels and Krog question unremembering, also in relation to everyday knowledge of state violence. Wessels quotes Krog as capturing white wilful unknowing during apartheid 'brilliantly': 'the day you woke up and heard Dulcie September had been murdered, what did you think?' (van der Westhuizen 2007: 319). In his autobiography, Wessels elaborates the point:

> If a person sees a truck full of police officers with sjamboks, you know they are going to use them. When someone is in solitary confinement, do you think there won't be pressure on that person to talk? We knew we were living in extraordinary circumstances. People had to suspect something. ... There were never serious discussions about alleged offences in NP meetings. So people did not know but there were also many things they did not want to know. (Wessels 2010: 345)

How unknowable was racialised poverty inscribed on bodies and landscapes? And reports of deaths and incarceration of black and also white people who resisted the system? A picture emerges of systemic complicity among white South Africans, of actions at structural and institutional levels converging to reproduce white supremacy, sustained by strategic unremembering and silences to claim a lack of knowledge and avoid apology and therefore accountability. In the next section, Gobodo-Madikizela's interpretation of knowledge and humanisation as figured by de Kock is discussed, starting with a consideration of the problematics of truth and knowing with reference to a court case that de Kock launched against me.

Eugene de Kock: the truth of (not) knowing

On 21 November 2007, a message arrived for me from the putrid bowels of apartheid. It came as a fax of 25 pages, some in long-hand scrawl, others typed, containing the demand that 'the truth' be heard. The fax included two smudged photocopies: one a news report on how South African history teaching had shifted from 'fact' to 'debate', and the other an excerpt from my just-published book, *White Power & the Rise and Fall of the National Party* (van der Westhuizen 2007). The scrawl was that of apartheid assassin Eugene de Kock and included the sentence: 'I am completely sick of all the lying, and will now start with her to tackle the issue'.[2] The 'her' refers to me, the author. De Kock was suing me from C-Max prison in Pretoria. Moreover, he had managed to have the book banned with immediate effect for the unlikely reason that it besmirched his 'good name'. This draconian decision was achieved by bringing an *ex parte* application, unheard of in similar cases but successful because of the apparent timing of the application to coincide with the presence on the Pretoria High Court bench of Judge Willie Hartzenberg, brother of former Conservative Party leader Ferdi Hartzenberg. The judge granted an interim interdict[3] that the book be withdrawn from all stores. I was only allowed a few weeks later to convince the court not to make the banning permanent.[4] When my publisher entered into a deal with de Kock, I parted ways with them and won the case with *pro bono* assistance from the law firm, Webber Wentzel, recognised for their work in defence of freedom of speech.

---

[2]   An excerpt of the handwritten communication (translated here from the Afrikaans by the author) by de Kock, as one of the attachments to the Founding Affidavit. See *De Kock v Van der Westhuizen and Others* (TPD) unreported case no. 54065 of 21 November 2007.
[3]   See *De Kock v Van der Westhuizen and Others* (TPD) unreported case no. 54065 of 21 November 2007.
[4]   See *De Kock v Van der Westhuizen and Others* (TPD) judgment of unreported case no. 54065 of 9 January 2008.

Incongruities, sometimes ironic, abound in this case. I discovered that de Kock and I share Boksburg, presently part of Ekurhuleni, as our home town. *White Power* starts with a personal reflection on growing up in the East Rand town, which notoriously reintroduced petty apartheid in the 1980s under a Conservative Party-controlled municipality. De Kock went to the same high school as my parents, who knew his brother. Boksburg is a springboard in the book to interrogate white denialism in contemporary South Africa. That the book provoked white reaction was therefore not coincidental. It was written to address white people's avoidance of the miserable demise in the mid-2000s of their once mighty National Party (NP). Former NP voters seemed determined to cast the party from public and personal memory, to avoid their own role in sustaining its system of apartheid. White people generally and Afrikaners specifically insisted they 'did not know' that apartheid was a deeply damaging and dehumanising system of dispossession, enforced through state and other violences. My quest to make sense of this Afrikaner nationalist legacy from which I had come collided with de Kock's campaign for early parole at the time. He was serving 212 years, plus two sentences of life imprisonment, after his conviction on 82 criminal counts, including six for murder. With his court bid against me, de Kock was hoping to reinstate the 'truth': he had 'never had a problem with' the 'truth', as he had 'always taken responsibility for his actions', according to his affidavit.[5] As seen in white denial over apartheid, the notion of 'truth' is fraught. The right kind of 'truth' could assist in de Kock's early release from prison, but this was apparently placed in jeopardy by a quotation in the book from Leon Wessels. It brought him back into public consciousness at an inopportune time.

Mamdani (1996) points out the problem of the TRC process replacing justice with 'truth'. De Kock is one of the few who had to face justice. For some, he is a 'fall guy' whose prosecution signals his disavowal by the people in whose name he perpetrated the dirty work of apartheid (literally 'dirty tricks', as extra-legal covert activities by state operatives have been called). But, for all de Kock's eagerness for the truth to be revealed in the case against me, the TRC had not granted him amnesty for certain crimes. His lawsuit to have *White Power* banned also involved the exclusion of details that would have confirmed the truth of the essence of the statement that he was contesting, namely that he was 'a cold-blooded killer' who treated his victims callously (Milo 2007: 14). Suspiciously, he demanded to know the 'sources' of the statement, (strategically?) ignoring that it came from

---

[5]   Para. 15.3 (translated here from the Afrikaans by the author) of the Founding Affidavit in *De Kock v Van der Westhuizen and Others* (TPD) unreported case no. 54065 of 21 November 2007.

his former political principal Wessels, despite the direct citation. He speaks in his affidavit of the 'incalculable damage and detriment' that my book's 'repulsive and humiliating insinuation' caused to his 'honour, dignity, good name and reputation'.[6] This portrayal of himself casts a shadow over the remorse he had shown previously, suggesting a person disconnected from the crimes he had committed to sustain white supremacy.

De Kock's approach in the lawsuit stands in contrast to his disclosures and apologies over time, including to Gobodo-Madikizela (2004) in the book *A Human Being Died that Night*. Her psychological study of repentance and forgiveness sheds some light on de Kock's knowing or unknowing of the terrible deeds he had committed. These deeds included killing and blowing up the body of an *askari* who had absconded (p 28). Despite the remorse he showed in his engagements with Gobodo-Madikizela and victims' families, he lied to her about the brutal treatment meted out to *askaris*, which echoes his omissions in the case against me. She explains his prevarication as that what he had done is not only beyond most people's comprehension but also 'beyond what *he* could understand, once he was removed from the day to day demands of the destructive life he had led' (p 23, emphasis in original). These crimes were committed 'in the name of white society' (p 113) – the same society which 'accepted his murderous protection of their privilege', only to excommunicate him afterwards (p 34). '[M]echanisms of denial' [were used] to enable a regime of terror to thrive, and … denial [was still used] to avoid facing responsibility for the past' (p 41).

The 'truth' that de Kock was confronted with is 'how a human life was destroyed' (p 130) – referring to the lives he destroyed, but also his own life. Gobodo-Madikizela argues that the perpetrator showing remorse enables mutual humanisation. Humanisation is understood as that 'there is something in the other that is felt to be part of the self, and something in the self that is felt to belong to the other' (p 127). Remorse opens the door to the perpetrator's admission that the victim was not an object but a human being (p 130), while encouraging the perpetrator to also admit 'that all along, he [the perpetrator] knew that he was human and knew right from wrong' (p 120). This mutual humanisation that Gobodo-Madikizela suggests, even in a case such as de Kock's, is a humanisation that is not about exoneration. Admitting both his victims' and his own humanity demands taking responsibility for what he had done. Extending this to white people complicit in the everyday reproduction of apartheid, apology towards mutual

---

[6]   Paras. 15.4 and 15.5 (translated here from the Afrikaans by the author) of the Founding Affidavit in *De Kock v Van der Westhuizen and Others* (TPD) unreported case no. 54065 of 21 November 2007.

humanisation would still require white people taking responsibility and therefore working towards redress for the effects of apartheid.

For Gobodo-Madikizela, the dialectic between remorse and forgiveness is central to the possibility of constructing a new democracy, especially in a case such as South Africa:

> How can we transcend hate if the goal is to transform human relationships in a society with a past marked by violent conflict between groups? The question may be irrelevant for people who do not have to live as a society with their former enemies. But for those whose lives are intertwined with those who have grossly violated human rights, ignoring the question is not an option. Not closing the door to understanding may be one of the ways in which people can redefine their understanding of atrocities and see them as something that is, like evil in the self, always a possibility in any political system that has emerged from a violent past. (pp 15–16)

This is needed to turn 'stalemates' from the authoritarian past into a reconstructed society based on a 'politics of contestation and compromise among equals' (p 126). This links with Wessels' (2020) understanding of reconciliation, which militates against it simply being a feel-good exercise (for whites). Instead, reconciliation is multifaceted, complex, and hard to attain, as it requires:

> an undertaking to accept each other's good faith; to understand that reconciliation and transformation are two sides of the same coin. Reconciliation is justice for me and for you. It means that differences will be resolved through discussion. It also means to listen to try and understand the other side of the argument without necessarily agreeing with it. (p 355)

The next section discusses the constitutive dynamics of white unknowing as read through his life.

Leon Wessels: the 'ought to have known' apology

Among his NP counterparts, Leon Wessels stands out as the one politician who has publicly grappled with apology since the transition to democracy. The only other comparable NP politician is his former superior as Minister of Law and Order, Adriaan Vlok. Vlok took to humbling himself in 2006 by washing the feet of victims of apartheid state violence, including the former head of the South African Council of Churches, Frank Chikane, and the mothers of the Mamelodi 10, anti-apartheid activists killed by operatives.

He started a charity feeding black children and granted interviews in which he confessed his racism (Fairbanks 2014). Vlok's actions stem from a strongly Christian motivation: he has not pondered questions of apology and knowledge to the extent that Wessels has. Hence, the focus in this chapter is on Wessels and particularly on his two autobiographical books, *Vereeniging – Die Onvoltooide Vrede* [Unification – The Incomplete Peace] (2010) and *Encountering Apartheid's Ghosts – From Krugersdorp to Constitution Hill* (2020). The later book is an English translation of the first, with some additional material on the TRC and political developments after the publication of the first book. Wessels' trajectory since apartheid would be regarded by some as an example of the lack of justice in the treatment of NP politicians compared with security force 'foot soldiers' like de Kock in the aftermath of apartheid. Wessels can be said to have been at the heart of P. W. Botha's 'Total Strategy' machinery after his appointment in 1988 as Deputy Minister of Law and Order under Vlok. In that capacity, he was required to finalise the State Security Council's (SSC) agenda, minutes, and documents for each fortnightly meeting, meeting with P.W. Botha at these intervals as then president and head of the SSC (Wessels 2010: 143). Apart from being a co-opted member of the SSC, Wessels was responsible as Deputy Minister for the National Joint Management System (NJMS) (p 214). This notorious structure was set up by the Botha securocrats to counteract the so-called 'total onslaught' of Communist and terrorist insurrection, as NP propaganda had cast popular agitation for democracy and against white supremacy. Wessels' job was to relay the NJMS's activities to the SSC, but he contends that he as Deputy Minister did not enjoy any executive powers in the SSC. Despite this role at the commanding heights of apartheid, in contrast with the postapartheid treatment meted out to de Kock, Wessels had risen from the NP's team in the transitional multiparty negotiations to Deputy Chairperson of the Constitutional Assembly that drafted the final Constitution of democratic South Africa. He went on to become a commissioner in the South African Human Rights Commission. His trajectory can be partly attributed to the political compromises struck in the transition to democracy. Such compromises in favour of the former rulers were due to the configuration of power at the time. Democracy was not brought about by military victory by the anti-apartheid forces but by a confluence of external and internal events, precipitating the unusual ceding of power by a militarily entrenched oligarchy in return for the constitutional securing of a market economy and liberal democratic rights (van der Westhuizen 2007).

This stay of retributive justice could be read as facilitating Wessels' soul-searching, but it can be traced back to the 1980s, when confrontations with foreigners during a visit to the USA sparked doubts about NP justifications of apartheid. He became one of the very first NP politicians to publicly apologise for apartheid. In 1990 he told international audiences – first in Toronto and then in Oslo, the latter event including just-released Nelson Mandela – that 'apartheid was a terrible mistake that wounded our country and its people' (Wessels 2010: 234). Recriminations awaited him upon his return to South Africa, with no colleagues supporting him, while de Klerk as party leader granted him the right to express his position but only with due understanding that it represented neither the party's, nor the government's stance (p 240). Wessels repeated the statement in parliament in 1991, adding that 'South Africans did not listen to the laughter or the crying of others. I am sorry that I was hard of hearing for so long' (pp 241, 267). His can therefore be described as an 'ought to have known' apology. He told the TRC in 1997 that apartheid 'blighted our land', and again apologised for having been 'hard of hearing'. Then he said:

> I believe that trying to hide behind a political defence of 'I did not know' is not appropriate in my case because in many instances I did not want to know … although direct orders to kill political opponents were never issued, speeches were made by members of the NP that created a climate for serious transgressions. I had suspicions about certain activities which caused discomfort in official circles. Because I did not have the facts to substantiate my suspicions, I must confess, I only whispered in the corridors. We managed the security forces poorly. (Wessels 2020: 267)

In his autobiographies, he admits to being one of those ministers congratulated for his rousing speeches. Wessels' galling reference to apartheid as a 'mistake' – also before the TRC – is part of the discourse that de Klerk is most known for: that apartheid was undertaken with 'good intentions' to manage the social complexities of South Africa (p 234). As Wessels the lawyer denies intention and therefore carefully evades culpability as former Deputy Minister, this position also suppresses the fact of apartheid as exploitative, violent, and justified by an ideology of racial inferiority, again an example of whiteness as wilful unknowing.

Wessels managed his role as member of the apartheid executive by asserting that he had acted lawfully in relation to the 1983 Constitution, which is why he did not apply for amnesty to the TRC because he 'juridically' had nothing to answer for, but he later conceded that his actions would not stand a constitutional test in democratic South Africa (Wessels 2010: 213, 307). His reason for appearing before the TRC seems to contradict this idea of apartheid as legal and therefore legitimate, as he testified out of a sense of 'public responsibility to explain the *wrongs* of that era to the TRC' (p 307, emphasis added). In the late 1990s, he and Roelf Meyer, also a former NJMS chairperson, were accused by an anonymous security force official in the Afrikaans press that they knew more than they were willing to admit. Wessels' retort was that he would take co-responsibility if any official was charged on the basis of a decision taken in the NJMS during his period as chairperson. Such a prosecution never transpired (Wessels 2020: 309). As chairperson of the NJMS, he was once told by an official:

> 'you ask so many questions in the meetings you chair. One day you will get an answer and then you will never be able to say you didn't know.' The comment was a puzzle that I did not pay much attention to … I didn't even think it was a warning that illegal things were happening … [W]e were not involved in illegal [actions] but stopping a revolutionary onslaught. We did not want to abdicate but to ensure that right and order would be maintained for a new [negotiated] constitutional dispensation … and not unilaterally with an AK-47. With this, the security management system helped excellently. (Wessels 2010: 213–14)

Here, he defiantly reasserts the NP *realpolitik* of the time: that the NP government used its security apparatus to manage the situation with a view to achieving their own, as opposed to their opponents', aims.

Wessels denies direct instruction or knowledge of killings: 'I still don't believe that the SSC where I served for 18 months – or any other SSC – would have approved the atrocities that were unearthed by the TRC' (Wessels 2020: 197). But he admits to being among those who facilitated the abuses while avoiding knowledge of the violence necessitated by continued apartheid enforcement:

> [W]e did create the atmosphere which provided the umbrella for these wicked, gruesome deeds. The truth is we – collectively and individually – were not sufficiently inquisitive to establish what was actually happening on the ground. It was easy to look away when 'our people' were involved in human rights abuses. (p 197)

He admits sitting in NP study groups where participants laughed

> when we were informed that a terrorist received a few slaps in the face because he was cheeky. Tongue in cheek it was told how they 'were worked over'. It was admissible. If this did not have the desired result he would receive more 'medicine' – stronger this time. All this resulted in the disgraceful transgressions that were disclosed to our shame. (Wessels 2010: 305)

He could have done more with his powers as Deputy Minister (2010: 213) to get to the bottom of accusations. When Botha publicly attacked Wessels about this admission before the TRC submission, Wessels (2020: 316) countered in the press that he had reported security force abuses to Botha four times during 1985–1990 and also to the NP caucus.

In the qualified declaration of accountability that Wessels, as a political figure, contributes to the ongoing debate about apology, one sees a delineation between types of knowledges about apartheid that speaks to whiteness. In a sleight of hand to avoid culpability as a senior NP politician, Wessels moves away from the TRC focus on government brutalities to interrogate the everyday unknowing that is constitutive of whiteness. His repeated 'ought to have known' apology is here read as admitting to Afrikaner whiteness as constituted through not knowing about what it took to sustain apartheid because of *opting* not to know. This is a white position akin to that of many Germans after 1945 regarding the Holocaust: 'those who are unaware know enough to know that they prefer not to know any more' (Geras 1998: 35). While Wessels argues that this position was not only that of the general white public but also shared by government figures, he takes it further to interrogate the agency of white people in the reproduction of apartheid itself. Eventually, Wessels (2020: 308) shifts to saying that he should also have told the TRC what he had told News24 in 2020:

> I might not have pulled the trigger on Anton Lubowski or sent the letter bomb which led to the unspeakable murder of Abram Tiro but it is for my account. You can say, as many do, 'look, I wasn't in politics then' or 'I wasn't involved in that' and 'don't be angry at me because I didn't kill him.' It's crap. I was an Afrikaner, I was a nationalist, the whole thing is on me. It is for my account.

While he limits his culpability as a politician to a narrow legalistic frame of what was legal under late apartheid laws, he conversely also extends it to confront his liability as a white person, an Afrikaner, and an Afrikaner nationalist. Answerability becomes a shared responsibility that Afrikaners and particularly Afrikaner nationalists carry for apartheid.

This sharing of responsibility could be read as an opportunistic ploy to divert attention from his own culpability, but it does allow for a reckoning with the production of whiteness in its ethnic Afrikaner form: intentional and intensified machinations of knowing and unknowing to constitute a narrowing lifeworld that ultimately gave rise to apartheid. This self-reflection mirrors an image that is horrifying at times, for example the tale relayed above about NP study group meetings' sadistic collective pleasure in jokes and hints about the torture of black people. The figure of the state functionary in the violent 1980s is captured by a nightmare vision that an experienced civil servant invokes on Wessels' first day as Deputy Minister.

Warning him about information from the security community or public service commission, the civil servant said: '[T]hey will spin their stories around you until you look like a mummy with just your mouth sticking out. Then they can feed you with a little teaspoon just what they want, and you will swallow everything' (Wessels 2010: 213). This cocooned figure, with only its mouth sticking out, serves as an apt metaphor for whiteness itself: a seemingly protective cocoon that does not harbour a chrysalis but a mummy, turning the subject into a consuming but dead and shrivelled larva. Wessels realises that 'I was in the system, I was the system, and I allowed that I be spun into a ball' (p 215). In the Wessels narrative, the intense kinship that he feels with other Afrikaners traps him in a cocoon. At first trained as a police officer, like his father, Wessels felt the police to be 'like family'. Belonging and knowledge converged: 'Tightly spun, I believed everything I was told … And you defend your family. You stand by them, because you believe them' (Wessels 2010: 216). He remains loyal to the 'highly competent and pleasant people that served the state … I will defend their honour' (p 213). His insistence on shared responsibility could be read in the context of the delightful togetherness with other Afrikaners, which acts from the start as an obstacle to any ethical reckoning with apartheid actions and effects.

Over the years, Wessels is increasingly forced to confront the implications of Afrikaner kinship, as he recurrently revisits how it was possible not to know, setting out over and again how ignorance is constructed as a bedrock of whiteness from the everyday to the heights of apartheid securocracy. After he was confronted about apartheid on his first trip to Europe in the 1960s, his 'feeling of uncertainty' caused by the conversations abroad 'quickly disappeared in the pleasure of socialising among my own people' (p 107). His commitment to believing everything he was told runs like a calcified vein through his narrative: as a young apartheid supporter 'just mov[ing] within the Afrikaner herd', he felt they 'had all the answers. There were no questions, because we had no questions, because we were not allowed to have any questions' (p 102). While holding leadership positions as President of the Student Representative Council and the *Afrikaner-Studentebond*, he was among those who 'built so many obstacles around us' to prevent 'open conversation' (p 114). The *Afrikaner-Studentebond*, or Afrikaner Students' League, was the Afrikaner nationalist alternative to the 'reviled' National Union of South African Students (NUSAS). Elected to the Transvaal provincial council, he aimed to learn as much of the 'practical politics, policy and organisation while *keeping my mouth shut*' (p 130, emphasis added). Later, as a member of parliament, he held the position that he was adequately informed and would take responsibility for his decisions without having to accept 'advice' (p 140). The TRC process ripped through the cocoon of unknowing: no longer in power and without the generals and his cabinet colleagues, he was 'alone':

> the most frightening thought was: what will my children think? … Is this my dad? Is this what he kept himself busy with? How could he not have known of this? … I was worried, not about anything I had done, but about that which I did not know about, but should have known about. (pp 266–7)

A white person is confronted with the moral wreckage of studiously maintained ignorance.

Wessels' first apology in 1990 upended the unremembering and forced the revisiting of all the repetitions of unknowing in a self-confrontation that intensified over time. He comes to grapple with racism, as he challenges himself, and Afrikaners and white people generally, to recognise their agency in responding to racialisation: 'The problem of who you are, who you were and who you want to be in a racial context can be approached from different angles' (Wessels 2020: 360). Such confrontation unravelled the kinship strands of the cocoon: with the adoption of the final Constitution in 1996, he identifies with the rejoicing Assembly Chairperson, Cyril Ramaphosa, and not his sombre NP colleagues. He links their heavy faces with an incident in 1987 in his ward of Krugersdorp where fellow churchgoers shouted at him to 'put forward your policy, k-boetie': 'After that, they were no longer "my people" … To be called a traitor by that camp is an honorary title' (p 282). His relationships with the security establishment went the same way (p 334). Years later, in 2014, he headed an independent team on the institutional culture of his alma mater, North West University, of which the findings brought a fundamental break with 'old friends' who he 'had travelled with for many years' (p 388). His investigation into initiation rites that included Nazi-like salutes uncovered an 'inhospitable' space that enforced a form of Afrikaner conformism that 'stripped students of their individuality, identity and human dignity, and … forc[ed] them to function only as a group' (p 386). Wessels had come full circle to confront his own experience as a student during the height of apartheid at the same university. He had shifted to new forms of kinship not on the basis of skin pigmentation, language, or religion, but on 'an inclusive South Africanism', with space for Afrikaners but not for 'Afrikaner arrogance' (p 388).

Wessels' apologies made him answerable to the Other, as the confrontation with white unknowing opened up his identification. From having 'no questions because we had all the answers', he is compelled to wrestle with his apartheid thinking. Breaking through the delusion of white respectability to expose the moral corruption at the heart of whiteness, he finally recognises the system's inhumanity, brutality, crudeness, and immorality (pp 312, 356). The repetitive revisiting of sites of South Africans' wounding, over and again, adapts his position to understanding it 'is a different world when you swap vantage points … It also helps to be inquisitive about the dreams and fears of your interlocutors. You don't have to abandon who you are but it certainly helps to understand that your skin pigmentation doesn't propel you to the centre of the universe – you are not the be all and end all of humankind' (p 369). He has to accept the humanity of the abjected black Other, the stirrings of which started when he felt a 'great missing' after the death of South African Students' Organisation (SASO) leader, Abram Tiro, in 1974, with whom he had become friendly as a student (2010: 121). Tiro was killed with a letter bomb while in exile in Botswana. Recalling his visit to the site of the massacre at Sharpeville as a child with his father, he remembers wondering whether the police officers' fear had led to the death toll. He notices that 'I never thought of the fear of the crowd … My father and I never tried to put ourselves in anybody else's shoes than those of the policemen. They were *our* people …' (p 106, emphasis in original). Facing racism's hierarchy of humanity is intrinsic to Wessels' shift. Discussing de Klerk's prevarication on apartheid as a crime against humanity, Wessels draws it back to kinship and 'the fear of going against your own people, of being excommunicated'. In de Klerk's case, his 'biggest fear is to be branded as having repudiated his father' (p 312). De Klerk 'grew up sheltered and isolated … in ministerial homes', with his father, Jan de Klerk, a minister in H.F. Verwoerd's cabinet and his uncle, J.G. Strijdom, a former Prime Minister. 'He never saw the cruelties of the Group Areas Act and Mixed Marriages Act' (p 312).

Cracking through the unknowing of whiteness demands an ongoing confrontation with racism, particularly one's own. The shame Wessels felt over Tiro and before the TRC (2010: 113) also struck him again '[d]eep into democracy, [when] it dawned on me that I was still looking at human beings through my racially tinted glasses. I was embarrassed!' (2020: 357): 'I battle to exorcise my own racial prejudices every day […] You never arrive because you never stop learning about your own hidden prejudices and the vulnerabilities of *your other*' (p 358, emphasis in original). Similar to Gobodo-Madikizela and Krog, Wessels is concerned about continuation in racialisation bedevilling possibilities for mutual humanisation: 'Our society is saturated with racial prejudice. The easiest part of the anti-racism campaign was the expunging of racism from our Apartheid statute books. The real challenge is to purge racial prejudice from our daily interactions with each other and to realise there is a racial sting to our inequality' (p 369). Indeed, racism 'will not let go as long as the disfigurement of inequality remains unresolved' (p 370). While noting the argument that colour blindness does not address the social reality of race-inflected inequality, he contends that on the back of 'inbred racism', race has become a 'commodity' accepted 'with glee' by 'new beneficiaries of racial classification' (pp 364–5).

As unresolved and still racially modulated socioeconomic pressures bear down on most South Africans, Wessels admits that the moment of apology passed 26 years ago – at the transition. When a journalist in a media interview serves up one of the embittered white right's favoured stereotypes of what black South Africans expect of whites, Wessels reflects on the changed political landscape for apologies. To the journalist's question of whether white people should be 'on their knees', asking forgiveness with their 'chequebooks at the ready', Wessels counters:

> there can be no future without an understanding of the past … [T]he time for pleading for forgiveness for the past has come and gone. The sulking and carefully formulated apologies of the past did not always impress and often fell well short – they are noted now as chances that have been trifled away. To cast a rich man's chequebook into the fray is simplistic and will not buy the intended positive outcome. What our fellow countrymen have longed for is an admission that Apartheid scorched our land, that we recognise it and that we want to join in building a better future together, as equal partners. Charity that is not offered with the right attitude and in all sincerity will disappear into a bottomless pit. (p 371)

Because of Wessels' position at the heights of apartheid securocracy, he shows how whiteness as an epistemology of ignorance worked throughout the social body to suppress the fact of apartheid's brutalisation. This was enabled by the denial of racialised Others' humanity, who could not be brutalised as they were cast as less than human. Hence, this particularist whiteness, inflected by a morally stifling and sadistic kinship, allowed Afrikaners to pull the wool over their own eyes, fixing them fast in a nightmarish cocoon. While Wessels' arguments about the legality of his actions under apartheid seem self-serving in obviating his own culpability, he, unlike most of his former colleagues, does not bow out of answerability as a white person, an Afrikaner, and an Afrikaner nationalist. Turning now to Krog, we see someone who adopted an anti-apartheid stance but still counts herself as responsible because of her Afrikanerhood.

Antjie Krog: apology as a release from whiteness

Poet, author, and journalist Antjie Krog represents 'arguably the most visible postapartheid white imagination on contemporary South Africa', given the national and international popular and critical acclaim for her work (Gqola 2010: 107). She was already celebrated for her extensive oeuvre of Afrikaans poetry before she achieved global recognition for *Country of My Skull* (1998), a creative mix of journalism, poetry, and fiction with an autobiographical slant, seeking to record and reflect on testimonies before the TRC. That was followed by *Change of Tongue* (2003) and *Begging to Be Black* (2009) to form a trilogy of works inventively blending fictional and non-fictional elements to ruminate on South Africa's postcolonial complexities in her 'attempt to understand what we say and have said about ourselves and others in the long conversation between black and white in this country' (Krog 2009: vii). Politically she has been regarded as an Afrikaner dissident. She attracted outrage from the Afrikaner nationalist establishment as an 18-year-old first-time poet for her 'blasphemous, communist and immoral' poems, published while still at school in 1970 (Visagie 2014: ix). Whiteness appears as a complex theme in her work from the very start. In her first collection of poems, titled *Dogter van Jefta* (Daughter of Jeftha), she conjures South Africa as a tiny thorn tree outside the biblical city Nineveh, in the poem *Buite Nineve* (Outside Nineveh). The thorns are white and apart, and it has 'a small Europe / in its Africa' (Krog 2004: 14, lines 4–5, own translation). Against those wishing for the demise of the tree, the narrator undertakes to sing songs and pray for the tree, because 'wherever I may sleep / I remain *your* thorn / I remain white' (Krog 2004: 14, lines 13–15, emphasis in original, own translation). The poem suggests that South African whiteness is a double bind, with white people compelled to provide succour to apartheid's racial order due to their insistence on maintaining their Europeanness with a prickly apartness from their Africa context. Whiteness is an intractable thorn in the side of South Africa, because the white subject finds her *raison d'être* in claiming both whiteness and South Africanness. The poem also foreshadows postapartheid debates about white belonging in South Africa and the (im)possibility of escaping whiteness.

In *Country of My Skull*, Krog does not merely report on the testimonies before the TRC but her 'authorial narrator embraces her role as chronicler of the past' as being about snatching testimonies from the 'death of forgetfulness' (Lütge Coullie 2014a: 3). Krog's work is criticised as misusing the testimonies of apartheid victims as mere 'backdrop' to her self-reflection on white and Afrikaner identity (see Gqola 2010). Others point out that the confessional sections form a relatively minor part of the work and that Krog grapples intensely with the ethics of attempting to represent such pain (Lütge Coullie 2014a). Krog bears witness in an attempt to bring individual memories of apartheid trauma into national remembrance (pp 5–6). The incorporation of victims' painful recollections into the narrator's documented memory renders them part of the readers' memories (p 4). In this attempt, which speaks to humanisation and mutual recognition in the face of apartheid dehumanisation of black people, she does not seek 'easy closure through artificial mourning' (Graham 2003: 25). Hence, she avoids 'solipsistic moral relativism' and instead uses literary innovations to conjure apartheid's human damages in the form of multiple experiences, acknowledging the insufficiency of language to represent trauma fully (p 23). Her later work, *There Was this Goat: Investigating the Truth Commission Testimony of Notrose Nobomvu Konile* (2009), co-authored with Nosisi Mpolweni and Kopano Ratele, springs from her problematisation of her own apparent inability to serve as a witness to Konile's narrative. Konile, one of the mothers of the Gugulethu Seven killed by apartheid security police, presented for Krog an incoherent testimony. She feels compelled to revisit it in *There Was this Goat*, as a self-examination of her own unwitting racism; it is part of her 'socio-political quest' to inhabit an African perspective, to achieve a fuller knowledge of the Other (Lütge Coullie 2014b: 315, 317). This quest to understand is a challenge to white ignorance, which Krog also captures in her interview with anti-apartheid activist Deborah Matshoba. Matshoba describes her frustration with white people who

> don't know that we only started having a democratic vote in 1994 … Oh really! Were you oppressed? Were you arrested? We did not know that! You could not be placed in a managerial position? You were in jail? Why? They do not know that they kept the National Party in power. (Krog 2003: 157)

Krog is slated for presenting

> the changing white subject [as] an insecure and somewhat passive one in its engagements with its historic Other; although provocative to imagined Afrikaner readers, it awaits invitation from Black people. … Krog's narrating subject insecurely addresses white audiences as she calls them to question and revisit older ways of being white/Afrikaner. However, her Other is an invented, all-powerful, active collective with the responsibility to invite her to a sense of belonging to the imagined country. (Gqola 2010: 108)

In Critical Whiteness Studies, this approach is regarded as a decentring of whiteness, in this case particularly Afrikaner whiteness. *Country of My Skull* is dedicated to 'every victim who had an Afrikaner surname on her lips'. Krog puts 'the victims of state violence, most of whom were black or coloured, at the center of her project' (Graham 2003: 21). She relentlessly reflects on whiteness in relation to its Other, thereby exposing and making highly visible an otherwise normalised centre point of oppressive power. This deconstructing and subverting confrontation includes her stepping up to interrogate her feelings of kinship with the perpetrators. She confronts her whiteness and her Afrikanerness, 'drag[ging] the corpse of white skin and Afrikaner tongue behind her' (Krog 2003: 169).

Krog's questioning of the penultimate apartheid president P.W. Botha's defiance of the TRC places lack of repentance at the heart of apartheid whiteness. Under his government in the late 1980s, she writes, '[a]partheid rule acquired its coldest, its most brutal and murderous edge' (Krog 1998: 267). Krog places P.W. Botha centrally as the engineer of extra-legal 'vicious oppression' (p 268). His refusal to appear before the TRC personified the 'unrepentant white rulers of yesterday, ensconced in so much financial and political privilege' (p 267). She recounts a press conference after Botha's court appearance on criminal charges, for failing to present himself to the TRC after being summonsed to do so. She asked him in person whether he would apologise. He 'snaps' at her: 'For what?' In response, she listed cross-border raids and death squads before he interrupted her with the defiant statement 'I don't apologise … I *pray* for them' (p 271, emphasis in original). She looked into the 'flat, mud-coloured surfaces of his eyes, grotesquely enlarged by his glasses' and thought, 'we have been governed by this stupidity for decades' (p 271). She tried to find a mental pathway to him: 'A link. An Afrikaner connection of a kind. No. I can still find common ground with those who are battling to deal with a dramatically changed order, with our part in the past – but with this swaggering fool there is nothing' (p 271). She mocked his public moniker as the *Groot Krokodil* (Big Crocodile), enjoying the 'uplifting thought' that 'he doesn't govern, thank God, the crawling, trotting, occasionally gliding crocodile, pushing itself along with its arrogant tail, does not *govern* anymore' (p 271).

Country of My Skull ends with an untitled poem about how the TRC created a 'flame of hope' (Krog 1998: 278) as the country that used to lie between South Africans, and in the process became wounded, now lies 'within' (p 278, lines 2–3). The TRC taught her to see more expansively after being 'scorched a new skin' by 'a thousand stories' (p 279, lines 13–15). She was 'changed forever', prompting her to say: 'forgive me / forgive me / forgive me / You whom I have wronged, please / take me / with you' (lines 16–22). Hence, Krog admits her own guilt due to the spoils of whiteness, shared by people racialised as white – even if they were active against apartheid and whiteness. In her poem *Litany* (pp 264–5), she takes apart whiteness and shows the dread within, obscured by its falsely claimed respectability: '[T]he long white shadow' once ran along 'white lustre and honour' but has been revealed to have 'the past in its teeth', which was 'a time of assassin and shame'. Krog captures white ignorance with this horror-invoking phrase: 'my past crawls forth on its deadly knees without once looking up' (p 264, line 8). The poem ends with her wishing to be set free from 'the long white scar lichen and ash', and 'into remorse' (p 265, lines 26–27). To be released into remorse is to be freed from whiteness with all of its violent horrors.

For Krog, memory stands central to mutual humanisation. She shares Gobodo-Madikizela and Wessels' concern about amnesia causing reactive repetition of racialisation, with concomitant violence. In *A Change of Tongue*, she recounts an interaction with a black computer technician that casts a critical light on her quest (Krog 2003). The technician notices the text on her computer, which includes observations made during a trip to Rwanda about the genocide, the South African War of 1899–1902 and its effects on Afrikaners, and an interview with an anti-apartheid activist. An interaction ensues, with the technician questioning her *'vroetel-ing'* (fiddling) with the past: 'why don't you forget, like the whole country is forgetting, and start afresh?' (p 153). She counters, in an echo with Wessels, that if 'you don't know where things come from, you won't be able to deal with them'. She would not be able to understand the prevalent violence and 'moral chaos'. He retorts that her only 'valid reason' for remembering is to create 'moral immunity' for herself, to do as she pleases, justified by her own background of suffering and by recording the suffering that apartheid caused. Moreover, he resents the humiliation of the older generation of black people, who are 'too soft with your kind'; he wishes for 'a country without whites' (p 154). Her response to him:

> You want whites out of the way so that you can forget the past. And certainly before you know you will be the heavy racists towards coloureds and Indians – or should they also leave the country so long? The answer is not in forgetting or ignoring the past, because you run the risk of becoming a racist yourself and creating a future that is no better than the past against which you fought. You become like a drug addict whose memory has been destroyed. Because he can't remember, he can't imagine a new kind of life. (Krog 2003: 154)

Her disdainful stance towards the politics of revenge as a dead end is confirmed in her poem *colonialism of a special kind* (Krog 2020: 125). The poem's title refers to the South African Communist Party's description of South Africa as a special kind of colonial state in Africa, the settlers never having left. The transitional politics of forgiveness and reconciliation was a response to this 'special' colonialism, for enemies to find a way of living together, to use Gobodo-Madikizela's phrasing. The poem describes the deterioration in the imaginary of forgiveness over time, as white racism and denial flare up and invoke black shame over forgiveness amid socioeconomic injustice. In response, South Africans turn to rage, hatred, and revenge.

Krog's project of knowing splices open the horror of apartheid whiteness, constituted as it was through the denial of black people's humanity. Far from centring whiteness, as she has been accused of doing, Krog relentlessly keeps whiteness in view to ensure that the losses of black victims do not become perpetrator-less crimes. She does not allow her reader to forget the relationality between black and white, forcing particularly her white reader into a reckoning with their own complicity in the white unknowing intrinsic to apartheid's dehumanisation of black people. Krog confronts her own racism and demands the same of Afrikaners and whites generally. By foregrounding racial relationality, her work also asks the difficult question: what do you do with the 'special colonialists', the still-settled settlers, of South Africa? One answer is apology, as a pathway out of unknowing and thus out of whiteness. It is the opposite of the murderous, reptilian morality of a white supremacist figure such as P.W. Botha, who eschewed apology. Proffering apology goes alongside her problematisation of revenge discourses, as Gobodo-Madikizela and Wessels also do. Krog's work suggests that subjects racialised as white should be salvageable if humanisation is to be fully pursued, with white people's apologies for the violences of race and racism an essential step.

Conclusion

With its focus on perpetrators rather than beneficiaries of apartheid, the TRC inadvertently set up a false division between apartheid state brutalities and the everyday reproduction of apartheid violences. The latter was excluded from consideration, despite its insidious contribution to the dehumanisation of racialised others. This knowledge division allows many white South Africans to conflate lack of knowledge about state brutalities with ignorance about generalised apartheid wrongs, including micro-level, intersubjective injustices. Claiming ignorance about the social wreckage in the wake of white domination demands a concerted unknowing, which is constitutive of whiteness. Unknowing facilitates white people pleading innocence and therefore as not responsible for racial injustice. By turning away from or denying the damages done, recognition of black people's humanity is also withdrawn, illustrated by the white denial that apartheid was a crime against humanity.

Apology provides a way out. Reconciliation with concomitant apology has been discredited as exoneration and hence a denial of justice, but it is argued here that remorse requires the white subject to overturn the individual and collective mechanisms of unknowing. This allows white subjects to confront not only extreme violations but also the everyday dehumanisations of racialisation and racism. Therefore, apology demands of the white subject to break through unknowing, which is epistemologically how whiteness is constituted. Three figures, Leon Wessels, Antjie Krog, and Eugene de Kock, the latter as interpreted by Gobodo-Madikizela, are analysed in this chapter as exemplars of how apology disrupts whiteness. Divergently situated as they are, they represent a strand of thinking that comes out of the transitional period, which emphasises mutual humanisation through reconciliation. Wessels' and Krog's painstaking work through Afrikaner whiteness shows how apology demands recognition of apartheid as unjust, which in turn compels the humanisation of black people. Racism is necessarily confronted, as the notion of an inherent superiority to whiteness is confronted as false. Apology therefore opens the door to the white subject assuming responsibility to undo the damages of racism, whether institutionalised or intersubjective in everyday settings. The damages of colonialism and apartheid extend to white people too: both Wessels and Krog revert to nightmarish metaphors as they wrestle with the horrors of apartheid whiteness. These insights align with Gobodo-Madikizela's position that a mutual humanisation of black and white people is required, partly to prevent racism from being reproduced in newly violent guises. Gobodo-Madikizela's analysis shows de Kock to have been dehumanised as he dehumanised black people. But her argument for mutual humanisation does not amount to the exoneration of white people; instead, it asks of white people to take up responsibility for the redress of apartheid legacies. She arrives at this position from the vantage point that '[p]hilosophical questions can and should give way and be subsumed to human questions, for in the end we are a society of people and not of ideas, a fragile web of interdependent humans, not of stances' (2004: 125). Gobodo-Madikizela is therefore advocating for adopting a position contrary to the Western frame of whiteness which, as I describe above, privileges ideas over (some) human life. This goes a long way towards answering Mbembe's (2011: 194) call for the 'acute ... need to experiment with new forms of ethical relations': to reimagine democracy not just as human mutuality and freedom but as a community of life. The need for new ethical forms of sociality is particularly acute in South Africa, with apology an essential component.

Reflections

Scarcely into democracy, an Afrikaans song was released with a title along the lines of 'Ons gaan nie meer jammer sê nie' (We won't apologise anymore). I was surprised. Who are the 'we' who have had enough of saying sorry? Apart from the few qualified apologies by Afrikaner politicians, white people and particularly Afrikaners apologising for apartheid were not really a feature of public life in South Africa. Indeed, the discourse of reconciliation and forgiveness seemed frequently to be missing the first step, the step before black people could consider any forgiveness and reconciliation: expressions of remorse from white people. By the 2000s, many Afrikaners wanted to enter the blissful white state of not needing to regret the wreckage left in the wake of their programme of social elevation and enrichment of themselves at the expense of everybody else living in this place. They wanted to un-know the damage of the intensified colonial system called apartheid. Those 46 years were already being repackaged in glossy, sepia-tinted nostalgia products by the newly burgeoning Afrikaans media and creative arts and crafts sectors. Why in such a hurry to forget? The obvious answer is to avoid reparations, particularly the redistribution of wealth. The less apparent answer, because of the optical trick that is whiteness, is that they would have to face the terror of their own culture. But I cannot but *remember*, growing up in Boksburg, east of Johannesburg, in the 1970s and 1980s. Physical violence, sexual violence, humiliation, hurt – everything it took to keep subjects obedient within Afrikanerdom, starting with the family. Antjie Krog's description of 'my past crawls forth on its deadly knees without once looking up' gets to the horror of what Afrikaner denial enabled and continues to enable. Pumla Gobodo-Madikizela captures this in her work on apartheid assassin Eugene de Kock, a contemporary of my parents who went to the same school as them in Boksburg. I was surprised to find Leon Wessels, who had the opposite experience of being an Afrikaner to me, providing a nightmarish vision of a cocooned figure spun tightly into submission, with only an ever-consuming mouth sticking out. He was describing becoming a National Party minister, but this metaphor strikes at the heart of Afrikaner identity. How can we tear through the silky, sticky strings of whiteness? Apology must be part of it, because it reinstates the suppressed relationality with the co-constitutive other that whiteness denies. It is one of the steps for us to take to become human. Perhaps we can then find the humans around us.

Christi

References

De Klerk, F. W., 2021, 'Text of de Klerk's video message to South Africa', *Reuters*, 11 November, viewed 14 February 2022 from www.reuters.com/world/africa/text-de-klerks-video-message-south-africa-2021-11-11/

Deutsche Welle, 2020, 'Namibia rejects Germany's reparations offer for genocide', 12 October, viewed 5 March 2020 from www.dw.com/en/namibia-germany-reparations/a-54535589

Etheridge, J., 2020, 'FW de Klerk Foundation apologises to SA, agrees apartheid was a crime against humanity', *News24*, viewed 15 January 2020 from www.news24.com/SouthAfrica/News/fw-de-klerk-foundation-withdraws-apartheid-statement-apologises-to-sa-20200217

Fairbanks, E., 2014, '"I have sinned against the lord and against you! Will you forgive me?"', *The New Republic*, 19 June, viewed 15 January 2020 from https://newrepublic.com/article/118135/adriaan-vlok-ex-apartheid-leader-washes-feet-and-seeks-redemption

Geras, N., 1998, *The Contract of Mutual Indifference: Political Philosophy After The Holocaust*, New York: Verson.

Gerber, J., 2020, 'Notion that apartheid is a crime against humanity is Soviet propaganda meant to agitate – FW de Klerk Foundation', *News24*, viewed 15 January 2020 from www.news24.com/news24/SouthAfrica/News/notion-that-apartheid-is-a-crime-against-humanity-is-soviet-propaganda-meant-to-agitate-fw-de-klerk-foundation-20200214

Gobodo-Madikizela, P., 2004, *A Human Being Died that Night: A Story of Forgiveness*, Claremont: David Philip.

Gqola, P. D., 2010, *What Is Slavery to Me? Poscolonial/Slave Memory in Post-Apartheid South Africa*, Johannesburg: Wits University Press.

Graham, S., 2003, 'The Truth Commission and post-apartheid literature in South Africa', *Research in African Literatures* 34(1), 11–30.

Krog, A., 1998, *Country of My Skull*, Johannesburg: Random House.

Krog, A., 2003, *A Change of Tongue*, Johannesburg: Random House.

Krog, A., 2004, 'Buite Ninevé', *Eerste Gedigte*, Cape Town: Human & Rousseau.

Krog, A., 2005, *'n Ander Tongval*, Cape Town: Tafelberg.

Krog, A., 2009, *Begging to Be Black*, Cape Town: Random House Struik.

Krog, A., 2020, *'n Vry Vrou. Gedigte van Antjie Krog*, Cape Town: Human & Rousseau.

Krog, A., Mpolweni-Zantsi, N. L., and Ratele, K., 2009, *There Was this Goat: Investigating the Truth Commission Testimony of Notrose Nobomvu Konile*, Pietermaritzburg: University of KwaZulu-Natal Press.

Lalu, P., 2009, *The Deaths of Hintsa: Postapartheid South Africa and the Shape of Recurring Pasts*, Pretoria: HSRC Press.

Lütge Coullie, J., 2014a, 'Remembering to forget: testimony, collective memory and the genesis of the "new" South African nation', in J. Lütge Coullie and A. Visagie (eds.), *Antjie Krog: An Ethics of Body and Otherness*, pp 1–23, Scottsville: University of KwaZulu-Natal Press.

Lütge Coullie, J., 2014b, 'A question of ethics', in *There Was this Goat: Investigating the Truth Commission Testimony of Notrose Nobomvu Konile'*, in J. Lütge Coullie and A. Visagie (eds.), *Antjie Krog: An Ethics of Body and Otherness*, pp 212–331, Scottsville: University of KwaZulu-Natal Press.

Mamdani, M., 1996, 'Reconciliation without justice', *Southern African Review of Books* 46, 3–5.

Mbembe, A., 2011, 'Democracy as a community of life', in J. W. De Gruchy (ed.), *The Humanist Imperative in South Africa*, pp 187–94, Stellenbosch: SUN Press.

Mills, C. W., 2007, 'White ignorance', in S. Sullivan and N. Tuana (eds.), *Race and Epistemologies of Ignorance*, pp 11–38, Albany: State University of New York Press.

Milo D., 2007, 'Of reputation, interdicts and freedom of speech: defaming Eugene de Kock', *Without Prejudice* 7(10), 14.

Posel, D., 2001, 'What's in a name? Racial categorisations under apartheid and their afterlife', *Transformation* 47, 50–74.

Steyn, M., 2012, 'The ignorance contract: recollections of apartheid childhoods and the construction of epistemologies of ignorance', *Identities* 19(1), 8–25.

Van der Westhuizen, C., 2007, *White Power & the Rise and Fall of the National Party*, Cape Town: Zebra Press.

Van der Westhuizen, C., 2016, 'Rejuvenating reconciliation with transformation', in K. Lefko-Everett, R. Govender, and D. Foster (eds.), *Rethinking Reconciliation: Evidence from South Africa*, pp 168–92, Cape Town: HSRC Press.

Van der Westhuizen, C., 2017, *Sitting Pretty: White Afrikaans Women in Postapartheid South Africa*, Scottsville: UKZN Press.

Van der Westhuizen, C., 2021, 'FW de Klerk: the last apartheid president was driven by pragmatism, not idealism', *The Conversation*, 11 November, viewed 14 February 2022 from https://theconversation.com/fw-de-klerk-the-last-apartheid-president-was-driven-by-pragmatism-not-idealism-164026

Visagie, A., 2014, 'Preface', in J. Lütge Coullie and A. Visagie (eds.), *Antjie Krog: An Ethics of Body and Otherness*, pp vii–xv, Scottsville: University of KwaZulu-Natal Press.

Wessels, L., 2010, *Vereeniging: Die Onvoltooide Vrede*, Cape Town: Umuzi.

Wessels, L., 2020, *Encountering Apartheid's Ghosts: From Krugersdorp to Constitution Hill*, Cape Town: Naledi.

9

(Re)Collections: Her Sorry, Never Mine

Diane Jefthas

I am back in my corner and I feel their eyes.

They watch me.

It happens every time. For those first few minutes while we wait, our backs to them, they're looking. At me, at her, at us. In judgment. And it stops only when they've had their fill, whispered their words, thought their thoughts. Only after they've drawn their conclusions and focused on their next target.

I wonder if she notices them. Can she also feel them looking the way I can? Does she also tingle the way I do?

She likes this spot. It's where she chooses to stand whenever we visit. Maybe she thinks it hides us. Maybe she thinks it hides me.

I cannot yet reach the surface. If I stand on my toes and extend my arms, the tips of my fingers can touch the edge. She doesn't like when I do that. I must face forwards, she says. I must stand still.

And so, I do. I face forwards and I stand still as she waits for someone to speak to her. For someone to listen to the story she has to tell them.

The minutes pass and I know the second I am forgotten. The second I become invisible, to both Mommy and them. The man I can't see starts talking, his voice deep and booming right above me. Mommy is answering, her words spoken softly as she leans forward, closer to the man, further away from the row of silent souls sitting side by side on the creaking bench behind us.

And because I am forgotten, because I am invisible, I am free to follow the adventure unfolding before me.

I too have been watching. Not the people, but the ants.

There are three of them travelling the dusty strip where the dirt-stained wall meets the side of the wooden desk. Two of them are in the lead and move quickly, so close together they seem almost like one. They're bigger than the third ant, the slower one, trying to follow them. He is not catching up and if he doesn't move faster, they will make the turn up ahead without him. They're nearly there. Will they stop and wait for him? Will he know which way they've gone if they don't?

I think I know where they're going. And if he goes the wrong way, maybe I'll help him. Because maybe they're a family. And maybe he's only the baby.

I trace their path but see no others. I search the wall, the desk, the floor, but no one's in front and no one's following. It's just these three. The bubble gum is theirs. Two pieces, stuck beneath the ledge, one a dull white, the other a bright pink. The pink piece is new. It wasn't here last time. And it looks fresh, still a little wet.

I wonder who put it there. Another child? Someone like me?

That's the piece they'll want, not the hard, white piece that won't have any sweetness left.

The leader ant continues on, nearing the intersection, as the second one falls behind. Then that second one stops, turns, and veers off the path they'd been following. Now, going in the opposite direction, further away from the other two, it gets ever closer to a spiky crack in the pitted wall.

Will it go in? And if it does, will it find its way out again?

It travels on and when it reaches the hole it slows and turns first to one side and then the other, as though checking whether it's safe to proceed. I watch but wonder if I should do something. Pick it up and make it go back? Place it on the original path? Perhaps closer to the baby? Or maybe nearer to where the bigger one now crawls?

Can they see each other? Are they aware that those with them have gotten lost? Do they know that they are now travelling alone?

Checking the lead ant's progress, I see that I was right. The bubble gum is the destination. But only for him. He has arrived and is now exploring his find.

There is no more hope for the baby. He has completely lost his way and I am too late to provide my help. Going at an angle and moving faster than before, he is now at a height I cannot ever reach.

When I look back to the crack, ant number two, so close to its edge only seconds ago, is no longer there. And when I again search on the opposite end, I see that the baby ant is gone now too.

The man with the deep voice is still talking to Mommy. He asks her a question and after she answers, he calls another for help.

That voice I recognise. That man was here the last time we came. He'd also had questions, and after she'd answered, he'd also got help. That was when I saw the lady again. Because the time before that, it was her. She'd asked the questions; she'd written the answers.

I liked the lady. I wonder if she is back there now. I wonder if she can see my Mommy.

I wonder if she knows I'm here.

She'd seen my hand that first time when I tried to see what Mommy was doing.

"Who do these little fingers belong to?" she'd asked, as she'd leant over the desk.

"This is Fabian," said Mommy. "Say hello, Fabian."

I'd said hello, tilting up to look back at her. She'd had kind eyes. Big brown eyes that first soberly scanned my face, and then lit with a smile when she'd noticed my shirt.

"Ooh, what's that on your shirt, Fabian?"

"A puppy."

"You like puppies, Fabian?"

I answered her question, but I don't think she heard me. She'd turned around, speaking to someone behind her and soon after she disappeared from my sight. When I again tried to stretch tall to see where she went, Mommy lifted my fingers and told me to stop. To stand still and behave.

I did stop leaning upwards. I did stand still as Mommy ordered. I did behave.

Later, the nice lady came back, bringing with her a juice. A cold one that had just been removed from the fridge.

"What must you say, Fabian?" asked Mommy, as I carefully took it, clutching it tightly in my hands.

"Thank you, Aunty."

She'd smiled bright at my response and remained there watching as I drank slowly, as Mommy instructed, sucking the orange drink through the curly straw.

Another time, on another visit, she'd given me three sweets and a bubble gum. Mommy said I could only eat one, so I made the easy choice and picked the fattest sweet and gave her the rest to put in her purse. I wonder if the aunty gave her gifts to others too. Maybe they'd chosen the gum and it was they who'd left it where it now is, hidden beneath the desk.

As the men finish speaking and the newer one leaves, I am again up on my toes straining to see if she's there. Mommy, now busy writing, doesn't see what I do, but I haven't escaped notice as the remaining man now studies my face. I watch his eyes and wait for them to meet mine, but they never do. Instead, when he concludes his inspection, he shifts his gaze away from me and refocuses on what Mommy is doing.

My feet start to hurt so I have limited time to complete my task. I look around quickly and my efforts bring success. I spot her. She is there, sitting at a table not too far from where we're standing. If she looks up right now, she'll see us. I hold on as long as I can, looking directly at her, hoping she'll turn my way. But she doesn't and I am out of time. I let go.

And it's just me in the corner again waiting for Mommy to finish so we can go home.

★★★★★★★★★★★★★★★★★★★★

We're leaving.

And I feel their eyes again as Mommy leads me to the door. They follow us, the tingling on my neck stronger than it was before. It stops when I step outside, disappearing completely as we leave them behind.

A lady pushing a baby in a pram is halfway up the ramp that leads to the entrance. Walking up the steps on the left side of the building is an older man, and alongside him, holding his hand the way I now hold Mommy's is a small, barefooted girl. She looks ridiculous, out of place, in a poofy pink dress that should only be worn on Sundays. Two butterfly bows sit askew in her messy hair. Mommy ushers me in front of her as we squeeze past the lady, then nudges my shoulder to make me face front.

But I don't. Not yet. Because I am watching the girl. And she is watching me.

I hadn't noticed the apple, the one she now bites into. They're waiting, the pram blocking their path, for the lady to enter first. Another bite. And while she chews, she smiles. At me. And I think it looks weird.

As Mommy walks faster, I must go faster too. But I twist around and continue to look at this girl who's looking right back. And when, with the hand still holding her fruit, she waves, I instinctively wave too.

The man leans down and speaks to her. Then he's pointing, towards an overflowing open bin standing against the brick wall. She doesn't hesitate, turns, and skips in that direction. One last bite and what's left she tosses on to the heap. And then she's twirling, once, twice, her poofy dress swinging wide, before launching herself at the man who is ready to catch her. When he does, they laugh, the sound carrying to where Mommy and I now stop. We've reached the road.

And then they're gone, through the doorway, following the lady who'd finally managed to guide the wheels of the pram across the threshold.

I keep looking, though the girl is no longer there. She is now behind those doors. Those ugly, dark brown, double doors that lead to what's inside.

Has she been there before? Or is this her first time entering?

Maybe she doesn't yet know about that sour smell that greets you. Maybe she hasn't yet seen those rusted windows that refuse to open no matter how hard you bang. And maybe she hasn't yet experienced the effect of those broken lights which create a strange darkness, so your eyes hurt when you first step back outside.

Maybe she doesn't yet know that it's not clean in there. That the floors and the walls are so covered in grime that any touch leaves a stain.

Maybe today will be the day she learns all those things.

Maybe today is the day she discovers that police stations are sad places, for sad people.

And that ants eat the bubble gum the visitors leave behind.

★★★★★★★★★★★★★★★★★★★★

We visit when Daddy must go away, and then we visit so he can come back again.

Today, he should not be home, because today he must go away. And because I was distracted, by a stupid girl in a pink dress eating an apple and smiling, I forgot to do what I must do on days like today.

I forgot to search.

Usually, her head swings one way, while mine goes the other. And that's when we start. Our scan. Of everyone and everything around us. Because we're looking. For his friends, for their cars. For his car. For him.

One time he'd jumped up from between two cars in the parking lot. By the time we saw him, it was too late to run, too late to go back to where we'd just come from.

He'd grabbed me, swung me up around his shoulders, and walked quickly to an empty taxi waiting at the corner. He didn't care that there were people standing close by and that they watched our approach. He headed straight to the door, pulled on the handle so it opened, and put me on the seat nearest the opposite window.

Mommy didn't care about the people either, running behind us and screaming at him to let me go and give me back to her.

He didn't.

What he did do was close the door so I was locked inside.

Then he turned around and punched Mommy in her face. Hard.

She'd stumbled back and fallen to the ground. He'd bent over, his head nearly touching hers, and screamed in her face words I couldn't hear. He'd stood back up, walked past the people still staring at him, and climbed into the front seat. And after slamming the door so the windows rattled, he'd ordered the man sitting next to him to go. The man listened.

We left her there.

I jumped up so I could see what was happening with Mommy, but Daddy leant over, across the back of his seat, and shouted at me to sit down and not move. Like the man who was driving, I also listened.

That time we went to Ma Edith's house, and stayed there for days and days until Mommy phoned to say it was okay for us to come home.

I don't want to go to Ma Edith's house again. I don't want Daddy to steal me away from Mommy. So, I must watch. Carefully. Right until the moment we walk through our front door.

And, if I see him I must run, back to the police, and I must tell them they must come. That is our plan. The secret one I'm not supposed to tell anyone about.

I look up at Mommy and see she is looking behind her, then off to her side. So, I must first start with the front and then look off to my own side.

We don't speak because we're focused. We walk and we look, all around us, all along the way, and even after we've reached and moved through the front gate with the still-broken latch.

Mommy unlocks the chain around the bars of the security door, removes the packet with the new lock from her bag, and using her teeth she tears through the plastic. Dumping the old lock with its key still attached right on to the centre of the brick path, she unlatches and opens the door, then pushes me into the house.

After the chain is again put into place, and the door is both locked and double-latched, only then does she turn to me, take a deep breath, exhale, and ask the question I have a ready answer for.

"Fish fingers and chips?"

"And cooldrink and cake?"

She smiles broadly as I say the words she expects. I'd remembered our game and it's made her happy. And because it makes me happy to see Mommy smile, it's easy, this time, for me to smile too.

I follow her as she double-checks the windows and the locked back door. I watch as she takes off her jacket and shoes and ties up her hair. When she lifts me to sit on the barstool at the counter and then gets what is needed to start making our lunch, I know that we're done. We've made it.

Again.

No familiar car. No taxis. No friends or family not on our side.

No Daddy.

And so, for now, and maybe for a little while, everything is fine. And it will remain fine, right until the moment it isn't.

★★★★★★★★★★★★★★★★★★★★

He is smothering her with the pillow.

It's the red one this time, the heart-shaped one with the white frilly edge. The word **LOVE** slants across the front in large black letters. I know it spells love because she told me so on the day that she made it. For him. As a gift.

When she'd finished, she'd taken my hand and guided my finger as she'd softly called out each letter, then whispered along with me as I did the same.

We'd both been eager to see if he'd like it.

He did.

And to prove it, he'd lifted her up, swung her in a circle, and rained kisses on her neck, till she laughed uncontrollably and begged for him to let go. When I excitedly shouted that I knew it spelled love, he'd picked me up, swung me around, and rained kisses on me too.

Now I stand at the entrance to their bedroom and watch as he sits on her stomach and presses her gift to him on to her face. She's scratching and pushing his arms, but it has no effect and neither does her kicking and tossing. He is so much taller and wider than she is, so it makes sense that she cannot move him.

The muffled sound coming from beneath that pillow scares me. I must act, though I know when this ends she'll be mad. What did I say? she will ask. First holding me still and then shaking me till I respond with the answer she wants.

I must listen when she speaks.

I must do what she says.

I must stay in my room when Daddy gets the way he gets.

I must turn on the TV and watch my cartoons. Or put on the headphones and play one of my games.

I must stay out of the way.

I must behave.

No argument I make persuades her.

She won't hear how I don't like it when he hurts her. How the sound she makes when she screams frightens me. How I know I can help.

How I don't mind when he hits me too because it sometimes means he stops hitting her.

And just like her tears don't matter to him, mine won't matter to her.

She will be mad and she will punish me. No TV or games for a week.

Because I must learn.

Because she knows what she's doing.

Because she is the mommy and I am the child.

Because she knows how to, and she will, handle Daddy.

I wonder if she knows that I don't believe her.

She'll make me say that I promise to never do it again.

And I will do it. I will promise.

But I'll be lying.

He is punching her now. On her face, through the pillow. First one side and then the next. Over and over again.

When he moves to her stomach, first one side, then the next, I know that she is tired now and that it is time. Her screams have turned to sobs, her kicks have stopped, and beside her head her arms lie limp.

She needs my help.

He lifts the pillow and in the voice I find scarier than his shouts, he talks to her. Softly, gently almost, he says the things I've heard him say to her before.

Why won't she listen?

Why must she always do this?

Make him behave this way.

Make him do what he doesn't want to do.

Does she understand what he is trying to teach her?

A slap to one cheek, and then another one to the other. Before the third one lands, I am on him, though I can't recall the moment I moved.

Both arms around his neck, I squeeze tightly, hoping he can't so easily fling me aside this time. He is shouting at me to let go, and he is trying to break my hold. In just a few seconds he will succeed. So I must try what's been circling my mind for these past few weeks. I regret that I hadn't thought of it sooner.

I bite him. Hard. And I don't let go even when he howls.

Because then he is up and she is free.

Soon I am too, and I am flying and falling. I can't see where I'm headed and I don't feel it when I land.

★★★★★★★★★★★★★★★★★★★★

She is walking me to school and all along the way she's preparing me.

I must lie.

And I must lie because what happened was an accident.

We are nearing the entrance and she is fidgety, nervous. Worried I won't perform as I should.

So she starts again, a reminder of what's happened these last few days. A search for agreement that we've had a wonderful time, while they kept me at home so my face could heal. Confirmation that I understand that Daddy is very sorry.

Daddy is very sad.

Daddy needs me to forgive him.

And the question that only has one answer – do I forgive him?

She's still unsure when she kisses my head and tells me to have a good day. But I am at the gate and Mr Jansen, the security guard, is ushering me along.

I move forwards, in the direction of my class, but I turn to see her standing there, watching me.

I give her what she needs. A smile. A wave.

And the comfort that later I will lie.

Mrs Langenhoven will ask. She always does. Why have I missed so many days of school? Again. Is everything okay at home? Is there anything I want to tell her?

I will give her my rehearsed answers and she will be satisfied. And be relieved that not more is demanded of her. Or them.

They tried. One time, when I told what I wasn't supposed to tell. When I asked what I realised too late I shouldn't have asked. For help.

They called their meetings and offered advice. Reasons were given, promises made.

And for a while I'd thought it worked. Because for a while everything stopped. But the while didn't last long and when everything again started, it all seemed so much worse.

So, yes, I will lie.

And they will all take their lead from me. The parents, the teachers, even my friends. It's in my voice, my actions. The way I move. What I say and how I say it. What I do and the way I do it.

If I am fine, then we can all be fine together.

And when I pretend, I give them the freedom to pretend along with me.

★★★★★★★★★★★★★★★★★★★★★

We are having a braai and I must be excited.

It's Friday night and he has bought sausage and chops, chicken and ribs.

"Make the potato salad," he tells her. And the one he likes so much, "the pasta one, with green peppers and pineapple".

He kisses her cheek when she says that she will, tickles her side, and makes her laugh.

But he knows it's not real, that she is not yet all the way there. That's part of what tonight is about. He's already given her the words, saw that they weren't enough, so now he's giving her more.

He has invited his friends, and he's allowed her to invite her family. None of his family will come because the two groups don't get along.

When the guests arrive, they bring cases of beer and many bottles of brown liquor. They've come ready to party, some even to spend the night.

Soon there is loud talking and laughter. Music and dancing. Dominoes and cards.

Two of my cousins escape to the street, take turns showing off their skill with a soccer ball, and within minutes draw a crowd. They invite me to play, but don't wait for a response, so don't hear my murmured "no, thank you". They're older and have never offered or wanted to play with me before. I think it's the bruise on my cheek that prompts the invitation.

No one asks what happened to me. There's no need to ask because they already know. Everyone partying with him tonight knows who he is and knows what he does. To Mommy and to me.

But though they know, they've never really seen. Never felt. Not all of it. And certainly not the worst of it.

Tonight, he'll be a different man. Drinking changes him. I sometimes wish he'd just drink all the time, because the daddy I know completely disappears and in his place emerges a stranger. This stranger is kind and affectionate. He likes wet, sloppy kisses and tight, crushing hugs. He has stupid dance moves and tries to sing, though he knows he sounds terrible.

This stranger loves Mommy and me and tells us so.

This stranger is safe.

And this stranger will make Mommy's smile real again. He is the one she will forgive.

I sit outside near the edge of the garden, inside my sandpit, right underneath the wide-open kitchen window. They're in there, Mommy and my aunties. And even when they whisper, I can hear them.

To anyone who bothered to look, my cars and the sand ramps have my full attention. I am in the exact spot he left me in earlier, seemingly preoccupied with the track he helped build. Should he come, or should she, they'll be happy to see that with the plastic bucket and spade he bought me, I have added to his design. My cars now have a place to park and an extra hill from which to race.

It's always what he does. After. Something he thinks is significant. Something he thinks matters. And how I respond is what he is looking for. He needs me to smile. To ask questions. To care. And so I do what I must. I smile. I ask questions. And, I care. Enough, so he'll believe me.

But the truth right now is that I am not interested in his construction, any more than I was interested earlier when he was alongside me.

Because I am listening. To what she tells them and what they're saying in response.

He knows what he did was wrong. It's frightened him.

They don't speak while she does, their silence her permission to make all her points. And she makes them. With strength and passion in her voice, she begins again her mission to convince them.

She defends him.

Does she not know who he is? Did she not know when she married him?

He is a complicated man, with volatile emotions. It's what attracted her in the first place. Yes, he's possessive, quick to anger, stubborn. But she knows he loves her. No matter what he does, she always knows that he loves her.

And she loves him.

You don't give up on people you love. You don't just give up on the life you've built.

He'll get better. They're working on it. And in the end, they'll be stronger.

So many of those words they've heard before. Not one thing of what's happened is new to them.

As always, it's Aunty Hannah who starts.

"You must leave him," words she's also said before. Words she often repeats.

"Look, don't start, okay," comes the familiar response.

"What about Fabian, Rissa? Are you right in the head to let him do that and get away with it?" Aunty Hannah's voice has gone softer and higher.

"Look, that was a mistake, okay? Fabian did something he wasn't supposed to do. Bryan didn't mean it."

"Doesn't matter if he didn't mean it, Ris – he did it. Have you looked at his face?" The softer and higher were fast becoming louder and stronger. "And this isn't the fucking first time!"

Aunty Sarah hates swearing, but she hates it even more when her sisters fight. The oldest, and always the peacemaker, she steps in.

"Okay, both of you need to stop this and be calm."

"She needs to mind her own damn business." This from Mommy.

"And you need to wise the fuck up!" is Aunty Hannah's instant comeback.

"I said stop it, okay? We're here to have a nice time. There's peace now, so stop this *kak!*"

Knowing that Aunty Sarah seldom swears and that when she does it means she's serious, and close to exploding, Mommy and Aunty Hannah obey immediately and say nothing further.

It's quiet inside, then a cupboard closes and water is running.

Outside, my red car travels over two steep hills and turns to make a second lap.

In the street, a goal's been scored, and spectators are cheering.

I'm still listening, but no one speaks. Is that it? Are they done?

A big smash-up is happening before me. The yellow truck has slammed into the mountain and is forcing its way through to the side where the red car has parked. Refusing to wait and see what damage the truck will bring, the red car speeds up the ramp and rams into the sand from the other end. Now, on a crash course, the two vehicles plough their way through, until they bang into each other, and the mountain collapses, crushes and buries them.

"What's the story with the caterer?" Aunty Hannah has listened to Aunty Sarah and she has stopped the *kak*. She's now asking about the plans for Ma's birthday.

As these more important matters become their focus, I think of Aunty Maureen and Uncle Clive. They don't visit us anymore. Daddy says Mommy's asshole brother and his stupid bitch are no longer welcome here. It's because of what happened. That one time. On another Friday night. At another braai.

Daddy was going to be late so Uncle Clive, who'd come straight from work, had started the fire. And when everyone else arrived, they'd started the partying without him.

But that was not the reason. That was not what started it.

It was the bruise on Mommy's face, the slow-healing one that everyone saw but no one commented on. Uncle Clive and Aunty Maureen chose that night to comment. Daddy had just moments before walked through the door, when Uncle Clive drunkenly asked why his "slim met die bek" sister was so okay with getting the shit kicked out of her all the time.

There was only a slight pause of stillness before everything went crazy.

Aunty Hannah told Uncle Clive to stop meddling in matters that don't concern him.

Aunty Sarah asked why we can't just have a nice family gathering.

Uncle Neill, Aunty Sarah's husband, said that it was not the time and place and pulled Uncle Clive's arm to get him to take a walk around the block.

And Aunty Maureen suggested that everyone sits and have a reasonable conversation.

The noise level rose as everyone spoke at once.

Then Daddy shoved Uncle Clive and said that he would fuck him up.

Uncle Clive shouted back that he was not his sister and that he'd like to see Daddy try it.

A bottle broke and someone screamed. Someone else swore. And Uncle Clive had Daddy up against the wall.

Then mommy was there and pushing Uncle Clive away. Turning to Daddy, she told him to chill out. Uncle Clive is already three sheets, she said, so let him go outside and cool off.

Aunty Maureen she told to fuck off. She has no ring on her finger, so she has no say in this family.

Aunty Maureen cried and said she would pray for Mommy.

Uncle Clive didn't like the way Mommy talked to his girlfriend, and Daddy didn't like the way Uncle Clive talked to Mommy. Uncle Clive said Daddy was a joker given what he did to Mommy on a daily basis.

Then Daddy exploded and ordered everyone to get out of his house.

I didn't see what happened next because Aunty Hannah told my cousins to take me and go outside. I didn't want to leave, but even though I said that, no one heard me. And when I pushed against Carl as he tried to steer me to the front door, he simply picked me up and carried me out. I didn't have a choice.

We were still outside, where I didn't want to be, when the police van arrived. And when the two men in uniform walked past us and into the house, all sound from inside almost instantly stopped. Carl said that I shouldn't be scared, that the police were there to help. He said it would all be better now.

I believed him.

But he was wrong.

And I haven't seen Aunty Maureen and Uncle Clive since that day.

"Meat is nearly done." Uncle Neill is in the kitchen now. They stop their conversation about the presents Ma has hinted at, and switch to who's doing the dishing.

Most of the track is now a flattened mess. I must fix it, rebuild, after I go inside and get my food.

And before he comes back this way and sees what I've done.

★★★★★★★★★★★★★★★★★★★★

Plate in hand, I stand there watching them, waiting for someone to notice me.

Aunty Hannah calls everyone in and instructs them to help themselves, gesturing to the many bowls and platters on the kitchen counter.

They've all come and gone and are now queuing outside to get their meat straight from the grill.

My cousins, the last to arrive, bypass the fruit and head straight for the potato salad. I am standing near the door, wondering again if I should climb on a chair and try doing this myself.

But then she is there. Aunty Sarah.

"You okay, cutie pie?" I don't like her calling me that.

"Yes, Aunty Sarah."

Aunty Hannah calls me sweetie. Aunty Maureen called me by my name.

She zeroes in on the bump, and as her eyes narrow, she gently runs her fingers down my cheek, careful to not press against the swollen part.

Then she smiles, takes my plate, and moves to the counter.

"Only potato salad, and some pineapple and watermelon." Mommy, now standing behind me, tells Aunty Sarah what I'd like. I twist around and on her face I see the expression I know so well.

She's uncomfortable. The bruising right next to my eye makes her uncomfortable. I make her uncomfortable.

"You want to sit at the table?"

"Can I go eat outside? I'm building a tunnel." She's going to say yes. She hardly ever says no when she looks at me like that.

"Okay, you go play and I'll bring your plate." She runs her fingers through my hair and then turns to take my plate from Aunty Sarah. I won't have to go into the yard to get the rest of my food from Daddy.

I wasn't thinking of how to build a tunnel but maybe I should consider it. When Mommy brings out the plate, she stands for a minute and watches me wet some sand and form a lump. I don't turn to look at her and know the second she places the plate on the grass behind me and quietly leaves to go back inside. She hasn't reminded me to eat. Or to pray, before I do.

She hasn't even told me to wash my hands.

I am alone again. No sound comes from the kitchen, which means they've all gone to eat in the yard or the dining room. My cousins should be coming this way, but they eat a lot so I have time.

To dig my holes.

I must eat, but I'm not hungry. So I dig, and then I bury. First the meat and then the salad. Little by little, it all disappears into the ground, until my plate is clean.

And by the time I am done I have formed a plan. I know exactly what to do and how to do it. So, I start.

I build my tunnel.

★★★★★★★★★★★★★★★★★★★★

She is holding my hand as we cross the road.

In her other hand she carries the bag. It is big and black and contains three large tins filled with cupcakes.

Mommy baked, because it's my birthday.

She's talking. I try to listen but my ear aches and my head still hurts. The blood on my pillow this morning scared me, and I'm wondering if I should tell her about it. Maybe she'll see if she tidies my room. But maybe she won't. I turned it around to hide the stain.

We'll have a party tonight. There'll be more cake, including a big, round chocolate one with caramel in the middle and chocolatey sauce on top. My favourite. And there'll be candles. I must take some time today, she says, to think about my wishes. One for tonight, for the family celebration, and one for Saturday, when we're having an even bigger party, for their friends and mine.

Am I excited?

"Yes, Mommy, I am", is my response, because it must be.

Am I looking forward to opening my presents?

"Yes, Mommy, I am", though I already know what the main one from them is.

He'd wanted to buy it. He'd had a plan. But she'd gone ahead and bought it without consulting him. Now they had the wrong one, not the exact one he'd wanted, the right version he'd planned to get. She'd messed things up, just like she always does.

So, he smacked her. And then he kicked her.

I saw those first strikes from my hiding place behind the arch. And as I watched I hoped that when she ran from him, she didn't run my way.

It was time for my bath. When he grabbed her hair and slammed her head against the fridge, I turned around, went into the bathroom, and closed the door. And then I locked it.

The running water drowned out the noise in the other room. Adding more bubble bath, I watched as the snowy foam rose higher and higher, nearing the edge.

When the water stopped, I listened for her sounds. But there was only quiet, so maybe they were done.

I jumped when the knock came, followed by his booming voice giving the order for me to "Finish up in there!" My obedience was swift. Still fully dressed, I pulled the plug and let the water drain. Only then did I remove my clothes and put on my pyjamas.

I must act surprised when I open my present. I must show excitement and joy. Maybe it won't be tonight, and she'll keep it till Saturday. Maybe I'll have more time to practise.

We're nearing the gate and she's greeting people as we pass.

Mr Jansen says hello and Mommy tells him she's coming in today, because there's cake to deliver.

He smiles and wishes me a happy birthday. And, as we enter through the gate, he asks Mommy how old I am today.

She doesn't answer but looks at me instead. "Tell Mr Jansen how old you are today, Fabian?"

"I'm 6, Mr Jansen."

★★★★★★★★★★★★★★★★★★★★

I am taller.

If I lift my head and tilt it only slightly back, I can see the top of the desk now.

Mommy is talking to the same man she was talking to on Monday. She is telling him she's changed her mind again. She is telling him the reasons why.

He looked at me once when I placed my fingers over the edge and raised on my toes to see how much I've grown. Then he looked away quickly when he caught me peeking right back.

He seems disinterested and rattles off what she's required to do to make what she started on Monday go away. He really shouldn't waste his time giving her information she already has.

I stand quietly and wait for the moment the tingles stop. The gum is in my hand, halfway to being opened.

When I know they've completed their watching, I carefully finish unwrapping the packet and pop the tiny green square into my mouth. I chew slowly, thoroughly, savouring the flavour.

Mommy is doing the writing part now, which means we are close to being done.

I must be ready. Ready to make sure no one sees what I'm doing. Ready to remove it from my mouth and form it into a ball. Ready to position it alongside the pieces already there.

I've been collecting them, hiding them. Saving them for our visits.

Next time, I'll be bringing piece number four. And next time the colour will be blue.

Reflections

Fabian's story is one I've wanted to tell for many years. His experiences, his thoughts, his feelings sat with me, uncomfortably at home in not just my consciousness. When the words finally came, they brought with them the expected and familiar reflections on issues like innocence, vulnerability, victimisation, responsibility, and accountability. I revisited my research work on domestic violence, reviewed data from complainant statements, reread my field notes. And committed to pacing myself when it came to consuming the information. Unexpectedly, the construction of sentences and the drafting of scenes also transported the accompanying images into my dreams. And my efforts to order and present them were frustrated by their unwillingness to be confined to my carefully designed daily schedule. Early morning and late evening writing sessions, which bookended my full days of work and family-related tasks and responsibilities, proved wholly inadequate as a method of accomplishing my goal of crafting and sharing a snapshot of occurrences in Fabian's life. After the last line was written, the question of what is untold remains. Because he remains. Though quieter now, and further hidden in the background, his presence still calls to be seen, to be acknowledged. The whispers of what continues to be invisible, dismissed, diminished, for him and for so many others, linger – a reminder that the picture isn't complete.

Diane

10

Beyond Words: Apologies and Compensation in Sexual Offences

Leila Khan and Dee Smythe

Introduction

Repairing the harm caused by sexual offences and obtaining justice through the criminal justice system is complex, given the nature of these crimes and the limited scope of criminal law. In South Africa, the state's response to rates of sexual violence, which exceed almost every other country in the world, have centred on more visible policing, stricter bail laws, increasing convictions, and harsher prison sentences. The public demand for more criminalisation in response to sexual offences is an understandable reaction to abhorrent acts of patriarchal violence in the context of a dysfunctional legal system. This prioritisation of carceral responses, and the prioritisation of retributive over restorative approaches to justice, has done little to deter or prevent sexual offences, while often exacerbating the structures and conditions that produce violence in the first place. Moreover, victims of sexual offences are largely excluded from participation in, and emotionally and psychologically devastated by, the criminal justice system and process.

Research points to a profound disconnect between victim conceptions of justice and the remedies offered by the criminal justice system (Herman 2005; Holder 2015; Clark 2015; Daly 2017; McGlynn et al 2017; McGlynn and Westmarland 2019). Where more restorative approaches are considered in the context of sexual offences, reservations have been raised by scholars and activists about their appropriateness to the seriousness of the crime and the context of unequal gendered power relations in which these violations occur. In respect of compensation, there are legitimate concerns that compensation as a remedy for sexual offences commodifies and objectifies women, plays into tropes of false reporting for financial gain, and lets rich offenders off the hook (Hamman and Nortje 2017: 13; Jeffries et al 2021). Some argue that for sexual offences this is a 'taboo trade-off', always already incommensurate with the nature of the violation (Fiske and Tetlock 1997; McGraw and Tetlock 2005; Shen 2013; Antonsdóttir 2020). There is concern that the transactional appearance of compensation creates the perception that compensation is a form of bribing or coercing the victim to accept a more lenient outcome than imprisonment, and that the availability of compensation may even further impede the complainant's credibility (Koss 2006; Smith and Galey 2018). In a country like South Africa, there are also practical constraints on implementing compensatory arrangements, given that a significant percentage of accused persons in South Africa live in poverty (South African Law Reform Commission 2004: 281–2).

While holding in mind the concerns expressed about apology and compensation as remedies, it is also true that many victims of sexual violence explicitly ask the courts for compensation, withdraw their complaints in preference for this outcome, or circumvent the criminal justice system altogether and go directly to the offender or their family to achieve it. This chapter is a preliminary effort to think through the apologetic meaning of compensation for victims of sexual violence and to tease out some of the questions that arise in this context. The lack of solutions in the criminal justice system for doing the work of repairing harms caused by sexual violence and providing meaningful recourse for victims requires that we learn from the outcomes and the forms of justice sought by victims themselves. Compensation can assist victims in recovering pecuniary and non-pecuniary losses, including lost wages, medical costs, therapy, and the cost of increasing security, as well as providing recompense for pain and suffering. Apologies are known to be useful and important in the realm of harm reduction, and to hold meaning and power for victims (Daly 2017; McGlynn and Westmarland 2019).

First, we set out the limited extent to which compensation plays a role in the current approach to sexual offences in South Africa's criminal justice system, which is overwhelmingly carceral in nature. We then consider compensation from the perspective of apology, using the framework of categorical apologies provided by Nick Smith (2008; 2014) to show the ways in which compensation overlaps with apology, both by giving greater meaning to apologies and by doing some of the work of apology on its own. We argue, given that compensation is instrumental or essential to apology, that it should not be so quickly dismissed by the criminal justice system. Because compensation, both as an end in itself and conceptualised in terms of apology, has meaning to victims of sexual violence, we suggest that it should be more intentionally included as a method of remediating harm for victims of sexual violence within the South African criminal justice system.

'Justice' for sexual offences within the current legal framework

The first decade of democracy in South Africa saw a marked turn towards progressive victim-supportive legislation and policy, which has since largely stalled, or been reversed. Reflecting the initial shift after 1994, the Department of Justice and Constitutional Development (DOJCD) published a *Service Charter for Victims of Crime in South Africa* ('Victims' Charter') in 2004 with the aim of cementing a move away from retribution to a more restorative approach (Department of Justice and Constitutional Development of the Republic of South Africa 2004: 3). Intended to come with this shift was a greater recognition of the impact of criminal justice processes on victims of crime and an appreciation that crimes are committed against a person and should not just be viewed in terms of the state. In line with this approach, the Victims' Charter enshrines a number of aspirational rights for victims of crime, including the right to be compensated for property loss or damage as a result of crime (DOJCD 2004: 8). South African law provides for the possibility of statutory compensation orders in the Criminal Procedure Act 1977 (CPA).[1] Section 297(4) read with s. 297(1)(a)(i) of the CPA allows a court, in relation to crimes with minimum sentences, to suspend the whole or up to five years of a sentence, to allow the convicted person to pay compensation to the complainant, or make reparation in kind, or perform community service. Section 300 of the CPA empowers a court to make a compensation award where the convicted person caused damage or loss to the complainant's property in the commission of the crime. Where a criminal court does not grant a compensation order, the victim retains the right to institute a civil claim directly against the accused. While the state may institute a criminal prosecution at any time, civil claims in sexual offences cases currently prescribe a mere three years from the time that the victim was first able to institute proceedings (ss. 10, 11 and 12 of the Prescription Act 1969).[2]

The way victims of sexual violence experience the criminal justice system is vastly different from the rights and procedures outlined in policy. When a sexual offence is reported, the state pursues the perpetrator with little involvement or input from the victim, who is a state witness. Upon conviction, the court may consider a victim impact statement in coming to a decision on sentencing. However, fewer than one in eight rapes is reported

---

[1] Act 51 of 1977.
[2] Act 68 of 1969. At the time of writing, the Women's Legal Centre is challenging the constitutional validity of civil prescription in sexual offences cases, in the Durban High Court in the matter of *AR v AB (and the Minister of Justice)* D8481/2020.

to the police; less than half of reported rapes lead to arrest; no more than 20 per cent of reported cases are prosecuted; and only around 5 per cent of all cases lead to a conviction (Smythe 2015; Nagtegaal 2018). Many reported cases are later withdrawn by complainants. Every stage of the victim's experience of the criminal justice system is traumatic, from unempathetic police who do not follow up on reports because they believe rape complaints are exaggerated, to insensitive health practitioners, disinterested prosecutors, and aggressive defence lawyers (Vetten 2014: 5). Where the trial results in conviction, 'justice' usually means sending sexual offenders to jail, in a context of underfunded and overcrowded gang-run prisons with inhumane living conditions and no scope for genuine re-education and rehabilitation (Makou et al 2017). Those who make it out of this environment, whether or not they were convicted of violent crimes in the first place, often reoffend violently (Murhula and Singh 2019). Because no sustained preventive programmes are in place to address patriarchal attitudes, and little has been done to address the overall structures and conditions that produce violence, this pattern of violence replicates and escalates. The psychological and emotional impact on victims of this time-consuming process cannot be overstated, and it remains the case that they do not receive adequate support in or after exiting the criminal justice system.

Apologies and compensation for serious crimes, even when requested by victims, have only been awarded in South Africa's criminal courts a handful of times, usually in lower courts and before being overturned in the Supreme Court of Appeal (SCA). In *Director of Public Prosecutions v Thabethe*,[3] the state appealed a sentence handed down in relation to the rape of a 15-year-old girl by her mother's partner. The accused reported himself to the police and was convicted and sentenced in the High Court to ten years in prison, suspended for five years so that the accused could pay 80 per cent of his income to the complainant and her mother. This sentence was imposed because the offender acknowledged responsibility, apologised to the victim, participated in a victim–offender programme, agreed to perform community service, and, in a number of other ways, cooperated in 'establishing conditions through which (the victim) may find closure' (*S v Tabethe* para. 36[4]). Even though the victim stated that she forgave the accused, and she and her mother made clear to the court that they could not survive financially without his monetary support, the SCA set this decision aside and sentenced the accused to the full ten years in prison. The court emphasised that the views of the victim, while important, are not decisive (*DPP v Thabethe* para. 21). Applying restorative approaches such as apologies and compensation in cases

---

[3]   (619/10) [2011] ZASCA 186 (30 September 2011).

[4]   (CC468/06) [2009] ZAGPHC 23 (23 January 2009).

where it was 'patently unsuitable', such as rape, could lead to a loss of faith in restorative sentencing options altogether; indeed: '[i]t is trite that one of the key ingredients of a balanced sentence is that it must reflect the seriousness of the offence and the natural indignation and outrage of the public' (para. 20). In *Seedat v S*,[5] the SCA again set aside a compensation order awarded in terms of s. 297 of the CPA. The complainant in that case had requested a community-based sentence as well as financial compensation and a motor vehicle because she struggled with transport. Setting aside this award, the court opined that:

> the courts are under a duty to send a clear message, not only to the accused, but to other potential rapists and to the community that it will not be tolerated ... Whilst the object of sentencing is not to satisfy public opinion, it needs to serve the public interest ... Indeed the public would justifiably be alarmed if courts tended to impose a suspended sentence coupled with monetary compensation for rape. (para. 39)

The implication of these judgments is that lengthy imprisonment alone is the only effective and acceptable resolution for serious violations like sexual offences. It is true that for the safety of the victim and the community, separation of the perpetrator can be a necessary arrangement. However, where the complainant explicitly requests compensation and asserts that incarceration would in fact be detrimental to their family, as in *Thabethe*, and the court is convinced that the accused poses no threat to others, the idea that imprisonment is the more just solution does not hold firm. Taking a long-term view, the ticking time bomb that is the South African prison system exposes the precarity of relying solely on imprisonment as punishment (and, for that matter, deterrent) in the 'public interest'. Ultimately, cases like *Thabethe* and *Seedat* suggest that 'justice' is more concerned at present with the performance of being tough on violent crime – even though prisons are ineffective at deterring or rehabilitating offenders – than the well-being of the victim and their stated need to receive some form of acknowledgement and remediation.

Notwithstanding the position of the courts, many victims and their families opt to enter compensation negotiations with the offender instead of going through the criminal justice system, and the matter is considered resolved once an apology and compensation is offered and accepted. The practice of settling disputes through apology and compensation, even where violent crimes are concerned, is not uncommon, especially in

---

[5] (731/2015) [2016] ZASCA 153 (3 October 2016).

Figure 10.1: Informal withdrawal template

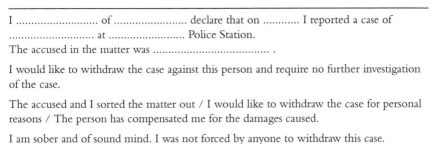

I .... of .... declare that on .... I reported a case of .... at .... Police Station.
The accused in the matter was ....

I would like to withdraw the case against this person and require no further investigation of the case.

The accused and I sorted the matter out / I would like to withdraw the case for personal reasons / The person has compensated me for the damages caused.

I am sober and of sound mind. I was not forced by anyone to withdraw this case.

Source: Smythe 2015: 118

vernacular forums. Mnisi Weeks (2018) recounts, for example, a case of attempted rape, where the accused was given the option of going through the criminal justice system, or of 'discussing the matter between the families and thereby coming to a mutually satisfactory agreement' (p 141). Smythe (2015) similarly describes a case in which the complainant's statement explicitly states that she and her family require police investigation only if negotiations for compensation fail (p 5). In both these cases, negotiation happens under the threat of criminal sanction. In another case documented by Smythe, the complainant writes: 'I have discussed the matter with my family members, the family of the accused have come to my family and apologised on the behalf of the accused. The matter has been resolved between the families and I came to the decision to withdraw the case' (p 121). The compensation component of these practices is acknowledged by detectives: 'You interview the victim and they tell you that the suspect's parents offered them some money. What can you as a policeman do? Nothing. And then you ask them "Is that the reason why they drop the case?" and they say "yes"' (p 125).

Smythe (2015) found that at one police station, this rationale was offered regularly enough for detectives to develop a standard withdrawal template (see Figure 10.1), to be signed by the complainant under oath, offering the payment of compensation as one of three 'reasons' for withdrawing a complaint, along with having 'sorted the matter out' and 'personal reasons' (p 118).

These practices raise many questions, but they also demand that we pay closer attention to the other avenues through which victims are seeking justice in cases of sexual violence. At the same time, they raise concerns around the potential limitations of these alternatives – to what extent are victims expected to prioritise the expectations of their parents and community, and disregard their own possibly differing desired outcomes? Won't apologies and compensation happen in ways that replicate unequal gendered power relations and once again sideline the autonomy of victims by denying them the opportunity to claim these remedies in their own right? Taking into account the difficulties around apologies and compensation, the marginalisation of such remedies in state law, and the reality that victims continue to ask for them both within and outside of the criminal justice system, a starting point is to unpack how apologies and compensation – where victims are making the choice to receive them – can be better understood so as to further shape effective criminal justice responses.

Compensation as apology?

Apologies are widely understood to be important social practices. They are often demanded from public figures, celebrities, or companies that break the law, cause offence, or otherwise transgress social expectations. Apologies are taught to children, and are regularly exchanged between romantic partners, friends, and family members. Apologies are given to end conflict, rebuild trust, and repair relationships. They can show the person to whom an apology is offered that their pain is taken seriously, and that the gravity of the wrong committed against them has been understood. Apologies can carry a commitment that the action which caused the harm will not be repeated, and that the apologiser will take responsibility to change their behaviour. In the context of criminal law, there is some evidence that where apologies are given by offenders, these offenders are less likely to reoffend; and where apologies are desired and accepted by victims, they feel more empowered and included in the criminal justice process. Studies suggest that even where victims are ambivalent about compensation, one of the predominant remedies they nonetheless seek is an apology (Antonsdóttir 2020). Where compensation is accompanied by an apology, victims see it more favourably than when they are offered compensation or an apology alone (Okimoto 2008; Antonsdóttir 2020). What then are ways to reconsider and better justify compensation as a remedy for sexual offences? And how does thinking about compensation in terms of apology help to make sense of its meaning to victims and its potential usefulness in repairing the harm of serious crimes?

Smith's conception of 'categorical apologies' (2008; 2014) provides a useful framework for understanding the key components of apologies in order to determine what an apology in the fullest, most robust sense might look like. Because apologies can take on a wide variety of forms, being able to classify them and distinguish meaningful, satisfying apologies from empty, insincere, or manipulative ones is helpful for victims seeking resolution through apology, or for anyone interested in interpreting apologies for that matter, including in a criminal law context. Smith points out that knowing the full potential of an apology is important for understanding the kinds of relief such an apology can offer to an offended person, including taking steps to repair some of the damage caused by the offence, providing some assurance that the harm will not be repeated, and being treated with dignity by the offender (2014: 20).

Smith's categorical apology is made up of 12 elements, representing the range of potential possible meanings this 'full' kind of apology can convey (2014: 16–19). These elements are:

1. Agreement and shared understanding of the events leading to the harm.
2. Acceptance of moral responsibility and blame.
3. Possession of appropriate standing to accept responsibility and blame.
4. Identification of each harm.
5. Identification of the moral principles underlying each harm.
6. A shared commitment to these underlying moral principles.
7. Recognition of the victim as a moral interlocuter.
8. Categorical regret, to the extent that the offender wishes they could undo the harm caused and commits to not repeat the harm.
9. Performing the apology to the victim as opposed to a third party.
10. Reform and redress.
11. Genuine intentions behind the apology.
12. An appropriate degree of emotions experienced by the offender, including guilt or sorrow.

Smith notes that it is not necessary for an apology to meet all 12 of these criteria to be satisfactory, as different elements or combinations of elements will be emphasised by different people. What is important is to clarify what kind of apology is sought by the person harmed, and to identify which elements are met, in order to determine more precisely what that person is getting from the apology, and what steps the offender is taking to rectify the harm done. By applying compensation to just a few of these elements, namely identification of each harm, recognition of the victim as moral interlocutor, performance of the apology, and reform and redress, the apologetic meaning of compensation and the ways in which compensation can do some of the work of apologies becomes evident.

Identification of each harm

Applying Smith, an apology that accounts for each specific injury caused by the offender is considered more meaningful than a general or partial apology. A specific and comprehensive apology allows the offender to come to grips with the true extent of the harm they have caused, and acknowledges the full extent of the pain and hurt experienced by the victim. Many victims of sexual violence ask for compensation precisely because they have been impacted and harmed by the offender's act in multiple ways, including through physical and psychological harm, as well as through loss of work and increased feelings of insecurity. Because of the specificity required in quantifying compensatory damages, compensation allows the victim to identify each harm and have the complexity of their pain recognised. This can also contribute to a broader understanding of the gravity of the offence, including by the offender and the court. For many victims of sexual violence who are regularly belittled or not believed, including by the criminal justice system, having their story heard and acknowledged can allow them to extract some meaning from the court process.

Recognition of the victim as moral interlocutor and performance of the apology

Recognition of the victim and the performance of the apology both concern the way in which an apology is expressed by the offender. Recognition of the victim as a moral interlocutor means that the offender acknowledges the victim as the person who was wronged and is owed the apology, and therefore as a person worthy of dignity. This is in contrast with an offender admitting to and apologising for the harm they caused in general terms by making no direct mention of or reference to the person they harmed. This recognition is crucial for victims, and particularly for those who have experienced sexual violence, given its extreme violation of and disregard for human dignity. The requirement for performance of the apology is that it be offered directly to the victim, as opposed to an apology that acknowledges the harm inflicted on the victim, but is then delivered to them indirectly, for example via a judge.

Since the victim is largely excluded from the criminal justice process, the provision of compensation, which is direct and personalised to the victim, is one way to ensure that the victim, at the very least, receives some form of acknowledgement and direct apology. It is for this reason that many victims of sexual violence pursue compensation via civil litigation, if they can afford to, after failing to find relief in the criminal law process. As shown by Des Rosiers, Feldthusen, and Hankivsky (1998), victims of sexual violence who enter into a compensation process are often doing so for the therapeutic effects of being heard and affirmed. This may explain why even small amounts of compensation can be considered meaningful by complainants (Greenbaum 2013: 253). Compensation can also play a symbolic role in sexual offences cases, standing in for an apology where a victim might desire acknowledgement, but is unable or unwilling to face the person who harmed them.

Reform and redress

For an apology to be categorical, the offender must undertake an ongoing commitment to changing their behaviour and not reoffending in the future. As part of this commitment, an offender should provide redress. The complication with this element, as Smith notes, is that its ongoing nature means it can be difficult to determine a point in time when it can be said that an apology has been made. However, this is not necessarily a drawback as its continuing nature means that more work is put into the apology, and the offender is prevented from superficially settling their harm and moving on without future remedial action. An apology of this kind can be considered a commitment, in which the victim can take some comfort and security, that the harm will not be repeated.

Compensation, both pecuniary and non-pecuniary, is a form of redress. The payment of compensation is one way for an offender to take 'practical responsibility' for the harm caused and is often sought by victims as a form of penance. The nature of sexual violence is such that the harm done can never truly be said to be 'undone' or 'repaired', but compensation can improve the material conditions of the victim. For some victims, this is the most important aspect or function of an apology: it is some way of making things right in an irreversible and seemingly irreparable situation. This is clear in *Seedat v S* where this outcome was, as she informed the court, the only way for the complainant to get some relief: 'He goes to jail, tomorrow or the day after he is released and walks away laughing, and I will still be sitting where I am sitting ... Why must I continue to struggle if I could benefit from the harm I suffered?' (para. 14).[6]

Compensation without apology and apology without compensation

Smith grapples with the fact that compensation on its own offers inadequate apologetic meaning, is ambiguous, and is, he suggests, a mere expression of sympathy at best. When compensation occurs without apology, it veers dangerously towards treating a person as a commodity, and creates the perception that payment is all that is required to remediate the harm caused. Conversely, an apology given without compensation can be viewed as meaningless and insufficient. This is particularly the case where the victim expects compensation, for example in the context of civil law or vernacular law where damages are a common remedy. As Pettigrove points out, 'while an apology absent reparation may be an apology in form it is not one in substance' (2003: 327), emphasising the weight and meaning that compensation can give to an apology – particularly where the victim has asked for this remedy.

---

[6]   *Seedat v S* (731/2015) [2016] ZASCA 153 (3 October 2016). Own translation from original Afrikaans.

Apology through vernacular compensatory arrangements

Another way of thinking through the extent to which compensation counts as or overlaps with apology is to ask what can be learnt from how it has historically been, and continues to be, conceptualised in South African vernacular dispute resolution settings. While on the surface such compensatory arrangements may seem transactional, they are often informed by a fundamentally different understanding of the function of money. Graeber (2011: 60) explains that money in many precolonial and pre-capitalist societies, including African ones, primarily played the role of rearranging and repairing social relationships and settling disputes, with economic exchange playing a secondary role. It is argued that prior to colonisation, money for Africans was not a commodity for creating, accumulating, and extracting value, but instead was relational, fulfilling critical social functions (Ferguson et al 2019). Prisons, Roberts (2013) reminds us, 'were rare in Africa during the precolonial period and crimes were primarily victim-focused, with victims or their kin receiving compensation' (p 182).

The relational importance of money is apparent in social arrangements such as *lobolo*, which involves property (usually in the form of cattle) being put forward in consideration of marriage between two families and which is also used as a form of compensation. While one interpretation of *lobolo* is a 'bride price' that perpetuates discrimination against women, others have interpreted it as a form of security against any threat to harmony within the marriage and wider community (Ngema 2012: 39). An act that disrupts cohesion within the marriage, such as domestic violence or adultery, can be resolved, when possible, through payment or forfeiture of *lobolo* between the families (Curran and Bonthuys 2004: 11). Compensation therefore exists as a means of repairing social fabric and regaining membership to the community. Following this understanding, many who practise *lobolo* do not view the practice as a sale transaction, which grants men ownership rights over women (Ngema 2012: 46–7; Claassens and Smythe 2015). The conception of money as a social relation dismantles the notion that compensation necessarily has the effect of commodifying human life and suffering. Instead, the exchange of money or property in kind within communities may be a pledge of good behaviour. Compensation is thus the logical result of wrongdoing, with payment interpreted as a sign of accepting responsibility for one's actions (Gabagambi 2018). In this way, compensation functions as part of a wider reading of the apology.

Another important function played by monetary compensation is to redistribute and reallocate both power and resources within a community, especially for those who are on the social margins. Mnisi Weeks' careful analysis of vernacular forums in Msinga shows that people turn to vernacular forums to request money and other forms of compensation as a way of reinforcing the veracity of a claim and the standing to bring it; as a way to attain peace and security through the reputational protection offered by resolution within the grouping; and as a way of restoring the 'social fabric' (2018: 216–17). This is in line with the fact that compensation is also a form of reparation, which is fundamental to an African conception of justice (Ramose 2001), with injustice considered to persist until reparative action is taken to restore equilibrium (M'Baye 1975: 138). The importance of this understanding is evident in the proposition that 'a debt or a feud is never extinguished till the equilibrium has been restored, even if several generations elapse' (Ramose 2001), so that extinctive prescription does not exist in African law. This approach underlines the fundamental importance within African philosophical conceptions of law of taking positive action to repair harm to the person and broader grouping that was wronged, aligning with the importance of ongoing reform and redress as a key element of apology. These differing expectations of justice, including in cases of rape and murder, mean that:

> even where state courts are turned to by local people ... for assistance, the relief these courts provide may not necessarily conclude the matter. Rather, the party who feels wronged may simultaneously or subsequently present his or her grievance in a vernacular forum, appealing for a form of relief other than that issued by the state court. (Mnisi Weeks 2018: 64–5)

In the meantime, in Magistrates' Courts, ad hoc reports are emerging of compensation payments being made that explicitly reference vernacular law. In one such case, in an urban Magistrates' Court, the magistrate is reported to have explicitly referenced the tradition of paying cows as compensation when a family has been wronged. On this instruction, the money was physically handed over between the families in the court room. Since her daughter had passed away during the trial, the mother said that she would use the money to pay for a tombstone (Mafokwane 2015). There seems little doubt that this practice is happening in other lower courts, including in prior engagements with police and prosecutors. In a constitutional dispensation that purports to take African jurisprudence, victims' rights, and restorative conceptions of justice seriously, a state legal system that emphatically rejects compensatory arrangements as unsuitable for resolving serious offences is likely to encourage attrition from the criminal justice system of those complainants who do not view prison alone as a just outcome and who seek both the material and social security (as tenuous as both may be) that comes from compensation.

More than words

South Africa is one of the most unequal countries in the world, and one of the most violent. The prevailing emphasis on police and prisons to solve the deep-seated violence that characterises South African society is inadequate – the inevitable outcome of an over-reliance on an offender-focused criminal justice system that has failed to meaningfully engage with victims' needs or the psychosocial and material consequences of the harm they have suffered. It is possible to bridge compensation, as a material acknowledgement of harms for which there are no words, and apology, being immaterial and potentially only words. Along with the understanding that compensation offered without an explicit apology (and vice versa) is generally more limiting, it becomes possible to think through the necessity to include compensation as a remedy for victims of sexual offences.

Learning from vernacular practices and incorporating these into the formal legal system can enable access to a broader range of remedies that align with 'justice' as determined by those victims who seek damages as a public affirmation and acknowledgement of the harm done to them. The practice of compensatory agreements is already happening in vernacular disputing forums, with survivors approaching these forums even after going through state procedures to obtain better or ancillary relief. This is similarly the case with the pursuit of delictual damages in civil courts following a criminal process. It is likely happening in an unregulated fashion in the lower tiers of the criminal justice system, where it is largely beyond scrutiny. Going through multiple channels to secure justice prolongs the survivor's emotional and psychological exhaustion and may build frustration with the law. This is ironic when, at the same time, perceived remorse continues to function as a basis for courts to reduce prison time, despite being 'a poorly formulated concept, lacking clarity and uniformity in both its definition and the characteristics that signal its presence or absence' (Zhong et al 2014: 39). At the very least, compensation for survivors of sexual violence, provided for in the Criminal Procedure Act, should be more deliberately incorporated into the criminal justice system and serious consideration given to a statutory compensation scheme that can serve as guarantor of those awards (South African Law Reform Commission 2004; Wessels 2018).

Incorporating compensation as a form of justice for serious offences is one pathway towards dealing with disputes beyond the prevailing rhetoric of meeting violence with violence. Along with comprehensive preventive solutions to violence against women that target systemic problems, a compensation-based approach can foreground principles of reconciliation and community care, provide an intermediary means of redistributing resources, improve the material conditions of survivors and others affected by sexual violence, and overcome a binary approach to civil versus criminal justice. Without a change in people's material conditions, there cannot be substantive resolution or acceptance of remorse. To return to Pettigrove, '… if we have no intention of making reparation, doing penance, and acting justly in the future, then the offer of an apology is infelicitous' (2003: 327). Compensation is integral to apology. Where African legal philosophies give more weight to the voices of those who were wronged and rely on accountability rather than violence, compensation is a method of harm resolution that can – as Smith's categorical apology illustrates – be applied to mitigate a harsh retributivist approach while at the same time making the system more responsive to victims' needs.

Reflections

Thinking through compensation for sexual offences, and writing about this within the framework of apology, was an incredibly difficult task. It seems unthinkable that payments or apologies could hold any power to remediate the many harms caused by such unconscionably violent acts. I struggled with this, and with how to write about 'justice' within the context of criminal law, given the law's role as a structure which itself creates and reproduces violence. I wanted to avoid presenting an essentially reformist argument. At the same time, it felt impossible to put forward abolitionist or decolonial arguments in a meaningful way while critiquing case law. For me, the process of writing this chapter was about responding to a prevailing carceral logic that cannot conceive of justice beyond police, prisons, and state-sanctioned death. It was also about trying to shift away from thinking about compensation in law as purely transactional, and towards thinking about it as a form of reparation or material security for people who are harmed. It was about taking seriously demands by women in legal processes for reparations (in the form of compensation and apology), and recognising these demands within a history of women's resistance that long predates South African law. Across Africa, women have always organised against violence and injustice, and have specifically demanded atonement and apologies from perpetrators in doing so. Ultimately, part of the work of this chapter was about learning from alternative forms of justice and finding pathways to these within a flawed criminal justice system.

Leila

References

Antonsdóttir, H. F., 2020, 'Compensation as a means to justice? Sexual violence survivors' views on the tort law option in Iceland', *Feminist Legal Studies* 28, 277–300.

Clark, H., 2015, 'A fair way to go: justice for victim-survivors of sexual violence', in A. Powell, N. Henry, and A. Flynn (eds.), *Rape Justice: Beyond Criminal Law*, pp 18–35, Basingstoke: Palgrave Macmillan.

Claassens, A. and Smythe, D., 2015, *Marriage, Land and Custom: Essays on Law and Social Change in South Africa*, Cape Town: Juta and Company.

Curran, E. and Bonthuys, E., 2004, *Customary Law and Domestic Violence in Rural South African Communities*, Johannesburg: Centre for the Study of Violence and Reconciliation.

Daly, K., 2017, 'Sexual violence and victims' justice interests', in E. Zinsstag and M. Keenan (eds.), *Restorative Responses to Sexual Violence: Legal, Social and Therapeutic Dimensions*, pp 108–39, London and New York: Routledge Taylor & Francis Group.

Department of Justice and Constitutional Development of the Republic of South Africa, 2004, *Service Charter for Victims of Crime in South Africa*, Pretoria: Department of Justice and Constitutional Development.

Des Rosiers, N., Feldthusen, B., and Hankivsky, O. A. R., 1998, 'Legal compensation for sexual violence: therapeutic consequences and consequences for the judicial system', *Psychology, Public Policy, and Law* 4(1–2), 433–51.

Ferguson, F., Seijo, M., and Saas, W., 2019, 'Confronting monetary imperialism in Francophone Africa: an interview with Ndongo Samba Sylla', *Africa's a Country*, 24 July, viewed 13 September 2021 from https:// africasacountry.com/2019/07/confronting-monetary-imperialism-in-fran cophone- africa

Fiske, A. P. and Tetlock, P. E., 1997, 'Taboo trade-offs: reactions to transactions that transgress the spheres of justice', *Political Psychology* 18(2), 255–97.

Gabagambi, J. J., 2018, 'A comparative analysis of restorative justice practices in Africa', *Globalex*, viewed 13 September 2021 from www.nyulawglobal. org/globalex/Restorative_Justice_Africa.html

Graeber, D., 2011, *Debt: The First 5,000 Years*, New York: Melville House.

Greenbaum, B., 2013, 'Compensation for victims of sexual violence in South Africa: a human rights approach to remedial criminal compensation provisions', doctoral dissertation, University of Cape Town.

Hamman, A. J. and Nortjie, W., 2017, 'Compensation orders in criminal proceedings – a fresh perspective', *Litnet Akademies* 14(1), 281–303.

Herman, J. L., 2005, 'Justice from the victim's perspective', *Violence Against Women* 11(5), 571–602.

Holder, R., 2015, 'Satisfied? Exploring victims' justice judgements', in D. Wilson and S. Ross (eds.), *Crime, Victims and Policy: International Contexts, Local Experiences*, pp 184–23, Basingstoke: Palgrave Macmillan.

Jeffries, S., Wood, W. R., and Russell, T., 2021, 'Adult restorative justice and gendered violence: practitioner and service provider viewpoints from Queensland, Australia', *Laws* 10, 13.

Mafokwane, P., 2015, 'Rapist free after paying R5000 to victim's family', *Sowetan*, viewed 13 September 2021 from https://pressreader.com/south-africa/sowetan/20151015/281513634991536

Makou, G., Skosana, I., and Hopkins, R., 2017, 'Factsheet: the state of South Africa's prisons', *Africa Check*, viewed 15 September 2021 from https://africacheck.org/factsheets/factsheet-the-state-of-south-africas-prisons/

M'Baye, K., 1975, 'The African conception of law' in R. David (ed.), *International Encyclopedia of Comparative Law*, Vol. 2, *The Legal Systems of the World, their Comparison and Unification*, pp 138–56, J. C. B. Mohr, Tübingen: Paul Siebeck.

McGlynn, C., Downes, J., and Westmarland, N., 2017, 'Seeking justice for survivors of sexual violence: recognition, voice and consequences', in E. Zinsstag and M. Keenan (eds.), *Restorative Responses to Sexual Violence: Legal, Social and Therapeutic Dimensions*, pp 179–91, New York: Routledge.

McGlynn, C. and Westmarland, N., 2019, 'Kaleidoscopic justice: sexual violence and victim-survivors' perceptions of justice', *Social & Legal Studies* 28(2), 179–201.

McGraw, A. P. and Tetlock, P. E., 2005, 'Taboo trade-offs, relational framing, and the acceptability of exchanges', *Journal of Consumer Psychology* 15(1): 2–15.

Mnisi Weeks, S., 2018, *Access to Justice and Human Security: Cultural Contradictions in Rural South Africa*, New York: Routledge.

Murhula, P. and Singh, A., 2019, 'A critical analysis on offenders rehabilitation approach in South Africa: a review of the literature', *African Journal of Criminology and Justice Studies* 12(1) 21–43.

Nagtegaal, J. 2018, 'The cost of rape: seeking justice in South Africa', *Daily Maverick*, 7 September, viewed 13 September 2021 from www.dailymaverick.co.za/opinionista/2018-09-07-the-cost-of-rape- seeking-justice-in-south-africa/

Ngema, N. M. M., 2012, 'Considering the abolition of *Ilobolo: Quo Vadis* South Africa?' *Speculum Juris* 2, 30–46.

Okimoto, T. G., 2008, 'Outcomes as affirmation of membership value: material compensation as an administrative response to procedural injustice', *Journal of Experimental Social Psychology* 44(5), 1270–82.

Pettigrove, G., 2003, 'Apology, reparations, and the question of inherited guilt', *Public Affairs Quarterly* 17(4), 319–48.

Ramose, M. B., 2001, 'An African perspective on justice and race', *Polylog: Forum for Intercultural Philosophy* 3, viewed 13 September 2021 from https://them.polylog.org/3/frm-en.htm

Roberts, R., 2013, 'Law, crime and punishment in colonial Africa', in J. Parker and R. Reid (eds.), *The Oxford Handbook of Modern African History*, pp 171–88, Oxford: Oxford University Press.

South African Law Reform Commission, (Project 82), 2004, *Sentencing (A Compensation Fund for Victims of Crime)*, Pretoria: South African Law Reform Commission.

Smith, O. and Galey, J., 2018, 'Supporting rape survivors through the criminal injuries compensation scheme: an exploration of English and Welsh independent sexual violence advisors' experiences', *Violence Against Women* 24(9), 1091–109.

Smith, N., 2008, *I Was Wrong: The Meanings of Apologies*, Cambridge: Cambridge University Press.

Smith, N., 2014, *Justice through Apologies: Remorse, Reform and Punishment*, Cambridge: Cambridge University Press.

Smythe, D. 2015, *Rape Unresolved: Policing Sexual Offences in South Africa*, Cape Town: UCT Press.

Shen, F. X., 2013, 'Rape, money, and the psychology of taboo', *Journal of Applied Social Psychology* 43, 1015–28.

Vetten, L., 2014, 'Rape and other forms of sexual violence in South Africa', *Policy Brief* 72.

Wessels, A. B., 2018, 'Developing the South African law of delict: the creation of a statutory compensation fund for crime victims', doctoral dissertation, Stellenbosch University.

Zhong, R., Baranoski, M., Feigenson, N., Davidson, L., Buchanan, A., and Zonana, H. V., 2014, 'So you're sorry? The role of remorse in criminal law', *Journal of the American Academy of Psychiatry and Law* 42, 39–48.

11

'She Told Me to Stop Making a Fuss': Undignified Treatment, Medical Negligence Claims, and Desires for Apology

Omowamiwa Kolawole

Introduction

Litigation has increasingly been used to air grievances and seek recompense for health concerns (South African Law Reform Commission, Project 141). This has especially been the case where genuine apologies and remorse have not been shown to health users who feel mistreated and, in some instances, taken advantage of. In a quest for some form of acknowledgement of the pain suffered and restitution for the same, litigation is increasingly becoming an avenue for seeking and sometimes getting closure. While in many instances, these legal claims are premised on the ability to prove actual medical negligence, as well as tangible damages suffered because of damages, the motivations for taking legal action are often not constrained to a desire for financial compensation. As studies on the uptake of medical negligence cases show, in many instances, these cases come as a response to the failure of medical personnel and their health institutions to adequately acknowledge the harm done to patients and offer what the patients perceive as genuine remorse, contrition, and acknowledgement of their pain.

The uptake in medical negligence litigation is also the case in the South African health system. Considering this development, there is an increasing need to better understand the factors responsible for the upsurge of medicolegal cases. Considerable scholarly intervention has been made to better understand this phenomenon and make recommendations addressing this growing field of the intersections of law and health systems. A lot of these efforts, however, have been on how to limit state liability, curtail the ability of health users to litigate, and on addressing the fallout of the increase in conservative medicine and health insurance (South African Law Reform Commission, Project 141). These interventions, while useful, do not fully capture the factors that have resulted in increased medicolegal cases. There is therefore a need to better understand the issues that influence the decision of health users to sue health care practitioners and the health systems for which they work. It is becoming more important to understand not just the institutional challenges that lead to more medical errors, but importantly, how such errors are managed and addressed. By exploring the motivations for litigation as a search for some form of catharsis, health practitioners may better understand the grievances of health users and the place of empathy and apologies in addressing them. I argue that the dignified and respectful treatment of patients regardless of medical outcomes is the ultimate acknowledgement of their pain and is a necessary first step in giving effective apologies for medical wrongdoing.

The rise of medical negligence cases and institutional responses

In March 2015, the South African Department of Health (DOH) held a medicolegal summit to discuss the growing 'crisis' of medicolegal claims in South Africa (South African Law Reform Commission, Project 141). The summit was attended by several key actors in the country's health governance structure at the national and provincial levels. At the summit, the Minister of Health stated that there were concerns that the 'lawsuit crisis' in South Africa could lead to the collapse of the health system. Citing the Australian health system, and its own prior collapse, the Minister stated that, unchecked, South Africa could suffer a similar fate. According to him:

> The nature of the crisis is that our country is experiencing a very sharp increase, actually an explosion in medical malpractice litigation which is not in keeping with generally known trends of negligence or malpractice. The cost of medical malpractice claims has skyrocketed, and the number of claims increased substantially. The crisis we are faced with is not a crisis of public healthcare. It is a crisis faced by everybody in the healthcare profession – public and private. (p 3)

This noted rise in legal claims against the health system and its personnel is premised on the rules of common law in the absence of any specific legislation to regulate the issue. This common law, which is a product of received English legal tradition, forms a significant portion of the legal norms of the country, which is also heavily influenced by Roman Dutch law and principles (Hahlo and Kahn 1968). On the basis of these existing legal traditions, many of the medicolegal cases against health care workers, service providers, and the health system are crafted as medical negligence cases, with ever-increasing damages being sought and being granted by the courts.

In the private health sector, an ever-increasing amount for medical malpractice premiums have also led to an increase in defensive medicine and an opposition to any action that may be interpreted as an admission of wrongdoing, which may be used to buttress a health user's claim of medical negligence. The opposition to early and relatively amicable resolution of health users' grievances against health practitioners, which may sometimes mean the use of informal channels and processes, may result in the eventual use of formal proceedings that are, by and large, more adversarial in nature. This is because, in these formal processes, as with litigation, the focus is on identifying the harm caused and apportioning blame to the relevant parties for said harm. This adversarial stance runs contrary to any hopes of conciliatory interventions, which could lay the foundation for the necessary acknowledgement of harm done to health users and the subsequent offering of apologies.

Unfortunately, however, in response to the increase in medicolegal cases, the focus has been on trimming the hedges around the adversarial nature of medicolegal claims. The emphasis of health practitioners and the health systems they work for has been on limiting the scope of those who can bring these medicolegal claims, as well as on proposing a cap on payouts. These efforts at limiting the scope and range of liability, while being understandably self-preservatory, run the risk of losing sight of the needs of health users and how failure to meet those needs translate into litigation. The resultant effect is the loss of critical opportunities to learn from individual mistakes and institutional failings, which would in turn help improve health systems and the nature of care they provide; a goal which itself has more long-term utility for all parties.

The centrality of health user dignity in health care provision

Dignity in the context of health care provision is concerned with the right of the health care user to be treated as a person in their own right and not as just another patient receiving medical care (World Health Organization 2000; Beach et al 2005). It is concerned with how health users feel, think, perceive themselves, and consequently act in relation to their worth. This sense of worth in turn affects how they perceive the treatment they receive during their interaction with the health system. By extension, to treat a person with dignity means to treat them as being of worth, in a manner that is respectful of their inherent value as human (Andorno and Pele 2015). In this manner, the health user is not simply an object/recipient of health care but is an autonomous þeing capable of agency, which ought to be recognised and respected. Treating the health user with dignity also entails respecting and protecting their other fundamental rights that are inherent to them. This respect and protection of the full gamut of health users' rights should not be restricted to their interaction with the health professionals seeing to their medical care directly. Rather, it should also occur in the course of their interaction with all the various aspects of the health care delivery structure. From administrative matters to the substantive medical care, to post-care management, it is pertinent that the health user always feels seen, heard, and respected by all health workers at all levels of service and care. This kind of treatment should involve being accorded respect by health staff, being given the opportunity to be fully informed of all health intervention options, and being given the chance to make fully informed decisions based on the options available (Baillie et al 2008). Being treated with dignity must also include the respect for a patient's privacy during examination and treatment. All these kinds of treatment, while being ethical and in keeping with best practices, are also intrinsic to the respect of health users' human rights and are an important part of ensuring high patient satisfaction (Beach et al 2005).

Health users have a legitimate expectation of being treated with dignity (World Health Organization 2000). In the absence of dignity, there can be a pervasive sense of being devalued, as well as feeling discomfort and lacking control. Under such unfavourable circumstances, health users are more likely to be unsure of their medical decisions, in which case, they are unprepared for their health outcomes. This may result in feelings of shame and humiliation at their lack of a sense of capacity (Baillie et al 2008). Patients have stated that they felt 'so small and so vulnerable' (Bell and Duffy 2009). In such times, what is required by patients, beyond the actual care given, is reassurance and as much of a sense of control (Baillie et al 2008). Human dignity here is not simply a principle for guiding the norms of biomedical issues. It is also a valued moral standard that should inform subsequent concrete and context-specific interactions with the health user as a 'person' and not just as a patient (Andorno and Pele 2015). It is key to the transition of perceiving the health user as an 'object' to being a 'subject' (Andorno and Pele 2015). As Valentine et al pointed out, in many priority lists, patients state the desire for 'humanness' as being important to them (Valentine et al 2003). In the course of receiving health care, patients are placed in a situation of special vulnerability where they are largely dependent on the assistance of others, both for the improvement of their health condition, but also for the meeting of their most basic needs. In such a state of susceptibility, patients are exposed to having their self-esteem affected if they see certain attitudes or behaviour by health care providers that appear to be dismissive or outrightly antagonising of their dignity and self-worth (Andorno 2013).

This becomes even more stark where the care they have received has either not produced the anticipated result or has been an outright failure.

While untoward health outcomes may not always be a direct result of not being treated with dignity, the situation is made especially worse when while addressing the substantive health concern leading to use of the health care facility, the patient's concerns are not given the regard and concern they are due. This kind of disregard, especially when layered over an undesirable health outcome after health care is provided, then becomes an expression of undignified treatment that may propel the affected patient to seek redress through the courts. Studies carried out in other jurisdictions have shown that the choice of litigation as a response to negative health outcomes during interaction with health care service providers is sometimes in response to a perception of not being treated with respect and dignity in the acknowledgement of the harm that has been suffered and the effect it has had on the health user (Robbennolt 2003). While the motivation for these kinds of actions by health practitioners in not admitting harm caused is usually to avoid liability, the resultant effect is the desire of the patient to seek redress outside of the health system and its managers. As such, the need to tangibly respect the dignity of patients becomes more imperative against the backdrop of increasingly bureaucratic, impersonal, and commercialised health care delivery. In the high-pressure and high-volume nature of health care provision, there is a tendency to be programmatic and utilitarian and, in the process, to inadvertently overlook the place of kindness and recognition of patients as individuals (Sinclair et al 2016). While this is more likely not a deliberate dismissal by health care workers, the ripple effect of such cold treatment is more likely a reduction in patient satisfaction, especially when the health outcome has been an undesired one. In these kinds of instances, it is possible to better understand litigation as a manifestation of discontent with the health system and as an outlet for the retrieval of lost agency that is a product of the violation of the health user's dignity.

Studies have been conducted to better understand when and why litigants go to court in civil cases for redress and what they aim to get from the courts (Lind et al 1989). Similarly, other studies have sought to understand how civil litigation may be mitigated, especially through apologies (Robbennolt 2003). The reasoning for this interrogation is that, by and large, apologies help to reduce tension, antagonism, and anger. In many instances, claimants have stated that receiving an apology would have prevented them from filing their suit (Robbennolt 2003). In these studies, patients emphasised a desire to receive an apology after a medical error (Gallagher et al 2003). In addition to this, another study found that health users were prompted to institute legal action when they realised that their health care providers had failed to be totally honest with them and either directly misled them or allowed them to believe the wrong things (Hickson et al 1992). In another study, up to 37 per cent of patients stated they would not have gone on to sue if they had received an explanation and apology, while 14 per cent stated that they would not have sued if there had been an admission of negligence (Vincent et al 1994: 1611). In South Africa specifically, a study has found that a leading cause of litigation, resulting from orthopaedic care, is a failure to properly communicate between surgeon and patient (East and Snyckers 2011). Another study in the South African context has also highlighted that, while the uptake in medicolegal cases has erroneously been attributed to legal practitioners and their 'predatory' practices, it is rather due to the more systemic problems of the South African health care system (Nwedamutsu 2020). In that study, alternative dispute resolution mechanisms are proposed as a viable alternative to litigation (p 83). However, not enough work has been done to better understand the non-medical motivations that drive medical negligence litigation, beyond the examination of damages and questions around quantum and whether or not they are enough or exorbitant. In this manner, the questions being asked can themselves fall into the trap of minimising the grievances of health users to simply being a desire for pecuniary interest.

Studies in other jurisdictions point to a connection between perceptions of undignified treatment and the decision to sue for medical negligence. The link between the two needs further enquiry in the South African context. Beyond instances where there is seemingly clear evidence of bad medical care, how often do patients feel the need to have an acknowledgement and reckoning of the wrong done to them? How are affronts to agency and autonomy confronted by health users? Is litigation used as an outlet for venting the grievances that occur from these affronts? The answers to these questions can help fill the knowledge gaps in our understanding of the place of apologies in resolving medical negligence claims. The case for apologies can be made stronger, if there is more proof that the result of medical interventions is not the only reason for taking action against health practitioners and the health system. It can also help in the quest to address the actual needs of health users, and in addressing their legitimate expectations. With a better understanding of the place of empathy in dealing with health users as being worthy of dignity, context-specific interventions may then be formulated which address the shortfalls in the treatment health users have received.

It has been noted also in other jurisdictions that a major limitation to the exploration of the viability of apologies as an approach to handling wrongdoing is the lingering notion that apologising would be tantamount to admitting liability, which may then be used in the substantive civil case against the party that apologised (Robbennolt 2003). However, it has been suggested that the opportunity cost of the apology may be well worth it, especially when it is done short of acknowledging liability. This approach itself has been critiqued by others as also lacking in the sincerity required for such a 'safe' apology to have a real effect on the recipient (Robbennolt 2003). What begins to emerge in this discussion around the nature and efficacy of apologies in medical negligence cases is the acknowledgement that, beyond any specific medical mishap, how the health user is treated goes a long way in determining how they perceive the care they have received. Where there is a power imbalance, as is usually the case with health care providers and their patients who are at their mercy, actions taken to reinforce the weakened position of the patient can be met with backlash, in a bid to reassert the sense of lost dignity that the untoward treatment created.

If the treatment of health users plays so much of a role in how they handle mishaps in their care, significant effort must be put into better understanding the phenomenon and to using it to inform how the non-medical aspects of health care service are handled. While there is no gainsaying that more action is needed to mitigate medical mishaps on both the personal and systemic level, the odds of total perfection at all times is next to impossible to guarantee. In this sense, we can understand medicolegal cases as not just about the actual medical error but also being about the mismanagement of the process of recompense. As such, litigation must be understood as not just the act of trying to right a medical wrong but as a process of getting vindication for a perceived affront of the health user's dignity.

Contextualising indignity and the treatment of health users in medical negligence cases in South Africa

A recurring theme that arises from the plethora of medical negligence cases in South Africa is an unfortunate penchant for treating patients dismissively, condescendingly, and without empathy. This poor and undignified treatment of patients becomes apparent in the retelling of the factual events leading up to and during the provision of medical care that ended up being medically negligent. In some instances, this undignified treatment is at the heart of the failure to provide the proper medical care, while in other instances, it is an ancillary fact that lends credence to a general culture of poor patient care.

A good example of dismissive conduct that resulted in poor and negligent medical care is seen in the 2019 case of *Gura v MEC for Health, Free State Province*[1] where the court noted:

> The Plaintiff was taken to the labour ward but was left outside the labour ward for many hours without being attended to. According to the Plaintiff the nurses were in their staff room when she called them

---

[1] (4632/2015) [2019] ZAFSHC 184 (3 October 2019).

again for assistance. One of the nurses *came to her and told her to keep quiet as she was disturbing the other patients in the ward.* She explained to the nurse that she felt something was coming out and she was not certain if it was the baby. *The nurse stood at the foot of the bed without helping her.* She gave birth to the baby without assistance. (para. 6, emphases added)

Unfortunately, as in this case, the dismissive treatment of the patient, who was in labour, was not merely a failure to prioritise her needs, but sadly proved to be instrumental in the botched delivery of her baby and its eventual death. The court here also highlighted the inhumane circumstances of the infant's birth. As seen in paras. 7 and 8 of the judgment, the court recounted:

The Plaintiff said after the baby was born, it lay between her legs, in [a] pool of water and blood without moving. The nurse then came and took the baby without checking if it was alive. The nurse put the baby in a waste plastic bag. The Plaintiff requested the nurse to hold the baby. The nurse took the baby out of the plastic bag and put it on her chest and at that moment she felt the baby move. She told the nurse the baby moved. *The nurse did not listen to the Plaintiff, but instead took the baby, placenta, and umbilical cord and put everything in a waste bag.* (para. 7, emphasis added)

The Plaintiff said a cleaner in the ward told her she heard the cries of a baby in the waste bag and called for assistance. The baby was taken out of the waste bag and taken to the Neonatal Intensive Care Unit (NICU). She mentioned that the baby was alive for approximately two days, and in that short period she was encouraged to express breastmilk for the baby to be fed via a feeding tube. (para. 8)

Rude and undignified treatment of the patient is once again highlighted in the 2017 case of *M obo M v Member of the Executive Council for Health, Eastern Cape Province*[2] where the plaintiff noted that the nurse who delivered her baby 'was harsh to her' and insisted that she must push, despite her hesitance, because, according to the nurse, the baby was tired (para. 10).

A particularly striking insight from the examination of medical negligence cases is how patients tend to remember the untoward statements made to them, with many recalling these statements verbatim. This recollection happens even when other relevant facts surrounding the events of their care have been forgotten or have become fuzzy. In these instances, the undignified

---

[2]   (1476/2014) [2017] ZAECMHC 42 (17 October 2017).

treatment appears to stay with the patients long after. This vivid recollection is often the seed that is planted in their minds, that reinforces the pain or discomfort they felt from the care personnel. Interestingly, also, even in the instances where these patients are unsure that the nature of care they received was of such a nature as to warrant a legitimate legal claim of medical negligence, their mistreatment without any consequent acknowledgement and redress sets the tone for their eventual legal claim.

In *Buys v MEC for Health and Social Development of the Gauteng Provincial Government*[3] of 2015, for example, the plaintiff says:

> It was then put to her that the sister or midwife who was in charge did not utter the words 'jy sal druk' (you will push) as alleged by the plaintiff. She gave the following response: 'Your honour, if I may just say, I mean I was the one that was in labour, I was the one that was there and if words like that were said to me it is very difficult or very unlikely that I would forget in a day or two, that type of words that were uttered to me it is, I will not forget it'. (para. 31)

Another good example is seen in the 2017 case of *S v Member of the Executive Counsel for the Department of Health, Eastern Cape*[4] where the plaintiff was in labour and stated to the nurses that she was exhausted and would like to have labour induced. Unfortunately, however, the response she received was one of dismissal. As the court noted:

> During the course of the following day, 12 November 2004, the same procedure was repeated over and over again despite the fact that she was suffering from extensive abdominal pains. At one stage a nurse placed something on her ears and on her stomach as a precursor to a vaginal examination and said to her 'Lady, still walk around!' (para. 9)

The court further noted:

> She (the patient) continued to approach the nurses during the remainder of that day and night to the extent that the nurses became annoyed. They continued to give her the same advice. On the 13th the pains had become severe and she requested that a caesarean section be performed. The response from one of the nurses was 'You seem to know a lot. You are going to deliver your child in the normal way like other people.' (para. 10)

---

[3] (16223/2013) [2015] ZAGPPHC 530 (18 June 2015).
[4] (2930/13) [2017] ZAECMHC 5 (28 March 2017).

In yet another case,[5] the court observed from the testimony of the plaintiff that 'when she complained to the nursing staff of the symptoms she experienced, she was told to stop being childish' (para. 29).

The assertion that unresolved, undignified treatment of patients is frequently at the root of eventual litigation is particularly highlighted in the 2015 case of *Nzimande v The MEC for Health, Gauteng*[6] where the court observed that '[t]he plaintiff was dissatisfied with the treatment she and her baby received but lacked the financial means to engage a lawyer' (para. 11). The court also noted that while the patient subsequently took up the quest for resolution of concerns into her own hands by seeking publicity in a magazine in order to raise awareness, no recourse was offered to her by the health facility that had mistreated her, all through that time (para. 12). As observed by the court in that matter, 'the plaintiff and her child were left in the lurch by an organ of state. *They were treated without empathy and without compassion*' (para. 27, emphasis added).

To further compound matters, the disdain shown to the plaintiff and her plight continued well into the process of litigation. As the court further noted, 'In this Court the defendant decided to play a role that was essentially obstructive. None of the essential features of the plaintiff's case were disputed or could be disputed, yet the defendant persisted in resisting both merits and quantum on the basis of a bare denial' (para. 27).

In this case, as with some others, the handling of the health system's case by its lawyers was done in a way that disregarded the plaintiff and the court. The lack of respect for the opposing party as both a matter of professional courtesy and as an acknowledgement of the solemnity of the issues being litigated on then add an extra layer on to the existing indignity that resulted in litigation in the first place. This kind of undignified prosecution of the health system's case in court, that is, legal representation that makes a mockery of the judicial process and or the seriousness of the health user's medical negligence claim, can manifest in various forms. This practice of disregard for the plaintiff and the court has also been highlighted in the 2014 case of *Zonele v Member of the Executive Council of the Department of Health of the Eastern Cape Government, Bhisho*[7] where it was observed by the judge in their judgment:

> This matter should not have proceeded to trial. It must have been clear to the defendant or the relevant official dealing with the claim that the plaintiff's treatment was sub-standard. The records at Grey

---

5   *V v MEC for Health: Gauteng Province and Others* (2014/69026) [2020] ZAGPPHC 223 (28 April 2020).

6   (44761/2013) [2015] ZAGPPHC 846 (8 September 2015).

7   (241/2012) [2014] ZAECBHC 17 (23 December 2014).

Hospital made it clear that no antibiotics were administered. The presence of infection over the weekend was apparent from the Frere Hospital records ... When the nurse discovered the greenish bandage and offensive smell, immediate action should have been taken. *Instead, the plaintiff was told to pray for a doctor. It is almost unbelievable that this could be said to a patient in a hospital.* No doctor attended to the plaintiff over that weekend. (para. 46, emphasis added)

Here, the court is quite clear that the harm suffered was manifestly obvious and the facts should not have been argued by the health care provider. This observation by the court in turn raises queries around why the choice was not rather to settle out of court through a more conciliatory attempt at acknowledgement, apology, and compensation. What situational or even systemic hurdles informed the choice to pursue the course of contesting the health user's claim, even when the facts showed clear liability? How much of the decision not to acknowledge wrongdoing factored in the health user's dissatisfaction and eventual choice to sue? While the answers to these questions are not evident from case law reports, other research carried out more broadly to better understand patients' motivations for going to court have pointed to a desire for acknowledgement of wrongdoing as a strong motivation (Hickson et al 1992). This observation is repeated in a number of cases, where the courts have expressed their displeasure with the decision to contest the plaintiff's claim, in some instances even querying the decision not to have addressed the issue, and allowing it to proceed to trial.

The pattern of undignified treatment becomes apparent from the kind of treatment the patient is subjected to during the events leading up to an eventual medical negligence claim. As noted by the court in *Maphosa v MEC for Health, Limpopo*[8]: 'In addition to this, it is clear that the plaintiff was sent from pillar to post and it was only after about three to four months that surgery was performed on his ankle' (para. 22).

In such an instance as that described in the case, the ill treatment of the patient was not only in the delay in being treated timeously but in the particularly unprofessional and inhumane way it was done, with no explanation offered or reasonable timeline set.

The courts have been adamant that the undignified treatment of patients, especially in their time of dire need, is an infringement on their dignity. As in the 2015 case of *M obo M v Member of the Executive Council for Health of the Mpumalanga Provincial Government*[9] the court noted:

---

[8] (29755/2011) [2017] ZAGPPHC 1259 (20 December 2017).
[9] (47217/2015) [2019] ZAGPPHC 935 (21 October 2019).

When O[…] was eight months old he had a fit whereupon she took him to the Mapulaneng Hospital for treatment where he was admitted. 'I was not advised by the doctor, nor did I consider the possibility that what occurred as a matter of fact could be as a result of the hospital staff's negligence during the birth during the birth process.' (para. 23)

In this case, the medical negligence is further exacerbated by the deliberate or tacit attempt to deflect and not bring to the attention of the health user the nature and gravity of the harm that they have suffered. This is yet another example of taking the health user for granted, insulting their intelligence, and, in the process, attempting to shirk responsibility and accountability. In such instances, the sense of helplessness that patients feel is then further compounded when the patients realise that their ignorance and/or lack of exposure has been unduly taken advantage of by the health system and its personnel. As the plaintiff in *M obo M*[10] recalled:

As stated above, even though I was told what the cause of O—'s brain damage was, I did not have the medical or legal knowledge to realise that someone could be held liable for such consequences and because I am not so directly involved in caring for O— (due to the fact that I am obliged to work in order to care financially for my family), I accepted his condition as 'one of those things in life'. (para. 23)

Apologies as restitution for patients' indignity

In the face of various instances that point to inhumane handling of allegations of medical negligence and undignified treatment of health users in South Africa, what solutions do a recourse to apologies present us? Can apologies be increasingly used in response to the legitimate grievances of health users. Can the use of apologies also achieve the health system's goal of minimised litigation and monetary compensation as a coincidental but welcome side effect? What would such apologies look like and what would they have to entail in order to be seen as genuine and thus effective? The answers to these questions are important in the quest to better treat health users, and are here explored.

On the question of what is entailed in an apology, Smith has pointed out that the nature of apologies often goes uninterrogated, with many who demand or claim to offer them being unsure of what is required (Smith 2005). And so, while there is a yearning for apologies that are heartfelt, givers and recipients are sometimes unsure of what that means in their particular context and

---

[10]   (47217/2015) [2019] ZAGPPHC 935 (21 October 2019).

thus can run the risk of having disjointed expectations and delivery. Worse still is the fact that in the face of seeming uncertainty around what a 'full' apology would entail, semblances to it that are more focused on deceiving and deflecting can masquerade as genuine (Smith 2005). In response to this, Smith makes the case for the use of a categorical apology. In his formulation of the term, a categorical apology is one that contains the various emotional and moral elements that together make up the most 'maximally meaningful' apology (Smith 2005). According to him, this categorical apology has a number of key elements, which, when put together, are most likely to assuage the recipient's desire for what I summarise as recognition, remorse, and restitution. He proposes that, while these elements may sometimes all need to be deployed, it may not always be the case, with a combination of any of those elements sometimes being sufficient together to convey the necessary contrition. He is also careful to note that, even where the intention is to offer a full and categorial apology, it may not always be possible to satisfactorily meet the conditions of a corroborated factual record; acceptance of causal responsibility rather than mere expression of sympathy; identification of each moral wrong; shared commitment to violated moral principles; expression of categorical regret; performance of apology; reform and reparations; standing; and the intention for apologising (Smith 2005).

Apologies and the form they take can vary, depending on the purpose for which they are made, and some, while being objectively less substantial, may be more meaningful in their context. The task is then to hold up the desired effect of the apology against the element of the categorical apology that can best provide such an effect (Smith 2005). As such, in the context of medical negligence, it is important to understand the desire of the health user and their preferred outcome in response to the injustice they have suffered. While each individual health user's desires are for the most part unique to them and will need to be considered on a case-by-case basis, there is considerable research available that provides us with broad themes around these desires. The quest to better understand and respond to these desires of health users are encapsulated in the scholarship of health systems' responsiveness. Interestingly, also, the study of health systems' responsiveness is less about patient's feedback on the substantive care they have received and determinations on their efficacy (Murray and Frenk 2000). Rather, it is concerned with understanding and then addressing the expectations of health users as to how they would like to be treated when interacting with the health system (World Health Organization 2000). Here, the population's legitimate expectations in this instance are defined in terms of international human rights norms and professional ethics. In measuring responsiveness, there are two broad areas of consideration, which are further divided into seven key elements. They are: (i) respect of persons, which entails the elements of dignity, autonomy, and confidentiality; and (ii) client orientation, which consists of the four other elements, which are prompt attention to the patient, quality of the amenities, access to familial and social support networks, and having a choice of provider (Mirzoev and Kane 2017).

With this understanding in mind, the role of apologies in the context of being a response to claims of medical negligence needs to be centred on restoring patients' sense of dignity, agency, along with recognition of any failure to give the patient prompt attention when it was needed. Furthermore, an apology that would be contextually relevant here would also seek to acknowledge and make amends for any fall in quality of care and support that was not provided in the course of care. The specific focus on these areas is especially necessary when bearing in mind that for the most part, patients interact with health care providers and the health system at their most vulnerable. Treatment with indignity only further worsens the sense of helplessness that the patients feel, regardless of the positive or negative outcome of their specific biomedical care. As such, the quest for the retrieval of dignity and agency is not limited to the confidentiality and autonomy that was desired in the course of medical care. Rather, it is centred on the desire for acknowledgement of the fact that one's humanity has been diminished and dignity assaulted, and to be consequently restored. As Smith points out, when a victim knows what they want from an apology, they can hold the offender to those standards, rather than 'artificially inflating the meaning of a few sympathetic words' (Smith 2005: 474). Therefore, the use of apologies in the context of medical negligence must be on the recognition and restoration of a patient's dignity, especially where its disregard was central to the poor treatment they received or, worse still, was an underlying factor in producing an undesirable health outcome.

Interestingly, also, fluency in the nature and language of apologies is also critical for those on the defensive end of the spectrum (Smith 2005). For if the offended is clear on what they require, it is in the interest of the party meant to give it to know how to do so, while naturally seeking to limit their exposure. This is particularly so in medical negligence cases, where the outcome of those cases has significant monetary implications as well as reputational ones. From the cases of medical negligence in South Africa reviewed, one of the main points of contention for patients arises from their interaction with the health care providers and the institutions they represent. First is the nature of shabby and undignified treatment they are subjected to in the course of their use of the health facility. Second is the consequent refusal to then acknowledge that those undignified events occurred, and to be accountable. The ill treatment of the health user then becomes compounded by attempts to discredit their pain as recollected by them. And while the refuting of the material facts takes various forms, ranging from dispute over minute details around the sequence of events or particular utterances made, sometimes, they go as far as an outright denial of the material facts, or worse, that the admitted facts are not actually the cause of the harm suffered. The South African courts examining these cases have noted that even when the issue in question is *res ipsa loquitor*, affected health care personnel can still be hell-bent on denying liability. A good example of a case where the facts seemingly spoke for themselves was that of *Goliath v The Member of the Executive Council for Health, Eastern Cape*,[11] where the basis of the claim was because a gauze swab had been left in the patient's abdomen after a prior surgical procedure. As the court in that case noted, 'in no other way could it have found its way into her body' (para. 13). The courts have found this kind of conduct particularly reprehensible and have gone on to express their displeasure in this regard by ordering punitive costs against the health care provider. In a scathing remark, the court noted the far-reaching effects of an approach hell-bent on diminishing the assertions of the health user about their experiences. The court stated in *M v Member of the Executive Council for Health, Eastern Cape Province*[12] that '[i]t is a salutary lesson to be observed that the defendant must bear the costs on the higher scale in the pursuit of defending a doctor's reputation rather than in keeping an objective mind about how the hospital collectively measured up to the standard expected of it' (para. 241).

In yet another case, *Smith v MEC for Health, Province of KwaZulu-Natal*,[13] counsel for the plaintiff argued that the court make an order as to punitive costs against the defendant (the Provincial Health Minister) for failing to admit the material fact that the patient had been given formalin, instead of water, and had unfortunately ingested it, which was the material fact upon which the substantive claim for medical negligence was made. The court obliged this request, stating that it did so as an expression of its displeasure with the health system's conduct, as well as that of its attorneys in defending the action against them in the manner that sought to discredit what appeared to the court to be manifest fact.

In response to what has been identified as a pattern of avoidance or denial of the facts, the court stated in the case of *Madida obo M v MEC for Health for the Province of Kwa-Zulu Natal*,[14] that '[t]he problem of medical and hospital records being unavailable timeously or at all is a recurring feature in medical malpractice cases that result in adjournments and extraordinary waste of legal and experts' costs at the expense of the public purse' (para. 74). Improper record keeping as a tactic to deflect from accountability further

---

[11] (085/2014) [2014] ZASCA 182 (25 November 2014).

[12] (1476/2014) [2017] ZAECMHC 42 (17 October 2017).

[13] (3826/12) [2016] ZAKZPHC 68 (2 August 2016).

[14] (14275/2014) [2016] ZAKZPHC 27 (14 March 2016).

highlights the grievances of health users in the quest for the recognition of the harm they suffered.

In the face of the challenges, the need for corroborated factual record, as well as the acceptance of causal responsibility – being the first two elements of Smith's postulation of the categorical apology – ring especially true. There must be recompense where patients are made to feel like their concerns, whether before, during, or after a medical procedure, are unheard or even outrightly belittled and dismissed. This is especially so when their recollection of those events is then unfairly and disingenuously called into question. In such instances, taking definite steps to corroborate the factual records as well as accepting causal responsibility must be central to any attempts at a resolution that makes the health user feel like their undignified treatment has been acknowledged and shown the remorse it is due. This is especially where the damage they have suffered is irreparable and no true form of restitution can be made. Where a patient has lost a child, limb, organ, or even just time, calculations of the quantum of damages in monetary terms are always with the intent of trying to, as best as possible, capture the gravity of loss suffered and compensate for it. The courts have stated several times that these damages cannot truly make up for the loss that patients have suffered. As such, it is risky to think that monetary compensation is all that is required. Often, this monetary compensation is sought in the stead of the acknowledgement so desperately desired by the plaintiff. Damages in these instances are only a matter of cause, which follow the acknowledgement of their suffering and the allocation of blame, by an impartial arbiter, having done the job of ascertaining the facts and determining that those facts are the causal link to the damage suffered.[15]

Tied to the acknowledgement of the harm suffered is the consequent need to show categorical regret, and then offer an apology. This should be followed by reparations to the party withstanding in the matter. These elements also line up with the desire of health users in medical negligence cases. Litigants usually state that when their concerns were laid to their health care providers or management within the larger health system structure, no attempts were made to express clear regret or offer to make reparations or reform. In the absence of such steps being taken by the health care providers, litigants have to seek these from the courts. In some instances, as in *Smith v MEC for Health, Province of KwaZulu-Natal*,[16] punitive damages have also

---

[15] For a successful claim of medical negligence to be made, the plaintiff must, on the balance of probabilities, show that harm was caused as well as show the causation between said harm and the damage claimed (Gittler and Goldstein 1996; South African Law Reform Commission, Project 141).

[16] (3826/12) [2016] ZAKZPHC 68 (2 August 2016).

been sought for initial denial of the facts. The need for responsibility to be taken by health managers in response to medical negligence claims has been highlighted by the courts in the case of *Member of the Executive Council for Health, Gauteng v Lushaba*[17] where it stated:

> *bureaucrats seem to get off scot-free, blithely taking no responsibility.* ... The quest to bring accountability to those who are responsible for the tragic proliferation of damages claims, and the seeming morass of never-ending litigation amidst which deserving claimants are sometimes made to suffer, must take a different form. (para. 11, emphasis added)

The question then becomes, if the outcomes of going to court are as likely to be the acknowledgement of harm, the apportioning of responsibility, and the provision of recompense for the same by the courts because of litigation, why then don't health care providers and managers take these steps themselves and save time and cost while doing so? In the face of the odds of reaching a negotiated out-of-court settlement that is a lower sum than what the courts would determine, an approach that is also less time-consuming, and that goes to the root of the contention, appears more pragmatic. In addition to this, the cost of litigation, especially when the facts are seemingly self-evident and show the health care provider to be in the wrong, further raises questions as to the choice to hold out on apologising to the health user and taking meaningful steps at restitution. Furthermore, by being proactive about acknowledging the harm done and accepting responsibility, apologies provided in these contexts are likely to be a more dignified approach for both parties, which can help manage what was hitherto an unpleasant experience with the health system. In the long term, this resort to apologies can help address the health system's concerns around ever-increasing litigation and, more importantly, feed into much-needed system-wide analysis of how health user dissatisfaction is received and managed, with the goal of being more responsive.

There must be a point at which the undignified treatment of the patient is put to a stop and the process of restitution begins. It is a further affront to the health user's dignity to have every level of health management refuse to acknowledge the harm done and to take steps to rectify it. This is even more so when that hard-headedness proceeds to trial and remains the conduct of the defendant during the case. The courts have shown displeasure at this and have noted in different instances that the cases should have been settled out of court, with the appropriate steps being taken to reprimand the affected medical personnel for their poor treatment of patients.

---

[17] (CCT156/15) [2016] ZACC 16 (23 June 2016).

Conclusion

As observed by the court in *Madida*, 'Malpractice suits are retroactive in the sense that they seek to remedy past wrongs. The litigation resolves the dispute but not the institutional problems' (para. 79).

The process of providing effective apologies must include and in fact begin with treating the health user with dignity. While the argument may even be made that treating the health user with dignity from the outset can in fact prevent the need for an apology altogether, such an assertion cannot be made in the case of medical negligence. To do so would be to presume that genuine medical errors cannot take place otherwise, or that it is possible to guarantee total perfection in the provision of medical care, without the possibility of human error. What is, however, emerging is that the treatment of the patient with dignity is closely linked to the decision to apologise for the harm they have suffered, as well as the choices on how to address that harm. Any apology that is not rooted in this acknowledgement is likely to inevitably come across as insincere and subsequently not be satisfactory to the patient receiving it. And while not every single element of the nine required for a categorical apology need to be met for it to be a sincere one, for it to be well received and accepted by the affected patient, it ought to be one that, above all else, acknowledges that their dignity has been disregarded and that seeks to restore dignity. This would particularly be in the context of medical negligence claims by acknowledging and corroborating the actual facts that occurred in the course of treatment, accepting causal responsibility, expressing categorical regret, and committing to reform and reparations for the affected health user.

While dignity may feel difficult to fully encapsulate as a concept, it remains integral to the expectations of health users who come to the health care system at their most vulnerable and in need. Taking the steps to better understand how they perceive their dignity and any affront to it must thus be at the core of any attempts to both provide better health care, as well as remedy any instances where such care has unfortunately fallen short.

Reflections

In the course of writing on apologies in the context of medical negligence litigation, I came to realise that the issues of closure and resolution were closer to my heart than I previously would have thought. With my own brushes with death over the years and my interactions with health systems with varying degrees of success, I have found that – beyond the immediate medical care I have been provided – what has determined how I recall my interaction with any medical facility is whether I felt *seen*, above all else. In the many instances where my concerns were dismissed, where I was made an object of curious fascination and poked and prodded by the next generation of medical practitioners in training as their class lesson for the day, the one thing that has stayed with me is that I was no longer seen as human. I was simply a curiosity to be solved. I was not someone's son, brother, friend, or lover; I was just a curiosity. Working on this chapter and seeing how often other patients too felt reduced to a case file by the health system and by the legal apparatus put in place to secure the interests of the health system did what all the years of my untoward interaction with health facilities never did: it made me feel seen. But, more importantly, it made me wonder: would it have made a difference if someone came to me and apologised for how I was treated? Would it have made a difference if they actually listened to my complaints and assured me that steps would be taken to reform the way medical care was provided? Now, more than ever, I believe it would have.

Omowamiwa

References

Andorno, R., 2013, 'The dual role of human dignity in bioethics', *Medicine, Health Care and Philosophy* 16(4), 967–73.

Andorno, R. and Pele, A., 2015, 'Human dignity', in H. ten Have (ed.), *Encyclopedia of Global Bioethics*, pp 1537–46, New York: Springer.

Baillie, L., Gallagher, A., and Wainwright, P., 2008, *Defending Dignity: Challenges and Opportunities for Nursing*, London: Royal College of Nursing.

Beach, M. C., Sugarman, J., Johnson, R. L., Arbelaez, J. J., Duggan, P.S., and Cooper, L. A., 2005, 'Do patients treated with dignity report higher satisfaction, adherence, and receipt of preventive care?', *The Annals of Family Medicine*, 3(4), 331–8.

Bell, L. and Duffy, A., 2009, 'A concept analysis of nurse–patient trust', *British Journal of Nursing* 18(1), 46–51.

East, S. C. and Snyckers, C. H., 2011, 'Orthopaedic litigation in South Africa: a review of the Medical Protection Society data base involving orthopaedic members over the last 10 years', *SA Orthopaedic Journal* 10(3), 71–9.

Gallagher, T. H., Waterman, A. D., Ebers, A. G., Fraser, V. J., and Levinson, W., 2003, 'Patients' and physicians' attitudes regarding the disclosure of medical errors', *Journal of the American Medical Association* 289(8), 1001–7.

Gittler, G. J. and Goldstein, E. J., 1996, 'The elements of medical malpractice: an overview', *Clinical Infectious Diseases* 23(5), 1152–5.

Hahlo, H. R. and Kahn, E., 1968, *The South African Legal System and its Background*, Cape Town: Juta & Co. Ltd.

Hickson, G. B., Clayton, E. W., Githens, P. B., and Sloan, F. A., 1992, 'Factors that prompted families to file medical malpractice claims following perinatal injuries', *Journal of the American Medical Association* 267(10), 1359–63.

Lind, E., MacCoun, R. J., Ebener, P. A., Felstiner, W. L., Hensler, D. R., Resnik, J., and Tyler, T., 1989, *The Perception of Justice: Tort Litigants' Views of Trial, Court-Annexed Arbitration, and Judicial Settlement Conferences*, Santa Monica: Rand/Institute for Civil Justice.

Mirzoev, T. and Kane, S., 2017, 'What is health systems responsiveness? Review of existing knowledge and proposed conceptual framework', *BMJ Global Health* 2(4), e000486.

Murray, C. J. and Frenk, J., 2000, 'A framework for assessing the performance of health systems', *Bulletin of the World Health Organization* 78(6), 717–31.

Nwedamutsu, T., 2020, 'Alternative dispute resolution in medical malpractice in South Africa', Master's thesis, Faculty of Law, University of the Western Cape, Cape Town.

Robbennolt, J. K., 2003, 'Apologies and legal settlement: an empirical examination', *Michigan Law Review*, 102(3), 460–516.

Sinclair, S., Norris, J. M., McConnell, S. J., Chochinov, H. M., Hack, T. F., Hagen, N. A., McClement, S., and Bouchal, S. R., 2016, 'Compassion: a scoping review of the healthcare literature', *BMC Palliative Care*, 15(1), 1–16.

Smith, N., 2005, 'The categorical apology', *Journal of Social Philosophy* 36(4), 473–96.

South African Law Reform Commission, Project 141, 2017, *Issue Paper 33, Medico-Legal Claims*, Cape Town: South African Law Reform Commission.

Valentine, N. B., de Silva, A., Kawabata, K., Darby, C., Murray, C. J., and Evans, D. B., 2003, 'Health system responsiveness: concepts, domains and operationalization', in C. J. L. Murray and D. Evans (eds.), *Health Systems Performance Assessment: Debates, Methods and Empiricism*, pp 573–96, Geneva: *World Health Organization*.

Vincent, C., Phillips, A., and Young, M., 1994, 'Why do people sue doctors? A study of patients and relatives taking legal action', *The Lancet* 343(8913), 1609–13.

World Health Organization, 2000, *The World Health Report 2000, Health Systems: Improving Performance*, Geneva: World Health Organization.

12

Unicorn Sightings: The Corporate Moral Apology in South Africa

Tracey Davies

In his book *I Was Wrong: The Meanings of Apologies*, Nick Smith (2008: 1) observes that 'we share a vague intuition that something has gone afoul with this ubiquitous gesture, a sense that apologies are rotting on the vine'. Apologies by corporations, or rather, by those representing corporations, in the rare instances when they are forthcoming, almost always evoke this sense of unease: a feeling that the apology is inadequate, evasive, or cowardly.

This is the case across the globe, and in relation to all types of corporate harm, from the unintentional to the incompetent and malign. It is indeed 'astonishing how many well-intentioned, sophisticated organizations completely botch apologies' (Schweitzer et al 2015).

South Africa's recent past is littered with corporate scandals and disasters. In each of these, those responsible have failed to apologise categorically to those they have harmed. This chapter will discuss failed apologies in relation to some of the postapartheid era's worst corporate tragedies and fiascos: the massacre of striking Lonmin workers at Marikana, the Tiger Brands listeriosis crisis, the implosion of Steinhoff, Tongaat Hulett's fraudulent accounting, and KPMG's complicity in 'state capture'.

However, in order to fully understand the responses of these companies, in the wake of exceptional failures in leadership and corporate governance, and in some instances extensive fraud and illegality, it is necessary to go back a little further in history.

The corporate sector's approach to the dismantling of apartheid, its submissions to South Africa's Truth and Reconciliation Commission (TRC), and the ultimate rejection by the African National Congress (ANC) of its own policy positions on forging a more inclusive post-apartheid economy, are integral to understanding South African big businesses' contemporary attitude to remorse and reparation.

Little remorse for apartheid

The TRC was established by the Promotion of National Unity and Reconciliation Act 1995,[1] with the objective to 'provide for the investigation and the establishment of as complete a picture as possible of the nature, causes and extent of gross violations of human rights committed during [apartheid]'.[2]

In addition to its hearings on human rights violations by the apartheid state, the TRC held a series of 'institutional hearings', on business and labour, the faith community, the legal community, the health sector, the media, and prisons. The aim of these was to try to better understand the 'old question' of how, 'over the years, people who considered themselves ordinary, decent and God-fearing found themselves turning a blind eye to a system which impoverished, oppressed and violated the lives and very existence of so many of their fellow citizens' (TRC Report 1999, Vol. IV: 1).

The 'Institutional Hearing: Business and Labour' was held to understand the role of business in the gross violations of human rights that were the hallmark of the apartheid state. The deep and enduring schism in views on the role of the corporate sector during apartheid was encapsulated in submissions to this hearing.

On the one hand, most of the companies that made submissions to the hearing maintained that they were, at worst, unwilling participants in a system imposed on them by an irresistible state. They argued that apartheid was 'essentially a politically inspired but economically irrational intervention that stifled business, distorted the economy and undermined long-term productivity growth' (Ibhawoh 2009: 274–5).

The opposing position, on the other hand, articulated in submissions from the ANC, the South African Communist Party (SACP), the Congress of South African Trade Unions (COSATU), and others, held that the apartheid state constituted 'a system of racial capitalism', one which 'was beneficial for (white) business because it was an integral part of a system premised on the exploitation of black workers and the destruction of black entrepreneurial activity' (TRC Report 1999, Vol. IV: 19). According to this view, the benefits of apartheid for white business were so great that it was simply not in its interests to challenge the system.

In submissions to the TRC, some companies and business associations expressed incredulity at the suggestion that corporations could commit

---

[1]   Act 34 of 1995.
[2]   Preamble to the Act.

human rights violations. Others were indignant at the idea that business might have had a moral role to play at all.

Old Mutual opened its submission by saying that, 'in principle, the mandate of the Commission which focuses on gross violations of human rights would almost certainly exclude Old Mutual from having to make any submission' (p 20).

Sanlam was shocked at the presumption that it could have done something to push back against the apartheid state:

> Any notion that business could have acted as a watchdog of the government as far as human rights violations are concerned is totally unrealistic and should be dispelled. Business was unable to act in that way in the past and will not be able to do so in the future. Government is so powerful and dominant that a business organisation will seriously jeopardise its prospects of success by crossing swords with politicians. (p 53)

Ann Bernstein, associated with the Urban Foundation set up in 1977 by Anton Rupert and Anglo American's Harry Oppenheimer, took a slightly different position, agreeing that business 'accommodated itself to the apartheid system' (p 53), but arguing that its activities provided the springboard for a new democracy:

> Corporations are not institutions established for a moral purpose ... They are not institutions designed to promote some or other form of morality in this world. ... Business in South Africa accommodated itself to the apartheid system. In doing so it provided jobs for millions of people, created infrastructure, unleashed democratising pressures (unintentionally) and sustained a base of economic activity that now provides a platform for economic growth in a democracy. (p 53)

At the most extreme end of the spectrum, South African Breweries (SAB) complained that 'English-speaking business leaders often felt marginalised under apartheid, having little or no influence over government policy ... in a real sense, such businesses were also victims of the system' (p 30).

The Commission was ultimately unsympathetic to these arguments. While acknowledging that there were different levels of corporate involvement in apartheid (the mining industry, for example, was 'involved in helping to design and implement apartheid policies'), the Commission found that 'business was central to the economy that sustained the South African state during the apartheid years' and that 'most businesses benefited from operating in a racially structured context' (p 58).

The Commission gave short shrift to the argument that corporations are incapable of committing violations of fundamental human rights. It found, for example, that denying black workers the right to join a trade union constituted a violation of human rights, and that the state's actions against trade unions, sometimes in cooperation with business, frequently resulted in gross human rights violations.

In response to the type of argument presented by Sanlam and Bernstein, the Commission found that '[i]t would be a sad day for the nation, faced as it is with the opportunity for renewal, if business were to dismiss social concern, business ethics and moral accountability in labour relations as being of no direct concern to itself' (p 54).

There were glaring gaps in the list of companies and industry associations that made submissions to the TRC.[3] The Commission also held an institutional hearing into the role of the media, at which it expected what it termed the 'Afrikaans media' to make submissions. The Afrikaans media declined to do so, however, and instead 'provided the Commission with a copy of *Oor Grense Heen*, the official history of Nasionale Pers (Naspers)' (p 177). In response, the TRC report states:

> Rather oddly in the context, the book repeatedly confirms that the various newspapers in the group were always pro-[National Party] government institutions. The opening paragraph states candidly that the NP victory in 1948 meant that the company became a pro-government institution ... Occasionally, doubts about apartheid do surface but, in the main, the book reflects a total lack of concern for the company's support of the racist system. (p 177)

Naspers' failure to appear at the institutional hearing into the media prompted TRC Chairman Archbishop Desmond Tutu to ask: 'Is silence from that quarter to be construed as consent, conceding that it was a sycophantic handmaiden of the apartheid government?' (p 177).

The view of the company's leaders, however, was not the view of all of its employees. After the hearing, 150 individual Afrikaans-speaking journalists submitted affidavits to the Commission in which they expressed 'disappointment at the Naspers decision not to appear', and 'maintained that, although the papers may not have been directly involved in violations, they should accept moral responsibility for what happened because they had helped support the system in which gross human rights violations occurred' (p 177–8).

In contrast to Naspers, those companies that did appear at the TRC hearings showed a measure of courage. However, with the notable exception of the

---

[3] For example, the Commission found that there was a reluctance from businesses to speak about their involvement in the former homelands, and lamented the absence of any submission from Sol Kerzner and Sun International.

Development Bank of South Africa, the corporate sector did not accept full responsibility for its role in supporting and enabling the apartheid state. Even in cases where corporates acknowledged that they could have done more, the acknowledgements fell far short of effective apologies. In particular, as is discussed in more detail below, none of these submissions demonstrated a clear acceptance of causal moral responsibility and blame, or an explicit identification of the moral principles and values at stake in the role that business played in, or the direct benefits that accrued to it from, apartheid.

Why did the TRC expect companies to apologise at all? What purpose are corporate apologies expected to serve? There is little difference between the reasons for apology in the personal and the corporate contexts: apology promotes healing and reconciliation, and the absence of apology sharpens resentment and makes it difficult for victims to move forward.

No individual company is likely to have been able to bring about the end of apartheid. However, it is clear, even from the anaemic admissions to the TRC, that little real effort was made to resist a system that protected white business. Failing to act, in the interests of personal and corporate financial gain, perpetuated and legitimised the apartheid state. At the very least, this constituted a vast and enduring moral wrong, the consequences of which still manifest themselves in the crippling inequality that defines our economy today.

Taft observes that 'apology leads to healing because through apologetic discourse there is a restoration of moral balance – more specifically, a restoration of an equality of regard' (Taft 2000: 1137). He links this to the concept of *ubuntu*, as expressed by Archbishop Tutu:

> [Ubuntu] speaks about the essence of being human: that my humanity is caught up in your humanity because we say a person is a person through other persons ... We set great store by communal peace and harmony. Anything that subverts this harmony is injurious, not just to the community, but to all of us, and therefore forgiveness is an absolute necessity for continued human existence. (Taft 2000: 1137–8)

Apology is such an integral part of forgiveness that even large financial settlements, when made in the absence of apology, often do not prevent victims from experiencing long-lasting anger and resentment (Smith 2008). Smith refers to studies that suggest that 'a few words of contrition, regardless of their sincerity by any measure, can dramatically decrease the likelihood of costly litigation' (p 3). Conversely, 'a refusal to accept blame for an injury often provides the fundamental grounds for a dispute arriving in the courts in the first place' (p 3).

In the South African context, however, the prospect of large financial settlements for the victims of apartheid is now a distant dream, and the majority of those victims do not have the means to litigate for compensation. The moral apology, therefore, takes on an enhanced importance in promoting reconciliation.[4] Govier and Verwoerd (2002: 71) observe:

> If a society pays no heed to brutalities and offences suffered by many of its citizens, it further damages these vulnerable people because moral contempt can be as devastating as the original wrong itself. In literature on the treatment of trauma, this lack of acknowledgement has been termed a second injury to victims, and its effects are referred to as the second wound of silence.

The reluctance of corporate leaders to accept moral responsibility for actions that harm others is often attributed to the fact that legal and public relations advisors recommend against doing so. Apology here is viewed as an admission of guilt, and therefore as a foundation for the imposition of financial penalties. Reliance on such advice may partly explain the inadequacy of the apologies described here, but it does not provide a full or satisfactory explanation.

What is an 'effective' corporate apology?

There are many interpretations of what constitutes an effective apology. In the business context, snappy advice from management gurus and crisis communications experts, promising three or seven or 13 steps to achieving an 'effective corporate apology', is ubiquitous. While the attention-grabbing format of this advice is often glib and superficial ('Leverage your vulnerability'), for the most part the recommendations are sensible and rather obvious: 'Be genuine, not defensive'; 'Don't make excuses'; 'Act like a human being' (Forbes 2020); 'Lose the corporate speak'; 'Move quickly: speed matters' (Casale 2017). But when a company has caused harm and the

---

[4] In 2002, a group of apartheid victims filed a suit in the Southern District of New York, seeking relief in the amount of $400 billion, on behalf of all historical apartheid victims, from more than 50 Western multinational companies that did business in apartheid South Africa (*Khulumani v Barclays National Bank Ltd* 504 F.3d 254 (2d Cir. 2007) (per curiam)). The plaintiffs did not sue companies based in South Africa during apartheid. The suit was filed under the US Alien Tort Statute, 28 U.S. C. §1350, which provides: 'The district courts shall have original jurisdiction of any civil action by an alien for a tort only, committed in violation of the law of nations or a treaty of the United States'. The case was dismissed in the first instances, and was pending before the Second Circuit Court of Appeals from 2010 until 2013, awaiting the Supreme Court's decision in the case of *Kiobel v Royal Dutch Petroleum Co.*, 133 S.Ct. 1659 (2013). The Supreme Court's decision in *Kiobel* in 2013 appears to have rendered the *Khulumani* case invalid.

pressure is on, corporate leaders find it extremely hard to remember even these basic tips.

An effective apology, however, is more complex than these quick-fix approaches suggest. The kind of apology that is required in cases of corporate harm such as those discussed here is the 'moral apology' (Govier and Verwoerd 2002) or the 'categorical apology' (Smith 2008). Such an apology requires, at the very least, an admission that the act was wrong, an acceptance of responsibility for that wrong, an expression of sorrow and moral regret, and an acknowledgement of the moral status of the victim.

Smith sets out 12 requirements for the categorical apology (pp 141–3). For our purposes, these can be summarised as follows:

- A *corroborated factual record*, in which the offender and the victim/s agree on what happened.
- An *acceptance of causal moral responsibility and blame* for the harm (as opposed to expressing sympathy for the harm, or describing it as accidental or unintentional).
- Possession of *appropriate standing*; in other words, the apology is not delegated to a representative.
- Explicit *identification of the moral principles and values at stake*, which means that the wrongdoer views the victim 'as a moral agent worthy of engaging in moral discourse and abandons the belief that she can disregard the victim's dignity, humanity, or worth in pursuit of her own objectives' (p 141).
- *Categorical regret*, as distinguished from expressing sympathy or regret at the victim's interpretation of behaviour which the wrongdoer considers justifiable.
- The wrongdoer *expresses the apology to the victim*, rather than sharing it only with a third party such as a judge.
- *Reform and redress*, in that the wrongdoer convincingly pledges not to commit the same harm again, and either offers to make reparation for it, or accepts proportionate sanctions imposed on him for committing the harm.

When thinking about the wrongs done during apartheid, the fourth (identification of the moral principles and values at stake) and seventh (reform and redress) requirements have particular resonance. Govier and Verwoerd (2002: 69) emphasise that 'in apologising, the offender is acknowledging the moral status of the victim(s)'. They also highlight:

> As the South African debate about reparations after apartheid highlights dramatically and painfully, victims and victim communities are likely to question the sincerity of an apology if the speaker is in no way

willing to commit himself to concrete measures to repair damage that has been done to the victim. (p 72)

When viewed in light of all of the above, the 'apologies' from South African corporates as reported by the TRC appear particularly meagre.

The Council of South African Banks expressed regret 'for acts of omission and commission committed by its members that contributed to the damage caused by apartheid', but insisted that it had no choice: 'Either you are in the business of banking, or you are not. It does not lie in the mouth of a bank to say that it will accept the instruction of its client to pay one person but not another' (TRC Report 1999, Vol. IV: 27) . The Commission found that the Afrikaner Handelsinstituut (AHI) was 'far more self-critical than other representative business organisations'. Even so, the AHI's admission that it had made 'major mistakes' was accompanied by the inevitable caveat: 'Without in any way detracting from the AHI's willingness to accept responsibility … it must be noted that support for separate development was part and parcel of the majority of the white community's thinking at the time' (p 31).

The Commission found that the mining industry represented 'first-order' involvement with the apartheid state, that is, 'direct involvement with the state in the formulation of oppressive policies or practices that resulted in low labour costs (or otherwise boosted profits)' (p 24). The Chamber of Mines' submission to the TRC, however, did not address or acknowledge this role, which the Commission found 'regrettable and not constructive', adding that such recognition, 'together with an appropriate apology, could contribute significantly to the reconciliation process' (pp 33–4).

The Commission found that while Anglo American's submission was an improvement on that of the Chamber of Mines, it too was flawed. Anglo's apology extended to an acknowledgement, with regret, that 'we did not sufficiently progress these and many other opportunities to oppose apartheid and hasten its demise' (p 34).

Sanlam 'accepted that its Afrikaans origins could have contributed to and facilitated cordial business relationships with government … However, apart from having easier access to government, [Sanlam] did not enjoy preferred status with the NP' (p 31).

The role that these and other companies played in apartheid was, and remains, highly contested, such that there is still no corroborated factual record of events. These apologies do little to explicitly recognise the moral standing of the victims of apartheid, and certainly do not accept moral responsibility and blame for their role in human rights violations. Overall, they are defensive and self-serving, and fall more into the category of excuse and justification than of apology.

No chance of reparation

Despite firm recommendations from the TRC, and even some willingness on the part of organisations like Anglo American, the corporate sector has also never been required to make any reparation for its role in apartheid. This has had a profound impact on the trajectory of our society.

The TRC recommended that serious consideration be given to the best way for businesses to provide restitution to the victims of apartheid. It suggested that various options should be considered as a means of 'empowering the poor' (TRC Report 1999, Vol. V: 318–19), including:

- a wealth tax;
- a one-off levy on corporate and private income;
- each company listed on the Johannesburg Stock Exchange to make a one-off donation of 1 per cent of its market capitalisation;
- a retrospective surcharge on corporate profits extending back to a date to be suggested.

None of these options were seriously investigated, and nothing resembling them has ever been implemented. The TRC's comment on inequality is even more pertinent in 2022 than it was in 1999: 'The huge and widening gap between the rich and poor is a disturbing legacy of the past, which has not been reduced by the democratic process. It is morally reprehensible, politically dangerous and economically unsound to allow this to continue' (p 318). The events leading up to South Africa's first democratic election, and the processes that were established to create new democratic institutions, could have had a far-reaching effect on business and the structure of the economy. Instead, as has been widely documented, the ANC ultimately abandoned its plans to use economic reform to tackle the economic and social legacies of apartheid.

The significant body of work and proposals prepared by the Macroeconomic Research Group (MERG) included evidence-based analysis and recommendations related to the restructuring of the domestic financial system, policies related to land reform and rural development (including innovative ideas relating to female-headed households in rural areas), and proposals for labour market restructuring (Michie and Padayachee 2019).

These recommendations were in the end ignored by the ANC. In their extensive analysis of the ANC's economic and social policy from 1943 to 1996, Padayachee and van Niekerk conclude that, rather than 'selling out', as it is often accused of having done, the ANC was 'intellectually seduced in comfortable surroundings and eventually outmanoeuvred by the well-resourced apartheid state and by international and local pro-market friendly actors' (Padayachee and van Niekerk 2019).

As a result, apartheid's huge economic and social inequalities were left largely intact, while the postapartheid economy has generated extremely high levels of corporate profits. Many of the companies the ANC, SACP, COSATU, and others argued were complicit in apartheid have become titans of the local economy.

Naspers, which famously refused to make any submission to the TRC, is now a global giant, and its senior executives, like many senior executives at South African companies, earn some of the highest pay packages in the world. These exceptionally high levels of real earnings among high earners, coupled with no real earnings growth among low and median earners, have resulted in income inequality in South Africa *worsening* since the end of apartheid (Stats SA 2019).

In 2015, at the centenary celebration of Naspers and *Die Burger* newspaper, Esmare Weideman, CEO of Media24 (part of Naspers), finally apologised for the company's role in apartheid, saying: 'We acknowledge complicity in a morally indefensible political regime and the hurtful way in which this played out in our newsrooms and boardrooms' (News24Wire, 29 July 2015).

In an opinion piece in August 2015, Dr Marjorie Jobson, national director of the Khulumani Support Group, a national membership organisation of family members of victims and survivors of apartheid atrocities, said: 'While Khulumani Support Group welcomes this important development, we also assert that the process of acknowledging complicity with the "morally indefensible apartheid regime", is incomplete without an accompanying commitment to make things right by helping to repair the damage done' (Jobson 2015). Khulumani therefore called on Naspers and its shareholders 'to complement their acknowledgement of their complicity with apartheid by establishing an independent reparations fund for victims of apartheid-era gross human rights violations, to support the endeavours of survivors to surmount through their own efforts the continuing constraints that are the legacy of the apartheid system'. There is no public record of any response to this call from the company.

The ANC's wholesale adoption of neoliberal economic principles effectively wiped the corporate sector's slate clean, setting it free to focus unhindered on the pursuit of profit for a privileged few. Unsurprisingly, the lesson learnt was that there are no consequences for corporations that cause harm (to people and the environment), as long as they are providing returns for shareholders. This message underpins the contemporary approach of big businesses to apology and reparation for wrongdoing.

Lonmin and the Marikana massacre

The 'Marikana massacre' is South Africa's most notorious postapartheid tragedy. On 16 August 2012, members of the South African Police Service opened fire on a crowd of striking mineworkers near Lonmin's Marikana platinum mine in the North West province; 34 mineworkers were killed, and 78 seriously injured. The massacre was the culmination of a tense week-long 'wildcat strike', with strikers demanding an increase in wages for rock drillers. Violence in the days leading up to the massacre also resulted in the deaths of ten other people, including six mine workers, two Lonmin security guards, and two South African Police Service members (South African History Online, 'Marikana Massacre 16 August 2021').

A few days before the massacre, Lonmin's UK-based CEO, Ian Farmer, had been diagnosed with cancer. He was therefore understandably not able to play a role in the way that the company handled the events. On 16 August, the company released a short statement in which chairman Roger Phillimore immediately distanced Lonmin from responsibility for the massacre:

> We are treating the developments around police operations this afternoon with the utmost seriousness. The South African Police Service (SAPS) have been in charge of public order and safety on the ground since the violence between competing labour factions erupted over the weekend, claiming the lives of eight of our employees and two police officers. It goes without saying that we deeply regret the further loss of life in what is clearly a public order rather than labour relations associated matter. (Lonmin 2012a)

Lonmin's management faced intense criticism in the days leading up to, and after, the massacre, for being 'unavailable for comment'. Reports indicate that at a memorial service held on 23 August 2012, Phillimore said that the incident was 'unquestionably the saddest loss in the history of this company' and that 'the company leadership is grieving and offered condolences to families' (Powell 2012). But it was only a year later that any actual apology was offered.

On 13 August 2013, new Lonmin CEO Ben Magara addressed crowds gathered at Marikana to mark the first anniversary of the mineworkers' deaths. He said:

> We will never replace your loved ones and I say we are truly sorry for that. It should not have to take the loss of so many lives for us as a company, as employees, as a community and as a nation to learn that this should have never happened and that it should never happen again. Each day we feel the effects of this tragedy. (BBC News, 16 August 2013)

In October 2013, Ian Farmer, who had quit as CEO of Lonmin at the end of 2012 due to his illness, was reported to have 'broken his silence to apologise to the victims' families and condemn the actions of South African police' (Smith 2013). His apology, however, was made at a conference in London at which none of the victims' families were present. Farmer spent more time criticising the South African government than he did apologising for his own company's role in the tragedy, opining that 'the rainbow nation's honeymoon period has ended' (Smith 2013).

The blame game was again evident in the 'Opening words from Roger Phillimore and Simon Scott' (acting CEO at the time) in Lonmin Plc's 2012 Annual Report (Lonmin Plc 2012b). Using language that wholly distanced themselves and their company from the events, Phillimore and Scott expressed their 'heartfelt sympathy for the families and friends who have lost loved ones' (p 2), before laying the blame for Marikana firmly at the door of 'all of South Africa':

> The scenes which unfolded shocked and horrified all who witnessed them. They placed this Company in the global spotlight and, crucially, they left the nation of South Africa seeking answers to some of the most difficult questions it has faced in a generation. ... Deep-rooted issues of poverty and inequality have been highlighted by what has taken place, but those go beyond mining and to every corner of South Africa. ... Nonetheless, no company, however large, can alone address the socio-economic issues facing the Republic. ... What happened at Marikana was a tragedy for the families and friends of those who died, and for those who still bear the physical and mental injuries of those events; but it was also a warning to all of South Africa. Together, we must heed that warning. (Lonmin 2012b: 2–3)

At the time of the massacre, Cyril Ramaphosa (now President of South Africa) was a non-executive director of Lonmin. Ramaphosa, a prominent former anti-apartheid activist and leader of the National Union of Mineworkers, left politics in early 1997 after losing the race for president of the ANC to Thabo Mbeki. By 2012, he was an extremely successful and wealthy businessman.

Lonmin was able to draw on Ramaphosa's powerful political connections to bring in an excessively large police presence to control its striking workers; when the police lost control, the company then abrogated responsibility for the ensuing catastrophe to the state. This double outrage was further compounded by the executives' failure to acknowledge the significant role played by Lonmin itself in perpetuating the poor socioeconomic conditions that gave rise to the discontent of its employees in the first place.

The Marikana Commission of Enquiry, chaired by retired judge Ian Farlam (the 'Marikana Commission'), was set up to investigate the massacre. During the hearings, the appalling living and working conditions of the miners came under the spotlight. Evidence emerged that Lonmin had failed to comply with the housing obligations set out in its social and labour plan, a condition of the grant of its mining licence.

These obligations dated back to 2006, and required Lonmin to convert 70 single-sex hostels to bachelor or family units, and to build an additional 5,500 houses for its migrant employees. By 2009, only three houses and less than half of the hostel upgrades had been completed.

At the Marikana Commission hearings, Lonmin's former chief operating officer, Mohamed Seedat, admitted that the living conditions in Nkaneng and other informal settlements where many of the mineworkers lived were 'truly appalling'. Seedat 'conceded that Lonmin had known about the critical housing shortage at Marikana and the squalid conditions in Nkaneng for years' (Marikana Commission Report 2015: 528).

In its report, the Commission concluded that it was satisfied that 'Lonmin's failure to comply with its housing obligations created an environment conducive to the creation of tension, labour unrest, disunity among its employees or other harmful conduct' (p 542). Lonmin has never apologised for this failure, which was in fact also a breach of mining laws. In the 660-page report of the Marikana Commission, the words 'apology' and 'apologise' do not appear.

The most famous non-apology for Marikana came from Cyril Ramaphosa.

The Commission heard how Lonmin management had appealed to Ramaphosa to use his political connections to urge government to intervene in the unfolding situation at Marikana. In an email from Ramaphosa to Albert Jamieson, Lonmin's Chief Commercial Officer, Ramaphosa said: 'The terrible events that have unfolded cannot be described as a labour dispute. They are plainly dastardly criminal and must be characterised as such. In line with this characterisation there needs to be concomitant action to address this situation' (p 423).

In 2017, five years after the massacre, and now back in politics and serving as Deputy President, Ramaphosa was asked, during a question–and–answer session with students at Rhodes University, to address his role in the tragedy. Ramaphosa replied that he had 'participated in trying to stop further deaths from happening', and that 'I have apologised and I do apologise that I did not use appropriate language but I never had the intention to have 34 other mine workers killed' (Tandwa 2017).

It is extraordinary that despite the deep understanding of the life of South African mine workers, which his history suggests he must have, Ramaphosa has never accepted any responsibility for the tragedy, nor has he ever been able to bring himself to express sincere remorse. But perhaps the saddest indictment of his role at Lonmin is that he felt comfortable accepting a role on the board of a company that had made so little effort to address the colonial and apartheid legacy of poor working and living conditions for its employees.

Lonmin the company no longer exists: it was purchased by gold producer Sibanye-Stillwater in 2019. But no one has been charged for the killings that took place on 16 August 2012 (Nicolson 2020). Families of the slain mineworkers have received some reparation in the form of compensation for loss of support, but negotiations with the government for constitutional damages are still ongoing.

South Africa has had no 'closure' on the tragedy. The Marikana Commission was harshly criticised for its relatively weak findings against Lonmin and the government, and for attributing some of the blame for the massacre to the striking mineworkers. The catharsis that so many hoped the Commission would bring did not materialise – in fact, it became the source of further hurt and resentment.

Almost a decade after the massacre, no one has been meaningfully held to account, and there has been no moral apology from the company or the politicians and police officials who should have prevented it from happening. There can surely be few better examples of the 'second wound of silence' referred to above.

Tiger Brands and the listeriosis crisis

Between January 2017 and July 2018, an outbreak of listeriosis, a serious bacterial infection contracted from contaminated food, infected 1,060 people in South Africa, killing 216 of them (Department of Health 2018a; Department of Health 2018b).

In March 2018, the National Minister of Health announced that the outbreak had been traced to meat-processing facilities owned by JSE-listed food and beverage company Tiger Brands (Department of Health 2018a). At a press conference the day after the Minister's announcement, the company's CEO Lawrence McDougall refused to apologise, stating: 'There is no direct link with the deaths to our products that we are aware of at this point. Nothing' (Mabuza 2018).

Three weeks later, Tiger Brands released a press statement in which McDougall said:

> The Department of Health has reported that people have lost their lives as a result of Listeriosis and according to the Minister of Health, 90% of these are as a result of LST6. Although no link has, as yet, been confirmed between the presence of LST6 at our Polokwane plant and the loss of life I deeply regret any loss of life and I want to offer my heartfelt condolences to all those who have lost their loved ones. Any loss of life, no matter the circumstance, is tragic. (Tiger Brands 2018)

The fallout from the crisis continues to shadow the company, which is facing a class action law suit. In September 2020 it announced the sale of the businesses falling under its meat-processing division. Although Tiger Brands claims that this sale was on the cards before the listeriosis outbreak, it seems more likely that, as one investment analyst put it, 'the massive reputational setback suffered from the value-added meat products scandal has forced them to dissociate completely from it' (Mahlaka 2020).

It is hard to view the Tiger Brands 2018 statement as an apology at all. Analysing the statement against Smith's (2008) criteria for a categorical apology, the only element met by Tiger Brands is that the person making the statement possessed 'appropriate standing'; the statements were made by the CEO, not delegated to a more junior representative.

Tiger Brands disputed the factual record, refused to accept causal moral responsibility and blame, and did not recognise the victims and their families as moral agents entitled to dignified treatment. The statement was not made in person, to the victims, and proposed no reparations. It is framed as an expression of condolence for a sad event that happened outside of the company's sphere of influence or concern.

In January 2020 Lawrence MacDougall retired. In the four years that he ran Tiger Brands, the company's share price declined by almost 31 per cent, compared with a 9.9 per cent gain on the JSE's wider share index over the same period (Kew 2020). His remuneration over that period totalled just over R50.8 million.

Perhaps there is a 'third wound' in the context of corporate behaviour that causes harm: when those responsible for the harm not only fail to apologise categorically to or compensate the victims, but are then also richly rewarded for their failures.

Steinhoff: South Africa's biggest corporate fraud

The Lonmin and Tiger Brands tragedies involved the devastating loss of many lives.

In contrast, the Steinhoff and Tongaat Hulett frauds had a different impact, including losses to pensions and savings for those invested in the companies, and the loss of jobs and livelihoods for many of the people who worked at these companies but who played no part in the scandals.

On the evening of 5 December 2017, the board of Stellenbosch-headquartered global furniture and household goods company Steinhoff International announced that CEO Markus Jooste, a billionaire businessman long venerated in the financial sector, was stepping down with immediate effect. The board added that information had come to light regarding 'accounting irregularities requiring further investigation'.

Over the course of the ensuing week, approximately R295 billion was wiped off the JSE as a result of the precipitous fall in the share price of Steinhoff and its associated companies, and knock-on impacts, such as the exposure of local banks to Steinhoff debt (Cairns 2017). By the end of the month, the company's shares were on the brink of collapse, as management had been unable to discover the extent of the irregularities.

The scandal has been described as South Africa's biggest corporate fraud. PwC's subsequent investigation found that 'the firm recorded fictitious or irregular transactions totalling €6.5 billion ($7.4 billion) over a period covering the 2009 and 2017 financial years' and that 'a small group of former Steinhoff executives and individuals from outside the company, led by an identified "senior management executive", implemented the deals, which substantially inflated the group's profit and asset values' (Motsoeneng and Rumney 2019).

By October 2020, Steinhoff's share price was R0.70, down from R55.81 on 1 December 2017. Investors, including pension funds managing the savings of millions of ordinary South Africans, lost billions in the collapse. The company faces investigations and legal action by regulators, as well as two class action lawsuits.

The story of apology in the Steinhoff context is a very short one, because the executives involved have never publicly apologised.

In a letter sent to some of his colleagues just before he stepped down, Jooste wrote that he would 'like to apologise for all the bad publicity I caused the Steinhoff company the last couple of months' (Fin24 6 December 2017). He added:

> Now I have caused the company further damage by not being able to finalise the year end audited numbers and I made some big mistakes and have now caused financial loss to many innocent people. ... It is time for me to move on and take the consequences of my behaviour like a man.
>
> Sorry that I have disappointed all of you and I never meant to cause any of you any harm.

For Jooste, 'taking the consequences of his behaviour like a man' has meant retreating to his seaside mansion in the town of Hermanus, and avoiding public interaction altogether. He has never apologised to – or even addressed – those 'many innocent people' who he systematically defrauded, and he and others responsible for the fraud have not yet faced any criminal sanctions. Jooste's apology to colleagues was an expression of regret at being caught, rather than an acceptance of blame and moral responsibility for his actions.

Tongaat Hulett's 'undesirable accounting practices'

In March 2019, the share price of South Africa's largest sugar producer, Tongaat Hulett, collapsed after it issued a cautionary statement (Tongaat Hulett 2019a). The statement announced that the company might have to restate its financial results for several years, after a strategic and financial review 'revealed certain practices which will require further examination'. The board appointed PwC to assist with a 'legally privileged investigation into alleged irregularities'.

The strategic and financial review was instituted in February 2019 following the appointment of Gavin Hudson as CEO. Hudson succeeded Peter Staude, who had led the company from 2002 until he retired in October 2018. In November 2019 Tongaat released key findings of the PwC investigation (Tongaat Hulett 2019b). The company said that it would not publish the full report, citing legal privilege and confidentiality restrictions. The investigation found that, among other things, various executives had 'initiated or participated in undesirable accounting practices'; that there was a 'culture of deference and lack of challenges' and that 'there were a number of governance failures' (Tongaat 2019b). The key findings report named ten senior executives, including former CEO Staude, who were involved in these practices, and signalled its intention to take legal action to recover bonus payments and benefits. Tongaat has also referred these matters to the relevant authorities, including the National Prosecuting Authority and the JSE (Njobeni 2020).

Shareholders have raised questions over the failure of Tongaat's auditors, Deloitte, to pick up the accounting misstatements. Tongaat is yet to take action against the audit firm, although it has stated that the case is not closed (Crotty 2020).

Despite the massive failures at Tongaat, there does not appear to have been any public apology from those responsible. Staude has largely avoided on-the-record statements, but is quoted as saying 'Have I made some mistakes with the benefit of hindsight? Yes. It would be odd if I did not do so' (Rose 2020).

Ironically, the only apology that appears to have been made in this saga was made by asset manager Investec shortly before Staude retired. In mid-2018 Investec publicly apologised to Staude after one of its analysts suggested in a report that the CEO should resign because of the company's 'appalling' financial results. Investec's spokesperson issued a swift assurance that this was 'not the view of the Investec Group', and that 'to the extent to which [the report] has caused embarrassment to Mr Peter Staude, with whom we have had a long and fruitful relationship, we apologise'. At the time, Investec provided investment banking services to Tongaat, and acted as a broker and advisor (Crotty 2018).

KPMG and 'state capture'

The term 'state capture' in the South African context refers to the close and corrupt relationship between Jacob Zuma and other senior members of the ANC during Zuma's term as president (2009–2014), and the wealthy Gupta family. Investigative journalists had been flagging the Guptas' political influence since 2010, but in 2016 allegations emerged about the Guptas offering cabinet positions, infiltrating state-owned enterprises, and influencing numerous sectors of government.

In 2017, two whistle-blowers 'leaked a vast cache of emails from inside the business empire of the Guptas' (Allsop 2018). Over the next three years, investigative newsroom amaBhungane published an exhaustive series of articles detailing the relationship between Jacob Zuma and the Gupta family, and implicating numerous senior politicians and high-profile companies in the corruption (see amaBhungane 2020). The companies implicated include global consulting firms McKinsey and Bain, public relations firm Bell Pottinger, and auditing firm KPMG, which worked for the Guptas for 15 years before finally cutting ties amid public outrage in 2016.

KPMG has made several belated apologies for its involvement in state capture. In September 2017, KPMG International's chairman John Veihmeyer said: 'I sincerely apologize for what went wrong in KPMG South Africa. This is not who we are' (*Reuters* 2017). Veihmeyer's apology followed the resignation of KPMG South Africa's CEO Trevor Hoole and seven other senior executives over the firm's links to the Gupta family (Cropley and Brock 2017; *Reuters* 2017).

KPMG's report into an alleged South African Revenue Service (SARS) 'rogue unit' that undertook illegal surveillance has also been discredited. The report was used to put pressure on then Minister of Finance Pravin Gordhan, who was previously SARS Commissioner, and to undermine sensitive investigations into Zuma allies.

KPMG's statement on 15 September 2017, which highlighted resignations, investigation outcomes, and governance reforms, tried to draw a line under the controversy. It also said that the SARS report 'should no longer be relied on' and offered to repay its fee for producing it (*Reuters* 2017).

However, the statement was criticised for being 'weak on admitting their own culpability in the problems they created for South Africa' (van Wyk 2017). Gordhan welcomed the withdrawal of the SARS report, but criticised KPMG's 'scant regard' for those damaged in the process and doubted whether their 'regret' was proportional to the damage caused (IOL 2017).

In December 2018, following another audit scandal, KPMG South Africa chairman Wiseman Nkuhlu said in an open letter: 'We know we made mistakes and we will accept responsibility, as appropriate, for our misdeeds', but appealed for the company to be given an opportunity to play a 'positive role in the business community and the life of the nation' (Nkuhlu 2018).

In September 2020, Nkuhlu announced that KPMG would contribute to reparations for those affected by the SARS report, but details were not provided. Former SARS executive, Johann van Loggerenberg, who was one of those implicated in the 'rogue unit' allegations, said in response to Nkuhlu's announcement: 'What was really significant – and different from Bain & Co, McKinsey, SAP and others who've issued apologies – is that this is an unequivocal owning of the fact that their report caused damage. KPMG went further, to say it would contribute to help those who were harmed' (Rose 2020).

The firm also took a significant step in early 2021. KPMG announced that it would no longer provide non-audit services (for example, consulting services and tax advice) to JSE-listed companies that it also audits (Rose 2021). The move is aimed at addressing the widespread loss of public faith in the integrity of the auditing profession, which has repeatedly failed to identify serious instances of fraud. The fact that auditing firms provide both audit and consulting services to large companies is widely viewed as creating cosy relationships that hinder the ability of auditors to robustly interrogate and challenge their clients.

KPMG's move is not without its critics, but it is nevertheless a rare instance of a concrete step – one which will cause financial loss to the firm – being taken by a corporation to address public loss of faith as a result of past wrongdoing, and to ensure that that wrongdoing does not happen again.

While there have been a number of apologies over a long period, each new apology does come somewhat closer to constituting a categorical apology than the last. The firm has accepted moral responsibility and blame, and recognised and acknowledged the harm that it caused, and the role that it played in the extraordinary attack on democratic institutions that occurred under Jacob Zuma.

However, KPMG's apologies came a long time after the harm was done, under a new political regime, and in the wake of the loss of many of the firm's clients. Crucially, none of these apologies were made by the people actually responsible for the harm.

Conclusion

There is a structural connection between the failure of the South African corporate sector to accept moral responsibility for its role in apartheid and the failure of major corporations to morally apologise for harms that they have caused in the post-apartheid era. This connection is most obvious in the context of Marikana.

Recall the TRC Commission's attribution to the mining industry of 'first-order' complicity with the apartheid state, which secured low labour costs and high profits at the expense of the human rights of mineworkers and their families. Lonmin, incorporated in 1909 as the London and Rhodesia Mining and Land Company Limited, and steeped in the colonial and apartheid-era oppression of black people, is surely precisely the category of company that the TRC Commission had in mind.

However, in the post-apartheid era, Lonmin not only did not make any reparation for its past complicity, it also then failed, by its own admission, to address the apartheid legacy of appalling socioeconomic conditions for its workforce. Then, when all of these injustices coalesced in the devastation of the events of August 2012, the company's executives blamed the government for failing to take sufficient action to address historic wrongs.

The failure by companies that benefited from apartheid to make moral apologies for their unjust enrichment, combined with the ANC's wholesale adoption of neoliberal economic policy, has cemented a culture in which the corporate executive is virtually untouchable.

A sense of exceptionalism and entitlement appears to lie at the core of the responses from the corporate leaders described in this chapter, as well as an unshakeable conviction that their success is due solely to sound business principles and their own superior abilities. There is no room for admitting that whatever they have achieved is, at least in part, attributable to historical and current privilege.

Our culture reveres rich, successful businessmen, but it does not prepare or expect them to face up to the consequences of their actions when those actions cause harm. When they fail, they are intellectually and emotionally unable to stomach the 'loss of power, or face' required in order to make a moral apology (Schweitzer et al 2015).

This exercise in humility appears to be particularly hard when the victims are members of a group perceived by those responsible to be socially inferior to themselves. This may go some way to explaining why Markus Jooste immediately apologised to his close friends and colleagues, but has never faced the millions of ordinary people who were the victims of his fraud.

The absence of meaningful reparation compounds the insult of the insincere apology, especially when those responsible continue to reap extraordinary financial rewards for themselves. Each of the executives mentioned in this chapter received total remuneration packages in the tens of millions of Rands in the years in which these disasters happened. In the case of Markus Jooste, the figure is over a hundred million Rand.

The costs of the human and environmental impacts caused by major corporations, impacts revealingly labelled 'externalities' by economists, are either ignored or borne by the rest of society. For over a century, South Africa's extractives-based economy has allowed corporate executives to run their companies from plush offices in Johannesburg or London, cocooned from the lived reality of their frontline employees, and unaccountable for the impacts of these 'externalities'.

In South African history, the list of wrongdoers who have escaped accountability is a long one. It includes many of the perpetrators of the gross human rights violations of apartheid, swathes of corrupt politicians and their corporate enablers in the post-apartheid era, and the richly rewarded executives of major corporations that have caused extraordinary harm.

We have not succeeded in achieving the healing and reconciliation that was so eagerly anticipated at the end of apartheid. There are many complex reasons for this, but these reasons must include the myriad failures of the rich and powerful to accept moral responsibility for wrongdoing, to show compassion towards those who have been harmed by their actions, and to make reparation.

The best form of reparation would be the implementation of policies and practices that address the pervasive structural inequalities which are a legacy of apartheid, but that continue to privilege a tiny elite today. The widening inequality in South Africa since the end of apartheid, in particular in relation to income and wealth, prevents social cohesion, sows the seeds of populism, and is in itself a barrier to building a more inclusive society.

The moral apology is 'an act of courage, not an expression of weakness' (Taft 2000). If the leaders of our corporate sector could see their way clear to perform this simple act of bravery when they have caused harm, whether intentionally or negligently, and take action that prevents such harm from happening again, it might go a little way to restoring our faith in the possibility of a more just and equal society.

Reflections

When the Marikana massacre took place, I was living in London, but on the brink of moving back to South Africa. I remember watching with horror the Channel 4 news bulletin reporting the massacre on the evening of 16 August 2012. On the day that I moved back to the country, the *Economist* cover was a picture of the striking miners, with the headline: 'Cry the beloved country: South Africa's sad decline'. I also remember well all of the other tragedies discussed in my chapter, and the outrage that I felt over each at the time. Researching and writing the chapter forced me to revisit my reaction to these events; but now, my renewed outrage was compounded by despair at how little accountability there has been for any of them. The TRC's finding that business must play a role in addressing the 'morally reprehensible, politically dangerous and economically unsound' gap between the rich and poor was particularly striking to me, because of my work as a shareholder activist, and because, 20 years later, that gap is even wider. If you let it, the tragedy of South Africa's lost potential can be an endless source of frustration and sadness. But, in spite of it all, living here is also a constant source of inspiration and joy, underpinned by the efforts of the many, many people – including those who have compiled this book – who refuse to give up hope.

Tracey

References

Allsop, J., 2018, 'Were the Gupta leaks South Africa's Watergate', *Global Investigative Journalism Network*, 24 September, viewed 25 February 2021 from https://gijn.org/2018/09/24/were-the-gupta-leaks-south-africas-watergate/

AmaBhungane, 2020, 'Special report: the #GuptaLeaks and more – all our stories on state capture', 10 August, viewed 23 April 2020 from https://amabhungane.org/stories/special-report-the-guptaleaks-and-more-all-our-stories-on-state-capture-2/

BBC, 2013, 'Marikana shooting: Lonmin apologises for South Africa deaths', BBC.com, 16 August, viewed 1 October 2020 from www.bbc.com/news/world-africa-23730268

Cairns, P., 2017, 'The funds most exposed to Steinhoff', *Moneyweb*, 6 December, viewed 30 April 2021 from www.moneyweb.co.za/investing/the-funds-most-exposed-to-steinhoff/

Casale, L., 2017, '7 steps to take when preparing a corporate apology', *Entrepreneur South Africa*, 13 November, viewed 25 February 2021 from www.entrepreneur.com/article/304424

Cropley, E., and Brock, J., 2017, 'KPMG's South Africa bosses purged over Gupta scanadal', *Reuters*, 15 September, viewed 30 April 2021 from www.reuters.com/article/us-kpmg-safrica-idUSKCN1BQ16P

Crotty, A., 2018, 'Sugar-coating unpalatable facts', *Financial Mail*, 7 June, viewed 2 October 2020 from www.pressreader.com/south-africa/financial-mail/20180607/281736975144377

Crotty, A., 2020, 'Tongaat: Deloitte in the firing line', *Moneyweb*, 29 September, viewed 2 October 2020 from www.moneyweb.co.za/news/companies-and-deals/deloitte-in-the-firing-line/

Department of Health, 2018a, '*Media statement by the Minister of Health Dr Aaron Motsoaledi regarding the update on the Listeriosis outbreak in South Africa*', 4 March (incorrectly dated on document), viewed 2 October 2020 from www.health.gov.za/index.php/2014-03-17-09-48-36/2014-03-17-09-49-50

Department of Health, 2018b, *Listeriosis Outbreak Situation Report*, 26 July, Johannesburg, viewed 2 October 2020 from www.nicd.ac.za/wp-content/uploads/2018/07/Listeriosis-outbreak-situation-report-_26July2018_fordistribution.pdf

Fin24, 2017, 'Steinhoff's Markus Jooste admits he made "some big mistakes"', 6 December, viewed 30 April 2021 from www.news24.com/fin24/companies/retail/steinhoffs-markus-jooste-admits-he-made-some-big-mistakes-20171206

Forbes Communications Council, 2020, '13 tips for crafting the perfect corporate apology plan', *Forbes*, 6 July, viewed 25 February 2021 from www.forbes.com/sites/forbescommunicationscouncil/2020/07/06/13-tips-for-crafting-the-perfect-corporate-apology-plan/?sh=1dee113e3703

Govier, T. and Verwoerd, W., 2002, 'The promises and pitfalls of apology', *Journal of Social Philosophy* 33(1) 67–82.

Ibhawoh, B., 2009, 'Rethinking corporate apologies: business and apartheid victimization in South Africa', in M. Gibney, R. E. Howard-Hassman, J. Coicaud, and N. Steiner (eds.), *The Age of Apology: Facing Up to the Past (Pennsylvania Studies in Human Rights)*, pp 271–84, Philadelphia: University of Pennsylvania Press.

IOL, 2017, 'Pravin Gordhan slams #KPMG apology', 15 September, viewed 2 October 2020 from www.iol.co.za/ios/news/pravin-gordhan-slams-kpmg-apology-11232779

Jobson, M., 2015, 'Let acceptance of apartheid complicity lead to reparations', *IOL News*, 14 August, viewed 26 February 2021 from www.iol.co.za/capetimes/opinion/let-acceptance-of-apartheid-complicity-lead-to-reparations-1899764

Kew, J., 2020, 'Tiger Brands CEO quits with listeriosis crisis still to play out', Bloomberg, 29 January, viewed 2 October 2020 from www.bloomberg.com/news/articles/2020-01-29/tiger-brands-ceo-quits-with-listeriosis-crisis-still-to-play-out?sref=KyesZvga

Lonmin Plc, 2012a, 'Lonmin statement on Marikana', 16 August, viewed 1 October 2020 from https://web.archive.org/web/20130729185918/https://www.lonmin.com/downloads/media_centre/news/press/2012/Lonmin_Statement_on_Marikana_-_16_08_12_-_FINAL.pdf

Lonmin Plc, 2012b, 'Annual report and accounts for the year ended 30 September 2012', viewed 1 October 2020 from https://thevault.exchange/?get_group_doc=166/1453812826-Lonmin_AR2012.pdf

Mabuza, E., 2018, 'In his own words: Tiger Brands CEO gets defensive amid listeriosis outrage', *Times Live*, 6 March, viewed 2 October 2020 from www.timeslive.co.za/news/south-africa/2018-03-06-in-his-own-words-tiger-brands-ceo-gets-defensive-amid-listeriosis-outrage/

Mahlaka, R., 2020, 'Not so fast, Tiger Brands', *Daily Maverick*, 17 August, viewed 2 October 2020 from www.dailymaverick.co.za/article/2020-08-17-not-so-fast-tiger-brands/

Marikana Commission of Inquiry, 2015, *Report on Matters of Public, National and International Concern Arising out of the Tragic Incidents at the Lonmin Mine in Marikana, in the North West Province*, Pretoria: Marikana Commission of Inquiry.

Michie, J. and Padayachee, V., 2019, 'South African business in the transition to democracy', *International Review of Applied Economics* 33(1), 1–10.

Motsoeneng, T. and Rumney, E., 2019, 'PwC investigation finds $7.4 billion accounting fraud at Steinhoff, company says', *Reuters*, 15 March, viewed 1 October 2020 from https://in.reuters.com/article/us-steinhoff-intln-accounts/pwc-investigation-finds-74-billion-accounting-fraud-at-steinh off-company-says-idINKCN1QW2C2

News24Wire, 2015, 'Media24 must pay for its role in apartheid group', *Businesstech*, 29 July, viewed 26 February 2021 from https://businesst ech.co.za/news/media/94495/media24-must-pay-for-its-role-in-aparth eid-group/

Nicolson, G., 2020, 'Marikana massacre: political will is urgently needed to deliver overdue justice', *Daily Maverick*, 14 August, viewed 1 October 2020 from www.dailymaverick.co.za/article/2020-08-14-marikana-massa cre-political-will-is-urgently-needed-to-deliver-overdue-justice/

Njobeni, S., 2020, 'Tongaat chair says those behind irregularities will be held liable', *Business Day*, 27 January, viewed 2 October 2020 from www. businesslive.co.za/bd/companies/land-and-agriculture/2020-01-27-tong aat-chair-says-those-behind-irregularities-will-be-held-liable/

Nkuhlu, W., 2018, 'Open letter to South Africa from chairman of KPMG South Africa, Professor Wiseman Nkuhlu', *Sowetan*, 10 December, viewed 2 October 2020 from www.pressreader.com/south-africa/sowetan/20181 210/281981788671512

Padayachee, V. and Van Niekerk, R., 2019, *Shadow of Liberation: Contestation and Compromise in the Economic and Social Policy of the African National Congress, 1943–1996*, Johannesburg: Wits University Press.

Powell, A., 2012, 'Thousands mourn South Africa mine shooting victims', *Voice of America News*, 13 August, viewed 1 October 2020 from www. voanews.com/africa/thousands-mourn-south-africa-mine-shooting-victims

Reuters, 2017, 'KPMG international chairman apologizes for South Africa failings', 19 September, viewed 2 October 2020 from www.reuters.com/ article/us-kpmg-safrica-chairman-idUSKCN1BU25A

Rose, R., 2020, 'KPMG's client dilemma', *Financial Mail*, 24 September, viewed 2 October 2020 from www.businesslive.co.za/fm/opinion/edit ors-note/2020-09-24-rob-rose-kpmgs-client-dilemma/

Rose, R., 2021, 'KPMG bites its own tail', *Financial Mail*, 18 February, viewed 26 February 2021 from www.businesslive.co.za/fm/opinion/edit ors-note/2021-02-18-rob-rose-kpmg-bites-its-own-tail/

Schweitzer, M., Brooks, A., and Galinsky, A., 2015, 'The organizational apology', *Harvard Business Review*, September, viewed 26 September 2020 from https://hbr.org/2015/09/the-organizational-apology

Smith, D., 2013, 'Mining boss condemns South African police over Marikana massacre', *The Guardian*, 10 October, viewed 1 October 2020 from www.theguardian.com/world/2013/oct/10/mining-boss-condemns-police-marikana-massacre

Smith, N., 2008, *I Was Wrong: The Meanings of Apologies*, New York: Cambridge University Press.

South African History Online, n.d., '*Marikana Massacre 16 August 2012*', viewed 1 October from www.sahistory.org.za/article/marikana-massacre-16-august-2012

Statistics South Africa, 2019, 'Inequality trends in South Africa: a multidimensional diagnostic of inequality', *Report No. 03.10.19*, Pretoria: Statistics South Africa.

Taft, L., 2000, 'Apology subverted: the commodification of apology', *Yale Law Journal* 109, 1135–60.

Tandwa, L., 2017, 'Ramaphosa apologises for role in Marikana massacre', *News24.com*, 7 May, viewed 1 October 2020 from www.news24.com/news24/southafrica/news/ramaphosa-apologises-for-role-in-marikana-massacre

Tiger Brands, 2018, 'Listeria update', 26 March, viewed 2 October 2020 from www.tigerbrands.com/sustainability/commitmentfoodsafety/listeriarelatedinformation/ListeriaPressReleaseArchive

Tongaat Hulett Limited, 2019a, 'SENS cautionary announcement', 8 March, viewed 30 April 2021 from www.inceconnect.co.za/sens-view/23907

Tongaat Hulett Limited, 2019b, 'Key findings of PwC investigation', 29 November, viewed 2 October 2020 from www.tongaat.com/wp-content/uploads/2019/11/Key-findings-of-PwC-Investigations-29-Nov-2019.pdf

Truth and Reconciliation Commission of South Africa, 1999, *Truth and Reconciliation Commission of South Africa Report*, Vols. IV and V, Cape Town: Truth and Reconciliation Commission of South Africa.

Van Wyk, P., 2017, 'KPMG: "weak" apology suggests company saw no evil, heard no evil – therefore did no evil', *Daily Maverick*, 15 September, viewed 2 October 2020 from www.dailymaverick.co.za/article/2017-09-15-kpmg-weak-apology-suggests-company-saw-no-evil-heard-no-evil-therefore-did-no-evil/

13

In Black and White:
The Hollow Apology
of Racialised State Compensation
to Freehold Landowners

Thuto Thipe

From its inception, the apartheid government focused particular attention on dismantling the property rights that underpinned multi-ethnic townships where black people owned land through freehold title deeds.[1] From the 1950s through to the 1970s, the apartheid government targeted urban black freehold townships across the country, physically destroying their infrastructure and forcibly moving their residents to far-flung locations and reserves, sometimes hundreds of kilometres away (Edwards 1994; Carruthers 2000; Jeppie 2001; Bonner and Nieftagodien 2008). Urban freehold townships stood as material counterarguments to apartheid constructions of black people's place in South African society and as an affront to the regime's aspirations of fixing the meanings attached to and possibilities available to people racialised as black. These areas existed as geographic islands. They were anomalies in the broader South African landscape where black people almost exclusively lived on land that the state owned. Black freehold townships were the result of different historical confluences across the four colonies that became South Africa. As in white freehold townships, title deed landownership offered black landowners distinct private property rights that restricted the state's and other actors' interference or encroachment on their land. On freehold

---

[1] Black is used here to refer to people who were legally classified as 'native', 'coloured', and 'Indian' under colonialism. Different freehold townships stipulated which groups of people among these three categories were eligible to own land in that township.

land, black people enjoyed relative freedom from the state's invasions into their homes and restrictions on how they lived.

These urban enclaves became sites of subversion and of imagination. Black landowners used their land as they desired; they built houses in the ways they wanted, some of them elaborate and grand in the architectural trends of their time; they housed tenants from around the country and the region in their yards; they established businesses of different scales; and, most importantly, they invested in putting down roots in the confidence of their permanence on their land. In keeping with the long settler-colonial tradition of forcing black people into the most restricted and insecure land tenure conditions, the apartheid government stripped the relatively small communities of urban black freehold landowners across the country of their freehold title deeds to force them into becoming tenants on state-owned land. Photographs in newspapers and first-person narratives from places like Sophiatown in Johannesburg and District Six in Cape Town captured international attention as they showed people being violently evicted from their homes by armed police and bulldozers demolishing their homes in front of them. Many more black freehold townships around the country experienced similar violence, destruction, and theft without as much public recognition. The dawn of democracy promised not only recognition of the injustice that black freehold landowners experienced, but, in the language of the 1996 Constitution[2] (the Constitution), 'just and equitable' compensation that took into account 'the public interest and the interests of those affected'.

Just seven months after the democratic state's assumption of power, the new South African government passed the Restitution of Land Rights Act 1994[3] (RLRA) to provide for the restitution of 'rights in land' to people who were dispossessed of their land to further 'the objects of any racially based discriminatory law'. The Act put forward a framework through which black freehold landowners who had been dispossessed of their title deed-owned land by the apartheid government expected restitution of land or compensation commensurable with what was taken from them. What they received, though, was blanket-rate compensation that ignored the individualised property rights that most landowners spent a lifetime paying bonds to acquire. The law that was intended to redress racial discrimination against black people became a vehicle through which black freehold landowners were differentiated from white freehold landowners to receive a fraction of the compensation that the state paid to the latter. Instead of their compensation being imagined through the legal framework of freehold land rights, their compensation was imagined through the lens

---

[2] Constitution of the Republic of South Africa Act 108 of 1996.
[3] Act 22 of 1994, preamble.

of their race. This framework turned the diversity of freehold stands that black people owned, with the substantial developments that many built on them, into a monolith whose value was defined by their owners' race. Under the Standard Settlement Offer policy, the state paid black urban freehold landowners between R40,000 and R50,000 for each property that they owned (Department of Rural Development and Land Reform 2009). At the exact same time, the state stalled land redistribution for over two decades while it tried to individually valuate white freehold landowners' property and negotiate terms to which these landowners agreed. In this exhaustive process of determining how to compensate white freehold landowners, the state showed tremendous 'willingness to pay land prices far in excess of the constitutional standard of "just and equitable" compensation' (Ngcukaitobi 2018a). In the infamous Mala Mala case, the state paid close to R1 billion for a single claim days before the case was scheduled to be heard by the Constitutional Court (Lorenzen 2014).[4]

The Commission on the Restitution of Land Rights, established by the RLRA, rationalised its payment to black freehold landowners, arguing that 'the standard settlement offer practice is based on the assumption that it is a "recognition" of rights lost, not an attempt to calculate exactly what was lost' (Department of Rural Development and Land Reform 2009: 4). At the same time as the state has treated white freehold landowners with astonishing care for individuals' well-being, their investment in their property, and the independent value of their land based on sophisticated calculations, it has treated black freehold landowners indiscriminately. Although title deeds to land were, and still are, identical in their method of acquisition, mode of registration, and rights guaranteed to their owner, whether black or white, the democratic state has differentiated the compensation that it pays freehold landowners based on their racial classification. Where the state has and is viewing white freehold landowners' property as an asset to which they are entitled market-related compensation, it has viewed black freehold landowners' property as primarily linked to sentiment, for which token payment is sufficient compensation. The state has given white freeholders material benefits where it has given black freeholders a gesture of recognition. Even though the Constitution 'permits the payment of compensation

---

[4] In *Mhlanganisweni Community v Minister of Rural Development and Land Reform* (LCC 156/ 2009) [2012] ZALCC 7 (19 April 2012), popularly called the Mala Mala case after the game reserve on the land in question, about 2,000 people filed for restitution of the seven farms that comprise the game reserve. This 2012 case was scheduled to be heard in the Constitutional Court over the high valuation of the land per hectare. The Land Claims Court decided in 2012 that the state pay the landowners above the valuated price per hectare. In total, the state paid to the owners of the Mala Mala Game Reserve just below R1 billion in compensation (Ngcukaitobi 2018a).

that is below, even *significantly* below, market value' the state has 'generally paid market value' to white freehold landowners (Ngcukaitobi and Bishop 2018: 2, emphasis added).

The RLRA's aim, set out in its preamble, to 'promote the protection and advancement' and the 'full and equal enjoyment of rights in land' for people disadvantaged by unfair discrimination, aligns with the Constitution's aspiration, as set out in its preamble, to 'heal the divisions of the past and establish a society based on democratic values, social justice and fundamental human rights'. Compensation to black freehold landowners presented the opportunity both for recognition of the dispossession, trauma, and disruption that they experienced, as well as material redress to make the apology real in impacting people's lives. In focusing on recognition to the detriment of materiality, the state offered black freehold landowners a hollow non-apology.

The RLRA becomes legible as an apology when read in the political and legislative context of its production and adoption. The final clause of the 1993 Interim Constitution[5] framed its role as providing 'a historic bridge between the past of a deeply divided society characterised by strife, conflict, untold suffering and injustice, and a future founded on the recognition of human rights, democracy and peaceful co-existence and development opportunities for all South Africans'. The 1995 Promotion of National Unity and Reconciliation Act[6] (PNURA), which provided for the establishment of the Truth and Reconciliation Commission (TRC), captured the legislative spirit of the moment that 'the pursuit of national unity, the well-being of all South African citizens and peace require reconciliation … and the reconstruction of society' through the 'establish[ment of] the truth in relation to past events as well as the motives for and circumstances in which gross violations of human rights have occurred, and to make the findings known in order to prevent a repetition of such acts in future'.[7] Like the PNURA, the RLRA underscored the centrality of state-driven investigation in determining violation, dispossession, and harm caused in the past, and it framed redress as following in response to evidence collected. Through investigation, the state determined the particulars of harm and loss that were caused and the ways that these were carried out. The state then offered acknowledgement to freehold landowners of their unjust dispossession, and mandated that they receive reparations for the wrongful seizure of their land.

The state's acknowledgement of black freehold landowners' unjust land dispossession was the first part of the apology to them. The RLRA's framing of restitution as 'the restoration of a right in land' or 'equitable redress' was the second part of the apology to landowners. The land restitution process

---

[5]   Act 200 of 1993.
[6]   Act 34 of 1995.
[7]   Preamble to PNURA.

succeeded in acknowledging racially discriminatory land dispossession. It fell short, though, of confronting the colonial state's 'motives' for undermining black freehold landownership and not only failed to 'prevent a repetition' of the undermining of these landowners' entitlements because of their race, but perpetuated this undermining itself in treating their seized property as an abstract entity that could be assigned arbitrary value, far below market rates, rather than an asset with calculable worth.

A significant difference between the TRC and the courts that the RLRA established was the former's exclusive focus on individual perpetrators and the latter's exclusive focus on structural perpetrators. Investigations into racially motivated land dispossession did not enquire into white landowners' potential fault. In compensating white freehold landowners, the state has universally assumed their innocence with regard to the processes through which they became landowners. In contrast with the TRC model where individuals took responsibility for violations, the land restitution process has centred the state as the wrongdoer and focused on the law in framing how black people were stripped of their property rights and forcibly moved from their land.

The outcomes of the early 1990s negotiated settlement imposed continuity between the apartheid and democratic governments to make the democratic state accountable for acknowledging and answering for black landowners' property dispossession and responsible for paying reparations. Through these agreements, the democratic state inherited the apartheid state's internal and external liabilities. Beyond imposing its financial debt on the new dispensation, 'by insisting on a regime of constitutional and legal continuity, the NP ... arguably sought to fetter the incoming democratic government's ability to radically alter the nature of established social and legal relationships, [and] legal norms' that had governed colonial South Africa (Sibanda 2018: 159). As the new government worked to build South African society anew, it remained constrained by legal frameworks that had been meticulously finessed over centuries to debase and disenfranchise black people in pursuit of white supremacy. This chapter argues that beyond being hampered by colonial legal architecture, the land restitution process has failed to understand and engage with black landowners as the freehold title deed holders that they were. The democratic state has reduced black freehold landowners into a monolithic category that, at great cost and through extensive manoeuvering, they had subverted and escaped during colonialism when they became freehold landowners.

The state's irreconcilable treatment of black and white freehold landowners illustrates the extent to which the democratic government has failed to fundamentally delink the relationships between land rights, citizenship, and race that the colonial government invested centuries in constructing and fortifying. To make white supremacy real at every level of society and to ensure that it permeated people's daily lives, the colonial state systematically cordoned off particular protections, services, and rights for white people. As in other settler colonies, 'the concept of whiteness was carefully protected because so much was contingent upon it. Whiteness conferred on its owners aspects of citizenship that were all the more valued because they were denied to others. Indeed, the very fact of citizenship itself was linked to white racial identity' (Harris 1993: 1744). In South Africa, land was central in the creation of ideas of citizenship and of people to whom the state owed protection. This chapter examines how the colonial state worked systematically and continuously to link land alienation and landlessness, and the vulnerability these engendered, to black identity. It shows how the state's hollow apology to black freehold landowners is rooted in its failure to divest its policy framework from the colonial model that could only imagine black people's land rights in collective terms and could not fathom, even when confronted with legally binding evidence, that black people could claim and be entitled to the same rights and protections in land as white people.

Freehold landownership and the settler state

European settlers formalised South Africa's founding sin of land theft from African people by writing themselves into newly created deeds records as the land's rightful owners. Deeds records became their justification for claiming the land and alienating indigenous people from their ancestral homes. Settler-colonial law, and the due process that its logic produced, became the fetish upon which settlers explained their domination and through which they produced a nation state that they claimed exclusively as their own. Freehold was the instrument through which settlers made stolen land their home and legal entitlement. Freehold's centrality in the creation and reproduction of the settler colony made it sacrosanct. Freehold was a right that was valuable in and of itself. It made possible the private industries that drove the country's economy and that attracted white people from around the world with the allure of riches.

The four settler colonies that formed the Union of South Africa in 1910 all worked to naturalise the relationship between freehold landownership and whiteness. At the same time as these administrations legally, politically, and socially linked the most secure land tenure system with the greatest protections of individual rights to white identity, they relegated people racialised as 'native' to state-owned reserves and locations (Delius 1984; Hamilton 1987; Campbell 1995; Dlamini 2011). These colonies systematically worked to construct black people's land rights and tenure security in collective terms, and at the mercy of the state.

From the early 1850s to 1868, the South African Republic (ZAR) government guaranteed Europeans settling within its borders two freehold farms and a township lot as their right, and continued settling claims to this entitlement into the 1890s (Braun 2005).[8] Simply arriving in the ZAR guaranteed settlers a claim to land that the state treated as empty and having no previous ownership. In 1855, Resolution 159[9] prohibited anybody who was not a *burgher* from owning land and specifically prohibited African people from having *burgher* rights in the region (Bergh and Feinberg 2004; Khumalo 2020). The Transvaal government explicitly linked the right to land and citizenship to European ancestry, and unambiguously excluded African people from the conjoined rights to landownership or citizenship. In the period immediately after the end of the South African War, as people began the work of rebuilding infrastructure and their lives, the Transvaal government passed the Settlers Ordinance 1902[10] that enabled 'agriculturists and other persons to become occupiers of the land' and eventually become freehold owners of Crown Land in the Transvaal (Thipe 2020). African people were implicitly excluded from both categories of agriculturist and person, showing the then British-controlled colony's continuation of the ZAR's political and legal conceptualisation of the relationship between land rights and race. Going beyond previous articulations of the relationship between citizenship and rights to land, Ordinance 45 of 1902 exposed the underlying logic of the Transvaal framework that imagined personhood as granting access to land rights and understood Africans outside the category of persons. The Transvaal similarly denied people, legally recognised as 'Asiatic' or as 'Coloured', from owning freehold title to land.

To circumvent their exclusion from freehold landownership, some black land buyers approached local missionaries to register this land in their names (Campbell 1995). These relationships with missionaries had varying outcomes for black landowners. Some missionaries dutifully honoured their agreements and respected that they served only as a European front for administrative purposes; other missionaries sought payment in money or land for the use of their names; and, worse yet, other missionaries claimed ownership of the land after its registration, double-crossing its rightful owners. As risky and costly as registration through missionaries could be,

---

[8]   The Zuid-Afrikaansche Republiek/South African Republic, also called the Transvaal Republic, and the Orange Free State (OFS), were the two Boer Republics established in southern Africa. Their founding leadership and citizenry were largely made up of European settlers who had previously lived in the British-controlled Cape and Natal colonies. The British government recognised the Boer Republics' sovereignty in the 1850s. The Boer Republics remained independent settler colonies until 1902 when Britain defeated them in the South African War, previously called the Anglo-Boer war. The Transvaal, OFS, the Cape, and Natal formally merged as a unitary state in 1910 as the Union of South Africa.

[9]   Act 2 of 1855.

[10]   Ordinance 45 of 1902.

for many black people it was their best or only option for seeking tenure security through landownership.

Black people briefly gained the right to register the title deeds in their own names in 1905 after the *Tsewu v Registrar of Deeds*[11] judgment in the High Court exposed that the wording of the law did not outlaw registration in black people's individual names (Campbell 1995; Ngcukaitobi 2018b). The Transvaal government responded by amending the law to explicitly deny black landowners' registration of their land in their own names. In the months before this amendment to the law came into effect, all of the freehold townships that would be available to black people for the next six decades were proclaimed (Thipe 2020). Alexandra Township, which was proclaimed in 1912, is the notable anomaly in this trend.

The 1908 case in the Transvaal Supreme Court, *Petlele v Minister for Native Affairs and Mokhatle*,[12] illustrates the extent of the state's intervention in preventing black people from enjoying individual rights to land that they purchased. In this case, a group, under the Bafokeng polity, sued to have land, which they had independently purchased, recognised as belonging to them rather than to the entire 'tribe'. The group of land purchasers had registered their land under Rev. Penzhorn, a local missionary, as the white intermediary whose name was recorded in the deeds registry. When Penzhorn died, the executor of his estate transferred the farm to the Secretary for Native Affairs in trust for Chief August Mokhatle and the Bafokeng tribe. Modisaking Petlele, the grandson of the collective of land buyers' leader at the time of the original purchase, sued the Chief and Minister for rectification of the title deed. In deciding who owned the land, Judge Bristow reasoned:

> If any individual or group of persons had been allowed to hold land separately from the rest of the tribe, it would have meant the destruction of the tribal system. ... For these reasons I feel strongly that the conclusion must be that, under pure native law and custom ... individual ownership was unknown, and the ownership was a common ownership by the whole tribe.[13]

The *Petlele* judgment spoke to the broader colonial attitude that black people could only legitimately exercise rights to land in the context of a collective. Through this lens, white people could be understood and treated as individuals, and their land rights similarly recognised, while black people could only be understood and treated in collective terms, and their rights

---

[11] 1905 TS 130.
[12] *Petlele v Minister for Native Affairs and Mokhatle* 1908 TS 267.
[13] At 271.

to land similarly recognised. Whatever they argued and whatever evidence they could produce to demonstrate their intention to individualised rights offered through freehold, the state insisted that black people be read as undifferentiated parts of a homogenous whole. In making the category of tribe the only one through which black people were legible, the state worked to formally invisibilise and erase the other terms on which they organised culturally, socially, politically, or otherwise, and positioned the state to decide the terms of this organising.

The Orange Free State, the other Boer Republic, stipulated through statute that 'coloured persons, with certain exceptions, may not purchase or lease land'. One exception was 'half-castes born of a lawful marriage' who were permitted to buy and sell land, provided they resided there (Matthew 1915: 5). This exception illustrates prospective landowners needing to demonstrate their proximity to whiteness through a white parent and needing to demonstrate the state's or the church's recognition of their parents' interracial relationship through marriage. Here, recognised distance from blackness opened opportunities for freehold landownership. Thaba Nchu was the one exclusion to the prohibition of African people's landownership and the only district in which Africans held freehold land titles (Murray 1992).

Black people's restricted access to freehold functioned differently in the two British colonies of Natal and the Cape. Like the Boer Republics, the Cape Colony and Natal both explicitly segregated particular areas for people racialised as native. Unlike the Boer Republics, though, African people were not exclusively restricted to living in reserves and locations. Land in the Cape Colony and in Natal was for freehold ownership 'without distinction of race' (Matthew 1915: 6). In the Cape, where African people enjoyed limited and qualified franchise, the parliament used landownership requirements to further restrict the numbers of African people on the voter's roll. The Cape Parliamentary Voters Registration Act 1887[14] extended the franchise to the Transkei and simultaneously raised the requirements for voter qualification to exclude voters who owned land under communal or tribal ownership. Twenty thousand, mostly African, voters lost their voting rights with this Act. Again in 1892, the Franchise and Ballot Act[15] in the Cape worked to purge African voters from the roll. The Act raised property qualification from land worth £25 to £75 and added a literacy test that required that voters write their name, address, and occupation. Two years later in 1894, the Cape government passed the Glen Grey Act[16] that set in motion the formalisation of locations where new taxes drove black people into working

---

[14]   Act 39 of 1887.
[15]   Act 9 of 1892.
[16]   Act 25 of 1894.

on white-owned farms and on the mines (Supreme Court of the Colony of the Cape of Good Hope 1896; Molema 2013).

Where black people, as individuals and as collectives, succeeded in acquiring freehold title deeds and asserting private land rights, colonial administrations worked to construct and demonstrate this ownership as exceptional and an aberration. Such political and legal manoeuvring was intended to show that these black people had transgressed racial boundaries and encroached on white racial entitlements. The colonies' restrictions on black people's freehold landownership alongside the normalisation of white people as freehold landowners worked to reinforce the idea that 'nature – not man, not power, not violence – had determined their [black people's] degraded status. Rights were for those who had the capacity to exercise them, a capacity denoted by racial identity. This conception of rights was contingent on race – on whether one could claim whiteness – as a form of property' (Harris 1993: 1745). The law and colonial policy made clear that only under the most exceptional circumstances could black people claim and access the land rights that were made default for white people.

For individuals, freehold promised independence and autonomy, and the type of authority in adulthood that black people were denied in virtually all public spheres, and in their own homes in state-owned locations and reserves. When black people secured the right to own land through freehold title, they gained the range of freedoms that settlers had spent centuries investing in regarding the idea and the law of freehold. It was difficult for white people and for the colonial state to attack or diminish the rights that black people gained through freehold without potentially undermining the meanings of freehold for themselves. As long as black people held freehold title, they were entitled to rights and privileges that attached to the idea of freehold. Black freehold landowners understood the power of their title and the position it afforded them in South Africa's legal landscape. They wielded these socially and legally recognised rights to protect their land, their autonomy on it, and their permanence in their homes.

Race and land in South Africa

From its 1910 founding, the Union of South Africa began consolidating law and policy that restricted black people's freehold ownership rights, and tenure security more broadly, and bolstering the numbers of white people owning land. In 1912, Parliament passed the Land Settlement Act[17] that outlined the provisions for the sale of state land to white people. Over the following four years, the state released 168,636 hectares to white farmers

---

[17] Act 12 of 1912.

(Pinilla and Willebald 2019). Similar to the ZAR, the South African government worked to normalise and socially and materially reinforce the idea of white people as freehold landowners and of the country's land mass as their entitlement. While increasing the number of white freehold landowners, measures such as the Land Settlement Act worked to entrench the idea that even if not all white people owned land, any white man could. In the context of ever-shrinking opportunities for freehold landownership, prior to apartheid, Harvey Feinberg explains that movements to buy land were marked by 'African initiative in identifying land for sale, success in persuading the state to approve a purchase, persistence in persuading officials if the answer was no, ingenuity in raising the money to meet financial obligations, and non-violent defence of ownership rights' (Feinberg 2015: 1). When the 1913 Native Land Act[18] restricted all African people to living on 7 per cent of the country's land mass, it also effectively banned Africans from buying and owning land anywhere other than in the designated reserves. In 1923, through the Urban Areas Act,[19] the state outlawed further granting of freehold property rights to black people on the grounds that they were not permanent urban residents and should only be permitted within municipal areas in so far and for so long as white people's wants demanded their presence.

Even with all of these increased restrictions on landownership, black people found ways to acquire freehold title and tried to secure for themselves some permanence and security in a country unrelenting in, and intensifying, the stripping away of their political, social, economic, and other rights (Margeot 1987; Lambert 1999; Khumalo 2013; Moguerane 2016). Harvey Feinberg and André Horn show that black people purchased more land between 1913 and 1936, through exemptions in the Land Act, than in the entire period before 1913 (Feinberg and Horn 2009). Within freehold townships demarcated for black people, the sale of stands increased across the decades of the first half of the century until there were no remaining empty stands in these townships (Thipe 2020). At every turn, black people who bought freehold land did so against hurdles and barriers that were intended to be insurmountable. They became landowners through sophisticated political and legal manoeuvring and at greater financial cost than their white counterparts. The state's consistent approach throughout these decades took as its basis the incompatibility between black identity and freehold landownership. Outside of existing state-sanctioned freehold townships, black people could only become freehold landowners where the state gave permission for it.

---

[18] Act 27 of 1913.
[19] Act 21 of 1923.

From the early 1950s, shortly after the National Party's election to power, the apartheid government began dismantling black people's freehold land rights, and particularly targeted, for forced removals and for demolition, townships demarcated for black people that were close to urban centres and townships demarcated for white people. The Group Areas Act 1950[20] permitted the government to establish separate residential areas based on race. In terms of the Act, black or white South Africans were prohibited from buying property or living in areas that had been proclaimed as an area for one racial group. The 1954 Natives Resettlement Act[21] gave the government power to remove African landowners and their tenants in urban freehold areas. The Act gave the state power to prevent Africans from living in or close to cities by forcibly moving them to faraway, sometimes remote, areas. The preamble to the Act provided for the creation of a Natives Resettlement Board that provided for the removal of African people 'from any area in the magisterial district of Johannesburg or any adjoining magisterial district and their resettlement elsewhere'.

In a hollow gesture to due process, the state offered urban freehold landowners compensation for the land from which they were forcibly removed. In Alexandra Township near Johannesburg, as the state began valuating properties for compensation, it adopted a policy that capped payment at two thirds of the value of property (Thipe 2020). The state acknowledged outright it had no intention of paying landowners what their property was worth. Because black people were excluded from accessing financing from banks, it was not uncommon for them to pay exorbitant interest rates from private lenders (Bonner and Nieftagodien 2008). The limited number of freehold townships in which they could buy land further drove up prices for individual stands in relation to similar stands available to white people. These factors, compounded with the significantly lower income that black people earned in relation to white people, meant that black freehold landowners often spent decades, if not a lifetime, paying for their property. As Jane Carruthers explained, 'once Lady Selborne residents received payment for their properties after expropriation or sale in the 1960s, much of the compensation money was spent on repaying outstanding bonds' (Carruthers 2000: 29). Beyond stripping landowners of the material base that they built and the potential for intergenerational wealth transfer that it presented, destroying the lives and homes they built, and tearing apart communities, Carruthers shows how the apartheid state's compensation to black landowners left them with little left with which to rebuild their lives in the locations and reserves to which they were relegated.

---

[20] Act 41 of 1950.
[21] Act 19 of 1954.

Land rights under democracy

The RLRA provided the framework for the Land Claims Court's establishment in 1996. Through the court, South African's newly formed democratic government invited people who lost their land because of racially discriminatory laws to lodge restitution land claims before 31 December 1998 (Walker 2008). The land claim form asked five broad questions: a description of the property; the street address and erf number on the deed; the department that acquired the property and the year that the department acquired the property; whether compensation was paid at the time to the land claimant; and the capacity in which the claimant was acting and whether any other family member might have an interest or claim on the land (Commission on Restitution of Land Rights 1996). Because freehold land is registered with the state, property sale records for every individual stand are housed in state-controlled deeds registry records. These records, which I have consulted extensively in my own research, detail the amount that each owner paid for the property, the year when they paid that amount, and any other transfers of the property, such as inheritance or subdivision of the land.

By 2000, the Commission on Restitution of Land Rights adopted the Standard Settlement Offer (SSO) for financial compensation to restitution claimants 'because of various challenges presented by the method of calculating financial compensation by establishing historical under compensation'. The Commission justified standardising compensation on the grounds of a lack of historical material to 'reconstruct' the past. Specifically, it decided that individual historical valuations 'were quite expensive and time-consuming' and that historical valuations were an attempt to restore exactly what was lost by the claimant, and resulted often in 'complicated formulae being applied in order to establish value' (Department of Rural Development and Land Reform 2009: 4). Based on the logic that compensation to freehold claimants would represent 'recognition' rather than an attempt at assessing what was lost, the Commission established the average in 2000 at R40,000. This amount was paid to claimants in Sophiatown, Payneville, and Lady Selbourne, among others. Larger claim areas, such Alexandra, where most individual stands measured 140 feet by 80 feet, received R50,000. In the Western Cape and Free State the average municipal value was set at R40,000; in KwaZulu-Natal, R50,000. In Limpopo the Office determined 'very few urban financial settlement cases and have therefore to date applied an area specific standard settlement offer'. The Eastern Cape 'applies both the method of under compensation and area specific standard offers', and in Mpumalanga 'though it has limited urban claims, has determined a provincial SSO amount of R60,000 which is used to ensure just and equitable settlements in the least time possible' (Department of Rural Development and Land Reform 2009: 7). While the SSO policy allows for factoring the land size, it does not consider improvements made on the land. The state's approach of considering land size but not the improvements on it ignored the extraordinary investments that landowners made on their land.

From its earliest days, the constitutional negotiations of the early 1990s led to the democratic state's adoption of the policy of 'willing buyer, willing seller' where the state paid for white freehold landowners' land at a rate agreed on by both parties (Hall 2004). In 2000, when the state decided individual valuation was too costly for calculating compensation for individual black freehold landowners, it was still negotiating individual settlements with white freehold landowners. These landowners exploited the fact that 'the state is the only buyer of land for restitution', to 'ask for exorbitant prices' (Ramutsindela et al 2016: 74). While the Standard Settlement Offer practice offered to black people aspires, at the most, to 'recognition of rights lost' and not even to 'an attempt to calculate exactly what was lost', compensation to white freehold landowners has been used a vehicle for personal enrichment (Department of Rural Development and Land Reform 2009).

Freehold landownership presents a scenario where black people lay claim to land on the same terms and through the same acquisition, registration, and recognition processes as white people. Unlike with other land tenure systems in the country, the only difference between landowners in the freehold title system is their racial classification. Even with the fundamental sameness in legal rights to land, the democratic government has treated financial compensation to black and white freehold landowners as dramatically different processes. The comparison of the state's treatment of black and white freehold landowners allows for an interrogation of the extent to which the democratic government has meaningfully departed from and worked to dismantle white supremacist valuing of people's rights through the prism of race.

Conclusion

White supremacy has perpetuated itself within the democratic state's logic of land compensation through policy on and popular imagining of the rights and protections the state owes differently racialised people. Over roughly a century, colonial administrations across the region that became South Africa went to great lengths to construct understandings of land rights that linked whiteness to freehold landownership, and freehold landownership to citizenship. Through the historical processes that excluded black people from universal access to freehold land and to a host of protections and entitlements guaranteed by citizenship, the colonial state normalised the idea of white people's rights to land as inalienable and of black people's rights to land as fundamentally and naturally expungable. At the same time, black people across the four colonies and then across South Africa found ways to buy freehold land and gain for themselves the protections, autonomy, and rights that title deed landownership promised. For several generations, black freehold townships offered relative shelter from the onslaught of state-driven invasion, violation, and insecurity that black people experienced in locations and reserves. Black freehold landowners and their tenants lost all of this when the apartheid government dismantled their property rights, took their land, and forcibly moved them to state-owned land.

The apartheid state stripped black landowners of their property on the sole basis of their racial classification. Decades later under democracy, these same freehold landowners found that the value of the compensation that they received for their property was determined solely on the basis of their race. The steps, which the state determined were too costly for valuating black freehold landowners' property, were applied to white freehold landowners. The token compensation that black freehold landowners received was justified as 'recognition' of their seized property, while white freehold landowners were paid market rate value and above for their property. The colonial state so effectively succeeded in constructing freehold rights as exclusively available to white people that even in seeking redress for racially discriminatory land dispossession, the majority-led state has not been able to imagine black people's freehold land rights existing on the same terms as white people's freehold land rights. The apology that the land restitution process promised to black people has revealed itself as an empty, gilded shell.

Reflections

In my oral history interviews with people who lived in black freehold townships before the forced removals, and in archival records of black people who bought land during colonialism, black freehold landowners consistently expressed their landownership as a victory and defiance. These landowners used South Africa's white supremacist law to claim for themselves the tenure security, freedom of decision, and protections from external interference on their land that European settlers selfishly guarded for themselves. Under every stage of colonialism, black people became freehold landowners at extraordinary personal cost and in the face of obstacles that were intended to be insurmountable. When the apartheid state seized black freeholders' land and property, it extinguished one of the few avenues black people had for building generational material security, it stole their biggest economic asset and investment, and it forced them to rebuild their lives from scratch on the state's terms. With knowledge of this history, it has been heartbreaking to read the democratic state's dismissive rationalisations in policy documents of why dispossessed black freeholders need not be compensated the actual value of their property. The state's betrayal of black citizens feels even more overwhelming when seen alongside its contortions to theorise and budget for ways to not only save white freehold landowners from economic hardship in land expropriation, but to address what it means and looks like to compensate them justly for their land. I know and love many people who received the standardised R40,000 or R60,000 compensation for their property. They have shared with me the very small dent this settlement made in their lives and offered me a glimpse of the depth of their loss from being violently removed from their homes. Writing about the democratic government's feeble attempt at apology to these landowners was painful, and made visible to me new wounds created by this attempt at apology.

Thuto

References

Bergh, J. and Feinberg, H., 2004, 'Trusteeship and black land ownership in the Transvaal during the nineteenth and twentieth centuries', *African Historical Review* 36(1), 170–93.

Bonner, P. and Nieftagodien, N., 2008, *Alexandra: A History*, Johannesburg: Witwatersrand University Press.

Braun, L., 2005, 'Spatial institutionalisation and the settler state: survey and mapping in the Eastern transvaal, 1852–1905', *South African Historical Journal* 53(1), 146–78.

Campbell, J. T., 1995, *Songs of Zion: The African Methodist Episcopal Church in the United States and South Africa*, New York: Oxford University Press.

Carruthers, J., 2000, 'Urban land claims in South Africa: the case of Lady Selborne township, Pretoria, Gauteng', *African Historical Review* 32(1), 23–41.

Commission on Restitution of Land Rights, 1996, *Land Claim Form*, Pretoria: Commission on Restitution of Land Rights.

Delius, P., 1984, *The Land Belongs to Us: The Pedi Polity, the Boers, and the British in the Nineteenth Century Transvaal*, Johannesburg: Heinemann.

Department of Rural Development and Land Reform, 2009, *Restitution Policy Guidelines: Standard Settlement Offer*, Pretoria: Department of Rural Development and Land Reform.

Dlamini, J., 2011, 'We now know: reform, revolution and race in post-apartheid South Africa', *Transformation: Critical Perspectives on Southern Africa* 75, 36–43.

Edwards, I., 1994, 'Cato Manor: cruel past, pivotal future', *Review of African Political Economy* 21(61), 415–27.

Feinberg, H., 2015, *Our Land, Our Life, Our Future*, Pretoria: University of South Africa Press.

Feinberg, H. and Horn, A., 2009, 'South African territorial segregation: new data on African farm purchases, 1913–1936', *The Journal of African History* 50(1), 41–60.

Jeppie, S., 2001, 'Reclassifications: coloured, Malay, Muslim', in Z. Erasmus (ed.), *Coloured by History, Shaped by Place: New Perspectives on Coloured Identities in Cape Town*, pp 80–96, Cape Town: Kwela Books.

Hall, R., 2004, 'Land restitution in South Africa: rights, development, and the restrained state', *Canadian Journal of African Studies* 38(3), 654–71.

Hamilton, R., 1987, 'The role of apartheid legislation in the property law of South Africa', *National Black Law Journal* 10(2), 153–82.

Harris, C. I., 1993, 'Whiteness as property', *Harvard Law Review*, June, 1707–91.

Khumalo, V. R., 2013, 'From Plough to Entrepreneurship: A History of African Entrepreneurs in Evaton 1905–1960s', master's dissertation, Department of History, University of the Witwatersrand.

Khumalo, V. R., 2020, 'Struggles for African independent education and land rights on the Rand and the significance of the Tsewu court case, 1903–1905: a new analysis', *Historia* 65(1), 14–37.

Lambert, J., 1999, 'African reasons for purchasing land in Natal in the late 19th, early 20th centuries', *African Historical Review* 31(1), 33–54.

Lorenzen, J., 2014, 'Compensation at market value for land reform? A critical assessment of the MalaMala judgment's approach to compensation for expropriation in South Africa', *Law in Africa* 17(2), 151–74.

Margeot, M., 1987, 'Freehold land tenure: problems and prospects', *Development Southern Africa* 4(3), 531–7.

Matthew, E. L., 1915, 'South African native land laws', *Journal of the Society of Comparative Legislation* 15(1), 9–16.

Moguerane, K., 2016, 'Black landlords, their tenants, and the Natives Land Act of 1913', *Journal of Southern African Studies* 42(2), 243–66.

Molema, S. M., 2013, *Lover of his People: A Biography of Sol Plaatje*, trans. D. S. Matjila and K. Haire, Johannesburg: Wits University Press.

Murray, C., 1992, *Black Mountain: Land, Class, and Power in the Eastern Orange Free State, 1880s to 1980s*, Edinburgh: Edinburgh University Press for the International African Institute.

Ngcukaitobi, T., 2018a, 'The land: ANC's date with destiny', *The Mail and Guardian*, 2 March, viewed 16 August 2022 from https://mg.co.za/article/2018-03-02-00-the-land-ancs-date-with-destiny/

Ngcukaitobi, T., 2018b, *The Land is Ours: Black Lawyers and the Birth of Constitutionalism in South Africa*, Cape Town: Penguin Random House South Africa.

Ngcukaitobi, T. and Bishop, M., 2018, 'The Constitutionality of Expropriation Without Compensation', paper presented at the Constitutional Court Review IX Conference, Constitutional Court of South Africa, Johannesburg, 2–3 August.

Pinilla, V. and Willebald, H., 2019, *Agricultural Development in the World Periphery: A Global Economic History Approach*, London: Palgrave Macmillan.

Ramutsindela, M., Davis, N., and Sinthumule, I., 2016, *Diagnostic Report on Land Reform in South Africa Land Restitution: Commissioned Report for High Level Panel on the Assessment of Key Legislation and the Acceleration of Fundamental Change*, Cape Town: Parliament of South Africa.

Sibanda, S., 2018, '"Not Yet Uhuru" – The Usurpation of the Liberation Aspirations of South Africa's Masses by a Commitment to Liberal Constitutional Democracy', PhD thesis, School of Law, University of Witwatersrand.

Thipe, T., 2020, 'Black Freehold: Landownership in Alexandra Township, 1912–1979', PhD thesis, Departments of History and African American Studies, Yale University.

Walker, C., 2008, *Landmarked: Land Claims and Land Restitution in South Africa*, Johannesburg: Jacana Media.

14

On Apology and the Failure of Shame in the TRC

Jaco Barnard-Naudé

Introduction

At bottom, this chapter concerns itself with the relationship between apology and reparation. The common (liberal) assumption as regards this relation is that the apology has a reparative dimension – saying sorry goes some way in making good for the wrong that one has committed. Indeed, Mia Swart (2008: 51) has, in the context of South African transitional justice, suggested that apology can be a powerful gesture of what she calls 'symbolic reparation'. In an early article about the South African Truth and Reconciliation Commission (TRC), Emily McCarthy similarly argued that the Amnesty Committee of the TRC should insist that 'the applicant apologise as a form of "reparation"' (McCarthy 1997: 245). She went on to argue that 'amnesty applicants have a moral obligation to apologise to the people they harmed. An expression of genuine remorse not only may help to ease the pain of victims and their relatives but also goes a long way towards fostering feelings of reconciliation among South Africans' (McCarthy 1997: 247).

Famously, the TRC's amnesty process did not require apology as a criterium for amnesty (Moon 2004: 191) and this contribution is, to a significant extent, concerned with the hidden ideological 'background' context that would explain such a silence in the amnesty criteria. But as a point of departure, I want to ask a different question, one that proceeds from the acceptance that, despite the structured silence in relation to apology in the amnesty criteria, many an apology was indeed forthcoming from amnesty applicants and even from those who did not apply for amnesty, such as the incomplete apology of F.W. de Klerk (McCarthy 1997: 245–6). The question is this: what if the discursive context of the TRC was so saturated with the ideology of pardon, forgiveness, and mercy that this discursive context in itself undermined the reparative dimension of apologies? What if the apology's performative force was so undermined by the discursive context in which it was delivered that, instead of 'symbolic reparation', we end up with a merely formal symbolic gesture, an instance of what Jacques Lacan would have called 'empty speech', that not only has no reparative effect but that risks (re)activating for victims the traumatic effect of the wrong? (Govier and Verwoerd 2002: 79). Clearly, this would be a paradoxical upshot of a discursive context that was meant to be therapeutic.

I will argue that this is precisely the kind of risk to which the TRC exposed postapartheid transitional justice and that this might, moreover, have everything to do with the reasons behind prominent refusals or failures to apologise or failures to apologise fully, such as that of de Klerk. It might also explain the structured silence in relation to apology in the TRC's amnesty criteria. In short, my sense is that a discursive context can be so intensely ideologically loaded that, instead of operating as the background context against which the utterance – in this case, the apology – is delivered, it rushes to the foreground and usurps the specificity of the utterance so that the communicative level that dominates and ultimately prevails – the level at which it matters whether the apology is accepted or not – becomes definitively the level of the big Other, the level of the Law, although, as we shall see, this is an altogether different kind of 'law' than the ordinary law of crime and punishment.

In relation to the concerns of this chapter, my argument will be that where the discursive context allows for the apology to anticipate its acceptance in advance – where the discursive context into which the apology is delivered overwhelmingly communicates the message that the apology is always already both acceptable and accepted, and, as such, not needed – apology's reparative dimension is seriously undermined. The reason why apology's reparative dimension is undermined under such circumstances is because, in a discursive context where it can anticipate its 'acceptance' (or the fact that it is not needed) in advance, the apology's relationship to the (ethical) dimension of shame is seriously called into question.

Thus, in this chapter it is the TRC as the big Other – as the network of socio-symbolic authority that determines a discursive context for a subject (Evans 1996: 136) – which will be of concern. This focus necessarily requires that we treat the TRC as an instance of Law, or the law, in a general sense. But what kind of instance of the Law was the TRC, if we understand that it was not an instance of the 'law' in the ordinary sense of crime and its punishment? What sort of instance of the Law can undermine the reparative dimension of apology in the way suggested above? What sort of instance of the Law *constrains*, instead of promotes, the experience of shame for wrongs done? In order to understand what sort of instance of the Law the TRC was, I suggest that we take a short detour to the opera.

La Clemenza di Tito and the South African TRC

W.A. Mozart's opera *La Clemenza di Tito* concerns a conspiracy against the Roman emperor Tito, instigated by Vitellia, the daughter of the deposed emperor, and her lover Sesto. The intricacies of the conspiracy against Tito need not detain us here. What is important is that the conspiracy ultimately fails, forcing the conspirators to confess their guilt and throw themselves in apology at the feet of the Emperor, who pardons them. In his discussion of *Clemenza*, the Slovenian philosopher, Slavoj Žižek (2009: 14–15), quotes a section from the opera's libretto that neatly summarises both Tito's predicament and his resolve. Just before the grand final pardon, Tito becomes exasperated by all the pardons he is faced with and exclaims as follows:

> The very moment that I absolve one criminal, I discover another. / ... / I believe the stars conspire to oblige me, in spite of myself, to become cruel. No: they shall not have this satisfaction. My virtue has already pledged itself to continue the contest. Let us see, which is more constant, the treachery of others or my mercy. / ... / Let it be known to Rome that I am the same and that I know all, absolve everyone, and forget everything.

What makes this section of Tito's speech in *Clemenza* relevant for the purposes of this contribution is the way in which Tito's words above testify to a discursive scene *saturated by forgiveness*. Tito forgives/pardons/absolves 'everyone', in advance, and he forgets 'everything'. This aspect of the opera has prompted Žižek (2009: 15) to remark that:

> [t]he ridiculous proliferation of mercy in Clemenza means that power no longer functions in a normal way, so that it has to be sustained by mercy all the time: if a Master has to show mercy, it means that the law failed, that the legal state machinery is not able to run on its own and needs an incessant intervention from the outside.

It hardly takes a leap of the imagination to recognise that the TRC qualifies as exactly such 'an incessant intervention from the outside' when the 'legal state machinery' was/became no longer able to 'run on its own'. Those familiar with the trials and tribulations of transitional justice in South Africa will recall how the clause that founded the TRC – the 1993 Interim Constitution's famous Epilogue and the provision therein that 'amnesty shall be granted'– was inserted into South Africa's first democratic Constitution at the 11th hour (Shore 2009: 112; Rowen 2017: 30), precisely at the moment when the 'legal state machinery' was no longer able to 'run on its own'. Acknowledging this is not to buy again into the narrative that the apartheid security forces 'blackmailed' the African National Congress (ANC) into amnesty by threatening to disrupt the first democratic election (du Toit 2018). Rather, it is to say, as Fanie du Toit has recently pointed out in his book on political transitions, that both the outgoing apartheid government and the incoming ANC-led coalition knew that they 'needed amnesty'. Without amnesty, the new legal state machinery, based as it was on a government of national unity, which included members of the old state alongside members of the armed struggle movements, could not have come into its own.

Thus, while the TRC itself was a creature of statute – the Promotion of National Unity and Reconciliation Act 1995[1] (PNURA) – of South Africa's first democratically elected parliament, its origin lies in an intervention – the Epilogue to the 1993 or Interim Constitution[2] – from outside this state legal machinery,[3] strictly speaking, and it was an intervention precisely aimed at ensuring that the ordinary law would, in the future, function in a normal way, indeed that the rule of law would finally take hold in South Africa. This view is certainly in line with the view that the TRC was created to consolidate the sovereignty of the new liberal democratic state. As Humphrey (2005: 204) pointedly writes:

> while national reconciliation addresses conflict between antagonistic groups, often defined along ethnic or religious cleavages, it does so with the larger purpose of re-establishing the authority of the state, more particularly, reinstating the liberal state based on the social contract between civil society and the state. Truth politics aimed at promoting justice and reconciliation have been at the heart of the recovery of the legitimacy of the state during political transitions to democracy.

This sovereignty could, under the peculiar circumstances that prevailed, only be secured at the cost of granting the exception in advance (exactly in the manner of Tito's mercy), in the form of an effectively a priori legal commitment that 'amnesty shall be granted', as per the Epilogue of the 1993 Constitution, so that the imperative 'shall be granted' becomes legally enforceable. In short, the birth of the TRC in the amnesty provision of the

---

[1] Act 34 of 1995.

[2] Constitution of the Republic of South Africa Act 200 of 1993.

[3] Indeed, in *Azapo v President of the Republic of South Africa* (LCC 156/2009) [2012] ZALCC 7 (19 April 2012) at para. 14, the Constitutional Court was at pains to insist that the Epilogue was as much a part of the Interim Constitution as any other provision thereof, a point made by the Interim Constitution itself. This, however, does not take away from the fact that the Epilogue was – as a product of the negotiations – imposed, both from outside the apartheid legal order and from outside the formal parameters of the first postapartheid parliament.

Interim Constitution's Epilogue was by itself an indication that power in the new South Africa could, at that point, no longer function in a normal way, so that it had to be 'sustained by mercy', by that form of the sovereign's relaxation of the rigour of the law that the Interim Constitution called 'amnesty' and styled imperatively.

Now that we have established via Mozart's *Clemenza* that there is enough to suggest that the TRC qualified as an intervention from outside the ordinary law for the sake of the ordinary law, I consider in the next section whether it could be said that, despite the fact that the amnesty dispensation was conditional, the TRC, like Tito's Rome, was nonetheless characterised by a 'ridiculous proliferation of mercy'.

The climate of forgiveness in the TRC

In a rare instance of strident criticism of the discourse of the TRC, Thomas Brudholm has argued that it stigmatised what he calls 'negative emotions' opposed to forgiveness. Brudholm (2006: 9) notes Martha Minow's observation that there is 'a striking prevalence of therapeutic language in contemporary discussions of mass atrocities', of which only one of the many institutional effects is that, according to Brudholm (2006: 9–10),

> [i]t allows the party to whom the angry protest is directed to reduce the resentment of 'objective' injury and injustice to trauma or a subjective disturbance and is seen as something that the victim/patient should 'get over' for his or her own sake and something in need of counseling and treatment rather than a moral-political response.

Brudholm (2006: 8, emphasis added) considers how '[p]opular as well as scholarly discourses about the question of how individuals and societies can "move on" in the wake of genocide are *permeated with references to "negative" emotions and attitudes like anger, hatred, and resentment*'. He argues that 'most of this discourse proceeds without much reflection as to the nature and value of these "negative" emotions and attitudes at stake and, indeed, with *a distinct discreditation of these emotions*' (p 8, emphasis added).

Against this backdrop, Brudholm considers the 'praise of forgiveness and reconciliation' that surrounded the TRC. He argues that the 'ideal articulated during the proceedings and in related writings was that of victims *overcoming* anger and desires for revenge or retribution, not the pacification of such emotions and desires by way of justice in the form of prosecution and punishment' (p 9). Brudholm believes that ' "negative" reactive attitudes' in a discourse permeated with reconciliation and forgiveness are often not given their due as authentic and valid human emotions. Instead, the discourse valorises the emotions that it regards as resonant with forgiveness and reconciliation. As such, it leaves little room for 'considerations of the possible value and legitimacy of victims' "negative" emotions. They are typically only considered in their function as a negative force to be overcome, labelled as hindrances to reconciliation, morally inferior, irrational, immoral, or pathological' (p 8). For Brudholm 'when forgiveness, healing, and reconciliation are promoted as overriding values', the advocates of overcoming the 'negative' emotions often assume that the overcoming 'leaves nothing to regret or consider' (p 10).

It is in this context that Brudholm (2006: 10) casts a critical eye on the writings of Archbishop Desmond Tutu, Chairperson of the TRC. He argues that in Tutu's writing 'resentment and desires for retribution appear only as destructive and dehumanizing forces that should be "avoided like the plague" because they are corrosive of "ubuntu" and social harmony' (p 10). Brudholm berates Tutu for a lack of concern, at least in his 'writings', for 'the possible moral value of anger or the possible legitimacy of some victims' resistance to the call for forgiveness' (p 10). Tutu describes the refusal to forgive in the TRC's hearings as 'exceptional' and he 'does not dwell on the cases of dissent, but hastily returns to the appraisal of the forgiving and more exhilarating kind of victim response' (p 10). Brudholm (2006: 10) continues:

> such lack of attention to the possible legitimacy of anger or the retributive emotions more generally, indeed the vilification of such emotions as destructive of our shared humanity and harmony, is troubling. It is troubling not only because of the way in which it licenses disregard of the possibly valid reasons of those who did not want to forgive, and not only because of the troubles arising from an elevation of social harmony to the status of supreme good. The disqualification of anger and resentment also insinuates and promulgates an uncritical conception of forgiving as always noble and praiseworthy.

Brudholm then considers the TRC itself and argues (p 10) that during its hearings, 'Tutu and other commissioners repeatedly lauded those victims and relatives who were willing to forgive and reconcile. They were held forth as models of the kind of personal magnanimity and nobility needed to secure the transition to a new and better South Africa'.

This impression of the TRC as an institution that practised a certain *injunction* to forgive, is not limited to Brudholm's criticisms. There is a considerable archive that documents the impression of the TRC as an institution that exerted pressure on victims to forgive. In a chapter on apology, Verwoerd (1999: 305) quotes the following statement from one of the victims who appeared before the TRC: 'What really makes me angry about the TRC and Tutu is that they are putting pressure on us to forgive.

For most black South Africans it is about us having to forgive ... I don't know if I will ever be ready to forgive'. Similarly, in an extensive survey concluding that a significant portion of victims and survivors did experience pressure from the TRC to forgive, the author quotes in conclusion one deponent as saying that 'the Government is telling us, saying that we must forgive the perpetrators. It is difficult to forgive someone who was an enemy' (Chapman 2008: 80).

As for the uncritical introduction of forgiveness in the moral discourse of the TRC, Jacques Derrida, in 2001, criticised Archbishop Tutu for 'christianising ... [w]ith as much goodwill as confusion ... the language of an institution uniquely destined to treat "politically" motivated crimes' (Derrida 2001: 42). Similarly, Claire Moon (2004: 186) echoes Derrida's point when she notes that the TRC's formulation of restorative justice 'made intrinsic to its political project of national unity a Christian interpretation of reconciliation'. As Moon (2004: 186) writes, this 'theological rendering of reconciliation' incorporated forgiveness and this became the defining feature of the TRC's contribution to both the articulation and the institutionalisation of the public discourse about the nation's 'moral and ethical reordering'.

When we move the focus to the TRC's own work product, its Report, the emphasis on forgiveness as an exception to the operation of the ordinary law is palpable. First, one should note that the Report describes the TRC from the outset as self-consciously an institution of restorative justice (TRC 1998, Vol. 1: 128). In the chapter on concepts and principles in the TRC Report, the Commission confirms that it operates according to the principle of restorative justice and *ubuntu* (TRC 1998, Vol. 1: 125). In this sense, then, the TRC was concerned to create an image of itself not merely as an institution 'uniquely destined to treat "politically" motivated crimes', but indeed as an institution that would be permeated by restorative justice and therapeutic jurisprudence which has been described as 'an alternative approach to law' (Scheff 1998: 97). It was particularly in relation to victims that the Commission was at pains to emphasise its function as an institution of restorative justice and to distance itself from the ordinary law: 'Through the public unburdening of their grief – *which would have been impossible within the context of an adversarial search for objective and corroborative evidence* – those who were violated received public recognition that they had been wronged' (TRC 1998, Vol. 1: 128, emphasis added).

There are several places in the Report where the Commission links restorative justice to forgiveness by emphasising that 'the key concepts of confession, forgiveness and reconciliation are central to the message of this report' (TRC 1998, Vol. 1:16). Similarly, in Vol. 5 of the Report, the Commission quotes with approval Archbishop Tutu's statement after a visit to Rwanda that 'confession, forgiveness and reconciliation in the lives of nations are not just airy-fairy religious and spiritual things, nebulous and unrealistic. They are the stuff of practical politics' (p 351). And in a telling statement on the relationship between forgiveness and reconciliation in Vol. 1 of the Report, it becomes clear exactly how primary the Commission considered forgiveness to be when it stated that '[i]t is also crucial not to fall into the error of equating forgiveness with reconciliation. *The road to reconciliation requires more than forgiveness*' (p 115, emphasis added). In this statement the TRC definitively revealed its ideological hand: we see the Commission taking forgiveness as the starting point, as that which *must happen* before reconciliation can be set on its course.

Brudholm's criticism coupled with the extracts from the TRC's Report tell us that at the level of ideology as moral discourse, the TRC was at pains to construct itself as the big Other of forgiveness, indeed as the protector and agency of the Law of Forgiveness. In a very literal, concrete sense, the TRC was principally concerned both with establishing the authority of forgiveness and with ensuring that it would be understood as the authority on forgiveness. It would, accordingly, not be overstretching the interpretation to say that many victims and survivors practically experienced the TRC as an institution in which forgiveness was the law to be obeyed and that such an experience was indeed (part of) the ideological intention of the TRC.

But was it simply at the level of ideological moral discourse that the TRC adopted and practised forgiveness as its law? Did it not in its application of conditional amnesty, at least, operate according to a set of principles that had less to do with forgiveness than with juridical mechanisms geared at obtaining as complete a picture as possible of the past (through the requirement of full disclosure, for instance)?

In order to have a comprehensive sense of the image that the TRC established of itself as an instance of the big Other figured as the Law of Forgiveness, we should move beyond the level of moral ideology and attend to the more specific juridical level at which the TRC operated in its Amnesty Committee. Only if it is the case that the TRC also in this aspect of its operations adopted forgiveness as its law – in other words, only if it can be shown that the TRC undermined its own juridical mechanisms in favour of an ideology of forgiveness – can one accept the proposition that it was permeated by a 'ridiculous proliferation of mercy'.

In this regard, Adam Sitze's (2013) criticisms of the Amnesty Committee's work are highly instructive. Sitze (2013: 4, 23) points out that much has been made of the fact that the TRC's amnesty was not a blanket amnesty – applications for amnesty had to meet a series of conditions before amnesty would be granted. Of these, the political motivation requirement and the full disclosure requirement became the most prominent. However, Sitze's argument is that much of the substantive conditionality of the amnesty process fell away as a result of the way in which the Amnesty Committee dealt with the proportionality and full disclosure requirements of the amnesty applications.

As a point of departure in his discussion of these aspects of the Amnesty Committee's practice, Sitze poses only one question as the test for the success or failure of the amnesty process, namely whether it managed to put 'out of commission' or render 'defeasible' the very jurisprudence in which it found its precedents (Sitze 2013: 100). That jurisprudence is the colonial-apartheid jurisprudence of indemnity, according to which the sovereign could, as a matter of convention, indemnify its agents for crimes that they committed in the genuine belief that they were protecting or promoting the safety of the population. As such, indemnity jurisprudence found its justification in the principle of political sovereignty: *salus populi suprema lex esto* (Sitze 2013: 66, 70).

With respect to the TRC's amnesty as the heir of colonial indemnity jurisprudence, Sitze's argument makes a compelling case that the way in which the TRC handled conditional amnesty did not displace colonial indemnity jurisprudence. Rather, it replaced it in the manner of a repetition under a different name. That name was 'amnesty'. The significance of the argument that the TRC's amnesty practice did not displace colonial indemnity jurisprudence should not be underestimated in terms of what this means for the question under consideration. For if the TRC's amnesty 'jurisprudence' did not displace colonial indemnity jurisprudence it means that this jurisprudence operated in close proximity to the sovereign 'right of grace' (Derrida 2001: 45) – in other words, a sovereign right of pardon – from which the indemnity convention in colonial jurisprudence was derived in the first place.

Sitze recognises that from the outset, the 'TRC Bill was a simple extension of what, in 1977, parliamentarians from all parties called the "principle of indemnity"' (Sitze 2013: 98). As Sitze writes, 'It was a classical Diceyan attempt to provide retroactive protection from civil and criminal prosecutions to those who violated the laws passed by the apartheid state's own sovereign parliament' (pp 98–9). Thus, the TRC *'re-used the very power whose abuse it criticized in the apartheid state'* (p 99, emphasis added).

But it is *also* the very use of these tools from within the decommissioned Master's house that provided for the TRC's 'unprecedented audacity and even genius' (Sitze 2013: 99). In short, the genius of the TRC lies in the way in which it used the techniques and powers proper to martial law as the 'juridical basis' upon which to build an exposure and critique of the inhuman acts that were committed under its aegis. From this point of view, the norm that would determine the TRC's success or failure was whether its deployment of indemnity *one last time* would render indemnity defeasible.

On the other hand, in this repurposing of the tools from the decommissioned Master's house lay also the TRC's greatest risk, namely that it would employ 'with little modification the same core mechanisms that defined indemnity jurisprudence under apartheid only now under a new name' (Sitze 2013: 100). The critical analytical question then becomes not whether the TRC reiterated indemnity jurisprudence but what 'the precise character' (Sitze 2013: 100) of such a reiteration was. This leads Sitze to an extremely thoughtful (and forceful) analysis of the work of the Amnesty Committee.

Sitze begins this analysis by noting the mandate of the Amnesty Committee according to the PNURA: 'the granting of amnesty to persons who make full disclosure of all the relevant facts relating to acts associated with a political objective committed in the course of the conflicts of the past' (Sitze 2013: 101). Sitze then argues that the Amnesty Committee's work revolved around two tests: the 'political objective' test and the 'full disclosure test' (pp 101–2). An important subset of the 'political objective' test was the 'proportionality requirement' which required the Committee to ask 'whether or not an applicant's illegal act was a suitable, necessary, and reasonable means to the end of accomplishing his or her stated "political objective"' (p 102).

Building on the work of Jeremy Sarkin and Antje Du Bois-Pedain, Sitze shows that the Amnesty Committee 'completely dropped' the 'evaluative or normative dimension to the "proportionality" requirement' – a normative dimension that was required by the Norgaard principles from which the 'political objective' test of the PNURA is commonly said to have derived (Sitze 2013: 106). Instead, the Amnesty Committee opted for 'nonnormative, descriptive distinctions between political objectives and nonpolitical objectives' and, accordingly, it *routinely* decided applications for amnesty on the basis of the applicant's 'bona fide belief in the necessity of a given illegal act' (p 108).

In dropping the normative dimension of proportionality (that is, in not asking itself the question of whether the applicant's act was *objectively* necessary), the Amnesty Committee *reiterated without difference* the indemnity jurisprudence from the apartheid era. How so? Because, as Sitze indicates, the necessity test for indemnity during the apartheid era became, precisely, a *subjective* test: whether the official concerned honestly believed that the act was necessary to preserve or restore the *salus publica* (Sitze 2013: 107). In point of fact, it was apartheid indemnity's restriction of itself to *this* test alone that caused the indemnity convention to enter decisively into crisis. The subjective test was indemnity's 'innermost pathology', the 'innermost norm for legalizing illegality' (p 108). Thus, in restricting itself to the question of the applicant's bona fide (subjective) belief, the Amnesty Committee allowed indemnity to silently survive in its practice. In this, the Amnesty Committee failed to apply a principle 'whose inclusion in the [PNURA] was to have turned that Act into more than just yet another indemnity act' (p 108).

One could have been forgiven for hoping that the 'full disclosure' requirement, at least, saved the amnesty dispensation of the PNURA from entering into an Agambenian 'real zone of indistinction' (Agamben 1998: 10) with indemnity jurisprudence. But Sitze (2013: 109) writes that this was not to be. Noting that, in the face of the Amnesty Committee's abandonment of the 'normative component of its "political objective" test, the "full disclosure" test became even more important' (p 109), Sitze argues that the 'inner norms and criteria' of this test were 'no more clear or distinct' than the political objective test. There was no guidance in the PNURA, nor, for that matter, in any other relevant legislation, as to what 'full disclosure' entailed. As a result, the Amnesty Committee 'conferred coherence on its "full disclosure" test in much the same way that it conferred coherence on its "political objective" test' (p 110).

The 'pivotal criterion' in the 'full disclosure' test became 'honesty' – whether the applicant had given an honest account of what actually happened (Sitze 2013:110). However, in comparison with the indemnity jurisprudence that immediately preceded it, the Amnesty Committee's full disclosure test reversed the onus as regards proof of honesty. In indemnity jurisprudence, the onus was on a plaintiff to show that the actions of the state officials were not motivated by an honest, bona fide belief in necessity. In the proceedings of the Amnesty Committee, on the contrary, the onus was on amnesty applicants to show that their actions were both bona fide and necessary (p 110). Did this make the crucial difference?

Sitze's answer is no. First, the indemnity jurisprudence referred to above 'was not categorically definitive of indemnity jurisprudence as a whole' (Sitze 2013: 110). In fact, 'full disclosure', where the accused had been presumed guilty unless they could show 'some legal justification for their conduct', was well known in colonial and apartheid South Africa, at least since 1900. Second, the individualised approach as such undercut a fundamental aim of the TRC, namely to 'narrate, as the common sense of the postapartheid state, the retrospective history according to which apartheid *as a whole* was a crime against humanity' (p 200). The individualised approach, as Jacqueline Rose has pointed out, shrinks accountability 'as the crimes of apartheid become more and more the acts of individuals, less and less the machinery of the unjust and illegal apartheid state' (Sitze 2013: 201).

The interpretation of 'full disclosure' that followed from the individualised approach put the Amnesty Committee at odds with 'the manifestly shared or common character of the political crimes it was charged with adjudicating' (Sitze 2013: 111). For it meant that amnesty applicants did not have to disclose their complicity in crimes in relation to which they had not applied for amnesty. Writing that the Amnesty Committee 'quietly rejected' an expansive version of the full disclosure requirement (put forth by George Bizos), which would have disallowed applicants the right to remain silent,

Sitze concludes that the Amnesty Committee's preferred, individualised, honesty-driven approach to full disclosure precluded the Committee from obtaining disclosure in relation to a vast number of acts in which amnesty applicants were complicit (p 113). And this approach severely constrained the normative force of the 'full disclosure' requirement.

Finally, as regards the work of the Reparations and Rehabilitation Committee, Sitze writes that the colonial antecedent of this form – the compensation committee – 'derived its authority not from the rule of law but from the highest form of exception to the rule of law, the sovereign right of grace' (Sitze 2013: 114). Sitze argues that the Reparations and Rehabilitation Committee defined reparation in terms that were 'almost identical' to the language that 'authorized the apartheid state to make *ex gratia* payments' (p 115). For instance, the description of 'reparation' as an 'essential counterbalance for amnesty' echoed the apartheid-era definition of 'compensation' as the 'counterpart of indemnity' (p 115). With reference to the Constitutional Court's decision in the *AZAPO* case, to the effect that the South African state was justified to limit apartheid-era compensation to individualised reparation payments, Sitze writes that 'the South African state justified its limited compensation scheme with reference not to the rule of law … but to the exception to law demanded by a specifically fiscal declension of the *salus publica*' (p 118).

In the TRC itself, this justification took the form of attempts to 'turn compensation into something more meaningful than just "symbolic" payment' (Sitze 2013: 118). However, the Mbeki administration's repudiation of the TRC's reparation proposals 'ruined the TRC's ability to differentiate itself' from apartheid-era compensation schemes (p 119). The tragic irony of this reliance on an exception to the rule of law, on a large-scale 'forgiveness' of the debt, one might say, was that in this very reliance on forgiveness, the postapartheid government prevented the victims of apartheid from obtaining adequate reparation for their injuries and losses.

The point of this lengthy excursion into Sitze's argument, then, is not only to show that the Amnesty Committee grossly neglected the most important substantive conditions for the granting of amnesty. Rather, it is to show that the entire TRC process was steeped in a proliferation of 'forgiveness' with devastating consequences for the victims of apartheid. It is to show that the ideological context became so saturated with 'forgiveness' that it permeated in the application of the TRC's innermost quasi-juridical mechanisms.

In short, the TRC, by foregoing the proportionality requirement, forgave indemnity jurisprudence its excesses; by foregoing the objective measure of full disclosure, it forgave indemnity jurisprudence its 'innermost pathology'; and, finally, the Mbeki administration, by foregoing the TRC's recommendations for comprehensive reparation, forgave the apartheid-era compensation committee its woeful shortcomings. Finally, then, the point of this excursion is to show that the TRC's ideological context, its status as the big Other, established itself as, and operated or operationalised, a 'ridiculous proliferation of mercy'. No wonder, then, that Sitze asks the following pertinent question about the process of the TRC as a whole:

> Have the normative excesses of transitional justice led it to embrace and affirm a discourse on forgiveness that, in genealogical terms, is little more than a newly moralistic shell for an old legal kernel – for the legalization of illegality that was at the core of indemnity jurisprudence? In other words, is 'forgiveness' simply the name that indemnity jurisprudence gives to its juridical forms under conditions where it is no longer able to recognize either itself or its byproducts, where indeed its basic forms silently survive even as indemnity jurisprudence itself has been legally proscribed? (Sitze 2013: 121)

Apology in a climate of forgiveness

Now that we have established that there is ample evidence to suggest that the TRC could be understood as an institution in which forgiveness was the law, both in its moral-ideological discourse as well as in its more conventionally juridical discourse, it is time to focus on the effect of this climate of forgiveness on apology at the TRC. The first thing to note in this regard is the conclusion of Weisman (2006: 234), after an extensive survey of the TRC's amnesty proceedings:

> Indeed, with few exceptions, the vast majority of applicants for amnesty either refused to apologise or show remorse even when invited to do so or, more frequently, offered statements that were so fraught with equivocation and qualification as to leave the victim and the Commission officials in doubt whether the perpetrator did feel remorse or had apologised for their gross violations of human rights.

Secondly, according to Govier and Verwoerd (2002: 67), '[t]he TRC transcripts provide examples of sincere and profoundly important apologies, illustrating the promise of apology as an important step toward rectifying relationships disrupted by wrongdoing. They also provide illustrations of apologies severely flawed by hypocrisy, grandstanding, and denial'.

Reading these statements together, one can discern that there was a severe deficit in the TRC as regards apologies which had the effect of 'symbolic reparation'. It is thus on this second, darker dimension of the apology that I would like to focus in what follows. My sense is that there is a profound connection between the lack of apology and 'severely flawed' apologies on the one hand, and the TRC's climate of forgiveness on the other hand, and my argument here is that *one* of the reasons that could explain the absence of apologies or the presence of severely flawed ones is that the TRC's climate of forgiveness occluded an essential dimension of apology. That dimension is shame.

I want, thus, to return to Brudholm's reference to the negative emotions in order to argue that one such 'negative emotion', which did not receive enough attention in the TRC as a result of the ideological context of 'forgiveness', is shame. I argue that, in the same way as the TRC, perhaps unwittingly, stigmatised the anger of victims, its ideological context of forgiveness also occluded the value of what the literature refers to as 'reintegrative shaming' (Braithwaite 1989; 2000). This is the kind of shame that has the potential to reintegrate a perpetrator into the community, and, as such, it operates in close proximity to the symbolic reparation of which an apology is said to be capable. In fact, my wager in this regard is that the reparative value of the apology is seriously undermined without a demonstration of shame on the part of the perpetrator. Accordingly, the occlusion of this kind of shame by an ideological context saturated by forgiveness makes it easier for perpetrators either to refuse to apologise, or to furnish apologies that are in fact not apologies at all: hypocritical, grandstanding, and denialist 'apologies' that not only have no reparative effect but that, moreover, risk re-traumatising victims.

Govier and Verwoerd (2002: 68), relying on the work of Tavuchis, thus argue that the apology 'realises its potential largely through the expression of shame and remorse. The sincere expression of sorrow is essential to a genuine apology'. For Govier and Verwoerd, this expression of 'sorrow' (their collective term for 'shame and remorse') 'indicates acknowledgement' which has three critical dimensions. First, the wrongdoer acknowledges wrongdoing and responsibility for it. Second, the wrongdoer acknowledges the 'moral status of the victims' as injured parties. Third, the 'offender is acknowledging the legitimacy of feelings of resentment and anger that victims may feel in response to being wronged' (Govier and Verwoerd 2002: 69). This form of apology 'presupposes moral agreement': the wrongdoer joins the victim in condemning the wrongful act.

While Govier and Verwoerd do not mention this explicitly, their implication is that at the level of affect, shame accompanies all three of the dimensions of effective acknowledgement. Without demonstrated shame – what Moon (2004: 188) calls the acknowledgement of responsibility 'made manifest in a sincere and outward show of remorse' – the apology does not translate into an acknowledgement that has the potential to move a victim to forgiveness, and thus to achieve symbolic reparation. Another way of putting this would be to say that the reparative dimension of the apology falls away without demonstrated shame. If, as Govier and Verwoerd (2002: 73) argue, there is a close connection between moral amends and material amends (a perpetrator who is not willing 'to commit himself to concrete measures to repair damage that has been done to the victim' is likely to have his apology dismissed as 'insincere or hollow'), then one can also appreciate that the presence of demonstrated shame in this context can be understood as the initial embodiment of the willingness also to make 'practical amends' (Govier and Verwoerd 2002: 73). It thus appears that shame in the restorative justice process operates like something of a threshold, in that it creates a gap or opens the door for both symbolic and material reparation which in turn can be the basis of a reintegration of the perpetrator into the community of victims and survivors.

It is thus here where the literature on the concept of 'reintegrative shaming' (Braithwaite 1989) becomes absolutely critical for the purposes of this contribution. In coining his theory of reintegrative shaming, Braithwaite (1989: 12) argued that the theory distinguishes between two forms of shaming: the 'shaming that leads to stigmatization – to outcasting, to confirmation of a deviant master status' and the shaming that 'is reintegrative, that shames while maintaining bonds of respect or love, that sharply terminates disapproval with forgiveness'. This latter form of shaming is, according to Scheff (1998: 102), critical to the process of 'symbolic reparation'. For it to occur, Scheff (1998: 102) writes, 'the offender must clearly express genuine shame and remorse over her actions'. If, as Swart (2008) suggests, apology is an important form of 'symbolic reparation', then the reparative aspect of apology is intricately connected with reintegrative shaming. Reintegrative shaming, argues Scheff (1998: 104), involves 'enough shaming to bring home the seriousness of the offense, but not so much as to humiliate and harden'. This involves 'two separate movements of shame' (p 105). First, it is crucial that shame felt by the *victim* in connection with the offence must be removed. This is the kind of shame that comes from a sense on the part of the victim that they are somehow at least partly responsible for the fact that the offence happened to them. It is critical that this shame be removed, because for the victim it 'leads to the most intense and protracted suffering' (p 105). Second, the victim's shame can only be removed if 'all the shame connected with the crime is accepted by the offender' (p 105). Scheff makes it clear that this second movement of shame can only take place through the offender 'acknowledging his or her complete responsibility for the crime' (p 105). In this way, Scheff confirms that what Govier and Verwoerd call 'acknowledgement' has shame as its affective component – a mere acknowledgement, one which is not accompanied by demonstrated shame, will not be reparative.

In order to offer an example from the TRC's proceedings in which there is an acknowledgement without any shame, consider the exchange between Clive Derby-Lewis, convicted for the murder of Chris Hani, and Advocate George Bizos at Derby-Lewis' amnesty hearing:

Mr Bizos:	Have you apologised about wasting a valuable life that may have made a valuable contribution to the people of South Africa, Mr Derby-Lewis?
Mr Derby-Lewis:	Mr Chairman, with respect, may I ask is this a condition and is this something over which the Committee should then be subjected to evidence? My impression was that an apology was not necessary and not part of the whole function of this Committee.
Chairperson:	Well, Mr Bizos, the Act does not require an applicant to apologise for what he did. He is required to make a full disclosure of what he did.
Mr Bizos:	I am not unmindful. The question was not for the purposes, but in order to test his sincerity on the supposed apologies to Mrs Hani, Mr Chairman. It is not only, I am not asking as a question of law. I am asking as to whether this person that is before you has ever expressed regret for killing a person who could have made a valuable contribution to the political life of this country or not.
Mr Derby-Lewis:	Mr Chairman, no. How can I ever apologise for an act of war. War is war. I have not heard the ANC apologising, the perpetrators of these deeds for apologising for killing people in pubs and blowing them up in Wimpy Bars. I have heard no apologies for that, Mr Chairman. Those people are just as important as Mr Hani was. (TRC 1997)

From the extract, it is evident that Derby-Lewis both acknowledges his 'act of war' and that he offered 'supposed apologies' to Mrs Hani, but that he is nonetheless incapable of publicly apologising for his act of killing Chris Hani. One sees how, instead of the apology for *this* deed, there is a deflection to the acts of others, an attempt to shame the other, instead of being (a)shamed yourself. One can discern from the transcript alone that Derby-Lewis demonstrates absolutely no shame for the killing of Chris Hani and how this lack of shame is displaced by projecting the shame on to the deeds of others, as if his apology is contingent upon theirs. This, then, is a textbook instance where an attempt (by Bizos) to shame the perpetrator into an apology fails dismally, where a perpetrator refuses to accept any of the shame connected with the crime. There is no chance for symbolic reparation in this instance, because the shame on which it critically depends is terminally absent. In this way, one can see that an acknowledgement of a deed may not be accompanied by the shame that would be necessary for reparation or 'reintegration'.

I have included the comment from the 'Chairperson' in this quote, because it provides an instance of where the TRC as the big Other speaks in(to) a context where apology is at stake. What the TRC says as the impersonal 'Chairperson' takes the form of a confirmation (and a reminder) that the law does not require Mr Derby-Lewis, as applicant, to apologise for the crime that he has committed. One could, of course, read this comment as the TRC 'merely' doing its job: reminding the amnesty hearing that the PNURA does not require an apology as a requirement for the granting of amnesty. But the point is that 'merely' doing one's job is always already also more than that, for it is also precisely to act in accordance with (and thus to reflect) one's ideological mandate. In this regard, it is significant that the 'Chairperson' goes no further than the confirmation that apology is not required – he does not join Mr Bizos in the attempt to elicit an apology. Thus, what the speech of the 'Chairperson' achieves at the discursive level in this context is to remind the context/everyone present that *the TRC* does not require Mr Derby-Lewis to apologise. As such, the 'Chairperson' comment illustrates how the TRC fulfils, in a specific instance, its general symbolic mandate, a symbolic mandate that is, on the terms of this chapter, steeped in an ideological logic of forgiveness that, much like that of Tito, is not in need of an apology but merely requires 'confession' in accordance with the TRC's repeated formula of 'confession, forgiveness and reconciliation'.

The further ironic consequence of the fact that the TRC is not in need of an apology here is that it is totally curtailed in terms of its ability to facilitate symbolic reparation (a task that it, as an institution of restorative justice, was supposed constantly to fulfil). For one thing, the logical implication of not being in need of an apology is that the actual insistence on apology can only come from elsewhere, as it does in this case through the voice of activist lawyer George Bizos in the cross-examination of Mr Derby-Lewis. And this means that the attempt to elicit the shame that would be critical for symbolic reparation to take place is also left to Mr Bizos as the representative of an ideological 'outside' of the TRC. In short, while it would have been reasonable to expect of the TRC to support Mr Bizos' attempt to shame Mr Derby-Lewis with a view to symbolic reparation, the TRC does exactly the opposite. By confirming to Mr Derby-Lewis that he does not have to apologise, the TRC facilitates his acknowledgement without shame – an acknowledgement that is not simply without any form of symbolic reparation but one that is indeed accompanied by the considerable risk of re-traumatising the victims, precisely because the perpetrator refuses to accept the shame connected to the wrong (Govier and Verwoerd 2002: 73).

The above discussion attempts to illustrate the importance of shame in apology and thus in the facilitation of reparation. It also illustrates that the ideological context of an institution such as the TRC can severely occlude shame where such context is permeated by a persistent logic and agency of 'forgiveness'. An example from the other side of the political divide can further illustrate this aspect. In the famous Human Rights Violations Committee hearing into the activities of the Mandela United Football Club, Winnie Madikizela-Mandela was in fact implored by the Chairperson, Bishop Tutu, to say that she was sorry:

> I beg you, I beg you, I beg you please – I have not made any particular finding from what has happened here. I speak as someone who has lived in this community. You are a great person and you don't know how your greatness would be enhanced if you were to say sorry, things went wrong, forgive me. I beg you.

To this, Ms Madikizela-Mandela responded that she had said 'how deeply sorry I am' to the mother of Stompie Sepei and then proceeded: 'I am saying it is true, things went horribly wrong. I fully agree with that and for that part of those painful years when things went horribly wrong and we were aware of the fact that there were factors that led to that, for that I am deeply sorry' (as quoted in Weisman 2006: 222–3).

In contrast with the Derby-Lewis example, here it appears that the TRC indeed does require and insist upon an apology. Yet, as much as Tutu's speech is punctuated by the words 'I beg you', he also says that he has 'not made any particular finding from what has happened here'. Once he has made this statement, he begs Madikizela-Mandela again to say sorry, to acknowledge that 'things went wrong' and then, *to ask for forgiveness*. What I am getting at is that Tutu's preoccupation with forgiveness as the end result of the apology overshoots the mark of the apology. It is as if Tutu is prepared to stroke Madikizela-Mandela's ego ('you don't know how your greatness would be enhanced') merely in order to elicit an apology from her, which could then serve as the basis of 'forgiveness'. What this attitude on Tutu's part evinces is an understanding of forgiveness 'as if it were an entitlement flowing from a contract' (Moon 2004: 188).

Tutu attempts to elicit an acknowledgement from Madikizela-Mandela in the form of an apology, but there is nothing in the transcript that indicates that he elicits this apology in an attempt to facilitate the *necessary* demonstration of shame – quite the opposite; he elicits the apology in an attempt to produce forgiveness *without a prior demonstration of shame*. And what Tutu gets in reply is precisely an apology in which no shame is demonstrated, an apology which deflects, ducks, and dives and merely expresses regret for 'that part of those painful years when things went horribly wrong'. The example illustrates that the attempt to use an apology as an instrument with which to obtain forgiveness, without at the same time closely attending to the necessary dimension of shame, can completely short circuit the aim of symbolic reparation.

When shame lacks

What happens, then, at the psycho-dynamic level, when shame fails, when there is a lack of shame where shame is expected or supposed to be? Rogers (2017: 172) notes that shame will not occur where the subject imagines he is 'master of knowledge', '*all* for the Other', for in such an instance there is no exposure of the behaviour as shameful. My sense is that this is precisely what happens in the Madikizela-Mandela example – Tutu's repeated implorations create and support a fantasy on Madikizela-Mandela's part in which she is, at that critical moment, '*all* for the Other'. Indeed, it is hard to shake the impression that Tutu would have the entire proceedings of the TRC in this case hinge upon not the apology, but upon the forgiveness of Winnie Madikizela-Mandela.

If the Other before whose gaze I am posed, 'does not accuse me of not knowing', then what is lost is precisely the Other in whose gaze I am, or could be, shamed. What arises, instead, in this instance, is an orientation to an entirely known, 'good' Other, which marks the inability to feel shame (Rogers 2017: 174). This is the (entirely fantasmatic) 'Other of the Other', whose inexistence Lacan announced in 1959 (Lacan 2019: 298). But the fact that Lacan announced its inexistence way back when does not mean that, in our capitalist 'postcolonial' societies in which enjoyment is the law, it is not continually being fantasmatically constructed, relied upon, and proliferated. Indeed, Jacques-Alain Miller (2006: 27) has gone as far as suggesting that this construction is the dominant feature of our discourse today, of our social bonds, at the present moment in civilisation: 'We are at a point where the dominant discourse *enjoins* one not to be ashamed.'

What then happens when this entirely known, 'good' and all-forgiving, non-lacking Other takes the place of the big Other in an institution such as the TRC? My sense is that the dominant discursive mode of the TRC ensured the construction of 'an Other of the Other' in the place where the Other in whose eyes I am shamed should have been. In discursively 'sanctioning' negative emotions and in neglecting the differential aspects of the amnesty dispensation's 'political motive' and 'full disclosure' requirements, the TRC, quite unwittingly I am sure, opened a discursive gap in which it could be constructed (and was constructed) as the 'good' Other before whom shame can either not be experienced at all or experienced only in a diminished and inconsequential fashion, that is, in a way that does not allow the shame to be/become 'reintegrative' and thus not reparative.

To be sure, I am not arguing that the TRC – in allowing itself to create this Tito-esque image of itself – entirely foreclosed the experience of reintegrative shaming before and in it. There were clearly examples of apology where perpetrators did experience or undergo reintegrative shaming before the TRC or as a result of its processes. What I am arguing is that the TRC's *dominant* discursive mode seriously diminished its status and function as an Other before whom perpetrators could be shamed. The dominant discursive mode of the TRC as all-forgiving, 'good' Other significantly affected its ability to elicit an affect of reintegrative shame. This, in turn, meant that the TRC, at least in this regard, undermined the reparative dimension of its own processes in relation to apology.

Eugene Baron (2015: 170) has argued that 'the exclusion of remorse and repentance as official requirements in the amnesty process brought about an incomplete reconciliation between victims and perpetrators'. Baron argues that there was an essential 'lack of justice in the process of amnesty' (p 170) and that this lack is intimately related to the exclusion of remorse and repentance from the requirements for amnesty. As Baron writes, 'If perpetrators envisaged themselves through the eyes of the other (victims), such a process could have brought about a deep sense of wrongdoing (remorse), but also active involvement in the reparations and the healing of the wrongs committed' (p 172). Implicit in Baron's argument that 'most perpetrators did not even understand that what they had done was immoral', is an inability on the part of the TRC to facilitate the experience of perpetrators seeing themselves 'through the eyes of the [O]ther' (p 172). This ability to see oneself in the gaze of the Other is critical when it comes to eliciting feelings of shame. As Copjec (2007: 75) writes, the 'radical point' is that 'the gaze under which I feel myself observed in shame is my *own* gaze'.

For Baron, these eyes of the Other in which I am to see myself are, critically, the eyes of the victims. Thus, what Baron is suggesting is that the TRC as the big Other of postapartheid reconciliation, truth, and forgiveness could not facilitate the experience of shame for most perpetrators, because it could not represent the gaze of the victims. The interaction of Clive Derby-Lewis with the TRC, quoted above, is a clear instance of a perpetrator's experience of the TRC as an institution that did not facilitate shame. The same can be said of Winnie Madikizela-Mandela's vague, strange, and shameless 'apology'.

To conclude this section by way of illustration, I want to cite two further instances of apologies that were offered in the course of amnesty proceedings in order to contrast them with each other. Both these examples come from Jonny Steinberg's book *One Night in Bethlehem* (2019). The first is an apology by Mandla Fokazi for the killing of a young white police constable, Cornelius Oosthuizen:

> The deceased and the one who survived, I would like to apologise to their families because *this is painful, nobody would enjoy this*. I would

like to ask for forgiveness for my involvement in this case and to the people of South Africa at large. And to my, the family of my co-accused I would like to ask for forgiveness because now in this country there is democracy and *I would like to build the nation, to build South Africa in a democratic country*. So I would like to *ask for forgiveness with my whole heart*, thank you. (Steinberg 2019: 143, emphases added)

In this apology, one can read that there is a marked agony at work in Fokazi's words. His expression that 'this is painful, nobody would enjoy this' is a reflection of the shame that he is feeling (the point is precisely that he is, critically, *not* enjoying the apology). One could even go as far as saying that Fokazi's statement is an *expression* of his shame, a demonstration of it. As Copjec (2013: 245) writes, shame as one form of *jouissance* 'names our capacity to put ourselves forward and determine our destiny'. This is what Fokazi does when he takes charge of his discourse by saying that '*I* would like to build the nation, to build South Africa' and '*I* would like to ask for forgiveness *with my whole heart*'. The phrase 'with my whole heart' indicates the sincerity with which his affect is present in the apologetic discourse. This is confirmed by the fact that he asks specific persons ('[t]he deceased and the one who survived', 'their families') for forgiveness.

On the other hand, there is the apology of Clement Ndabeni for the same incident:

I would like to say to the South Africans, I ask for forgiveness and I ask for forgiveness to the families of the police who died and to the people who were with us, I would like to ask for forgiveness to their families and to the families of the police and the families of the deceased that were with us and South Africa at large. (Steinberg 2019: 145)

Apart from the fact that this apology is also offered to the families of the police officer who died, there is at the same time a certain formulaic ring to it as well as a sense of incoherence. In contrast with Fokazi's apology, there is no indication of an agony at work here, no sign of shame for the deed that has been committed. Discursive signs of the presence and sincerity of the affect of shame are missing. Ndabeni also deftly avoids using the signifier 'apologise'. There is only the repetition of the request for forgiveness as if this – the three times repeated request – was the only thing that was (still) required of him. Moreover, the perpetrator in no way puts himself forward and takes charge of his discourse. While he, like Fokazi, says 'I would like to ask for forgiveness', his discursive 'I' becomes lost in the fixation on 'forgiveness'. Here, it is as if forgiveness only has to be spoken in order for it to be granted, as though forgiveness is a simple formality of the amnesty process, an 'entitlement flowing from a contract'.

This is the kind of empty 'apology' for which the TRC opened the door when it decided that its dominant discursive mode would hinge on the pivot of 'forgiveness'. It reflects a TRC in which the gaze of the Other has, ironically, been lost, one before which the perpetrator is not exposed, but indeed covered by his repeated invocations of forgiveness. It is as if the signifier 'forgiveness' itself becomes the discursive cover that prevents the subject's exposure and, hence, the demonstration of shame. In apologies like these, the perpetrator does not (have to) fear abandonment by the big Other, because the big Other has him covered in and by forgiveness in advance – all that he has to do is speak the word 'forgiveness' for the Other to come running.

Conclusion

In 1957, Lacan proclaimed that the big Other does not exist (Evans 1996: 136). In his book, *Less than Nothing: Hegel and the Shadow of Dialectical Materialism*, Žižek (2012: 86) interprets this declaration to the effect that while the big Other is the 'virtual ideal agency', it is 'kept alive by the work of individuals participating in it'. The big Other, therefore does not have an autonomous existence all of its own and in this sense it does not exist. However, while the big Other does not exist, it is nonetheless effective; it 'works' (Žižek 2012: 104). For Žižek, the task of ethical action today is to assume fully the sense in which the big Other is inexistent or, as he calls it, 'barred' (p 263). Assuming the inexistence of the big Other means that we become aware of the ways in which it is 'inconsistent or lacking': 'its very functioning depends on subjects whose participation in the symbolic process sustains it.'

In this contribution, we have seen that a substantial part of the problem with the TRC as the big Other has been the way in which it exposed itself, by way of its ideological discourse as well as in its practical work ethic, to the risk that it would be understood by perpetrator, witness, and victim alike as an all-forgiving, non-lacking, consistent big Other. In other words, the TRC relied and could not but rely, to a significant extent, on its own existence as the big Other of forgiveness. The further risk to which the TRC exposed itself in this regard is neatly described by Žižek (2009: 16) in reference to Tito: 'Tito's acts display features of hysterical self-staging: Tito is playing himself all the time, narcissistically fascinated by the faked generosity of his own acts'. In other words, in staging itself in the manner of an all-forgiving big Other, a big Other which forgives in a hysterical fashion, the TRC risked the authenticity of its discursive intentions.

I further considered the way in which this discursive construction of the TRC of itself as the big Other of forgiveness, indeed as the subject *supposed to* forgive, impacted on the reparative value of apology in the TRC. The conclusion I discerned in this regard is that the TRC, instead of eliciting or procuring shame, positioned itself in the discourse in such a way that the demonstration of reintegrative shame was occluded. I illustrated this by way of the examples of Clive Derby-Lewis' refusal to apologise at the TRC and Winnie Madikizela-Mandela's shameless apology before it. I then argued for a psycho-dynamic understanding of the lack of shame as the fantasmatic construction of an Other of the Other – an Other before which the experience or demonstration of shame cannot be borne. I concluded that the TRC, in constructing itself (and in having itself constructed as) the Other of the Other, seriously diminished its capacity to be a big Other who could represent the gaze of the victims of apartheid, before which shame could be experienced and demonstrated.

Claire Moon writes that '[i]f, and this is a very big "if", the gift of forgiveness could present a rupture to the exchange cycle, it might performatively constitute the break with the past that is repeatedly cited by the TRC as a desirable outcome of its investigations' (Moon 2004: 192). Žižek's and Lacanian psychoanalysis' position here would be that such a rupture depends on us fully assuming the big Other's inexistence. Indeed, it is at least two psychoanalytic (and ethical) steps away from the TRC as an Other of the Other. Moon's reference to the fact that it is a 'very big "if"' that is at stake here resonates with Žižek's (2012: 963, emphasis added) argument that the 'inexistence of the big Other signals … that every ethical and/or moral edifice has to be grounded in an *abyssal* act which is, in the most radical sense imaginable, *political*'. In short, ethical action – the action of forgiveness – is always already only realised through the assumption of radical political responsibility.

The importance of shame in this regard is that it confronts us with what Žižek (2012: 963) calls the 'zero-level of politics' in that the *jouissance* of shame 'opens up the space for the political act to intervene'; it creates a 'gap' which can be 'saturated by the political effort to impose a new order'. This imposition of a new order is, of course, the break with the past, which the TRC was at pains to underscore. In the context of this contribution, that political act which constitutes a break with the past, that political effort to impose a new order, is the act of reparation, the action that the perpetrator and/or beneficiary embarks upon to 'make good' or make up for the wrong that has been committed – and this reparative act critically depends on the emergence of reintegrative shame.

As paradoxical as it may sound, I think that the lack of reparation in South Africa today is, to a significant extent, a function of our continued belief in the big Other of 'forgiveness', figured in the TRC at first and today in a dysfunctional postapartheid state where accountability remains at an all-time low, despite Commissions of Inquiry in which the worst merely becomes public, without apology and especially without demonstrated shame. This lack, then, becomes a function of the belief that we can take our cover in the big Other, that the big Other will not expose us. In failing to accept that the big Other is barred, inconsistent, and itself lacking, we continue to allow it to determine a reality in which political responsibility is not only severely lacking, but is so severely lacking precisely because no demonstrated shame results from the process. The paradoxical upshot of this state of affairs is that we fail to realise the very forgiveness that the TRC advocated as central to its work. Jacques Derrida (2001: 43) cites a critical moment in the TRC when 'a black woman comes to testify before the Commission' and says: 'A commission or a government cannot forgive. Only I, eventually, could do it'. This is a woman who was well aware of the inexistence of the big Other. Her words critically continue to challenge each one of us to undertake the 'abyssal' *political* act on which the future of South Africa, to a great extent, depends.

Reflections

The provocation to write about apology has been a uniquely rewarding experience for me as a researcher and as a white person living in postapartheid South Africa. What the exploration of the relationship between apology and shame has taught me is that we can only really speak about reparative apologies where there has been a clear and unequivocal demonstration of shame on the part of the perpetrator. It seems to me that with the proliferation of apology on the geopolitical scene today, there is a disastrous lack of shame when it comes to these all to easily offered apologies. I think that white South Africans have, in the aftermath of the TRC, been certainly willing to apologise for apartheid. But, in general, they have been unwilling to accept and demonstrate the shame that should come with such an apology. What I have learnt from writing this chapter is that if I, as a white South African, want to say sorry about apartheid, and if I want this apology to make a difference, to go some distance in the quest for reparation, I absolutely have to be prepared to be ashamed; I have to be prepared to demonstrate my shame in a concrete and practical way that attempts to make good for the wrong that I have perpetrated or that was perpetrated in my name. Shame and its demonstration in the apology may, in turn, open the door for the kind of lasting and authentic forgiveness that remains as a gift that can only ever come from the Other – a forgiveness that is not an entitlement flowing from a contract, a forgiveness that no truth commission nor any other political institution can ever give in the Other's name.

Jaco

References

Agamben, G., 1998, *Homo Sacer: Sovereign Power and Bare Life,* trans. Daniel Heller-Roazen, Stanford: Stanford University Press.

Ahmed, S., 2004, *The Cultural Politics of Emotion*, Edinburgh: Edinburgh University Press.

Baron, E., 2015, 'Remorse and repentance stripped of its validity: amnesty granted by the Truth and Reconciliation Commission of South Africa', *Studia Historiae Ecclesiasticae* 41(1), 169–84.

Braithwaite, J., 1989, *Crime, Shame and Reintegration*, Cambridge: Cambridge University Press.

Braithwaite, J., 2000, 'Shame and criminal justice', *Canadian Journal of Criminology* 42(3), 281–98.

Brudholm, T., 2006, 'Revisiting resentments: Jean Améry and the dark side of forgiveness and reconciliation', *Journal of Human Rights* 5(7), 7–26.

Chapman, A. R., 2008, 'Perspectives on the role of forgiveness in the human rights violations hearings', in A. R. Chapman and H. Van der Merwe (eds.), *Truth and Reconciliation in South Africa: Did the TRC Deliver?* pp 66–89, Philadelphia: University of Pennsylvania Press.

Copjec, J., 2007, 'The descent into shame', *Studio Art Magazine* 168, 59–80.

Copjec, J., 2013, 'The censorship of interiority', in S. Jöttkandt and J. Copjec (eds.), *Penumbra,* pp 239–64, Melbourne: re.press.

Derrida, J., 2001, *On Cosmopolitanism and Forgiveness*, London: Routledge.

Du Toit, F., 2018, *When Political Transitions Work: Reconciliation as Interdependence*, Oxford: Oxford University Press.

Evans, D., 1996, *An Introductory Dictionary of Lacanian Psychoanalysis*, London: Routledge.

Govier, T. and Verwoerd, W., 2002, 'The promise and pitfalls of apology', *Journal of Social Philosophy* 33(1), 67–82.

Humphrey, M., 2005, 'Reconciliation and the therapeutic state', *Journal of Intercultural Studies* 26(3), 203–20.

Lacan, J., 2019, *The Seminar of Jacques Lacan, Book VI: Desire and its Interpretation*, Cambridge: Polity.

McCarthy, E., 1997, 'South Africa's amnesty process: a viable route toward truth and reconciliation?', *Michigan Journal of Race and Law* 3(1), 183–253.

Miller, J.-A., 2006, 'On shame', in J. Clemens and R. Grigg (eds.), *Jacques Lacan and the Other Side of Psychoanalysis: Reflections on Seminar XVII*, pp 11–28, Durham: Duke University Press.

Moon, C., 2004, 'Prelapsarian state: forgiveness and reconciliation in transitional justice', *International Journal for the Semiotics of Law* 17, 185–97.

Rogers, J., 2017, 'Shame, pain and melancholia for the Australian constitution', in B. Sheils and J. Walsh (eds.), *Narcissism, Melancholia and the Subject of Community*, pp 161–87, Cham: Palgrave Macmillan.

Rowen, J., 2017, *Searching for Truth in the Transitional Justice Movement*, Cambridge: Cambridge University Press.

Scheff, T. J., 1998, 'Community conferences: shame and anger in therapeutic jurisprudence', *Revista Juridica Universidad de Puerto Rico* 67(1), 97–120.

Shore, M., 2009, *Religion and Conflict Resolution: Christianity and South Africa's Truth and Reconciliation Commission*, Abingdon: Routledge.

Sitze, A., 2013, *The Impossible Machine: A Genealogy of South Africa's Truth and Reconciliation Commission*, Ann Arbor: University of Michigan Press.

Steinberg, J., 2019, *One Day in Bethlehem*, Cape Town: Jonathan Ball Publishers.

Swart, M., 2008, 'Sorry seems to be the hardest word: apology as a form of symbolic reparation', *South African Journal on Human Rights* 24(1), 50–70.

Truth and Reconciliation Commission of South Africa, 1997, 'Amnesty hearing transcripts: Pretoria: killing of Chris Hani (part 2) Derby-Lewis, C.; Walusz, J. on resumption on 19 August 1997 – day 7', viewed 5 May 2021 from www.justice.gov.za/trc/amntrans/pta/derby07.htm

Truth and Reconciliation Commission of South Africa, 1998, *Report*, Vols. 1–7, Pretoria: TRC.

Verwoerd, W. J., 1999, 'Toward the truth about the TRC: a response to key moral criticisms of the South African Truth and Reconciliation Commission', *Religion and Theology Journal* 3(3), 303–24.

Weisman, R., 2006, 'Showing remorse at the TRC: towards a constitutive approach to reparative discourse', *Windsor Yearbook of Access to Justice* 24(2), 221–39.

Žižek, S., 2009, 'Mercy and its transformations', *Muzikološki Zbornik Musicological Annual* XLV(2), 7–16.

Žižek, S., 2012, *Less than Nothing: Hegel and the Shadow of Dialectical Materialism*, London: Verso.

15

Amnesty, Amnesia, and Remembrance: Self-Reflections on a 23-Year-Old Justification

Heinz Klug

Shortly after arriving as a junior faculty member at the University of Wisconsin Law School, I was approached by a colleague who edited a legal-cultural magazine entitled *Graven Images* who asked me if I was willing to write about my response to the Truth and Reconciliation Commission (TRC) in South Africa. At first, I was very unsure about what I would write but when I reflected on my own trajectory, I felt compelled to consider my own ambivalence and to justify to myself how I could accept the compromises so necessary to the democratic transition I had been a part of in the years between 1990 and 1996. My own political role included spending 11 years in exile in Botswana, the United States, and then back in Southern Africa before returning to South Africa in 1990. I had served in the African National Congress (ANC) underground, both inside and outside South Africa, including six months' military training with *Umkhonto we Sizwe* (MK) in Angola in the second half of 1982. After being required to leave Botswana in 1985, I had studied Law in San Francisco and qualified as a member of the California Bar, which meant that on my return to Southern Africa, Zola Skweyiya, then head of the ANC Legal Department in Lusaka, asked me to serve as his researcher. I later became a member of the ANC Land Commission secretariat after the ANC was unbanned and I returned to South Africa in June 1990. Asked to contribute to this volume, I thought of my earlier essay and decided that it would be useful to reflect on it explicitly. This chapter thus begins with the text of the original 1998 publication, marked as 'justification', which is then followed by a reflection on that justification as a way for me to understand why, for me, 'sorry', as a speech act, is just inadequate and why apology must be matched with accountability, even if that is limited to truth-telling and acknowledgement. 'Sorry' would be so much more meaningful if matched with deeds, making even small reparation for the harm that was done.

1998 justification

Each time we buried our friends and comrades who had been killed by the apartheid regime, we made a commitment – singularly and collectively as a political movement – to pick up their fallen spear, to avenge their death, and to achieve victory over apartheid in the name of the fallen. Today apartheid is vanquished, yet the killers are free, they receive amnesty, are guaranteed their government employment (where applicable), and are accepted as partners in the creation of a new South Africa.

Viewing this new reality, in which Mandela's government stumbles forward daily against the legacies of apartheid strewn in its path, I am forced to recognise that we have always been trapped in an irreconcilable conflict between our past promises and our moral duty to the future. While we fought against evil and promised peace and justice, the needs of peace and the future generation required a forward-looking vision, one in which justice is resolved without endangering the future. What place then for truth and reconciliation?

While we (who argue that the TRC has unfinished business) might point to international legal norms and instruments that deny amnesty for such crimes, others decry South Africa's TRC as a 'witch hunt'. These voices either demand collective amnesia in the form of a general amnesty for the past or continue to assert that their policies were merely misguided. The abuses of human rights, which they now acknowledge did occur, they characterise as infrequent aberrations and even equate them with the actions of those who fought against apartheid. Yet as the hearings of the TRC have traversed the South African landscape, from cities to remote rural communities, the broad patterns of abuse and horrifying detail of each individual case has revealed to all that these atrocities were never isolated incidents but rather formed the very basis of the system. Are we to forgive this crime against humanity – as apartheid was defined in the 1974 International Convention on the Suppression and Punishment of the Crime of Apartheid[1] – without even a decent demonstration of remorse or apology from the leaders and perpetrators of that system?

While democracy has not resolved the vast inequalities created by apartheid, there is no doubt in my mind that the compromises of a negotiated transition, even accepting the political participation of the creators of apartheid in South

---

[1] 1015 U.N.T.S. 243, entered into force 18 July 1976.

Africa's first postapartheid government, was a moral and political necessity in which the demands of the 'past' and even of many of the 'present' – such as the generation of youth who gave up their chance for education to make apartheid ungovernable – were in part sacrificed in order to establish a viable future for the younger and future generations.

It is in this context and in the face of an ongoing conflict between the voices of victims and the strategies of denial, avoidance, and justification by the perpetrators that we must try to evaluate the process of truth and reconciliation in South Africa. On the one hand are the victims, like the Biko and Mxenge families who, demanding justice, have challenged the TRC in court and continue to reject the amnesty it promises to the murderers of their loved ones. On the other hand, there are the former apartheid leaders and functionaries who either continue to justify their actions as a 'natural and necessary result of revolutionary conflict … justifiable under international law'[2] or express no remorse at all. Take, for example, police agent and later apartheid police spokesman Craig Kotze, who told the TRC's hearing on the role of the media under apartheid that he had 'no regrets' for his role 'as a soldier/policeman', in which he infiltrated newsrooms and planted false information as part of the state's covert disinformation campaign.

And in the face of this I reflect back on the not-so-distant past – on the singing, speeches, and searing emotions of so many funerals – and I wonder about our commitments to the past and how they have been sustained in the complex interactions of South Africa's democratic transition. I recognise that peace and democracy was achieved – a 'small miracle' to quote Nelson Mandela (Nelson Mandela Foundation 1994) – with a promise of reconciliation and even a recognition of the dignity and rights of our nation's former oppressors. Yet, as I witness the continuing pain of the families of those who gave their lives and the many other victims bearing their souls before the TRC, I am returned to thoughts of those we left behind.

Thoughts that send my mind reeling and stumbling across so many memories. Of little Katryn as a precocious toddler, a child of hope born in exile to my comrades Marius and Jeanette Schoon, a political prisoner released after 12 years and a trade union activist banned from social contact and political activity, who met illegally and married before fleeing to Botswana. And of the cowardly parcel bomb that killed Katryn and her mother before she was old enough to go to school. Of 'Rogers' Nkadimeng,

---

2   Niel Barnard, former head of the National Intelligence Service, before a special hearing of the TRC on the role of the former State Security Council (the highest decision-making body in the apartheid security apparatus, which functioned as a subcommittee of the Cabinet), Cape Town, 4 December 1997, viewed 7 May 2021 from www.justice.gov.za/trc/special/security/ssbarn.htm.

the smiling young man whose shattered body was laid in its casket before the same alter where he had been married only two months before the bomb – wired to the ignition of his vehicle – ended his activities as an underground trade union organiser. Of Thami Mnyele, the exquisite graphic artist who was machine-gunned to death amid his art works as the apartheid regimes' commandos sowed death among refugees, activists, and Motswana bystanders, killing 12 in a night of horror, which the South African media boastfully headlined 'The Guns of Gaborone'. Of the all too many whose lives were destroyed or crippled by a system, whose former leaders – political, social, and economic – now wish to distance themselves from what they describe as the activities of 'rogue elements' for whom they deny direct responsibility.

These memories and thoughts overwhelm me with the pain of survival and outrage against those who demand amnesia as an imperative for reconciliation. My sense of outrage is not focused on the horrors of torture and callous acts of killing that we have all been so aware of for so long, but rather on those more articulate perpetrators who would erase distinctions between oppressors and resisters and who still work so hard to suppress truth in order to elide history. I am also concerned about the focus on Christian forgiveness, which has become such a marked feature of so many of the TRC's hearings, and of course I am troubled by my own ambivalent attitudes towards this process. I recognise that it is these tensions which motivate me to search for a position from which it will be possible to justify a forward-looking vision without turning my back on my past commitments.

These concerns remind me of my attitudes towards Craig Williamson, the South African Police Colonel who was among the planners of the Botswana raid and who has publicly admitted, without remorse, to having sent the bomb that killed little Katryn and her mother, and who reluctantly applied for amnesty only after losing his motion to dismiss the civil law suit brought against him by Marius Schoon. I know I can never forgive him for the murders of Jeanette and Katryn, which can never be justified as a proportional response to Marius and Jeanette's resistance activities. Does this mean that I could not accept his receiving amnesty from the TRC? Not necessarily.

While I cannot accept the standard definition of amnesty as a 'complete forgetfulness of the past', as articulated in the 1996 judgment of *Azanian People's Organization (AZAPO) and Others v President of the Republic of South Africa and Others*,[3] I do believe that pardons, based on a 'full disclosure of all the relevant facts relating to acts associated with a political objective', as required by the 1995 Promotion of National Unity and Reconciliation Act in South Africa,[4] are one essential part of achieving the reconciliation required

---

[3]   (CCT17/96) [1996] ZACC 16 (25 July 1996) at para. 35.
[4]   Act 34 of 1995, s. 3(1)(b).

to rebuild community in the aftermath of violence and gross violations of human rights. The justification for pardon cannot, however, rest merely upon the assertion of political necessity – that South Africa's democratic transition was the product of a political compromise which required amnesty in order to avoid a military backlash and as the basis for agreement. In fact, the apartheid regime first insisted on a blanket amnesty and attempted, even in its final hours, to grant amnesty to some of its minsters to avoid the need to account for their actions.[5] It is this last element, the need to account, which for me provides the essential link between our obligations to the past and the needs of the future.

It is only by requiring a full accounting of the events and circumstances surrounding these violations that it is possible to judge whether pardon may lead to acceptance and reconciliation, even if forgiveness is impossible. First, as in the case of Williamson, the statute requires a finding that the motives of perpetrators were political and not based on 'personal malice, ill-will or spite'.[6] In the case of Katryn and Jeanette, this will require a distinction between his decision to kill in order to curtail the family's political activities and the possible personal grudge that Williamson may have held as a result of the contribution Marius and Jeanette made in exposing him as an apartheid spy while he posed as an exiled anti-apartheid student activist and managed to become a senior official in the Geneva-based International University Exchange Fund. Second, it is only through a full accounting that it will be possible for the TRC to achieve its primary goal, which is to establish the truth about the gross violations of human rights that occurred. Third, it is only by establishing the truth of these events that it will be possible to ensure remembrance instead of amnesia, and thereby to work towards the goal of preventing 'a repetition of such acts in future'.

Remembrance then becomes both the justification for granting pardons to the perpetrators, who have acted with a 'political motive', and the basis for resolving the quandary posed by the need to reconcile our present and past commitments. By recording and elucidating the memory of those who suffered for their resistance to apartheid, we are able to both fulfil our commitment to never forget their efforts and also to continue their mission by using them as an example to future generations of what should never be repeated. Thus, it is neither amnesia nor forgiveness that is the basis of

---

[5]   Amnesia continued to plague apartheid's last leader, F.W. de Klerk, who as recently as February 2020 claimed that apartheid was not a crime against humanity and was soundly criticised by among others Bishop Malusi Mpumlwana, Secretary General of the South African Council of Churches, who called on de Klerk to retract his statement that 'apartheid was not a crime against humanity but a soviet propaganda ploy' (Seleka 2020).

[6]   Act 34 of 1995, s. 20(3)(f)(ii).

reconciliation, but rather the recognition of past suffering as a lesson to the future and a symbol of what has been overcome.

Although I am able, in this way, to reconcile myself with the purpose and work of the TRC, my understanding of amnesty requires a clear rejection of the present attempts to shape the work of the TRC into an examination of human rights violations that refuses to make a moral distinction between the actions of those who fought apartheid and those who acted in its name. Instead of making a distinction between retributive justice and restorative justice as a means to justify amnesty over prosecutions, our understanding of truth and reconciliation should rather focus on the slow but steady process of accountability that the TRC is working to achieve. While individual cases have been addressed, the TRC has also attempted to grapple, through its institutional hearings, with the wider evils of the apartheid system, drawing heated criticism from even 'liberal' white South Africans. Their attempts to avoid the wider implications of apartheid policy saw even Hermann Giliomee, the noted Afrikaans political scientist and now president of the traditionally liberal Institute of Race Relations, argue that apartheid was not a crime against humanity, despite the revelations of the TRC hearings (Giliomee 2020).

While the false arithmetic of moral equivalence is easily propagated, it is important that the TRC help reveal all gross violations of human rights, including those committed in the name of the liberation movements. However, the task of remembrance requires that there be accountability, not only of those who engaged in the countless acts of violation but also of those who enabled and sustained the system that provided the opportunities for such deeds. While the 'justice' Archbishop Desmond Tutu promised in his eulogy at Griffith Mxenge's funeral in 1981 (Rosenberg 1996: 88)[7] has not materialised to the satisfaction of the Mxenge family,[8] the amnesty granted Mxenge's murderers may be sustained so long as the life and work of Griffith Mxenge is elevated in remembrance, above the deeds of his killers and the continued denials of those who benefited from the system those killers upheld. It is only through direct public accountability, and hopefully eventual remorse, that a collective memory can be created, which will provide a fitting acknowledgement of those who suffered and will present a barrier against a repetition of the past.

---

[7] As quoted in Rosenberg (1996) Bishop Tutu, speaking at the funeral, said that 'when the government of the people takes over, justice will be done'.

[8] The Mxenge family joined the Biko family and others in challenging the validity of the TRC, see, *Azanian People's Organization (AZAPO) and Others v President of the Republic of South Africa and Others* (CCT17/96) [1996] ZACC 16 (25 July 1996).

2021 reflection

While it is 23 years since I wrote those words, my sense of outrage now focuses on our failure to adequately recognise the lives of those who paid the ultimate sacrifice for freedom in South Africa. Although Nelson Mandela refused to accept the attempt by de Klerk to impose a blanket amnesty for apartheid crimes, in fact the TRC process and the failure of subsequent ANC governments to even prosecute cases where amnesty was denied by the TRC[9] has amounted to a near blanket amnesty for those who committed crimes recognised as such even under apartheid law, as well as for the broader violations of human rights committed in defence of and in the name of apartheid. What follows is a critical evaluation of my own maybe naïve hopes about the potential of acknowledgement and remorse from 23 years ago when I believed that a commitment to a better future may have justified a willingness to forego the justice and accountability that trials may have offered. While at that time I may not have accepted the potential of apologies, with their implications of acknowledgement, responsibility, and remorse, looking back today it seems that even the naïve hope that we might build a more just society in the name of the lives sacrificed is being confronted with denial and assertions of victimhood from those that benefited from apartheid. A denial that is further compounded by those who attempt to avoid accountability, or call for amnesty, for their corruption, on the grounds that this is nothing compared with the crimes of apartheid for which the perpetrators were never called to account.

In the early years following the 1994 election, before the threat of a right-wing coup or violence slowly receded and before the new government managed to overcome some of the initial bureaucratic resistance within state structures, the role of the TRC was essential, at least when we think of the impact of the victim's hearings. As the TRC held victims' hearings across the country, communities and the nation heard the heart-wrenching details of individual and family suffering that had been wrought by apartheid officials in their capacity as public servants (Boraine 2000; Wilson 2001). The value of this process was that it affirmed the horrors of apartheid brutality and made it difficult for all South Africans, and white South Africans in particular, to deny the truth of suffering at the hands of the apartheid regime. The direct impact of these victims' hearings, I believe, was that it prevented those who sought to resist the new democratic order through violence – by plotting a campaign of terror or encouraging a coup d'etat – from gaining the moral and material support of the white community that they would have needed

---

[9]   In 1998 the TRC gave more than 300 names to the National Prosecuting Authority for investigation and prosecution (Sooka 2006).

to take up arms against the new democratic government. Instead, most whites now began to view the reconciliation offered by Mandela's government as a preferable alternative to civil war.[10] This was, of course, premised on their own ability to adopt a strategy of denial in which they told themselves and the world that it was merely 'bad apples' that had caused the torture and killings that were the focus of victim testimony,[11] and that they were thus absolved from their own accountability for apartheid. An extreme version of this amnesia is the self-presentation of Niel Barnard, apartheid's last intelligence chief, whose memoir, *Secret Revolution*, makes claim to a role 'together with Mandela, of preparing the way for a political settlement in our fatherland' (Barnard told to Wiese 2015: 275) but never acknowledges any responsibility for any of apartheid's consequences, let alone the torture and deaths for which he denies all responsibility (pp 139–41).

It is also important to recognise that there was little chance of justice being attained within the judicial and prosecutorial institutions in the early years of democracy (Dyzenhaus 1998). We need only recall the case of General Magnus Malan, who was implicated in a 1987 massacre committed by a South African Defence Force unit in KwaZulu-Natal. The trial of Malan and 18 co-accused on 13 charges of murder, conspiracy to commit murder, and attempted murder began in Durban in March 1996 and within seven months the judge dismissed all charges, arguing that the prosecution's case was fundamentally flawed (Schmidt 2020: 260–1). While old order investigators and prosecutors were rumoured to have destroyed evidence and deliberately sabotaged the trial (p 261), the accused could now proclaim their innocence, making it clear that the judicial system was not able or prepared at that time to address the crimes of apartheid, even when they involved murder. A more contemporary example was the failed trial of Wouter Basson who remains staunchly 'unapologetic' for his role in the murder and disappearance of captured combatants in both Namibia and South Africa (pp 275–80).

The productive value of the victim's hearings, even accounting for the criticism that they often triggered anew the suffering of victims and brought pressure on victims to contemplate 'forgiveness' in deeply religious overtones (Tutu 1999: 257–82), has to be distinguished from the other aspects of the TRC process. As detailed in the law, the TRC had three pillars: the victim's hearings, the amnesty process, and a means of providing reparations to those identified by the TRC as victims (see Dyzenhaus 1998: 4; Boraine

---

[10] Michael Schmidt (2020: 262–5) details continuing negotiations between the security forces and the newly elected democratic government from 1996, creating what is referred to as the 'pact of forgetting'.

[11] The prime example of this was the case of Eugene de Kock (de Kock told to Gordin 1998), who was tried and sentenced to two life terms plus 212 years in prison.

2000: 47).[12] Neither the amnesty hearings nor the process of reparations for recognised victims under the statute met the aspirations of those who saw the three pillars as a means of addressing or overcoming the past (Asmal et al 2006: 17–33; Abrahams and Seekoe 2006: 34–52). These remaining pillars of the TRC process were deeply compromised. First, in the case of the amnesty hearings, the insistence on individual perpetrators and the requirement of political motives meant that apartheid officials (predominantly police and special unit members who had been identified as perpetrators by victims or the media) would only acknowledge their personal involvement and then justify their actions in the exact terms that the apartheid regime had long articulated – that the victims were terrorists or communists or intent on using violence against the state – justifications they continued to assume legitimated their actions. Furthermore, the TRC's equation of the violence employed to defend apartheid with the violence used to resist apartheid, only added legitimacy to the claims of apartheid's perpetrators.

The refusal of the TRC to distinguish between the legitimate acts of violent resistance against apartheid oppression and the acts of those defending the system of apartheid was exacerbated by the TRC's decision to interpret the Promotion of National Unity and Reconciliation Act of 1995[13] to focus only on individual acts of torture, disappearance, and extrajudicial killings. When challenged to investigate forced removals as an example of the systematic violence of apartheid, the TRC argued that forced removals were part of apartheid policy and that the Commission was created to investigate 'gross violations of human rights',[14] not policy. The statute then defines 'the violation of human rights' as

(a) the killing, abduction, torture, or severe ill treatment of any person, or
(b) any attempt, conspiracy, incitement, instigation, command, or procurement to commit an act referred to in paragraph (a).[15]

In effect, then, the TRC only considered acts that had, in fact, already been declared illegal under the laws of apartheid South Africa as violations requiring amnesty. The effect was to legitimate 'normal' apartheid law despite the Commission's claim in its final report that it found apartheid to be a crime against humanity.

---

[12] The three pillars reflect the three committees that were established to do the work of the Commission: the Committee on Human Rights Violations; the Committee on Amnesty; and the Committee on Reparation and Rehabilitation.
[13] Act 34 of 1995.
[14] See s. 3(1)(a).
[15] See s. 1(1)(xix).

While 20 years ago the promise of a democratic government implementing a programme of reconstruction and development gave hope to the notion that the past may be sacrificed for a better future (ANC 1994), the reality of South Africa at the beginning of the second decade of the 21st century raises serious questions about our justification in deferring justice in order to build a better future (Mbatha and Kathrada 2017). This is not to argue that the present is not a significant change from apartheid; however, the fact is that the majority of South Africans continue to live in conditions that are unjustifiable in a country as wealthy as South Africa (Seekings and Nattress 2005). Even if there is now a black middle class as large numerically as the white middle class, it is the persistence of gross inequality, in which less than 20 per cent of the population is able to live a life secure from the threat of hunger and economic deprivation, that undermines the legitimacy and possibly the sustainability of the constitutional settlement (Southall 2013: 17–38).

While the international community declared apartheid to be a crime against humanity as early as 1974,[16] and the crime of apartheid is now recognised as a prosecutable crime with individual responsibility under the 1998 Rome Statue of the International Criminal Court,[17] the architects and beneficiaries of apartheid continue to deny either the criminal nature of the system or the benefits they gained from it. Failure to acknowledge or offer genuine apology is, I believe, closely tied to the question of memory. The role of memory has as much to do with shaping the future as it has to do with confronting the past. Recognising the impact of the projects of denial – involving the conscious and unconscious envisioning of the futures of nations, ethnic minorities, communities, institutions, and individuals – in the framing of past events, deeds, and ideas, provides a particular way of understanding the role of memory. This orientation towards past events requires a construction of the past that either highlights good intentions, emphasises sincere aspirations and goals, excuses mistaken understandings, or simply denies.

To see these processes, we need only to consider the presentations and arguments of perpetrators – individuals and institutions – in a wide range of contexts. Consider only the reconstruction of the nature of apartheid presented by F.W. de Klerk on behalf of the National Party before the TRC or the arguments of lawyers for apartheid's security forces in amnesty hearings, who continued to assert that the past abuses of those they represented were justified as part of a more general anti-communist campaign rather than in

---

[16]   International Convention on the Suppression and Punishment of the Crime of Apartheid, 1015 U. N. T. S. 243, entered into force 18 July 1976.

[17]   2187 U. N. T. S. 3, 17 July 1998, Art. 7(j).

an unjustifiable defence of apartheid. To this end some perpetrators have gone beyond denial and have even attempted to reconstruct the personal histories of their victims, or even of the witnesses for the victims, seeking to deny their status as legitimate anti-apartheid activists. In this sense the struggle to shape memory, memorial, and history continued throughout the TRC process.

When approached from the perspective of the future – in which we all wish to imagine honourable and productive roles for ourselves and our communities – it is possible to understand what drives and shapes these forces of forgetting and denial that shape the struggle over memory. However, when considered from the perspective of either the victims or those from all sides who believe that a stable future must be premised on an adequate confrontation and addressing of the legacies of authoritarianism, the practices of forgetting and denying become major obstacles to a just and sustainable future. Furthermore, the vision of the future – in which perpetrators of past violations wish to recreate their own self-esteem, respectability, authority, and even power – has implications not only for how the past is reconstructed but also for how they act in the present. Thus, the consequences of forgetting and denial of the past have a direct impact on the present and the shape of the future.

This impact may be witnessed in the way denial has produced significant consequences for post-1994 South Africa. The denial of accountability and the canard that the violations of human rights that occurred were either unintended or perpetrated by a few bad apples has enabled two distinct pathologies. On the one hand is the assertion that the system of apartheid was the product of good intentions that did not work out as planned and thus the leaders, policymakers, and bureaucrats that perpetrated the crime of apartheid are free of any responsibility for its consequences. This canard continues to be repeated by F.W. de Klerk and his Foundation, which even claims that the regime, which they served and led, is responsible for ending apartheid (Varney 2007; McGreal 2021). On the other hand, the failure to hold the perpetrators of the crime of apartheid, separate from individual perpetrators of gross violations of human rights such as torture and extrajudicial killings, accountable for their internationally recognised crimes has produced a climate of impunity in which legal violations, especially non-violent acts of corruption and self-dealing, are discounted when compared with the horrors of apartheid. This has produced the notion that some are above the law and only have 'smallanyana' skeletons in their closets compared with those responsible for apartheid who are free to enjoy their ill-gotten benefits in the new South Africa. This is a view of the world that threatens dire consequences for the rule of law and its legitimacy today.

For me, in the case of Williamson and others who actively fought to preserve the apartheid regime, the only basis for amnesty and reconciliation would be a genuine recounting of the truth of their actions. This would need to include the naming of those accountable for making the relevant decisions and their own involvement in the planning and perpetuation of these crimes, as well as an acknowledgement that apartheid was a crime against humanity and that their actions could therefore not be justified in any way, including as they often repeated, as preventing terrorism and communism.[18] The fact that they continued to avoid revealing who gave orders or how decisions were reached about specific targets, as well as justifying their actions as protecting a legitimate government, raises serious questions about the claim that amnesty was given in exchange for truth. Even with their false accusations and denials, they continued to receive amnesty and avoid accountability. When the child of one of Williamson's victims sought to appeal the decision to grant him amnesty, Williamson promised to pay compensation in exchange for the withdrawal of the appeal; however, after the appeal was withdrawn, Williamson failed to pay.

It seems to me – also – that a proper account of the crime of apartheid must include an acknowledgement of both the evil of colonialism and racism upon which the system was built, as well as some reflection on the social and economic harms inflicted on the majority of South Africans as a result of specific policies and laws. The violence of apartheid includes the separation of families and destruction of family life, forced removals and dispossession of homes and land, the denial of education, and the exploitation of labour, not merely the direct violence of the state inflicted upon those who resisted apartheid. Only with such recognition might we, as South Africans, both beneficiaries and victims of apartheid, collectively address the continuing legacies of apartheid, whether it is the geography of apartheid that continues to shape South African cities, or the lack of opportunity, whether in education or employment, that continues to shape the lives of most South Africans. Such an acknowledgement and commitment to change will require a differential contribution from former beneficiaries and the institutions that were founded on the riches that apartheid bestowed. However, it is still the case that the beneficiaries of apartheid are quick to reframe their situation as being that of a victimised minority and to point to the postapartheid government's programmes, designed to address racial inequality, as both a 'violation' of the ANC's commitment to 'non-racialism' and as a form of discrimination. The fact that some members of the government and new elite have engaged in increasingly brazen forms of corruption that today undermine the very programmes designed to address the legacies of apartheid cannot be an excuse for the denial of apartheid's role in creating

---

[18] On Williamson's refusal to accept responsibility, see Ancer (2017: 219).

the degrees of social and economic deprivation that continue to characterise South African society.

As South Africa continues to strive for a viable future in the early 21st century, questions of accountability and reparation remain central to the building of a sustainable society. While a repeat of formal apartheid or minority racial domination by law is indeed consigned to the rubbish bin of history, threats to democracy and the rule of law are, as in all societies, ever-present. Despite a quarter century of democracy, racial and economic divisions remain and continue to threaten our beautiful land, which still harbours some of the highest levels of inequality in the world. Under these conditions what might justify any hope for a 'viable future'? If our failures to address the legacies of racism, colonialism, and apartheid, whether in the realm of accountability or material inequalities, has left us hamstrung by amnesia, denial, and a rejection of accountability, what might we embrace today as signs of hope for building a better and even 'viable future'?

Accepting the danger that I am once again embracing false optimism, I feel that it is essential that we recognise the enormous, if fragile, achievements of our democratic transition. First, while there was horrendous violence, the country avoided the disaster of an extended civil war that has and continues to befall so many other lands (Garson 2020). Second, despite its many limitations, South Africa has maintained an uninterrupted formal democracy for longer than most countries in history, especially among postcolonial states. Third, and I believe most significantly, the institutions created by our Constitution have thus far proven resilient, despite often concerted attempts to co-opt and undermine them in the pursuit of illegitimate ends such as state capture. Unlike the average constitution, which according to empirical scholarship is on average significantly redesigned every 19 years, the South African Constitution has remained central to the country's governance for a quarter century – an achievement that is often overlooked.

While there are serious criticisms raised against the constitutional settlement and the failure of our democratic governments to address the serious problems of unemployment, poverty, and criminal violence that continue to plague our land, I believe that the embrace of constitutionalism by the liberation movement and the rejection of attempts to fragment the country through claims of group rights and extreme regional autonomy remain unrecognised achievements of the democratic transition. Instead, the embrace of rights and innovative constitutional institutions has thus far frustrated attempts, such as the campaign of state capture and corruption engaged in by the Zuma faction within the ANC, to fully capture undemocratic and unaccountable power. The resilience of these institutions, I would argue, has been bolstered by degrees of freedom and restraints on power that are often now taken for granted. Despite the autocratic ambitions of some, attempts to limit the ability of the media to expose malfeasance or to undermine the ability of civil society to organise and question the actions of those in power have been repeatedly thwarted. It is in this struggle for accountability that I find hope.

However, for our society to move in the direction of a viable and sustainable future, it will take more than formal accountability for corruption and poor governance. If amnesia, denial, and the rejection of accountability are to be the legacies of the democratic transition, there will be little grounds for hope. It is only by extending accountability to a broader acceptance of the common responsibility collectively shared by all the beneficiaries of apartheid that it will become possible to imagine a full implementation of the constitutional promise. Instead of asserting colour blindness and the unrestricted protection of property as the 'postapartheid deal', we need to recognise that accountability requires us to embrace both the truth of our history and the constitutional logic of affirmative action that seeks to achieve redistribution through legal process rather than graft and unconstrained appropriation. It is only a shared commitment to the physical and social reconstruction of the country that will fulfil the promise of a viable future.

References

Abrahams, C. and Seekoe, M., 2006, 'The TRC's unfinished business: reparations', in C. Villa-Vicencio and F. du Toit (eds.), *Truth & Reconciliation in South Africa: 10 Years On*, pp 34–52, Cape Town: David Philip.

African National Congress, 1994, *The Reconstruction and Development Programme*, Johannesburg: Umanyano Publications.

Ancer, J., 2017, *Spy: Uncovering Craig Williamson*, Johannesburg: Jacana.

Asmal, K., Asmal, L., and Roberts, R. S., 2006, 'Reconciliation through truth: a reckoning of apartheid's criminal governance; the TRC's unfinished business: prosecutions', in C. Villa-Vicencio and F. du Toit (eds.), *Truth & Reconciliation in South Africa: 10 Years On*, pp 86–98, Cape Town: David Philip.

Barnard, N. (as told to Tobie Wiese), 2015, *Secret Revolution: Memoirs of a Spy Boss*, Cape Town: Tafelberg.

Boraine, A., 2000, *A Country Unmasked: Inside South Africa's Truth and Reconciliation Commission*, Oxford: Oxford University Press.

De Kock, E. (as told to Jeremy Gordin), 1998, *A Long Night's Damage: Working for the Apartheid State*, Johannesburg: Contra.

Dyzenhaus, D., 1998, *Truth, Reconciliation and the Apartheid Legal Order*, Cape Town: Juta.

Garson, P., 2020, *Undeniable: Memoir of a Covert War*, Johannesburg: Jacana.

Giliomee, H., 2020, 'The "apartheid as a crime against humanity" question revisited', *Politicsweb*, 26 February, viewed 30 April 2021 from www.politics web.co.za/opinion/the-apartheid-as-a-crime-against-humanity-question

Mbatha, K., 2017, *Unmasked: Why the ANC Failed to Govern*, Johannesburg: KMM Review Publishing.

McGreal, C., 2021, 'De Klerk seeks accountability. What about his own?' *The Guardian*, 22 March, viewed 30 April 2021 from www.theguardian.com/global-development/2021/mar/22/fw-deklerk-apartheid-crimes-accountability-south-africa

Nelson Mandela Foundation, 1994, 'Address by Nelson Mandela announcing the ANC election victory, Johannesburg, 2 May 1994', viewed 30 April 2021 from www.mandela.gov.za/mandela_speeches/1994/940502_anc.htm.

Rosenberg, T., 1996, 'Recovery from apartheid', *New Yorker*, 18 November, p 88.

Schmidt, M., 2020, *Death Flight: Apartheid's Secret Doctrine of Disappearance*, Cape Town: Tafelberg.

Seekings, J. and Nattrass, N., 2005, *Class, Race, and Inequality in South Africa*, Pietermaritzburg: University of KwaZulu-Natal Press.

Seleka, N., 2020, 'SACC calls on de Klerk to retract his remarks and apologize', *News24*, 15 February, viewed 30 April 2021 from www.news24.com/news24/SouthAfrica/News/sacc-calls-on-de-klerk-to-retract-and-apologise-for-his-apartheid-remarks-20200215

Sooka, Y., 2006, 'The TRC's unfinished business: prosecutions', in C. Villa-Vicencio and F. du Toit (eds.), *Truth & Reconciliation in South Africa: 10 Years On*, p 17, Cape Town: David Philip.

Southall, R., 2013, 'The power elite in democratic South Africa: race and class in a fractured society', in J. Daniel, P. Naidoo, D. Pillay, and R. Southall (eds.), *New South African Review 3: The Second Phase – Tragedy or Farce?* pp 17–38, Johannesburg: Wits University Press.

Tutu, D., 1999, *No Future without Forgiveness*, New York: Doubleday.

Varney, H., 2007, 'De Klerk and the Truth Commission', letter to *The Guardian*, viewed 7 May 2021 from www.theguardian.com/world/2007/aug/17/southafrica.leadersandreply

Wilson, R. A., 2001, *The Politics of Truth and Reconciliation in South Africa: Legitimizing the Post-Apartheid State*, Cambridge: Cambridge University Press.

Index

305

disappearances 37, 297, 298
discursive context of the TRC 265
dispossession 14, 32, 247, 249, 250, 260, 301
District Six 247
domestic violence 13, 172–5, 177, 178, 181
DPP v Thabethe 187

E
Eastern Cape 258
education 78, 83, 187, 292, 301
Electoral Commission v Mhlope and Others 78
elites 31, 66, 69, 241
El Salvador 36
emotions 121, 268–9, 277, 282
equality *see* inequality
Equality Act 77–80, 95–6
  Chinese Association 89, 91, 92
  Equality Courts 8, 12, 75, 86, 93
European settlers 251, 260
evictions and displacement 247, 257, 298

F
Falati, X. 106
Fanon, F. 125
Farmer, I. 231–2
Feinberg, H. 256
Fokazi, M. 283–4
forced evictions and displacement 247,
  257, 298
forgiveness 5, 7, 15, 37, 99
  and accountability 45
  and apology 276–82
  Christian forgiveness 293, 297
  climate of forgiveness 266–75
  and remorse 150
Fose v Minister of Safety and Security 78, 80
fraud 14, 221
  accounting fraud 221, 235–6, 237, 239
freehold
  landownership 251–5
  law 255
  townships 246–51
Free State 258
full disclosure 36–7, 100, 272–4
  and de Klerk 41
  and Vlok 44

G
gender 44
  gendered expectations 103
  gender harms 102
  gendered power relations 184
genocide 32, 33
Germany 32, 144, 154
Giliomee, H. 295
Glen Grey Act 254
Gobodo-Madikizela, P. 149, 164
Goffman, I. 5
Goliath v MEC for Health, Eastern Cape 215
Govier, T. 226, 227, 276–7

Gqola, P. D. 146
Graeber, D. 194
Gregoriou, P. 86
Group Areas Act, 1950 257
Guatemala 34
Guattari, F. 123
Gupta family 238
*Gura v MEC for Health, Free State
  Province* 207

H
Haffejee, H. 47
Halsmith, M. 62
Hani, C. 278–9
harassment 43, 75, 77, 78, 91
harmony 59–61
  ideologies 12, 65–8
  within marriage 194
  and traditional courts 56, 68–71
harms 2, 4
  caused to patients 201, 212
  corporate harm 221
  generational harms 2
  identification of 191–2
Harper, S. 102
Hartzenberg, Justice W. 147
hate speech 12, 75, 77, 78, 79, 91–5
  and apology 75
  effectiveness of apology 95–6
  homophobia 85–90
health insurance 202, 203
health litigation *see* medical negligence
health systems, responsiveness of 213–14
health users and care 205–6
Hicks, D. 60
Nkomo, N. 119
Holocaust 32, 154
homophobia 85–90
Hook, D. 125–6
Hudson, G. 237
human rights 14, 36, 100, 213, 222, 224
  UN declaration 30–1
Humphrey, M. 267

I
imprisonment 8, 32, 79, 106, 120, 185
  lack of rehabilitation 187, 188
impunity, climate of 14, 30, 46, 47,
  95, 300
individual acts 3, 29, 45, 116, 250
  and amnesty 36, 298
  and apartheid 274–5
Indonesia 31
inequality 10, 196, 225, 230, 232, 240, 241,
  291, 302
  socioeconomic inequality 143, 155–6, 299
  structural inequalities 241
  TRC proposals 229
Institute for Justice and Reconciliation
  (IJR) 143